Robert Peel

Robert Peel

A biography

DOUGLAS HURD

Weidenfeld & Nicolson
LONDON

First published in Great Britain in 2007
by Weidenfeld & Nicolson

1 3 5 7 9 10 8 6 4 2

© 2007 Douglas Hurd

A CIP catalogue record for this book
is available from the British Library.

ISBN: 978 0 297 84844 8

Typeset by Input Data Services Ltd,
Frome

Printed and bound in Great Britain by
Butler & Tanner Ltd, Frome and London

Weidenfeld & Nicolson

An imprint of the Orion Publishing Group
Orion House, 5 Upper St Martin's Lane,
London WC2H 9EA

www.orionbooks.co.uk

Contents

List of Illustrations

The House of Commons, by Sir George Hayter, 1833 (National Portrait Gallery, London)

Lord Liverpool, by Sir Thomas Lawrence, 1827 (National Portrait Gallery, London)

Henry Goulburn, engraving by J. Holl after Pickersgill (National Portrait Gallery, London)

John Wilson Croker, by William Owen, c. 1812 (National Portrait Gallery, London)

William Ewart Gladstone, by George Frederick Watts, 1859 (National Portrait Gallery, London)

Benjamin Disraeli, by Sir Francis Grant, c. 1840 (National Trust Picture Library)

Daniel O'Connell, an engraving by Joseph Hagerty (private collection/Bridgeman Art Library)

Lord George Bentinck (Mary Evans Picture Library)

Edward Stanley, 14th Earl of Derby, by Frederick Richard Say, 1844 (National Portrait Gallery, London)

Drayton Manor, Staffordshire, an engraving of 1842 (private collection)

The grand gallery at Drayton Manor (private collection)

Between pages 312 and 313

'*Punch*'s monument to Peel', by John Leech (Mary Evans Picture Library)

'Stag at Bay', John Doyle's parody of Edwin Landseer's famous painting, 1846 (private collection)

'The Fall of Caesar', an engraving of 1846 (private collection)

Julia Beatrice Peel, by Sir Thomas Lawrence, 1828 (Christie's Images/Artothek)

Queen Victoria, the Duchess of Kent, Prince Albert, Wellington and Peel in Windsor Great Park, by Henry Barraud, 1845 (Christie's Images/Bridgeman Art Library)

'I'm afraid you're not strong enough for the place, John', an engraving of 1846 (private collection)

'Manager Peel taking his farewell benefit', an engraving of 1846 (private collection)

Wellington and Peel, by Franz Xavier Winterhalter (The Royal Collection © 2007 HM Queen Elizabeth II)

Sir James Graham (Bridgeman Art Library)

Sir Henry Hardinge, by Sir Francis Grant, c. 1849 (National Portrait Gallery, London)

Peel on his horse (Mary Evans Picture Library)

'The Preaching of John Knox', by Sir David Wilkie (Petworth House, West Sussex/Bridgeman Art Library)

Anxious crowds waiting for news of Peel, 1850 (Illustrated London News Picture Library)

Endpapers

Peelers assembling at Bow Street, London, 31 January 1837 (Hulton Archive/Getty Images)

Introduction

We liked to watch the portly figure of Dr Kitson Clark as, black gown swirling, he made his way across the Great Court of Trinity and disappeared up the staircase. During tutorials in his rooms on that staircase I first learned about Robert Peel, whose career Kitson Clark had already studied for more than twenty years. His first book on Peel, published in 1929, is a young man's work, rich in florid phrases and ambitious analyses. By the time he taught me Kitson Clark had allowed the Cambridge air to mellow his views, but he was still a staunch supporter of Peel. As a shallow undergraduate politician, holding cavalier views to compensate for my sober style of life, I moved the other way. The savage wit of Disraeli as he tore into the Prime Minister and Peel's pompous, defensive replies seemed to sum up the difference between a first-rate and a second-rate orator; I hardly looked beyond the oratory.

In a different mood I came back to Peel as Home Secretary in 1988. I was reminded that it would be decent to commemorate his birth two hundred years earlier. He was remembered by most people mainly as the founder of the London Metropolitan Police. But I read more widely, including the masterly biography in two volumes by Professor Norman Gash. From these Peel emerged as a man of government, indeed the first modern Prime Minister of Britain, who dedicated himself through ceaseless work and difficult decisions to the welfare of the whole nation. Disraeli wrote that Britain was two nations, the rich and the poor; but it was Peel who exerted himself to soften the difference and fuse us into One Nation. That phrase seemed to need emphasising in 1988, the high point in the reign of Margaret Thatcher, whose Government was often accused of divisiveness. I had no wish to put myself on a pedestal alongside Peel, but the Peel Society organised a dinner in the remaining fragment of Peel's home outside Tamworth. I made a One Nation speech praising the active citizen as a necessary counterpart of the free market. The Prime Minister complimented me on the speech, more I think because of some favourable headlines than because she had read and agreed with it.

Peel was indeed a man of government. He became a Minister as a young man of twenty-four and held office during twenty of the next thirty-four years. But the holding of office lodges no claim to greatness. For Peel, office was not an end in itself but an opportunity for action. His appetite for facts and figures was insatiable, and he was never content with what he found. But the changes he made were conservative in spirit. They were designed to protect the institutions and way of life in which he believed. The list is impressive. Peel founded the modern police, first in Ireland, then in London. He completely overhauled the criminal code, not so much in a humanitarian spirit as to bring order out of a system of cruel chaos. He reformed the revenue of the Church of England. He settled the crucial border between Canada and the United States, as part of a foreign policy which preferred reasoned diplomacy to noisy bluster. He established firm rules for the banking system. He removed the barriers which prevented Catholics from sitting in Parliament. In the new situation which followed the Great Reform Bill of 1832 he founded the modern Conservative Party. He provided it with its first election manifesto. He was the first Prime Minister to be chosen as the result of victory in a general election.

The list is long. There were few intervals of leisure. But alongside the burden of work Peel collected pictures, helped the arts and sciences, built two large houses, shot grouse and partridges, and married a beautiful wife to whom he was entirely devoted. Overarching all this stands the repeal of the Corn Laws and the lowering of tariffs across the whole range of imports. Peel moved slowly in this direction, until the Irish famine induced him to quicken his pace. The high drama which followed brought about his own downfall, and the fracturing of his party.

What drove this proud man forward into destruction? The answer was poverty. Peel was strongly moved by concern for what was the called 'the condition of the people', in particular distress in the industrial north. He became keenly and personally involved in the misery of the weaving town of Paisley. He was not alone; many others concerned themselves with poverty. The Chartists looked for an answer in radical political change.

Lord Shaftesbury pressed for social legislation to improve working conditions. Marx and Engels out of their research hatched the theories of Communism. Disraeli toyed with the romantic notions of Young England. But Peel was the man who acted. He worked out a clear analysis and remedy. The answer was to make food and other necessities cheaper for ordinary people, and above all for that great majority which did not have the vote. With them in mind he reduced the cost of living by cutting tariffs and eventually repealing the Corn Laws. Sweeping aside sectional interests, he argued and governed on behalf of the nation as a whole. The ideas owed much to others, but the action was Peel's.

The results flow through into our own times and ways of thought. A hundred and fifty years is not an immense gap in the history of a nation. Some of the dilemmas with which Peel wrestled are with us today. The relationship between a leader and his party is defined and redefined in each generation, but never settled. Leaders of the Conservative Party have struggled to prevent the kind of split which destroyed Peel when he repealed the Corn Laws. Once I found myself warning that the Party might split on Europe as it had on the Corn Laws. The Conservative Party will always contain within its ranks those who in Peel's time were called the Ultras – men, and now women too, who instinctively resist change and pine for a golden age that never was. Sometimes the Ultras are negative and vengeful, the sour Right. Sometimes they have the charm of Trollope's favourite characters. Few Conservative leaders have in practice accepted their belief that government is just the dignified protection of the status quo. Peel challenged the Ultras in open conflict to achieve the changes he thought necessary. He succeeded in doing what he wanted, but in that process forfeited their further support; they no longer felt that he was one of them. Those, then and now, for whom party unity is the great prize and jewel of politics, believe that Peel deserved his eventual punishment. But he was using his skill and courage for a wider purpose.

Now the scene is shifting again. The question is not whether a political party can stay united, but whether political parties are any longer the acceptable vehicle for political thought and action. Today's intelligent citizens remain deeply interested in political issues, but do not see why they have to be discussed in the raucous way normally adopted by political parties. They turn instead to pressure groups outside Parliament which offer a clear though narrow message. Supporters of Greenpeace or

Amnesty International or the World Development Movement would have felt at home in the Anti Corn Law League or O'Connell's Catholic Association. But pressure groups cannot balance out the different arguments and interests; only Parliament and politicians can do that. Peel was the first to manage this in a modern context, at great cost to himself, and great benefit to his successors. His legacy has been crucial to the relative stability and success of our system.

Peel saw more clearly than any of his predecessors that Britain's well-being depended on the success of industry and commerce operating freely. But the free enterprise system had to work in a way acceptable to the new electorate. This meant that government had to watch its operation carefully and be ready to act before any sore places became dangerously inflamed. The same line of thinking ran through the policies of two of his formidable successors, Gladstone and Thatcher. These three leaders wore different party labels and applied different specific policies. But each had enormous willpower and a similar clear vision – of a free enterprise system encouraged by government and yet modified when necessary in the interests of the nation as a whole.

The impact spread beyond the shores of Britain. Peel steered a firm economic course for Britain at a time when we were the world's dominant economic power. He set the pace for universal free trade and free enterprise. No doubt regardless of Peel, the United States would one day have taken over that role and led the world towards a global free enterprise system. But because of Peel, Britain and the United States have worked with ups and downs on the same economic philosophy – to the benefit, I would argue, of the world as a whole. That is why Peel is one of the founders of globalisation.

Peel was loved by a few, disliked by many, respected by almost all. When he died he was mourned by thousands who normally took no interest in politics. In each generation the controversy swings to and fro about this strange man who decisively shaped our nation.

One

From Cotton to the Commons

'The only ancestry we care about is the shuttle'
Lady Henley, great-granddaughter of 'Parsley' Peel

'Industria'
Peel family motto

'Only think what a head he must have'
Peel's Oxford contemporary, George Chinnery, on Peel's Double First

For several days the November fog had lain thick on the Staffordshire countryside surrounding Drayton Manor. Sir Robert Peel, 1st Baronet, began his letter to his son by remarking on the weather. But he went on to serious matters, using phrases which must have been carefully prepared:

> It will afford me much pleasure to hear from you that you have been introduced to your new Society and that you have a prospect of having rooms to your satisfaction ... You have hitherto afforded me unspeakable pleasure in the manner you have conducted yourself, and I have no fears for the future. Your good sense will convince you of the importance of being distinguished among those with whom you live and study.[1]

In the autumn of 1809, when he received this letter, young Robert was, at the age of twenty-one, beginning to study law in London at Lincoln's Inn. The Baronet phrased his letter to his son in terms of congratulation. But he would not have been human if he had not leant back in his chair, gazed out at the fog, and reflected that whatever his son's future might hold, up to that point the achievement had largely belonged to himself and his own father.

Two generations of steady work, sound judgement and adventurous exploitation of new technology brought the Peel family a long way from the small farm near Blackburn in Lancashire where the 1st Baronet's father had grown up. He was known as Parsley Peel from one of his own experiments in pattern printing. Born in 1723, Parsley Peel had no special pretensions for himself. Over a long life he built the prosperity of his family but was content to remain a Lancashire cotton manufacturer. Through commercial acumen he mastered the processes of carding, spinning, weaving and printing. John Wesley met Parsley Peel in 1787 and was impressed, up to a point. 'I was invited to breakfast at Bury by Mr Peel, a calico printer who a few years ago began with £500 and is now supposed to have gained £20,000. Oh, what a miracle if he lose not his own soul.'[2] Whatever the state of his soul, his mills, warehouses and factories spread across Lancashire and later Staffordshire, and when he died in 1793 he left his family a substantial fortune of nearly £140,000.* In the last year of his life Parsley Peel pointed that family in a new direction when he obtained the grant of a coat of arms. There was no search for improbable ancestors. As one of his descendants remarked, 'The only ancestry we care about is the shuttle.' And the shuttle could be admired there on the coat of arms, clasped by a silver lion, accompanied by a golden bee and three bundles of arrows, all above the new family motto, *Industria*.[3]

This was social mobility indeed, of which Parsley Peel's generation provides many examples. But the Peel story shows that it was hard-earned. The new technology, boldly embraced in Lancashire, meant that skilled workers lost their jobs and were replaced in the factories by unskilled men, women and children. Violence and rioting followed, machinery was destroyed; Parsley Peel moved most of his manufacturing out of Lancashire. The family learned to prize law and order as the prime political virtue, indeed the only guarantee of progress.

The existence of a coat of arms showed that with the old man's blessing the next generation was moving sharply out of the social

---

*Throughout I give sums of money their value at the time. When Peel became Prime Minister in 1841 £1 was worth the equivalent of about £40 today.

surroundings which had satisfied Parsley Peel. His son Robert was still a mill-owner first and foremost. He married his partner's daughter and the family wealth continued to grow. He employed about 15,000 work people. But he also bought and rebuilt a country house at Drayton, and in 1790 entered Parliament as Member for the nearby borough of Tamworth. He spoke seldom, always in support of Pitt and his successors, and became known as an expert on the cotton industry. 'No minister', he said of Pitt, 'ever understood so well the commercial interests of the country. He knew that the true sources of its greatness lay in its productive industry.'[4] He read widely and wrote a pamphlet on the National Debt. One year before income tax was invented he and his partners made a voluntary contribution of £10,000 to the Treasury. When Pitt created a supplementary militia to cope with the threatened French invasion, Robert Peel helped raise the necessary men in both Lancashire and Staffordshire. By these sizeable but conventional decisions he moved quietly but quickly up the English ladder, and accepted a baronetcy from Pitt in 1800.

The first Sir Robert emerges as a quiet, determined and honourable man, steady in his ways and opinions, loyal to his friends, family and country. His thinking was that of his time and class, harsh by our standards, but not static. Sir Robert brought pauper children from the London warehouses to work in his mills for twelve hours or more a day; but he was the first to see the need for legislation, and himself promoted the Factory Act in 1802 which limited the hours for children to twelve, and made provision at least in theory for clothing, education and conditions of work.

Sir Robert's wife, Ellen, bore him eleven children in eighteen years. The eldest of these, also named Robert, was born in Bury, before the move south, on 5 February 1788. His mother's natural liveliness and energy suddenly deserted her after the birth of her youngest daughter, and she died when Robert was fifteen. Sir Robert married again, but Peel was never close to his stepmother. The disappearance of his mother may have brought and kept him nearer to his father than would have been normal at the time. The letters between them are formal in the style of the day, but they show that each spent much time thinking with careful affection about the other. Old Sir Robert was ambitious for all his children, but particularly his eldest son.

Tall, handsome, with blue eyes and a touch of red in his hair from the start, Robert Peel looked the part prepared for him. His education started early. At Bury until he was ten, Peel with his brother and two sisters was taught for two hours a day by the local curate. After the family's move to Drayton, Peel was sent to a school run by the Reverend Francis Blick. He enjoyed the open-air pursuits which Drayton provided. He quickly found that he was an excellent shot, and throughout his life this was his favourite pastime. But *Industria* was a motto which had to be justified in each generation. His father made Peel repeat after church on Sunday the substance of each sermon, and learn by heart great chunks of eighteenth-century poetry. We can discount some of the stories about early predictions of greatness for Peel – such stories cluster round the childhood of many great men. But he emerges early as exceptionally hard-working and intelligent, more popular with adults than with contemporaries, a boy with a future.

Old Sir Robert was clear that this future should involve another swift move up the social ladder, this time to the top. Like Parsley Peel before him, Sir Robert was shrewdly content with what he had achieved for himself. He had won respect, but knew his limits. It was not for a cotton manufacturer to mingle with royal dukes, to gamble at Brooks's, to govern India or Ireland, to make or destroy ministries. But there was no reason why the next Baronet should not aim as high as he pleased, provided the preparations were properly made. Sir Robert did not worry whether he himself was regarded as a gentleman; the title, Drayton Manor, the seat in Parliament, and 15,000 men, women and children at work were enough for him. But there should be no doubt about his eldest son, or indeed about any of his sons. All five should go to public schools. The Reverend Blick had not taught the art of composing Latin verse, an art unknown to Sir Robert but evidently essential for his sons on their upward march. The time had come to move on. After careful consideration Sir Robert sent his eldest son at the age of twelve to Harrow.

Harrow, like other public schools, was riding the crest of a wave in the first years of the nineteenth century. More parents could afford the fees of a boarding school, but this increased prosperity was not the only reason. Society was becoming less quirky, more competitive, better organised. The British Empire did not yet demand that yearly output of soldiers and district officers which, in the second half of the century, sustained the traditional public schools and created many new ones. But the British aristocracy increasingly recognised that the private tutor, the local rector and the gamekeeper might not be adequate guides to launch their offspring into this new and more complicated world. The rising men of business saw the same point from a different angle, and sent their sons to mingle with young ragamuffins who would one day be dukes.

In 1793–5 Harrow had 120 boys, ten years later (when Peel went) more than 300. In picking out Harrow, Sir Robert was probably swayed by the high reputation of the Headmaster, Joseph Drury, who had by then reigned for nearly twenty years. Unlike Keate at Eton, who flogged mercilessly, Drury treated pupils with patience and consideration. He devolved discipline onto others, confining himself to gentle reprimands. His pompous style of teaching was not based on deep scholarship, and Harrow had no high reputation in the universities for learning. Drury excelled in the rather different art of attracting to Harrow the children of the great, and equipping them to keep or even improve their places on the social ladder. In 1803 the school contained one actual and three future dukes, a future marquess, two actual and five future earls and viscounts, four lords, twenty-one honourables and four baronets. But the acquisition of titled teenagers was not Drury's main achievement. Between August 1827 and October 1865 there were only three brief periods when an Old Harrovian was not either Prime Minister or Foreign Secretary.[5] The young noblemen from Harrow somehow learned to succeed in a world where merit had begun to compete with birth as a qualification for high office.*

The teaching at Harrow was almost entirely concerned with Latin and Greek. Outside the classroom there was time and some encouragement to read more widely and to learn other subjects, but knowledge of the classical languages and literature lay at the heart of a good education. Peel carried through life a wide acquaintance with Virgil, Homer and the like. More important was his mastery of the techniques which a classical education developed. These included a prodigious memory and an ability to muster arguments quickly, forcefully and in good order. The boy who could be found helping laggard friends compose their urgently needed

---

* Eton has produced more Prime Ministers but scattered over a longer period. Harrow lists her Prime Ministers on the programme of the annual festival of Harrow Songs. Speaking at this occasion I commented that it must be convenient for Harrow to be able to print all its Prime Ministers on one page. This very Etonian remark was received with hisses.

exercises became the man who astonished the House of Commons hour after hour with his control of complicated facts and arguments.

Oratory was part of the classical curriculum. On Speech Day in July 1804, Peel acted part of Virgil's *Aeneid*. He took the role of Turnus, the feared enemy of Aeneas and the Trojans, while King Latinus was played by a lame younger boy called Byron. Byron was closer to Peel's younger brother. He wrote later that Peel was a better scholar than himself, but not so well grounded in history and general information. Peel was never a great orator. He often went on too long, and rarely sparkled. But he was never obscure or confused. Mastery of substance, clarity of presentation, self-confidence in private and public argument were talents he acquired and sharpened at Harrow.

Beneath the genial surface of Mr Drury's rule and the tranquil surroundings of church and village, there was another Harrow, tense, chaotic and sometimes violent. The boys were crowded together in the school itself and bullying was left unchecked. Palmerston, Peel's contemporary and later political rival, wrote in 1798 that the school was awash with swearing and fighting and claimed that heavy drinking was 'fashionable at present'.[6] Peel was beaten in his first year for refusing to fag for an older boy. But boys could roam the surrounding countryside following their own desires. Though cricket and football were played, there was nothing like the later structure of organised team games. Peel was strong, intelligent and by instinct law-abiding. Unlike Byron, he rarely got into trouble, but quietly developed the talents which he had brought with him from Drayton. With his closest friend Robert Anstruther he kept a gun secretly in a nearby cottage. The two boys used to beat the hedgerows for small birds, and carry back any trophies to school, pretending they had been brought down by a stone.

Most Victorians looked back on their schooldays with sentimental affection. Only Lord Salisbury was so miserable that in later life he used to cross the street to avoid former Eton schoolfellows. The Harrow songs are full of sentimentality, made palatable by splendid tunes. That was not Peel's style. He told a friend who asked for advice that he had misspent his time at Harrow and hoped it was now better conducted. But there is no evidence that while he was there he disliked a school which, though not academically brilliant, gave him the confidence he needed.

Peel anticipated modern fashion by taking a nine-month gap between school and university. But he had already begun to organise his life with rigorous regard for the future. At Drayton, two hours a day were allotted for shooting with his brother William. He studied at his desk behind a tag from Horace, 'nocturna versate manu, versate diurna' – work by night, work by day. He had plenty to do. Oxford required a knowledge of mathematics for success, which Harrow had not even begun to provide. It was typical of his father that once he grasped the need he engaged a senior wrangler from Cambridge to coach Peel at Drayton.[7]

Peel went up to Christ Church, the leading Oxford college, in October 1805, the month when Nelson at Trafalgar finally removed the fear of a French invasion. The University of Oxford had already begun to stir out of the comfortable lethargy of the eighteenth century that had provoked Gibbon to criticise his teachers and their 'dull and deep potations'. As happens once educationalists develop a taste for reform, new systems tumbled over each other in some confusion. Peel entered the university under the regulations of 1800 but at the end of his time was examined under those of 1807. Greek and Latin still dominated the teaching, and Peel's classical reading list was formidable; but there was now to be a separate School of mathematics and physics. Peel set himself to tackle both Classics and these new subjects.

At first he did not allow academic ambition to cramp the rest of his life. He played cricket, rowed on the river, dressed well but not extravagantly, joined in the occasional practical joke, and made a host of friends. But as the final examination approached the time available for pleasure was swallowed up in work.

He was urged on by two formidable Christ Church figures. Cyril Jackson, Dean of the College since 1783, had spotted Peel as one of a rare breed, the Harrovian scholar, and began to press him forward. He developed a closer relationship with his tutor, Charles Lloyd, later Regius Professor of Divinity. Peel wrote a huge number of letters in his life. Dipping into them, I have become used to the formal style, elaborate though (unlike Gladstone) never obscure, in which Peel usually expressed himself. But to a small number of correspondents he wrote with a direct frankness born of personal intimacy. Charles Lloyd was the first of these.

The examination for the two Schools (Classics comprised one School; maths and physics the other) would take place in public on the same day in November 1808. Peel had set himself to obtain honours in both schools. He realised, perhaps further in advance than most students of any generation, how much hard work this would involve. Through his life, Peel often complained about hard work, but always enjoyed it. He particularly relished the task of organising the work in an orderly framework and setting out its results in logical order. He studied tirelessly during the summer term, for five weeks during the summer vacation, and then for up to eighteen hours a day during the last term before Schools.[8]

But out of inexperience he misjudged himself. Short of sleep and exercise, he lost his nerve. He wrote to his father suggesting that he withdraw from the examination since he was convinced he could not succeed. Once again Sir Robert, dealing with matters of which he had no personal experience, supported his son as a friend and encouraged him to proceed. Peel regained his nerve, and went forward to the examination, having very sensibly played tennis the day before.[9]

The examination was oral, and held in public. Because of his high reputation, the Examination Schools were crowded. The strain on Peel must have been tremendous. As one eyewitness wrote to his old tutor at Harrow, 'The crowd that went to hear him resembled more the assembly of a public theatre than that attending a scholastic examination, and it was hard to decide which seemed more diffident of entering upon the business, the examiners or the examined.' The examiners began with Divinity, and then went on to Aristotle, but Peel's answers were 'so comprehensive that they passed quickly to Sophocles, Aeschylus, Pindar and Lucretius'. His construing was so perfect that 'it seemed as if the whole assembly was actuated with one sentiment of applause'.[10]

Another eyewitness, George Chinnery, wrote to his mother:

> I among the rest of our Christ Church men went to hear Peel's examination yesterday, which even all the Out-College men confessed to be the most splendid thing they ever heard. He was equally perfect in Divinity, Ethics, Logic, Classics and Mathematics, and in each of these he was superior to any man who has yet appeared in the Schools ... The Schools were as full as they could hold. Only think what a head he must have, not to have been puzzled in a single question, and to have rendered himself so completely master of every single thing in which he was examined ... He asked me to breakfast this morning and I went out with him and nine other men for a long walk.[11] *

What Peel achieved in 1808 was a Double First in the true sense: a First Class degree gained simultaneously in both the two Schools then existing. He was the first to achieve this feat, and the event was long remembered. His was an extraordinary performance, particularly given the imperfect grounding he had received at Harrow. Peel carried himself modestly at this time. He did not yet feel the need for defensive boasting which came to him later in life. But the outcome must have given him huge satisfaction, and more important, the underlying confidence in his own abilities which is a condition of success in politics. When Sir Robert wrote that letter to his son a year later, stressing that he had 'hitherto afforded me unspeakable pleasure', he must have cast his mind back in particular to the amazing scene in the Examination Schools at Oxford.

Being a man of action Sir Robert had already prepared the next steps. Law and politics could be careers run in tandem. Earlier in 1809 he had saluted his son's coming of age by arranging for him to be elected to the House of Commons at a by-election for Cashel in County Tipperary. He had spoken a word in the ear of the Chief Secretary for Ireland, who passed that word down the line. No doubt money was spent, the two dozen electors saw their duty, and the great reformer of the nineteenth century began his parliamentary career by representing a corrupt Irish borough.

---

* Young Mr Chinnery was warding off a complaint of idleness from his mother by stressing his friendship with this paragon.

Two

Not a Timid Man

'Be assured that I shall pursue you, as long as I live, with a
jealous and watchful eye. Woe be to you if you fail me.'
Dr Cyril Jackson, Dean of Christ Church, to Peel, 1810

'In Glasgow I hired a humble but faithful steed and I
traversed, partly on horseback and partly on foot, the best
part of the country which lies to the southward of
Inverness'
Robert Peel on travelling in the summer of 1809

I n 1809 Peel entered the House of Commons at the age of twenty-
one. Britain had been at war with France for sixteen years, with one
interval of a few months. After the collapse of the Treaty of Amiens
in 1803 the country returned almost with a sense of relief to what seemed
its normal state, namely war with France.

Yet by 1809 each side despaired of knocking out the other. Four years
earlier, the victory at Trafalgar had destroyed Napoleon's hope of invading
Britain. For her part Britain had encouraged and financed coalitions of
Continental powers to resist France, only to see these repeatedly routed. In
1809 the Austrians were again beaten at Wagram and Napoleon summoned
their Emperor's daughter to his marriage bed as a trophy of war. In the same
year British expeditions were twice forced to retreat from the Continent, Sir
John Moore gloriously from Corunna, the Duke of York ingloriously from
the Dutch island of Walcheren. The newest General, Arthur Wellesley, and
his Spanish allies beat the French at Talavera in July. Wellesley as a result
became the Duke of Wellington; but British losses were heavy, the French
rallied, and once again forced the British back into Portugal.

Each side, without hope of sudden victory, tried to wear the other down by economic blockade. The result was hardship, but in neither case starvation or the disruption which might cripple its ability to fight.

By 1809 Britain had run out of heroic figures. King George III was relapsing once more into madness; his heir, who became Prince Regent in 1810, was sensationally unpopular. Nelson rested in St Paul's Cathedral. Wellington was not yet a full-blooded hero. Most important of all was the death of Pitt. He contained in one frail body the contrasting characteristics shown by Chamberlain and Churchill in the Second World War. Like Chamberlain, he was happiest with detailed statistics and proposals for fiscal reform, avoiding war as long as he possibly could. Like Churchill, once war began he found the willpower which gave energy and determination to the nation. Unlike Churchill, he had no zest for military matters, and the defeats which he suffered did not call from him any great exclamations of heroism. But Pitt was honest, highly intelligent, and he stuck it out. He became, as Canning wrote, the pilot who weathered the storm.

But in 1809 the pilot was dead and the storm still blowing. The Tories, followers of Pitt, limped back into power. The Duke of Portland, ill and anxious, yielded the premiership to Spencer Perceval. The new Prime Minister began to show competence and courage, but the political scene remained clouded. The Government contained two men of outstanding ability, Canning at the Foreign Office and Castlereagh at the War Department. Unfortunately they were incapable of working together. Canning intrigued for Castlereagh's dismissal. Castlereagh discovered this and the two men fought a duel on Putney Heath, from which both emerged with damaged reputations and Canning with a flesh wound in his thigh. Tired of opposition, the Whigs hoped that their old friend the Prince of Wales, once he wielded the power of the Crown as Prince Regent because of his father's madness, would contrive to give them office. Ever inconsistent, he let them down.

Gossips hovered like dragonflies over the surface. For these the excitement of 1809 was the allegation that Mrs Clarke, the mistress of the Duke of York, had been involved in selling Army commissions. Indeed all the King's sons were unsatisfactory, though in a variety of ways which kept the gossips busy.

The substantial issue of politics was the conduct of the war against Napoleon. But serious men knew of another struggle at home, rarely debated in the open at this time, but too dangerous to be ignored.

The French Revolution in its first years had attracted wide support in Britain. It seemed at first that the French, as usual over-dramatic and in a hurry, were attempting in a year or two the splendid process which in Britain had needed a century and a half of evolution, including the Glorious Revolution of 1688. Fox proclaimed his enthusiasm for the French Revolution; Paine declared the Rights of Man; Wordsworth found it bliss to be alive. Burke was the first thinker to draw the contrast between gradual reform in Britain and violent revolution in France. When he published his passionate *Reflections* denouncing the French Revolution they seemed exaggerated. But for most of Britain the guillotining of Louis XVI in January 1793 proved Burke's point. In theatres across the land, audiences and performers joined night by night in singing 'God Save the King'.* Others continued to nurse the revolutionary hope. It was not easy to recognise the Emperor Napoleon as the embodiment of the Rights of Man; but it was also hard to see the Prince Regent and the British aristocracy as valid examples of a thriving constitution dedicated to enlightenment, freedom and toleration.

Political unrest in a country without a police force was a nightmare. During the nineteenth century the British built up to their own satisfaction the legend of themselves as a moderate law-abiding nation. That was not how men like old Sir Robert Peel or his son saw their fellow countrymen in 1809. The London mob was famous throughout Europe for its sudden violent eruptions. The destructiveness of the Gordon Riots of 1780 was within living memory. In 1810 the descendants of the same mob rioted for four days in support of the radical MP Sir Francis Burdett, smashing windows and putting up barricades in Piccadilly.[1]

To political discontent were added the inevitable hardships of a rapid industrial revolution, intensified by the damage done to trade by Napoleon's economic decrees against Britain's trade with the Continent. Exports and manufacturing output fell, thousands lost their jobs, angry and frustrated men destroyed machinery. Those in charge closed ranks. Pitt, who had begun as a reformer, clamped down on dissent. The wartime measures taken against radical speech and action set the tone for three decades. Manufacturers like Sir Robert Peel and his son saw the maintenance of order as by far the most important task of government. They were protect-

---

* A political song which had lain dormant for forty years was quickly promoted to be the National Anthem.

ing their own mills and the farms of their tenants, but also the institutions of their country. Their logic was simple. The government had the duty to protect property because the right to hold property without arbitrary interference was one of the inherited liberties of an Englishman. The destructive horrors in France showed what happened once this principle was lost. The French King and nobles had tried to compromise and as a result lost their heads to the guillotine. The courage of Britain's fleets and armies had to be matched by determination at home. Far from the minds of most Members of Parliament in 1809 was the thought that another duty of government was to improve the condition of the people.

Peel was silent during his first few months in the Commons, but watchful eyes had already noticed him. Then as now the Sovereign opened each session of Parliament with a speech setting out the Government's programme. Then as now two backbench supporters of the Government were chosen by the Prime Minister to move an address of thanks for the speech. In 1810 the Prime Minister, Spencer Perceval, chose Peel as the second of these speakers. Peel spoke for forty minutes, twice as long as would now be acceptable. Maiden speeches rarely contain much exciting substance, and Peel's was no exception. He defended in detail the Government's handling of the war and praised British commerce for finding new markets to replace those blocked by Napoleon.[2]

Interested observers were watching the style rather than the substance and were greatly pleased. Foremost of course was his father, sitting in the gallery opposite, tears rolling down his cheeks as he listened to the cheers when Peel sat down. Sir Robert wrote to an old friend, 'You will be pleased to hear that my son's first speech was judged to be, by men the best qualified to form a correct opinion of public speaking, the best first speech since that of Mr Pitt.'[3] In those years that was the comparison in everyone's mind. The diarist Creevey wrote, 'Peel ... made a capital figure for a first speech. I think it was a prepared speech, but it was a most produceable *Pittish* performance, both in matter and manner.'[4] *

---

* In researching his *William Pitt the Younger*, William Hague came across a copy of the first biography of Pitt which had Robert Peel's stamp and coat of arms inside it. Peel had clearly prized this possession and proudly placed his own coat of arms at the front. The life of Pitt was a model and benchmark for all aspiring politicians, and Peel would have been well aware of the example held up before him.

One difference from Pitt was Peel's Staffordshire accent, traces of which remained with him through his life. Regional accents were much more common in the unreformed Parliament than in these ostensibly democratic days, but snobs noticed. Lord Campbell once tartly remarked: 'Peel can always be sure of an "H" when it comes at the beginning of a word, but he is by no means sure when it comes in the middle.'[5] During his early years in the House of Commons Peel's nickname was Spinning Jenny, in mockery of his industrial background.

Old Cyril Jackson, now retired as Dean of Christ Church, was delighted by this first speech. He had received half a dozen letters praising Peel and wrote to him: 'I do therefore most graciously condescend to tell you that I am very much pleased – more than I thought I could be with anything of the sort – and if I had you here I would feed you with ling and cranberry tart.' Dr Jackson had no doubt of the key to Peel's future success. The old Dean urged the continual reading of Homer, who 'alone of mortal men thoroughly understands the human mind'. Peel should read him over four or five times every year, and let no day pass without having him in his hands.[6]

Regardless of their knowledge of Homer, Ministers were in deep trouble over the failure of the expedition to Walcheren. The military and naval leaders quarrelled in public; the opposition moved a vote of censure which the Commons debated over five days. Two months after his maiden speech Peel spoke on the fourth night, 30 March 1810, concentrating on the diplomatic need to help Austria rather than the disastrous military details. This was a shorter, less ornate speech, but Dr Jackson was even better pleased. It was clear that his former pupil had been reading Homer. Only one conclusion remained: 'Work very hard and unremittingly. Only retain which is essential, your former temperance and exercise, and your aversion to mere lounge, and then you will have abundant time both for hard work and company, which last is as necessary to your future situation as even the hard work I speak of, as much is to be got from it. Be assured that I shall pursue you, as long as I live, with a jealous and watchful eye. Woe be to you if you fail me.'[7]

Within months of entering Parliament Peel was thus established as a promising backbencher. Party lines were less firmly drawn than today, but his support for Spencer Perceval's Government was clear enough. The next question was whether and when he would be offered a place in that

Government. Dr Jackson thought he should wait for something really worthwhile. His father had already dropped a hint to the Prime Minister. When writing to thank him for giving Peel the opportunity of moving the address he added, 'If my son has the good fortune to be honoured with your confidence I flatter myself he will be found deserving of the trust reposed in him. He possesses capacity, industry and virtuous habits; and under the guidance of a judicious and well-informed friend, he may become a useful member of society.'[8]

The offer came from Lord Liverpool who, as Secretary of State for War and Colonies, invited Peel in June 1810 to serve as one of the two Under Secretaries. Sir Robert was delighted.

Hidden among the mountains of papers on Peel is a note from Lord Bathurst recalling this moment in 1810. Peel had told him that he was reluctant to accept office so soon. He fully supported the Government on foreign and defence matters, but there were domestic issues which he had not had time to think about. He would have preferred to remain independent for longer before committing himself. He had only accepted Lord Liverpool's offer because his father pressed him to do so. There is no reason to doubt this story. Peel was naturally cautious, and there were cross-currents of domestic policy, particularly on Catholic Emancipation, which he had not yet navigated. But he owed everything so far in his life to his father, and if Sir Robert advised him to take the bird in hand, he was not ready to disagree.[9] *

Lord Liverpool gave Peel his first taste of an experience which he came to relish more than any other in politics, namely the hard grind of departmental work. Under the British system a junior Minister benefits hugely from apprenticeship under an experienced senior Secretary of State who is prepared to delegate but in the end takes responsibility. The Department of War and Colonies covered a vast field of action by a country at war. To Peel was delegated much of the routine work on

---

* Years later Guizot, senior French statesman, recorded in his book on Peel that Sir Robert wrote to Lord Liverpool in 1809 advising that his son had Whiggish instincts which could best be countered by giving him early office. Though his views were not fully formed, Peel's instincts at this time were Tory. A suggested variation that Sir Robert might have written in this way after 1818, when his son was out of office for four years, equally lacks supporting evidence. This seems a clear case of history being written backwards.

colonial matters. When Liverpool or his fellow Under Secretary was away Peel moved closer to military matters, in particular the equipping of Wellington for his successful defence of Portugal against Napoleon's Marshals. The opposition became impatient at the slow progress of the war, which Peel defended warmly and to good effect.[10]

So much for the hard work. By providing Peel with a small home next to his own off Whitehall, Lord Liverpool made it easy for him to follow the other half of Dean Jackson's advice and entertain company. Even as early as this Peel became well known for his dinner parties with a strong political flavour. Professor Gash gives an attractive description of the young Peel:

> [He] presented to the outward observer an enviable combination of good looks, good clothes, wealth and talent ... He was still very much the Oxonian in society, attentive to dress and following the fashion. It was still modish to wear powder at dinner or in the evening, and this custom, which concealed the reddish colour of his hair, and suited his complexion, became him very well. With good features, a pleasant smile, a well formed head, and a countenance which when animated took on a certain fire and expressiveness, he was an extremely presentable person ... To these physical graces were added a sense of fun, a keen eye for absurdities and a quiet, slightly malicious relish in exposing them.[11]

As Peel's reputation grew, so did the number of his friends. It was an unclouded start to what seemed to all a highly promising career. What was lacking so far was any direct exposure to dangers and difficulties. He had made none but obvious choices. The House of Commons, the Departmental work under the guidance of Lord Liverpool, the dinner parties at Fife House, his father's watchful affection, his holidays at Drayton were fine so far as they went; the real work was yet to begin.

It was probably during the parliamentary recess of 1809 that Peel took a holiday alone in Scotland. Many years later he described this expedition memorably at a dinner in Glasgow:

> I wished to see something more of Scotland than I could have seen by hasty glimpses from a luxurious postchaise. I wanted to see other

habitudes and manners of life beside those which the magnificent castles and hospitable mansions of the nobles of the land might present ... Yes, in Glasgow I hired a humble but faithful steed and I traversed, partly on horseback and partly on foot, the best part of the country which lies to the southward of Inverness ... Many a day have I climbed the mountain side with no other companion than a highland shepherd. Many an hour have I passed with him, listening to his simple annals and his artless views of human life. Such was the intercourse which taught me to admire the proud and independent spirit, chastened and softened by a natural courtesy. I have seen him with intelligence apparently above his condition, but with intelligence that taught him patience under his privations, confidence in his own exertion, submission to the law, loyalty to the King (cheers) and reverence for his God.[12]

On the afternoon of 11 May 1812 the Prime Minister, Spencer Perceval, was shot dead in the lobby of the House of Commons. The assassin, John Bellingham, was a commercial agent indignant at the ruin which the war had inflicted on his business.

Perceval had been building a reputation for steadiness and competence among those who knew him. Had he lived he might have pulled the Tory Party together and finished the war in a style worthy of Pitt. His death revealed again the gulf between the narrow political world of London and the country outside. Wilberforce describes the state of the West Riding of Yorkshire at this time as 'dreadful – next to rebellion, smouldering rebellion'. The London mob cheered Bellingham loudly on his way to Newgate Prison.[13] Political rivalries delayed the formation of a new government for three weeks. Wellington's brother, Lord Wellesley, tried his hand. The Prince Regent put on a first display of that indignant vacillation which was his main contribution to affairs of State over the next eighteen years. Finally the lot fell on Lord Liverpool, with momentous consequence for his Under Secretary Robert Peel.

Lord Liverpool continued as Prime Minister for fifteen years without interruption. He persevered through the last years of the war, through the excitement of victory and the disillusionment of peace, through great economic hardship to the beginnings of a more solid prosperity. In such stormy times one might think that the Prime Minister would need dramatic qualities of leadership, up to the level of Pitt or Churchill or at least Palmerston or Lloyd George. Lord Liverpool possessed no such qualities. In his novel *Coningsby*, Disraeli described him as the Arch-Mediocrity. He looked awkward and untidy, suffered from poor health, was increasingly irritable, and often broke down in tears.

Two qualities kept him going: he was a competent administrator and everyone trusted him. By 1812 he had just shown that competence as Secretary of State for War. It was easy to cheer British victories in Spain; it did not follow that everyone would help build and supply Wellington's armies. That was Liverpool's task, which he had carried out with determination and success. By the time he left the War Office he had increased the British Army in the Peninsula from 33,000 to 48,000 men. He was trusted by all, partly because, unlike Canning, he showed no particular desire to shine. Quietly as Prime Minister after 1812 he supervised the main branches of government and was the dominant influence in the slow liberalisation of economic policy. More gifted and more ambitious men rose and fell during his premiership.[14] They shaped and reshaped the map of Europe, quarrelled, made memorable speeches, suffered dramatic mishaps. Their chief, Lord Liverpool, did none of these things. He survived; he was indispensable.

The Government badly needed reinforcement in the Commons now that the Prime Minister was in the Lords. Liverpool wrote to Wellington in Spain that the fate of the Government would depend on its young supporters in the Commons. If a new Pitt would arise among them he would willingly resign the Government into his hands.[15] Events moved much more slowly. It was necessary to find a new Chief Secretary for Ireland to serve under the Lord-Lieutenant, the Duke of Richmond. There was much manoeuvring. The Duke was anxious to have a colleague who shared his robust Protestant views. In the political parlance of the day 'Protestant' and 'Catholic' did not refer to personal faith but to a man's views on lifting the barriers which prevented Catholics achieving high office or entering the House of Commons.

'Pray don't let them send me a Catholic or a timid man,' Richmond wrote to Lord Bathurst on 12 June.[16] When he was told that Peel was to be appointed he was cross that he had not been properly consulted. The Prime Minister hastened to reassure him: 'I can speak with more confidence of Mr Peel than I could of most persons to whom such an office might be offered. He has been under me in the Secretary of State's office for two years and has acquired all the necessary habits of official business. He has a particularly good temper and great frankness and openness of manners, which I know are particularly desirable on your side of the water.' On 1 September 1812 Peel arrived in Dublin to take up his new office. Nothing in his education, early career, Scottish travels or in the works of Homer could have prepared the twenty-four-year-old for the world he now entered.

Three

Orange Peel

'I believe an honest despotic government would be by far
the fittest government for Ireland'
Peel to Gregory, 1816

'In Ireland the man of blood is not secret; and neither the
law of his country, nor his own conscience have any terrors
for him'
Peel in the House of Commons, 1 March 1833

'The packet was full of passengers. The men were all sick
and the women and children thought they were going to the
bottom, and filled up the intervals of sickness with a chorus
of lamentation and cries of "Steward, are we sinking?"'
Peel to Croker, 1815

Dublin in 1812 was beginning to look a little drab. Only a little,
because the streets and squares which make the city a masterpiece of Georgian architecture were still new. The Lord-
Lieutenant ruled Ireland from the Castle, lubricating his use of the
Crown's authority with patronage and abundant hospitality. The present
incumbent, the Duke of Richmond, was particularly noted for generous
entertainment. Peel, though himself no enemy of dinner parties, worried
that by Dublin standards he was not up to the mark in enthusiasm for
port and the many toasts which accompanied it.

For Dublin the moment of greatest glory had passed. Ireland overflowed with discontent. Hopes of peaceful progress were evaporating.
During Pitt's premiership there had at first been bright moments, when
his own reforming instincts coincided with the aims of moderates in the
Irish Parliament. For a few years the eloquence of Henry Grattan in that

Parliament gave impetus to the reforming tendency, but beneath the surface fundamentals were going wrong. Ireland was not following England in the turbulent but enriching experience of the Industrial Revolution. Dublin and Belfast were the only centres of new industry. The rest of Ireland stayed within an agricultural system dominated by English landlords, and the cultivation by their tenants of one particular crop. The formidable productivity of the potato enabled the average tenant to keep his many children reasonably fed from the output of even a tiny holding. But as the population grew, so did emigration with its inevitable bitterness and heartache. The children who stayed were before long to pay a heavy price for dependence on the potato.

Yet the heart of the difficulty was not economic but political. Britain and Ireland were growing apart. The facts of history were damaging enough to any hopes of lasting reconciliation. The myths which were multiplying round that history led most of the Irish to believe in separation from England as their rightful ambition. This was the age of Thomas Moore and his Irish Melodies.

> *Let Erin remember the days of old*
> *Ere her faithless sons betrayed her; . . .*
> *Ere the emerald gem of the Western World,*
> *Was set in the crown of a stranger*

So Lord-Lieutenants came and went on behalf of the Crown, the best being those with the fewest Irish relatives and Irish friends asking for favours. Politicians as always wrote pamphlets and mulled over proposals for bettering the condition of Ireland. In Dublin the educated Irishman saw the bustle of the red-coated English soldiers and sadly recalled the misty past when Ireland had ruled herself in glory. Most tenants in the countryside resented the harshness or the neglect of their absent English landlords, and were forced to pay tithes to the Protestant Church of Ireland whose doctrines, as good Catholics, they rejected as heretical.

The last and fatal outbreak of violence had been suppressed in 1798. The 1798 rising was fatal, not because it posed a real threat to British rule, but because it was linked with a French attempt to invade. The French made a hash of their intervention, but the damage was done. There would be no more talk in London or Dublin of reforms or greater self-government for Ireland once Irish rebels were seen as part of Napoleon's effort to invade and conquer Britain. In 1801 Pitt secured the abolition of the Irish Parliament and the Union of Ireland with England, Scotland and Wales. The task of persuading the Irish Parliament to vote for its own dissolution fell to the young Lord Castlereagh. He used to the full the instruments of threat and promise which were normal for governments at the time. Both he and Pitt genuinely believed that they were doing Ireland a service by yoking her indissolubly with her larger neighbour; the Union would make possible better government and wider prosperity. The United Kingdom came into existence.

By 1812 the new Union Jack in its present form, with the Irish cross of St Patrick amalgamated with those of St Andrew and St George, was a familiar sight over Dublin Castle. The initial hubbub of protesting Dublin crowds had died down, and by the time Peel arrived as Chief Secretary the Union seemed an accepted fact. But one piece of business which Pitt and Castlereagh planned had never been accomplished. Every man, Catholic or Protestant, who registered in an Irish county and enjoyed a modest level of prosperity (the forty-shilling freehold) had the vote, which they could now use under the Union to send 100 Irish Members to Westminster. But none of those Members could be Catholic. Qualified Catholics could vote, but not elect Catholics. Pitt and Castlereagh believed this to be untenable, and there had been wide agreement in London that these and other discriminatory rules should be abolished once the Union was in place. But in 1801 King George III had violently objected, inconveniently remembering his Protestant Coronation Oath. Pitt, ill and exhausted, had resigned at once and the expected reform was postponed indefinitely. For nearly thirty years the issue of Catholic Emancipation was the running sore of British politics, dividing families and parties, arousing passions beyond its actual importance, frustrating coherent government and distorting individual careers, not least that of Chief Secretaries such as Robert Peel.

Peel, like any ambitious Minister, was keen to keep open his existing direct line of communication with the Prime Minister. He was a little too quick to analyse the state of Ireland within a fortnight of his arrival in a country in which he had never before set foot. He wrote to Lord Liverpool on 14 September 1812 describing 'the extraordinary tranquillity of this country in every part of it. Even this state of quiet however does not satisfy the very loyal, and I was told that they would greatly prefer a little agitation in so dead a calm.'' Peel had not yet understood an unwritten law for British Ministers in Ireland: they should be careful not to appear satisfied with the calm state of the country since it is then likely to change sharply for the worse. But he had quickly grasped another truth, that those most loyal to the Government liked a little agitation to justify their own anxieties and prejudices. Peel arrived in Ireland well prepared, at least in theory. He had already learned that thorough preparation, however tedious, is a necessary art of government. On a high shelf in one of the corridors of the House of Lords stand bound volumes of over a thousand pamphlets on Irish affairs from the years before 1812, with a note saying that these had been assembled for the use of Robert Peel on his appointment as Chief Secretary.

The Prime Minister himself disrupted the calm of Peel's first weeks in Ireland. Lord Liverpool decided to call a general election throughout the United Kingdom. The harvest was good, and Wellington's war in Spain had taken a decisive turn for the better. Liverpool could reasonably hope to increase his majority in the Commons. His decision threw an exceptional burden on his Chief Secretary for Ireland. Elections in Ireland have rarely been innocent and straightforward affairs. After the Union they had become much more important in political life as a whole. No longer was it a matter of choosing Members for an Irish Parliament with limited powers. One hundred Irish Members of Parliament now sat at Westminster. Their support could be crucial to the survival of the Government. How would they turn out? Notional party labels were not much use in reading these hundred Irish riddles. Far more important was personal influence, often amounting to virtual ownership in the different counties and boroughs. To the magnates concerned this influence was a cashable asset, a factor in their relationship with Government in London and Dublin to be withheld or bestowed by calculation of personal advantage. To be sure, there were issues to be debated, for example the conduct of the war, the rules of trade between Ireland and Britain, the legislation against disorder. But it would have been thought bizarre, in Ireland even more than in Britain, that differences of opinion on political issues should decide an election. These were matters to be discussed and decided by King, Government and Parliament afterwards; they should not get in the way of the reconciliation of interests, the balancing of advantages, the settlement of old debts and old scores, which were involved in the choice of fit persons to sit in Parliament.

The Lord-Lieutenant was the head of the Government of Ireland, and the fountain from which honours and patronage flowed. But as Chief Secretary Peel was expected to do the hard work, constituency by constituency. Lord Liverpool set out his general requirement: 'You will of course send us all the information you may obtain and make every exertion which can be safely made for the support and assistance of our friends.'² There was a certain opaqueness about the Prime Minister's prose, and for good reason. Three years earlier Parliament had passed an Act forbidding the sale of parliamentary seats for cash. Peel explained to a friend the consequence for his own work in a letter dated 1 October 1812: 'I am placed in a delicate situation enough here, bound to secure the Government interests if possible from dilapidation, but still more bound to faint with horror at the mention of money transactions, to threaten the unfortunate culprits with impeachment if they hint at an impure return, and yet to prevent those strongholds at Cashel, Mallow and Tralee from surrendering to the enemies who besiege them.'³

Cashel in County Tipperary was Peel's own seat. What had become a convenience when his father bought it for him was now a liability. The Government had decided that its Ministers must now find seats without any history of buying and selling. Peel gave up Cashel; his father was as ever prompt with help. Property was bought in the Wiltshire borough of Chippenham. There was an argument over the exact terms of this arrangement. The deal went through and Peel was elected, but Peel had what he described as a 'very unpleasant' meeting lasting two hours with the owner of the property, who believed that Sir Robert had agreed to buy it outright, and not just for one election.⁴ In truth Chippenham was no purer than Cashel. The new transaction was just as financial as the old one; but at least it occurred outside Peel's sphere of operation in Ireland.

Peel could turn his attention to negotiations with those who controlled the seats in Ireland for the return of Government supporters – for example with Lord Clancarty in Galway, Sir Edward Denny in Tralee, and a Mr Handcock in Athlone. Mr Handcock was particularly difficult, threatening to stand himself for Athlone, with no commitment to support the Government, unless he received an English peerage.⁵ He was not alone in making this request. Lord Charleville had the same idea for the borough of Carlow. But Lord Liverpool drew a line, to Peel's satisfaction. 'You must do the best you can without the promise of an English peerage.'[6]

Politicians, like other human beings, are tempted to exchange something they have got for something they want. In politics this is called corruption. Recently under governments with low standards, such as those of Lloyd George and Blair, the focus has been on allegations that honours and in particular peerages have been given in return for party funding. In 1812 the parties did not need funding. They needed the political support in the Commons which is now usually secured by the modern system of party discipline. In exchange politicians were accustomed to offer not just honours and peerages, but jobs and promotions across the whole public sector. Peel used the system in Ireland but then and later steadily reduced its scope. Merit became increasingly the test for jobs and honours. This was a crucial part of the Victorian cleansing of public life.

In 1812 the election process dragged on, but the final result was not too bad. The acknowledged master of these dark arts in Ireland was Lord Castlereagh and on 16 November Peel could write to him: 'Although our gain in Ireland may not have been great I think considering the exertions which have been made by our opponents, the incredible activities of the [Whig] Duke of Devonshire and the Catholics, we have done as much as we could be expected in maintaining our ground.'[7] The tone is defensive, but the difficulties in Ireland were understood in London. In Britain the Government had increased its majority and Liverpool was well satisfied.

The 1812 election gave Peel a clearer idea of Irish politics than any number of tracts. He was required to administer a system which depended on the consent not of a majority of Irish men but of a small number of Irish and English individuals connected with the Protestant ascendancy. That consent in turn depended on favours from government across the whole range of patronage. Peel saw from the beginning how the granting of favours demeaned and weakened the quality and integrity of government. But deny the favours and the necessary consent would be withheld. The process offended Peel's fundamental seriousness. But he was a man of government; he could not destroy the system on which the Government of Ireland depended. The process told heavily on his patience and his temper.

Peel quickly organised the pattern of his new life with its awkward division between London and Dublin. In Dublin he was the senior executive of government under the Lord-Lieutenant. In London he was the ministerial spokesman on Irish matters in the Commons and in discussion of policy between government departments. The role was not in principle entirely different from that of the modern Secretary of State for Northern Ireland under direct rule, who has the same two tasks, and whose life is similarly divided. The modern Secretary of State deals with six counties rather than twenty-six. But the main difference is the method of travel. The Secretary of State can now be in his office in Stormont two hours after leaving the House of Commons. Peel had to travel over bad roads to the Welsh port of Holyhead, from which the journey to Dublin took at least seven hours, or in bad weather fourteen. Once in 1815 he described the voyage, which took thirty-three hours in a storm, as wretched beyond description; 'The packet was full of passengers. The men were all sick and the women and children thought they were going to the bottom, and filled up the intervals of sickness with a chorus of lamentation and cries of "Steward, are we sinking?" '[8] In his first two years of office Peel crossed the Irish Channel nine times, usually in winter because of the timing of the parliamentary sessions at Westminster which he had to attend.[9] Each journey meant a gap of about a week in the regular flow of work.

In Dublin Peel's home was the Secretary's Lodge in Phoenix Park, though he also had official apartments in the Castle. He found the Lodge a pleasant house with abundant gardens, though the sanitation was primitive and the drawing room ceiling bulged dangerously. Peel set about organising the necessary water closets, and marble columns to strengthen the ceiling. In London he took a house in Stanhope Street in Park Lane. His property was more at risk in London than in Dublin. His London neighbour and colleague, Lord Palmerston, wrote to warn him that the mob were expected to attack the street the next day.[10] Palmerston had boarded up his fanlight and instructed the servants to fire small shot from the bedroom windows as soon as the first stones were thrown.

The main hazard in Dublin by contrast was excessive hospitality. He had written soon after arrival, 'I have scarcely dined once at home ... I see no great prospect of it for some time to come, excepting with about twenty-five guests. I am just opening up the campaign, and have visions of future feasts studded with Lord Mayors and Sheriffs elect.' The vision was realised. The departure of a Lord-Lieutenant was a particularly popular occasion for farewell banquets. The Duke of Richmond left his post in 1813, and observed, drawing on expert knowledge of his own, 'The Lord Mayor has a very pretty method of getting drunk. He is so well used to it that he knows his way back in the dark. And is always sober when he gets up next morning.'¹¹ The heavy drinking was linked to politics by innumerable toasts. The most important of these was to the Protestant King William III who had won the Battle of the Boyne, thus rescuing Ireland from Catholic rule, 'to the pious, glorious and immortal memory of William III'. If he went to the dinner Peel could hardly avoid the toast, and he was observed drinking it in the traditional attitude, standing on his chair with one foot on the table.¹²

Nevertheless, among the clatter of Dublin society Peel led a lonely life. He was twenty-four when he went to Ireland and thirty when he left. The social whirl in which he lived overflowed with gossip, but there is no suggestion from friend or enemy that he had affairs in Dublin. There is something portentous yet plaintive about his efforts in 1813 to drum up a visit from his school friend Bache Thornhill:

> There lives not one with whom I am more anxious to renew, not my friendship, for that requires no renewal, but my former habits of daily intercourse ... You are of an erratic and adventurous turn, you have not been in Ireland, and what reason can you urge for not paying me a visit at the Phoenix Lodge on my return? Choose your companion. Where is James? Where is Browne? I am sure they cannot doubt of the real satisfaction that it will give me to have them the inmates of my house.¹³

Through his life Peel wrote letters morning, noon and night. He varied the style to match his closeness to his correspondent. The above is the example of his clumsy-playful mode. Most of his political correspondence was roundabout and stately, even pompous. But he had made one particular political friend to whom he wrote with special frankness.

John Wilson Croker, now almost forgotten, became a formidable figure in British political and literary life during the first half of the nineteenth century. Eight years older than Peel, he had progressed by way of Trinity College Dublin to the Inns of Court in London. Once the Irish

Parliament was abolished, Irish Protestants like Croker with political
ambition were drawn inexorably towards the House of Commons. Like
Peel, Croker at first made rapid progress and by the time Peel reached
Ireland was not only a Member of Parliament but a junior Minister at the
Admiralty. He held the job for twenty years, proving himself a competent
administrator and turning down offers of promotion. For his real talent
and interest did not lie in the front line of politics. Croker was a critic
and commentator, who loved controversy for its own sake. His views were
not entirely of one piece. He supported Catholic Emancipation and
called himself a rational reformer; but in practice his views on other
matters were hard, Tory, unsentimental and legalistic. As outside pressures
for change began to bear increasingly on the House of Commons, Croker
persuaded himself that the whole country was on the edge of revolution.
He became a master of the slashing attack, plundering history for examples of fatal vacillation and compromise with which to frighten the
Whigs and stiffen Conservative backbones. His vehicle was the *Quarterly
Review*, which became the leading exponent of intellectual Tory opinion.

When Croker met Peel, Croker was at the start of his career. He had
not yet fully formed the friendship with Lord Hertford, who became his
patron in a relationship which drew down on him the lethal scorn of
Disraeli. The caricature of Croker as Rigby in Disraeli's novel *Coningsby* is
as venomous as anything he wrote.*

In those early days Croker was a congenial companion for Peel in the
crowded loneliness of Ireland. With another friend, William Vesey
Fitzgerald, they dashed over for a spree in Paris a few days after the battle
of Waterloo. Sitting next to Wellington at dinner, Peel heard one of the
first of the innumerable accounts which the Duke told of his victory. The
Duke of Richmond, whom all three had served in Ireland not long
before, gave them hospitality in Brussels.† In pouring rain the three
young men roamed the battlefield, still littered with caps, helmets and

---

* 'The world took him at his word,' begins Disraeli's portrait, 'for he was bold, acute and
voluble; with no thought, but a good deal of desultory information; and though destitute of
all imagination and noble sentiment, was blessed with a vigorous mendacious fancy, fruitful in
small expedients, and never happier than when devising shifts for great men's scrapes.'
†His Duchess must still have been tidying up after her ball on the eve of battle made immortal
by Byron.

cartridges among the mass graves; Peel bought a French cuirass for two napoleons.

Yet even then something jars in the correspondence between the two friends. Too often Croker asks for something. In 1812 he asked for £100 to help with his election in County Down, which he lost. Peel turned him down, but next year he was at it again, on behalf of one of his supporters. 'Is there a coast officer's place at Annalong in County Down vacant? Can you give it to one of my martyrs? 'Tis but £35 per annum.' He goes on in a vein which at once arouses suspicion. 'Oh, my dear Peel, the horror of refusing a friend is nothing at all to the horror of asking a friend.' This time Peel did his best, replying that he had found the man a messenger's job at £60 a year, though adding drily, 'no part of whose duty, I fancy, is the conveyance of messages'.

There was a hint, too, of political difference. Peel was warned that Croker was flirting with Canning and his group of malcontents within the Tory Party. The friendship and its steady flow of letters continued. Peel wrote 620 letters to Croker between 1810 and 1846. Until he became Prime Minister, Croker with one interruption was his closest political confidant; but they were two different characters, and in the end it showed.

Peel quickly realised that his complacent first letter to the Prime Minister about Ireland had simply recorded a short peaceful interval between bouts of disorder. He soon grasped the underlying cause of disorder. It was not created by the French; it would not be removed by greater prosperity or better administration, nor even by admitting Catholics to Parliament or by reducing the burden of the Protestant Church of Ireland on the Catholic majority. It arose from something more fundamental, the rejection of British rule, a rejection strengthened by a growing sense of Irish history and therefore Irish nationalism.

Yet Peel was clear that British rule in Ireland was essential to Britain. Ireland was not a distant colony, but part of the fortress of the British Isles. Peel owned no Irish property and had no particular regard for the importunate representatives of the Protestant ascendancy. For traditional Tories the argument for British rule in Ireland was not economic, but strategic. History showed how quickly and dangerously Irish discontents were exploited by Britain's enemies; first Spain, then France. British rule of Ireland, which was crucial to Britain's security, depended on the apparatus of Dublin Castle and of the Protestant ascendancy. By making this apparatus more efficient, more honest, and more reasonable, the Government could lessen its dependence on military force and reduce the garrison; that was the most that could be hoped for.

Nowadays we draw a distinction between peaceful and violent pressure for political change. This distinction lies at the heart of the peace process in Northern Ireland, begun under John Major and continued under Tony Blair in the 1990s. Could Sinn Fein be persuaded to renounce force, to replace the bullet by the ballot, while retaining its belief in a United Ireland? The question has waited long for a definitive answer. But this distinction between political and violent action depends on possibilities which hardly existed between 1812 and 1818 when Peel was in Ireland. We take for granted the existence of peaceful groups moulding opinion and a parliamentary system which everyone recognises as broadly representative. Neither of these assets existed in Peel's early years. Political action rapidly became violent for lack of a peaceful outlet. Men like Peel in his early years, and Croker even more, saw political agitation outside Parliament as simply the prelude to violence. It was therefore wise to act against such agitation before it took hold.

The leader of Irish Catholic opinion at this time was Daniel O'Connell. Thirteen years older than Peel, he had already established himself as a skilful lawyer with a taste for theatrical confrontation. O'Connell was a romantic radical, but no revolutionary. Indeed he had been harassed out of France after the Revolution and actually joined the volunteers raised in 1796 to resist a French invasion of Ireland. He campaigned against the Union throughout his life, but supported the British monarchy. He professed to oppose any resort to physical force as a remedy for Ireland's problems.[14] Yet to Peel this was simply a pretence, and he described O'Connell to the Home Secretary as one of the two leaders of the violent party.[15]

Peel had half a point. O'Connell's direct actions were not violent, but his oratory certainly was, and that was the trouble. He excited people with his words, then looked away if their excitement led them to riot or murder. O'Connell was quick to assault Peel for his youth and fashionable appearance denouncing 'the foppery of perfumed handkerchiefs and thin shoes'.[16] The two men settled into a relationship of strong antagonism. In 1815 it came to a head. At a Catholic meeting O'Connell accused Peel of lack of courage. 'Mr Peel would not dare, in my presence, or in any place where he was liable to personal account, to use a single experience derogatory to my interest or my honour.'[17]

Neither his grandfather Parsley Peel nor the first Sir Robert would have been greatly bothered by O'Connell's remarks. But Harrow and Christ Church had pushed Peel into a society where such words had to be taken seriously. Duelling was illegal and disapproved of, but it still happened, particularly in Ireland. If Peel had not reacted, O'Connell would have repeated and intensified the attack. After an unsatisfactory private exchange Peel issued a challenge against the slur on his integrity. It was agreed that the two men should fight with pistols, at Ostend, beyond the reach of the authorities. Peel was taking a big physical risk; O'Connell had killed a man in a duel the previous winter. O'Connell was an excellent pistol shot, as a result of long practice shooting dogs which came out at him as he rode on legal business through the Irish countryside. But through his life Peel showed himself exceptionally sensitive to any attack on his honour. The son of the cotton manufacturer had been turned into a gentleman and a gentleman had to defend his honour.[18]

There was no heroic sequel to this heroic decision. Peel slipped across the Channel to keep his appointment. But the news leaked, and O'Connell was detained in London. The press began debating the matter as if it was a political tournament. Peel spent three weeks hanging about incognito on the Continent, unable to do any official work. His friends began to worry that he was carrying the matter too far. His brother William wrote: 'I think you have done perhaps more than was required of you.'[19]

The two seconds started a mini-quarrel between themselves and held a mini-duel in Calais at which neither was hurt. A grave defence of Peel's honour was dwindling into farce. The whole episode petered out, and Peel returned to Dublin. Ten years later O'Connell apologised, at a time when he hoped for Peel's support on Catholic Emancipation; but the two men were never on reasonable personal terms.

Peel's political duel with O'Connell had begun earlier and continued longer than this personal fracas. O'Connell dodged in and out of the law, forming, dissolving and re-forming bodies with different names and rules to continue his struggle against the Union. In June 1814 Peel persuaded his colleagues to outlaw O'Connell's current organisation, the Catholic

Board. It was a long tussle, and in private Peel criticised Liverpool for being much too pacific a Minister for Ireland.[20] The ban did indeed deprive O'Connell of a legal vehicle for organised agitation for several years. For a moment Peel sat back content. 'I never saw a document in print which gave me so much satisfaction – a new era, to use a fashionable phrase – in the policy of the Government.'[21] But the essential problem lay below the surface of O'Connell's eloquence.

Peel received a steady flow of reports from all over Ireland of intimidation, violence, disorder and murder. Particular victims were magistrates, witnesses, members of a jury, and anyone who actively helped the Government. Peel read of Mr Lawrence of Carrick whose daughter was raped by four men before his eyes; of the small farmer in Westmeath murdered at Mass after he had killed three men who attacked his home; of James Connell, who had given evidence in a case for the prosecution, barbarously murdered with his wife; of a whole family burned to death in their home in County Louth after three men had been hanged for an earlier attack on them.[22]

Throughout Peel's life bad news acted as a stimulus. He often thought and spoke with deep pessimism, but pessimism was usually a prelude to action. The 'aversion to lounge' of which old Dean Jackson had spoken remained dominant. In Ireland it did not take him long to decide and get agreement on a fresh policy, with two main components. He revived the old Insurrection Act which empowered local magistrates to call out the yeomanry or British garrison to deal with disorder. Peel accepted that the prompt use of military force was often necessary. But though he defended the Act as a temporary measure, he was never enthusiastic about its use. Some magistrates who were local landowners were too quick to spread alarmist reports or to protect their interests with unnecessary use of force.

Ireland was increasingly divided on sectarian lines. While Peel himself was staunchly loyal to the Union, the language and tactics of loyalists were a different matter. He distrusted the Brunswick Clubs which had sprung up to express, sometimes violently, what were already called Orange opinions. Such opinions were particularly strong in the local yeomanry. When the yeomanry were in 1816 accused of unnecessary killings in Roscrea, Peel wrote 'if the corps of yeomanry have acted improperly as a body, for God's sake as a body let them be punished. There is enough bad blood in Tipperary without the blockheads aggravating it with their party tunes.'[23] Peel was clear that the Government should not use its monopoly of legal force to favour one section of the community against another. The law was the best safeguard. Peel began to stress the importance of using the ordinary law rather than exceptional measures whenever possible. In his view, as he wrote to a correspondent at the end of 1816, it was often 'better to bear with some disturbance than to repress it by the means of unusual and extreme authority'.[24]

More was needed. Even discounting the cries of alarmists, even with the help of the Insurrection Act over and above the ordinary law, the Government and local magistrates often had to choose between inaction and the use of troops to shoot and kill. Moreover, it was increasingly difficult to find the troops. While the war against Napoleon lasted the Irish Government had to argue in Whitehall the case for troops against the more dramatic needs of Wellington in Spain and Flanders. But at least no one in London could during the war doubt that Ireland must be defended against the French and Irish rebels who sided with the French. During Peel's first years in Ireland regular troops and local yeomanry amounted together to about 30,000 men.

After Waterloo the French threat disappeared. Retrenchment became the rule in London and pressure to reduce the garrison in Ireland was irresistible. Even before Waterloo Peel began to work out a proposal for a professional force of police to be deployed first of all in counties with the worst disorder. To his surprise the proposal, skilfully christened the Peace Preservation Bill, passed through the Westminster Parliament early in 1814 and recruitment started. Anyone who knew Ireland understood that at this point the real difficulty would begin. New jobs created by government meant a new honey pot round which the friends of government would buzz. Demands poured in on behalf of deserving friends and impoverished relations. By then Peel knew Ireland well. The 1812 election had shown him that Ireland could not be governed without patronage verging on corruption. He could not destroy that system, but he was not going to let it infect his new creation. Confronted with this torrent of applications he was clear: 'We ought to be crucified if we make the measure a job and select our constables from the servants of our parliamentary friends.'[25] Merit and only merit must be the test for the new constables. Peel was learning to look to the long term. He wrote to an official, 'the Bill was rendered necessary by the past state of Ireland for the last fifty years, and by the probable state of it for the next five hundred'.[26]

In the short term the new police provided only a patchy improvement. It was possible to reduce the British garrison to 22,000 by 1817. Peel in 1816 actually supported the Chancellor of the Exchequer in resisting the claims of his Irish colleagues for extra troops. Law and sound administration were for Peel better palliatives for Ireland's problems than expensive military occupation. But the palliatives produced minor improvement rather than cure.

The disorder continued, bringing with it atrocities of a cruelty which made a deep impression on Peel. He was determined to convey to his colleagues and to Parliament in London a sense of the outrage which he felt. In 1816 the Prime Minister showed signs of favouring reprieves for individuals condemned to death for crimes of violence. Peel remonstrated, 'You have no idea of the moral deprivation of the lower order in that county [Tipperary]. In fidelity towards each other they are unexampled, as they are in their sanguinary disposition and fearlessness of the consequences of indulging it.'[27] Peel rammed the point home in a debate in the House of Commons in April 1816.

> The disturbances which now prevailed had no precise or definite cause. They seemed to be the effect of a general confederacy in crime – a conspiracy in guilt – a systematic opposition to all laws and municipal institutions ... The records of the courts of justice would show such a settled and uniform system of guilt, such monstrous and horrible prejudices, as could not ... be found in the annals of any country on the face of the globe, whether civilised or uncivilised.[28]

He followed up with specific examples of murder. One of these cast a shadow on his mind so dark that he recalled it many years later. He was supporting coercive measures in Ireland after a year in which there had been 196 murders:

> Why, you have fought great battles and achieved famous victories at a less cost of English blood. But why do I talk of battles? Oh how tame and feeble the comparison between death on the field of honour and

that death which is inflicted by the hand of Irish assassins! It is not the fatal hour of that death that is most terrible: it is the wasting misery of suspense, the agony of expectation, listening for weeks and months to every nightly sound lest it be the fatal knell to summon a whole family to destruction. These are the real terrors, from which the act of murder is too often a merciful relief. In Ireland they can afford to give you notice of death, and woe to the victim that receives that notice and neglects it. I am still haunted by the recollection of the scenes of atrocity and suffering with which I was once familiar.

Peel went on to describe the Dillon family in Kilkenny – father, mother and three children, the eldest a girl of nine. The father had helped with his evidence to bring about the execution of a wanted man. He asked that his home be 'slated' by the government. Peel explained why a slated roof, as compared to thatch, gave some protection against arson. But the slate roof was no help to Dillon. Murderers came, dragged him outside and killed him with pitchforks. Peel recalled how the mother spoke to her eldest daughter:

'Those are the cries of your dying father. I shall be the next victim. After they have murdered him they will murder me; but I will not go out when they call me: I will struggle with them to the last, that I may give you time to do that for which I put you here. My last act will be to throw this dry turf on the hearth; and do you, by the glare of it watch the faces of the murderers, mark them all narrowly, that you may be able to tell who they are, and to revenge the death of your father and your mother.' So it happened: the dry turf blazed long enough; five murderers were hanged on the unshakeable evidence of a child.

Peel quoted Macbeth:

Blood will have blood they say.
Stones have been known to move and trees to speak;
Auguries and understood relations have brought forth
The secretest man of blood.

He ended: 'In Ireland the man of blood is not secret; and neither the law

of his country, nor his own conscience have any terrors for him.'[29] Peel's
anger is manifest and genuine, yet anger did not lead him to the cry for
vengeance which similar atrocities provoked in public opinion during the
Indian Mutiny. His private conclusion had been reached by 1816: 'I believe
an honest despotic government would be by far the fittest government for
Ireland.'[30]

Even the most awful tragedy becomes trite when often repeated.
British opinion hardened through the nineteenth century, providing itself
with a thick protective layer of mixed tedium and irritation against the
steady flow of Irish troubles. The same phenomenon became apparent
during the renewed troubles of the 1970s and 1980s. As Secretary of State
I was constantly surprised that IRA atrocities failed to stir opinion, either
one way or the other, for or against our policy in Northern Ireland.

There was one aspect of the Irish problems which could not be
shunted into a siding. The barrier which kept Catholics out of the House
of Commons was not the most important Irish grievance, but because it
lay at the heart of British politics it was the most discussed. The question
of Catholic Emancipation had divided every Cabinet since the days of
Pitt. Cabinet government was only possible on the basis that, whatever
individual Ministers thought, the government as a whole was neutral on
the Catholic issue. Neutrality meant inaction, and the formula therefore
particularly suited the Prime Minister, Lord Liverpool, who wanted no
change in the foreseeable future. More important, it suited the King –
both George III, who believed that his Coronation Oath prevented him
from agreeing to Emancipation, and his son who as Prince Regent and
then as George IV discovered rather late in the day that it was his duty to
obey his father's wishes. The opinion of the Crown still weighed heavily,
and it was this rather than stalemate in Cabinet which enabled the
formula of neutrality to survive for so long.

But it was not a stable formula; it could not go on for ever. The balance
of opinion in the Cabinet and in Parliament began to shift towards
Emancipation. Castlereagh and Canning, bitter rivals in other respects,
were both 'Catholics'; so were most of the younger more liberal Tories; so
were the Whigs in opposition; so even was voluble, right-wing Croker.
The periodical debates in the Commons became increasingly desperate
rearguard actions. During Peel's time in Ireland the Commons still contained a majority against Catholic Emancipation, but the margin was

narrow and the 'Protestants' were conscious that in terms of quality of argument the battle was becoming unequal. On the other hand the Prince Regent was impervious to argument. So indeed was public opinion outside Parliament. People no longer worried seriously about a new Guy Fawkes or a new James II; but anti-Catholic prejudice was part of the English cultural tradition which ordinary Englishmen were slow to abandon and rather enjoyed.

Against this background Peel found himself pushed to the front of the 'Protestant' cause. In those ranks youthful energy and eloquence were in short supply, and he could provide both. Some who knew him well were surprised. Palmerston was forthright: 'I can forgive old women like the Chancellor, spoonies like Liverpool, ignoramuses like Westmorland, old stumped-up Tories like Bathurst, — but how such a man as Peel, liberal enlightened and fresh minded, should find himself running in such a pack is hardly intelligible.'[31]

But Peel did not find the choice difficult. He might already be working out in his mind a concept of the national interest, but letting Catholics into Parliament need not necessarily be included. Peel accepted the traditional argument that in one important way Catholics were outside the nation: they refused allegiance to the Crown. He expressed this in a letter to the Duke of Richmond as early as 2 March 1813:

> At no time and under no circumstances, so long as the Catholic admits the supremacy in spirituals of a foreign earthly potentate and will not tell us what supremacy in spirituals means, so long as he will not give us voluntarily that security which every despotic sovereign in Europe has by the concession of the Pope himself, I will not consent to admit them. They are excluded from privileges for which they will not pay the price that all other subjects pay, and that all other Catholics in Europe find themselves bound to pay.[32]

The boundary between the spiritual and the temporal had been blurred by the Catholics themselves. So long as that boundary was blurred, the British Crown could not be sure of their loyalty.

Opponents of Emancipation at first began to talk about what were called securities in order to appear reasonable, whereas in their hearts they opposed the principle of Emancipation. But by the time of the

Commons debate of May 1817 the question of securities was at centre stage. Grattan, formerly the brightest star of the Irish Parliament, introduced a detailed motion in Westminster approving Catholic Emancipation with securities and with some exceptions. Peel made the wind-up speech opposing the motion.[33]

At first sight when one reads the speech in full, its success is slightly surprising. It is not particularly eloquent, and until the close there are no memorable passages. Peel devised a skilful debating speech in which he picked to pieces the details of Grattan's proposals on securities. He did not defend the history of British involvement in Ireland, but argued that the House had to recognise where we stood today. There was an inviolable compact between Britain and Ireland, of which one essential part was the recognition of Protestantism as the established and favoured religion of State. Peel continued with a rhetorical device which became his favourite. He listed with an appearance of objectivity the policies between which his audience could choose. They could at one extreme outlaw the Catholic Church in Ireland: no one proposed that. Or they could make it the established Church; no one proposed that. They could go on as at present, excluding the Catholics 'from those offices which are immediately connected with the administration of, and may be said to constitute the government of the country – admitting them generally to all other offices, privileges and distinctions'. Or they could approve Grattan's plan for Catholic Emancipation.

Peel drew attention to the failure of attempts to gain the approval of the Vatican or the Irish clergy to the securities proposed by Grattan. Grattan wanted Catholics to be eligible to be Chief Secretary of Ireland, but not Lord-Lieutenant; to be Cabinet Ministers but not King. This would divide the King and his representatives in Ireland from his advisers. It would not satisfy the Catholics, who would press for access to the very top positions and the disestablishment of the Protestant Church of Ireland. Emancipation as proposed by Grattan would in practice bring no benefit to the people or Catholic clergy of Ireland, only to the aristocracy and the Bar. He ended with an off-the-peg peroration on our glorious constitution, asking any undecided Member to 'weigh the substantial blessings which he knows to have derived from the government that is, against all the speculative advantages which he is promised from the government which is to be'.[34]

In a Parliament of loose party loyalties, Members listened to the arguments before deciding on their vote. By speaking last on his side Peel seized the tactical advantage; his detailed arguments were still fresh in the mind of Members as they voted. Contrary to their expectations, the Protestants defeated Grattan's motion by twenty-four votes. Peel's speech was greeted as a sensational success. 'There was never a speech did so much for a man,' wrote one observer. As early as 1814 O'Connell had christened him 'Orange Peel' before there was much justification for the unsubtle joke. Peel did not regard himself as a champion of the Orange cause in Ireland. He had removed orange facings from the livery of his servants in his house at Drayton. Not for him the crude partisanship for that cause which later distinguished Lord Randolph Churchill, Carson and Bonar Law. But after the speech of May 1817 he could not help himself. Partly because there was no other, he became at the age of twenty-nine the Protestant hero. Dean Jackson was among the first to send congratulations; copies of the speech were widely distributed; Canning on the other side of the debate praised its consummate ability; the Corporation of Dublin asked him to sit for his portrait.

One greater prize followed immediately. In the spring of 1817 the parliamentary seat of the University of Oxford fell vacant. In the unreformed Parliament the reputation of constituencies varied hugely. A county Member representing a sizeable electorate had greater prestige than a man who sat for a rotten borough. In the highest rank shone the University seats of Oxford and Cambridge. For Peel to sit for his old university, to which he was deeply attached, would be a big step upward from tiny corrupt Chippenham. The difficulty was that Canning wanted the seat badly. Canning was fed up with his present constituency of Liverpool, far away and full of hard work. Also a Christ Church man, he was senior to Peel and much better known. But that was the difficulty: Canning was widely known and widely distrusted. Peel on the other hand was young, and, the wise professors thought, malleable. He had just scored a splendid victory for the Protestant cause, in which the University believed and on which Canning was unsound. A wave of enthusiasm led by Christ Church swept Peel into the seat. It remained for his old tutor, Dr Lloyd, to point out that the University, unlike Chippenham, expected its Member of Parliament to respect their views.[35]

Peel had now worked in Ireland for five years. When politicians have a talent for administration, given time they change the nature of any job they are given. Peel transformed the job of Chief Secretary. His predecessor had floated uncertainly in ill-defined relationships with the Lord-Lieutenant and with the Prime Minister and Home Secretary in London. Peel established an efficient, well co-ordinated partnership with successive Lord-Lieutenants, within which he took over the massive work of daily administration. He thus became the real power in Irish politics.[36] He kept open a direct line of communication with the Prime Minister, elbowing to one side the Home Secretary Lord Sidmouth, whose interest in Ireland was fleeting and indifferent. He worked closely with those Irish officials whom he found efficient.

Peel took administration seriously. He discounted the idea that government was just a matter of reconciling interests and keeping things quiet. For Peel administration consisted of positive decision-taking, based on facts.

'There is nothing like a fact,' he wrote to one official in 1814, and again two years later, 'Facts are ten times more valuable than declamations.'[37] But Ireland, while awash with declamations, rumours and exaggerations, was short of demonstrable facts. Peel persisted. There were serious food shortages in 1817. Peel organised what were by the standards of the time significant relief measures, the harvest turned out favourably, the famine receded and his reputation was further enhanced. When the food shortage was at its height he received a proposal that the Government should ban the export of potatoes from Ireland to Britain. At first sight it seemed an obvious way of keeping food in the country. But Peel asked for figures of those exports. No figures were available. Peel remonstrated, but if the plan was to be effective it must be applied at once; urged on by the Lord-Lieutenant and Irish officials Peel put it to his colleagues in London without figures. When the figures turned up they showed that the export of potatoes from Ireland was negligible whereas imports were three times as high. Peel had been made to look ridiculous. This experience hardened Peel's heart against sloppy vagueness of all kinds.

Indeed for him this whole period marked a hardening of heart. As he learned more of human frailties, Peel's character changed. The clumsy jollity which had imbued earlier letters to friends disappeared. Ireland turned Peel sour. Against the background of tragedies like that of the Dillon family the tone of Dublin society struck him as extraordinary.

When in England for the big Irish debate in 1816, Peel sent for the latest news from Dublin. The Military Secretary, Sir Edward Littlehales, replied 'with an account of vice-regal dinners, adding that everything had gone off perfectly well, except on one unfortunate night, on which Lady Manners had a party at the time there was another party at the Castle. I think Sir Edward is rather surprised that these subjects formed no part of the debate on the state of Ireland.'[38] Peel had no time for such social niceties. He saw that in Dublin to frivolity was added incessant greed. Government depended on patronage; the demand for places greatly exceeded the supply. 'I am in the midst of all these vultures, and must throw a little food among them occasionally,' he wrote to an official.[39]

Peel developed irony as a vehicle for his refusals. One man wanted a baronetcy so that he could get married. 'I fear I must request you to advise your friend not to postpone his marriage in expectation of a baronetcy. I am sure he cannot want that in addition to his other recommendations.' Of another claimant Peel remarked that when he wanted a baronetcy he was very rich, but when he wanted a place he was very poor. A notorious gambler applied for the Collectorship of Taxes in Belfast. 'Considering how careless he has been of his own money perhaps some office not connected with the collection of public money and requiring incessant vigilance to prevent fraud would be more suited to him.'[40]

But the facts of political life in Ireland remained unchanged. Votes were needed, and votes had to be found. In a typically jaunty letter Palmerston, still Peel's colleague, asked in 1817 if there was likely to be a contest in the next election in Sligo. If so he could manufacture 280 to 290 votes by creating new tenancies on his estate. The assumption, still just valid in 1817, was that the new tenants would vote as their landlord wished.[41]

After five years of this Peel had had enough, not just of Ireland, but of government office. He wanted a break, and began to urge this on the Prime Minister. There was a problem of timing. The Duke of Richmond's successor as Lord-Lieutenant was Lord Whitworth, a skilful diplomat who worked well with Peel, being content to let his junior carry most of the daily burden. But Whitworth's time was coming to an end, and it was agreed that Peel should remain to see in his successor, Lord Talbot. He remained until the summer of 1818, having supervised one more general election. His spirits rose. 'This is the hottest day I remember in Ireland. Old women say there must be a rebellion this year for it is as hot as it was in 1798. However as I leave Ireland in a fortnight I hope to close my accounts without one.'[42] This closing of accounts was as near a triumph as any British Minister could achieve in Ireland. Peel left at a quiet moment, the press and Dublin opinion were loud in his praises, and the administration of Ireland had been much improved by his efforts.

He forgot the sourness of Ireland when he wrote to Croker:

A fortnight hence I shall be free as air – free from ten thousand engagements which I cannot fulfil; free from the anxiety of having more to do than it is possible to do well; free from the acknowledgements of that gratitude which consists in a lively sense of future favours; free from the necessity of abstaining from private intimacy that will certainly interfere with public duty; free from Orange-men; free from Ribbonmen; free from the Lord Mayor and Sheriffs; free from men who pretend to be Protestants on principle and sell Dundalk to the Papists of Cork; free from Catholics who become Protestants to get into Parliament after the manner of ——, and of Protestants who become Catholics after the manner of old ——; free from perpetual converse about the Harbour of Howth and Dublin Bay haddock; and lastly, free of the Company of Carvers and Gilders which I became this day in reward of my public services.[43]

On 3 August 1818 Peel left Belfast for Scotland. Ireland was to return often to his thoughts and emotions in coming years; but he never went there again.

Four

Bullion and a Bride

'But where thou art is home to me, And home without thee
cannot be'
Peel to his wife Julia

'Do not you think that there is a feeling, becoming daily
more general and more confirmed, … in favour of some
undefined change in the mode of governing the country?'
Peel to Croker, 23 March 1820

'Peel has declined accepting office, but whether it is because
he wishes to live retired with his pretty wife, or that he
thinks the Ministry will not stand, I know not'
Mr Wilbraham to Lord Colchester, 1821

*T*he thought of Scotland softened Peel's prose style. 'We had
supreme dominion, so far as the chase is concerned, over
uncounted thousands of acres. Loch Ericht, and Loch Laggan
and Loch Dhu, and the streams from a thousand hills were ours. We had
hind and hart, hare and roe, black game and grouse, partridge and ptarmi-
gan, snipe and wild duck.' Peel went straight from Ireland in August 1818
to rent a castle near Badenoch in Inverness-shire. He and his party shot
thirteen hundred grouse during their holiday of five weeks. He brought
with him his cook 'to gild the decline of day'.¹ Peel was attracted by the
wide spaces and the contrast between the chatter of politics and the
monosyllabic wisdom of ghillies and gamekeepers. He had deliberately
sought and now genuinely enjoyed this long rest from government office.

But this did not mean a rest from politics. Peel was soon deliberately
preparing himself for the next chapter. As usual he had approached Dr
Lloyd, his old tutor at Christ Church, this time for examples of the art of

reasoning, particularly in reply to argument. 'There is not half reasoning enough in politics – not half. Burke's speech on the Nabob of Arcot's debts is good, but he sets out with a distinct enumeration of the arguments of his opponents.'[2] Peel himself soon perfected this technique of fair-mindedness as one of the arts of persuasion. He became a master of defining his opponent's argument before knocking it down.

He soon faced a task which taxed to the full this growing gift for clear exposition of a complicated theme. There was widespread confusion and unrest about the banking system. The Napoleonic Wars had created hardship for some and prosperity for others. Farming had thrived on high prices, some industries connected with the war effort had done well; others had been ruined by the restrictions on trade. The Government and the banking system had managed somehow to cope with the costs of war, but had strayed far from the firm principles of financial management laid down by the younger Pitt. The obligation of the Bank of England to pay gold in return for notes had been suspended in 1797, with the effect of depreciating the currency in terms of gold. There was an uneasy feeling that this was disreputable; even while the war was still on the Horner Committee had recommended in 1810 an immediate return to the gold standard. But the Government and many businessmen were scared at the prospect of tighter money and the deflation which might result. The change back to gold was accepted in principle but in practice repeatedly postponed.

Britain after Waterloo suffered a multitude of economic ills, notably chronic unemployment and agricultural hardship. It became increasingly fashionable to blame these on obscure manipulation of the banking system by the Bank of England, by Chancellors of the Exchequer and shadowy international financiers with names like Baring and Rothschild.

The debate was complex, which sometimes helps an uncertain government to postpone a decision. But by 1819 obfuscation could no longer benefit government. The Cabinet was faced with a parliamentary revolt when they proposed yet another postponement of cash payments. They decided, as Cabinets do, to set up an immediate parliamentary Committee of Enquiry. Peel asked if he could be a member; after discussion with the Prime Minister, Lord Liverpool, he was appointed chairman. It was a striking achievement for a young man just over thirty who had no experience of finance. His ability and honesty were not in doubt; he was at a loose end; those were sufficient qualifications.

It was just right for Peel too. He set himself to accumulate and study the facts and draw objective conclusions. Eight years earlier as a new MP he had voted against an immediate return to the gold standard. More important, his father, always the practical businessman, feared the result of a return to the gold standard on those who relied on easy credit to run a profitable business. But Peel set these considerations aside. He threw himself into the new work.

The Committee met twenty-five times between February and May: Peel never missed a meeting. Bankers, economists and businessmen gave copious evidence. The pamphlets poured in. There was no doubt about the way the intellectual tide was flowing. Radicals such as Attwood in Birmingham, joined by some agriculturists, might argue like old Sir Robert for a loose monetary policy. But the Whigs, the leading economist Ricardo and an increasing number of liberal Tories on the Government benches felt that the time had come to return to honest money. They distrusted the Bank of England. They felt that they had tolerated long enough the half-hidden devices by which old-fashioned Chancellors of the Exchequer like Vansittart, the current occupant, had shuffled their way through each financial crisis.

The leader of this campaign was William Huskisson. He held the unpromising job of First Commissioner for Trade, Forests and Land Revenues. The Prime Minister preferred to keep energetic policy makers out of the Cabinet for as long as possible. His own views on economic matters were liberal, and there was no sudden breakthrough. But Huskisson's clear mind and forceful advocacy were gaining ground, with Liverpool himself and also with up-and-coming politicians like Peel. 'In finance, expedient and ingenious devices may answer to meet temporary difficulties; but for a permanent and peace system [*sic*] the only wise course, either in policy or for impression is a system of simplicity and truth.' Peel could have written this at any time in his life, but they are the words of Huskisson on cash payments in 1819.[3]

An impressive pamphlet reached Peel from the Reverend Edward Copleston, later Bishop of Llandaff. It showed how intellectual and moral impulses joined to flow down the same channel. Honest men should believe in honest money just as, increasingly, honest men were coming to believe in clean government or indeed (a little down the line) in free trade. It was for Providence to guide the fortunes of individuals and nations. The less that imperfect men interfered with the workings of Providence the better. So monetary doctrine was fed by evangelical fervour. To suspend cash payments in 1797 had been a device justifiable at the lowest moment of the war against France. To resume them was a sign of a God-fearing nation, confident enough to clear away the clutter of the past and keep bankers and politicians in their place. Providence allied to good English common sense should see to the rest.

Peel was an orthodox Anglican who disliked religious controversy. He rarely himself brought religion into political argument at a time when it was quite common to do so. But his alert mind caught and was influenced by this increasingly dominant spirit. It brought him together with the reforming group within the Government – Huskisson, Lord Liverpool himself, even Canning, with whom on the question of Catholic Emancipation Peel deeply disagreed.[4] As a particularly shrewd historian of this episode put it, '[i]n 1819 Englishmen embraced gold, seduced by its moral force as a symbol of truth and stability ... like swimmers leaping into the cleanness of fixed parities'.[5]

The real difficulty for his Committee lay not with the principle, but with timing and detail. A transitional period was needed, for example to deal with repayment of loans made by the Bank in the depreciated currency. The Committee put forward, and Parliament approved without much difficulty, a complicated set of proposals. From May 1823 the Bank would fully return to gold. Peel's speech introducing his report on 24 May dealt competently and at length with the technical proposals, but also put the question in the perspective of history. He described with magisterial authority what should in his view be the correct, that is subordinate, relationship between the Bank of England and the sovereign Parliament.

Peel's Act of 1819 was never short of critics, and Peel had often to return to the subject. Attwood and the worried businessmen of Birmingham were right to argue that the short-term effect was deflationary. But it was not sudden. Over the four years between the passing of the Act and the resumption of payments sterling rose of its own accord and at the moment of convertibility the remaining gap between sterling and the price of gold was described as 'trifling'. Cobbett had been far off the mark when he predicted universal ruin and a million people dying of hunger.[6] In the long run convertibility rooted the gold standard deep in the British economic system and entrenched sterling as the leading world currency.

In 1819 Peel was not in government, but the Government and the House of Commons had in effect delegated the currency issue to him. Politicians devising a major policy have to cope with a mix of practical and intellectual thoughts and emotions. For some the practical is everything: they work for a decision which accurately reflects the sum of the arguments and the pressures mobilised to influence them. In others the intellectual conviction comes first, and they wrestle to minimise the concessions which they have to make to practical pressures. At least three times after 1819 (on Catholic Emancipation, Parliamentary Reform and the Corn Laws) Peel worked out this balance within himself in politically desperate circumstances. He was by nature a man of government, emphatic on facts as the basis of a decision, devoted to clarity, order and good administration, impatient of wild concepts and empty phrases. Gladstone wrote that Peel was 'not a far sighted man, but fairly clear sighted'.[7] But beyond that he was a man of conviction. He needed to believe in what he did; his decisions had to fit his beliefs. These were based on the traditional Anglican pillars of reason and Christian faith. He rejected, often with scorn, propositions which collided with either of those pillars. But on each occasion the balance between the practical pressures and the intellectual conviction was in the end struck in a different place from his starting point.

On the Bullion Committee in 1819 Peel felt few practical pressures. He was not in charge of the Government or the Exchequer. He led no party. Because of the safe wealth he was to inherit he felt none of the prejudices which go with personal economic anxiety. He did not enjoy disagreeing with his father, but knew that the old gentleman would bear no grudge. The result was a cool dependence on rational process which he traced back to his mathematical training at Oxford. He wrote to Charles Lloyd,

I believe the demonstration of the Bullion report to be complete. Still there are facts apparently at variance with their theory. If the demonstration is complete, this can only be so apparently. They are like the triangles that I used to bring to Bridge [his maths coach] and declare that the angles of these particular triangles amounted to more than two right angles. The answer in each case is the same: There is some error in the fact, and in the triangle, not in the proof ...[8]

A familiar fallacy lurks inside this comparison. Economists often parade their theories as if they were as absolute as a mathematical proof, concealing the subjective assumptions on which they rest. The newcomer is tempted to support the economic theory simply because he understands it; he is attracted precisely by its neatness. The fact that the bullionist doctrine of return to gold was aesthetically attractive may have helped Peel to believe that it was intellectually inevitable and morally right. This underlying simplicity informed the detail of his own later Budgets. He would have enthusiastically welcomed successors who worked in the same purifying spirit. He would have congratulated Geoffrey Howe when he swept away exchange control in 1979 or Gordon Brown when he transferred interest rate decisions from suspect politicians to an independent Bank of England operating within published rules. In later years Peel would not have been as ready as in 1819 to crush facts into a theory, or to treat political economy as a form of mathematics. But he would never let pragmatism dominate his mind completely. He always needed a valid moral and intellectual shield for each main decision.

The bullion question, added to the pursuit of partridges and grouse, could fill Peel's days, but hardly made a full man. He was thirty-one, good-looking, a rising political star and heir to a considerable fortune. He clearly needed a wife, or at least feminine companionship of some kind. That was certainly the view of Lady Shelley, who fancied herself as a political hostess and drew Peel into her net during 1819. Frances Shelley was not attracted at their first meeting; Peel talked too much about partridges. But soon she became interested in his knowledge of English literature and his lively stories about Ireland. He told her the tragic story of the dry turf cast on the fire to light the face of the murderers. She decided that he was the English Metternich and 'a most delightful person'. The high point of her friendship was a dinner party at Peel's home at which she was the only lady present. The conversation was political and there was no scandal. Peel saw no harm in flirting with a skittish married lady who enjoyed political gossip, but he was not the man for a flaming affair.

And anyway, he was committing himself elsewhere. Another lady on the prowl was the widow of Sir John Floyd, a distinguished General who had fought gallantly with the cavalry in Germany and India. At the close of his career Sir John was posted to Ireland where he and his family were on friendly terms with Peel. Sir John was old-fashioned: he wore blue breeches and a triangular hat. He died in 1818 leaving an Indian fortune, a vigorous Irish lady who had been his second wife, and the children of his first marriage including, most importantly, a beautiful daughter called Julia. Lady Floyd, eager to find a husband for her stepdaughter, played Peel on a long line. In Dublin it had transpired that his Dresden dinner service lacked ice picks. Lady Floyd promised to trace the missing items for him. She invited him to call in London to inspect her findings, carefully baiting the hook with a reference to Julia: 'Miss Floyd joins me in requesting that you will remember us and that you will believe that we never do or can forget your kindness to us at Dublin.' The friendship between Peel and young Julia grew into romance. Julia had many admirers, including the future Tsar Nicholas of Russia; but Peel won her heart, and in March 1820 she accepted his proposal. She was twenty-five, seven years his junior.

For reasons which are not clear Peel then imposed on himself a period of exile which went beyond any reasonable convention. In March 1820 he went to stay with his sister Mary in Bognor. Ineptly, he wrote to his dearest Julia that he did not intend to make impassioned declarations of his love. Her response was to keep her own letters few and short. More skilfully he developed a habit, carried on after their marriage, of criticising harshly those of his experiences which she did not share. 'We are about a quarter of a mile from the sea, with an imperfect view of it.' 'Bognor ... must be the paragon of dullness. There is nothing whatever to gratify the test of those who delight in the festivities of Brighton or Margate. No theatre, no balls, no society, not even a walk. Mary and I toiled over a shingle beach yesterday which must have been precisely in the same state at the creation of the world.' 'Our days pass in the unvarying sameness. I can hardly tell you what we do. I for my part do nothing but write to you and look at the sea, and sometimes pretend to read a book, and when I think I have been particularly attentive, awake from a sort of reverie and ask myself in vain what it is I have been reading about.'[9] Remembering the Highlands while contemplating the flatness of Bognor in March, he hoped that Julia shared his taste for solitude and rocky uninhabited wilderness.

Searching for diversions, Peel and his sister visited Arundel Castle, but found it melancholy and everything in bad taste.[10] It was a great relief to return to London at the end of the month and dine with Julia and her mother in Seymour Street.

Peel marked his love with a poem for Julia:

There are those who strangely love to roam
and find in wildest haunts their home,
and some in halls of lordly state
who yet are homeless, desolate.
The sailor's home is on the main,
The warrior's on the tented plain,
The infant's on the mother's breast
But where thou art is home to me,
And home without thee cannot be.[11]

Equally conventional, though definitely generous, was a string of seventy-eight pearls which he bought for her in May at a price of £1,080, roughly £45,000 in modern money.

Finally, on 8 June 1820, Peel and Julia were married in Lady Floyd's drawing room in Seymour Street. They spent the honeymoon in a rented house at Mickleham in Surrey, from which Julia wrote to her stepmother: 'I believe myself to be the very happiest of all human beings. I am thank God united to a thoroughly amiable man, and one whom I adore, for whom I would willingly risk existence itself.'[12]

Julia's charm shines out of the brilliant portrait by Lawrence in the Frick Museum in New York. Peel commissioned Lawrence to paint her in dress and hat of the seventeenth century as a companion piece to Rubens' picture 'Le Chapeau de Paille', which he bought in 1823 for upwards of £3,000. Julia was dark, with an oval face; she wore her hair in ringlets and was an acknowledged beauty. Theirs was a perfect match; they were happiest in each other's company; their love for each other never varied. Both had lost their mothers in childhood, so that there were channels of affection which only now flowed freely. Lady Shelley put it about that Peel's bride knew nothing of politics, but Julia learned the hard way, through the overflow of her husband's worries. She herself had no particular interest in causes and initiatives apart from her husband's part in them.

Politicians sometimes found her hard to talk to, and she did not intrude on Peel's decisions. But she entered fully into his anxieties, and felt criticisms of him as if the lash fell on her own shoulders. When Peel wrote to her about his work it was usually in terms of personalities rather than policy. Like most husbands of his time, he decided where they should live and what they should spend. They were both devoted parents. In their letters there is much happy chatter about the children who year by year filled the nursery, later interspersed with problems of schooling and later still, in the case of their eldest son Robert, with headshaking about his friends and way of life.

In sum, twenty years before Victoria married Albert, Peel and Julia settled down to the best kind of Victorian family life. They supplied each other with continuity, comfort and sustained love.

For a few months Peel seemed genuinely detached from politics. Early in 1820 George III died. A few of his subjects remembered the promising young man who had come to the throne sixty years earlier, then the monarch whose stubbornness had helped lose the American colonies, finally the man who emerged to popular rejoicing from his first bout of madness to become Farmer George, the plain patriotic wartime King. But all that seemed a long time ago. George had been kept invisible so long, old, blind and mad at Windsor, that his death caused no stir.

Under the rules of the time it meant a general election. The election campaign was in full swing while Peel walked the beach at Bognor in March 1820. There was no contest in Oxford University, but several candidates vied for the county seats in Sussex. Peel and his sister drove from Bognor to the hustings at Chichester, but more for entertainment rather than any serious political purpose.

This appearance of detachment was unreal. Peel had taken a break from active politics, but his mind was hard at work. As usual his thoughts quickly found their way onto paper. 23 March 1820 was a particularly dreary day at Bognor. A storm blew hard on the shore, and the post brought Peel nothing from Julia. He wrote her a letter of three loving paragraphs and then settled down to compose a reflective piece for Croker:

Do not you think that the tone of England – of that great compound of folly, weakness, prejudice, wrong feeling, right feeling, obstinacy and

newspaper paragraphs which is called public opinion – is more liberal
– to use an odious but intelligible phrase – than the policy of the government? Do not you think that there is a feeling, becoming daily more
general and more confirmed, ... in favour of some undefined change in
the mode of governing the country? It seems to me a curious crisis –
when public opinion never had such influence on public measures, and
yet never was so dissatisfied with the share which it possessed. It is
growing too large for the channels that it has been accustomed to run
through. Can we resist, I mean not next session or the session after
that ... but can we resist for seven years Reform in Parliament? – And
if reform cannot be resisted, is it not more probable that Whigs and
Tories will unite, and carry through moderate reforms, than remain
opposed to each other?[13]

Peel's question was general – it applied not just to the question of parliamentary reform, but to all the main issues of the day. Peel was no
natural liberal reformer. A year earlier he had supported the Manchester
magistrates in their handling of the Peterloo Massacre in which
troops had killed eleven Radical demonstrators. He had spoken in
favour of the Seditious Meetings Bill which for five years severely limited
the scope of public meetings. He was well known as the leading
champion of the restrictions on Catholics in public life. Yet here in
private he was beginning to question the whole basis of this resistance to
change.

Nor was he alone. Lord Liverpool's Government had been in office for
eight years. Some of its Ministers like Eldon, Sidmouth and Castlereagh
were famous for their harshness. Shelley paraded them one by one in his
Masque of Anarchy, written after Peterloo:

> *I met Murder on the way –*
> *He had a mask like Castlereagh –*
> *Very smooth he looked, yet grim;*
> *Seven bloodhounds followed him.*
>
> .   .   .
>
> *Next came Fraud and he had on,*
> *Like Eldon, an ermined gown –*

His big tears, for he wept well —
Turned to millstones as they fell.

. . .

Like Sidmouth next, hypocrisy
On a crocodile rode by.

Yet behind that grim façade new ideas and new men were stirring. The last years of Lord Liverpool's Tory Government produced unexpectedly a change of mood among Ministers, and the first steps in the reforms which both Whigs and Conservatives later carried forward and which gave a special character to the Victorian age.

The men pilloried by Shelley were not bigoted or selfish tyrants. Castlereagh in particular was a perceptive and deep-thinking Foreign Secretary who held views on Ireland more enlightened than Peel's own thoughts in 1820. But even Castlereagh found it hard to move out of the shadow of the French Revolution. That threat to lives, to the Church, to property, to the rule of law, to the whole familiar structure of society dominated Tory ideas and instincts. The fear lingered on long after Napoleon's defeat at Waterloo. Napoleon had been a threat to Britain, like Philip II and Louis XIV before him and Hitler and Stalin after. Napoleon, like Stalin, had embodied not just a military danger but also the threat of revolution. True, these two rulers were heirs of revolution rather than revolutionaries themselves, but they had been brought to power on a surge of ideas which, once let loose in Britain, could lead to disaster.

But there was an important difference between Britain after Waterloo and Britain after the fall of the Berlin Wall. In the West, including Britain, we could be sure that we had defeated Communism in the battle of ideas long before the Wall came down. Men like Castlereagh, Eldon and Sidmouth felt no such confidence that they had won the battle against revolutionary ideas in Britain. For them the only way to check revolution was to be absolute in defence of existing institutions, to resist the kind of change which, even when argued in good faith by reformers, would soften those defences. After all, they thought, Burke and Pitt had both started as reformers, but both had learned the danger of radical change when the storm broke and the waves rode high. Pitt Clubs up and down the

country toasted his memory over the port, and quoted those phrases of
Burke which seemed to justify resistance to any change.

Peel was different. He had been only five years old when the guillotine
had ended the life of the King of France. He spent his formative years
under the same shadow as his elders, but was young and intelligent
enough to see before long that the shadow had lifted. In the new world
after Waterloo there was a need to understand and discuss the pressures
for change. Peel's reaction to these pressures was still unfocused, as his
letter to Croker showed; but the question marks now hung in his mind.

The Prime Minister, Lord Liverpool, was moving in the same direction. More immediately he had to handle a drama which had nothing to
do with reform, and a lot to do with public opinion. A royal scandal, particularly if drawn out and bubbling with sexual detail had (and certainly
still has) the power to seize the whole attention of the British press and
public. The ordinary excitements of politics seem pale and dull by comparison. A right royal crisis accompanied the new King George IV to the
throne. That crisis was his Queen.

Queen Caroline, long separated from her husband, was noisy, coarse,
promiscuous and wholly unsuited to the throne; but hardly more so than
the King. As her misdemeanours came to light George IV worked himself
up into passionate indignation. He was particularly anxious that the
Queen his wife should not be prayed for in church. This vituperative conflict about prayer between two self-indulgent adulterers greatly entertained the press and the London mob, who on balance sympathised with
Caroline. The Government, caught in the middle, mishandled the matter
and suffered badly.

As soon as he was on the throne George IV pressed for a divorce. The
Government, anxious to avoid scandal, persuaded him to drop this
request if they agreed to remove the Queen's name from the Church's
liturgy. The Queen would no longer be specifically prayed for in the
morning and evening services of the Church of England. It seemed a neat
compromise, but Caroline herself was not a lady for compromise. As
soon as she heard of her father-in-law's death she hurried to England, and
on 6 June drove in triumph into London in an open carriage. She was
determined to vindicate her honour by having her name in the liturgy.

The wretched Cabinet, boxed in between the King and his people,
decided to lay the evidence of the Queen's misdemeanours in a Bill before

the House of Lords. Here indeed was a feast for the prurient. Caroline's tawdry comings and goings were vividly described and analysed. Where, when, and precisely of what kind had been her adulteries? Had she, when sleeping on deck at sea on a hot Mediterranean night, had sex with her Italian valet who called himself Count Pergami? Lawyers with solemn faces argued to and fro while the public giggled. Eventually the Government won the vote in the Lords, but only by a margin of nine votes. They decided they could not proceed. Canning had spoken with mistaken chivalry about the Queen. The King, driven by ever wilder furies, believed that Canning had been her lover. Eventually in December 1820 Canning resigned.

Liverpool, anxious to strengthen the Government in the Commons, asked Peel to take Canning's place as President of the Board of Control with a seat in the Cabinet.* Lord Liverpool's offer was made in private. Peel declined on the grounds that he could not defend in public all the decisions of the Government on the question of the Queen. With the clarity that comes easily to those without responsibility he had told Croker how the matter should be handled: 'If she be worse than Messalina nothing but the united voice of King, Lords and Commons should have degraded her. I certainly would have tried her the moment she set foot in England, but I would have prayed for her as Queen till she had been tried.'[14]

The terms of Peel's reply to Liverpool suggested that he might be open to a later offer, and Liverpool tried again next spring. He had discussed with his colleagues the possibility of making Peel Chancellor of the Exchequer. This post was less important then than now, since no one in 1821 supposed that the Chancellor of the Exchequer could presume to guide the national economy. The man's job was simply to raise in taxation or borrowing the sums which Ministers had decided to spend. But it was important enough, and Castlereagh, Leader of the House of Commons, felt that Peel's promotion would threaten his own authority. The idea faded.

---

* The Board of Control controlled the East India Company. India was governed in tandem between the Government and the company – a curious halfway house which caused Peel trouble later and was swept away after the Indian Mutiny.

In May Liverpool talked again to Peel, this time vaguely, inviting him to join the Government, but not specifying a post. There was much coming and going. Croker in particular buzzed to and fro as a self-appointed go-between. It emerged that Liverpool once again had in mind the Board of Control, and Peel again declined. This time he pleaded poor health, and indeed had suffered from eye trouble earlier in the year. But Croker thought that 'with a great fortune and domestic habits like his the stormy sea of politics can have little temptation for him'. Another observer put it more bluntly. 'Peel has declined accepting office, but whether it is because he wishes to live retired with his pretty wife, or that he thinks the Ministry will not stand, I know not.'[15]

Certainly Peel was enjoying himself at home. His first child, named Julia after her mother, was born in April 1821. But Peel would never make a final decision to abandon politics. He did not relish the idea of the Board of Control. Its President was sandwiched uncomfortably between his colleagues in Government, the directors of the East India Company and the Governor General out in India. The line of authority was blurred; there seemed no scope for the firm exercise of administrative authority and the parliamentary work which Peel enjoyed. Lord Liverpool was irritated by his second refusal. But the Government's need of new strength in the Commons remained, and a fresh opportunity to recruit Peel soon came round.

The Queen's drama entered its final phase. As before, in each episode the element of personal tragedy was quickly transmuted into farce. When the King was crowned in July 1821, she knocked vainly on the locked doors of Westminster Abbey. Three weeks later quite suddenly she died. There were riots as her coffin passed through the streets of London; but by then the public had had enough of their improbable heroine. The arguments died down. The Government suffered no penalty for their mistakes.

Ordinary politics resumed, and Lord Liverpool could once again turn his mind to a reshuffle. Old Lord Sidmouth was willing to step down from the Home Office as part of a general reshuffle while remaining in the Cabinet. Liverpool proposed to offer the Home Office to Peel. Because of the King's aversion to him Canning was urged to accept a sumptuous exile as Governor General of India. He suggested that Peel might be willing to wait and that he, Canning, should take the Home Office. But the King and Liverpool held to their plan. The messenger from the Prime Minister who offered Peel that job came back the same day from his holiday home at Lulworth with Peel's acceptance. Peel received the Seals of Office from the King and was sworn in as Home Secretary on 17 January 1822.

Five

The Disturbance File

'Why not treble the duty upon all Sunday newspapers? The
King reads everything of this kind, and feels it a duty to do
so; hence the King can judge of the mischief resulting from
this absurd liberty of the press.'
George IV to Peel from the Brighton Pavilion, 1823

'It is difficult to reconcile an effective system of police with
that perfect freedom of action and exemption from
interference, which are the great privileges and blessings of
society in this country'
Report of Commons Select Committee, 1822

'There is not a single law connected with my name which
has not had as its object some mitigation of the severity of
the criminal law, some prevention of abuse in the exercise of
it, or some security of its impartial administration'
Peel, House of Commons, 1827

*A*s Home Secretary Peel escorted the King on his visit to Edinburgh
in August 1822. George had been warmly received in Dublin a few
months earlier and found the same welcome in Scotland, in contrast to the irreverent treatment usually meted out by his subjects in
London. Though the Scottish August was blowy and wet, the King was in
high spirits. The visit has passed into history because of the royal decision
to wear and be painted in a kilt, setting the tone for the romantic cult of
everything Highland. Peel had his doubts about this display of royal flesh
and would not have agreed with Lady Hamilton Dalrymple's comment: 'As
he is here for so short a time, the more we see of him the better.'[1] Luckily
this was not a matter on which the Home Secretary had to advise.

On the visit Peel became close friends with Sir Walter Scott, who performed brilliantly as impresario of the whole occasion. The two men walked up the old Edinburgh High Street together, Peel the young English Home Secretary unrecognised while all passers-by hastened to salute their great novelist.

The royal visit was interrupted by news of disaster. On 12 August Lord Liverpool wrote asking Peel to inform the King that Castlereagh,* Foreign Secretary and Leader of the House of Commons, had killed himself that morning, slitting his throat with a letter opener. 'There never was a clearer case of insanity,' wrote Liverpool. 'The King is in some degree prepared for the sad event; he knows what was the state of his mind when he saw him on Friday last. My first idea was to come down, but I felt that public duty ought to retain me. What a sad catastrophe this is, private and public! What a conclusion to such a life! May God have mercy on his soul.'[2]

Peel hurried to the royal yacht, the *Royal George*, anchored in the Firth of Forth. That afternoon the King, protected from the weather by a flowing blue cape and an oilskin cap, was responding to loyal greetings from the boats surrounding the yacht, tossing one steamboat a bottle of claret with which to drink his health. Peel found that the King was indeed prepared for the bad news. He and the Duke of Wellington had been shocked by recent conversations with Castlereagh. Already exhausted by hard work, the Foreign Secretary had been unhinged by a belief that he was being blackmailed for entering a male brothel.

Peel had never been personally close to Castlereagh. He must have known that Castlereagh had blocked his promotion to Chancellor of the Exchequer a year earlier, and they differed on Catholic Emancipation, which Castlereagh favoured despite his staunch Tory views on most matters. Nevertheless, the news came as a painful shock. Castlereagh, deeply unpopular, had never cared for popularity. He was a poor speaker who never spoke foolishly. He worked tirelessly at detail, aiming at the public good. His foreign policy, pragmatic, careful, co-operative, became a model for Peel. The two men had more in common than either realised.

---

* He had recently succeeded his father as Marquess of Londonderry, but it is easier to stay with the familiar name.

Castlereagh's death created a critical gap in the Government. This was immediately understood by all concerned. Canning had just agreed to go to India as Governor General. The King, who detested Canning because of his support for Queen Caroline, was anxious that this arrangement should stand, and wrote accordingly to Liverpool from Holyrood Palace in Edinburgh, only telling Peel two days later. Above all George did not want Canning to succeed Castlereagh at the Foreign Office. Nevertheless, this was an almost inevitable move – provided that Peel would agree that at the same time Canning would also take over Castlereagh's other post as Leader of the Commons. Canning was not content to return to the Foreign Office, which he had already held, unless he was also clearly recognised as the Government's central figure in the Commons.

Peel behaved correctly in his stiffest manner. Croker meddled as usual, creating the false impression that Canning would concede the leadership of the Commons to Peel despite the fact that Canning was many years his senior in parliamentary terms. When this misunderstanding was cleared up, Peel declared that he was happy with his important work at the Home Office, and would do nothing to hinder Canning's promotion. Lord Liverpool thanked him warmly for his handsome behaviour.

Peel could now begin to master the tasks of a Home Secretary. The Home Office confronts each incomer with a tangle of problems emerging from the entrails of our society. To put it mildly, it is not a department of fun and laughter. Two themes dominate most of the work. The first is the protection of society as a whole from public disorder; the second is the protection of the individual citizen from the individual criminal.

For many years protection of the individual was dominant. An interminable procession of Criminal Justice Acts have defined and redefined the means of preventing and punishing crimes against the individual.* By contrast public order has been called into question at rare intervals as a result of strikes or inner city riots, but on the whole has been taken for granted. Recently the balance has shifted. The terrorist threat since 11 September 2001 has created more commotion and dismay than the previous efforts of the IRA. The protection of our towns and cities against

---

* As I write the House of Lords is pondering the fifty-second Home Office Bill to be introduced in Parliament since the arrival of Mr Blair's Government in 1997.

this new form of public disorder has become a paramount responsibility, producing its own trail of special legislation. Peel would have understood this priority. A few days spent among the Home Office files at Kew are enough to show that the preservation of public order was his main concern. He was confronted day by day, report by report, city by city, county by county, with threats of public disorder. These incidents and his efforts to deal with them fill volumes of what the Home Office labelled 'Disturbance Reports'.

Order in civilised societies rests on silent consent. The physical force available to the government will always be less than that theoretically available to the governed. By calculations of physical strength a prison is at the mercy of the convicts, an army at the mercy of mutineers from the ranks, a city at the mercy of a mob. There will be groups or individuals whose anger or greed will tempt them to cause a breakdown in public order. They are defeated or deterred partly by the actual forces of order, but mainly by the knowledge that the forces of order operate by the consent of most of us. This acceptance is the basis of the modern state.

In Britain and most western countries institutions have grown up to reflect and buttress this consent. Britain has a democratic parliamentary system, a civilian police force operating under laws approved by Parliament, an independent judiciary with a particular regard for individual liberty, a trade union movement with powers defined by Parliament, and a welfare system designed to soften the effects of poverty. None of these institutions is perfect, and we argue endlessly about their failings. But they all in different ways make it less likely that angry men and women will take the law into their own hands; they separate strong feelings from violence. Our institutions provide remedies against the abuse of authority and some of the other harshnesses of life. They lessen the urge to lash out, to burn, smash and kill.

The British are apt to believe that we are a law-abiding and peaceable race. History teaches otherwise. We have tended on the whole to fight and win ruthless wars, to impose our views on other nations, and at home to quarrel strenuously among ourselves. The London mob was once notorious through Europe for its fury. There is still plenty of disorder in Britain and what is now called antisocial behaviour in our streets. We keep a higher proportion of our people in prison than any other big European country. By the creation of these modern institutions we have learned to protect ourselves to a large extent against our own violent instincts. But all this is relatively new. Peel as Home Secretary was expected to keep order in a country which had none of these institutions, except to some extent the independent judiciary. Discontent ran high against the corruption and unfairness of the political system, and overwhelmingly against unemployment and poverty.

Historians argue fiercely about the condition of the people at this time. These were the decades in which Britain changed more rapidly than at any time in our history. We became an industrial society, dominated by great cities in which a new working class and a new middle class lived together. Even the most distinguished historians approach this phenomenon with their own views about the merits and vices of our society today. We all nurse prejudices, however disguised, about the events which created that society. Moreover there is simply no reliable statistical basis for calculating the wellbeing of the British people in the 1820s. On the whole the standard of living was improving and real wages rose. On average people grew taller and lived longer. The rich became richer and the poor did not become poorer. But averages, even when validated by better statistics than we have, are deceptive in describing the scene.

The fluctuations year by year and place by place were immense. Clothing became cheaper as the Lancashire mills got going, but food prices rose and fell dramatically. The rapid movement into the cities brought squalid slums, disease and degradation of all kinds. As late as the 1840s three children out of twenty died in the first year of life. In Sheffield and Manchester more than half of the children died before they were five. In the industrial north the fierce working of the trade cycle created months of acute distress; during these months more than half the workforce might be out of work and another third on short time. In the countryside of the south and east of England, which we are accustomed to think of as comfortable and conservative, low wages ensured continuous and desolate poverty. Desperate and angry men came together in trade unions. Many turned against the new cotton looms in the north and the new agricultural threshing machines in the south, blaming for their poverty the techniques which would in the end rescue them from it.[3]

The 'Disturbances' file in the Home Office archive at Kew gives the bitter flavour of this surging world which Peel had to confront. In Monmouthshire, strikes interfered with the transport of coal to the iron

and tin works. The disorder spread to the Forest of Dean. There were disturbances near Wolverhampton. A strike in Newcastle for ten weeks
obstructed the coal traffic on the Tyne.

His predecessors had faced similar outbreaks, but Peel's diagnosis differed from theirs. Old men like Sidmouth and Eldon still lived with vivid
memories of the French Revolution. Disorder to them had a political
motive; it was attempted revolution, a prelude to Jacobinism and the
horrors of the guillotine, and had to be dealt with accordingly. But Peel,
who insisted on accurate information, came to know better. He found
himself in a similar position to the American leaders who had to explain
at the time of Senator McCarthy that not all American problems could
be blamed on Communism. Peel saw clearly that the Industrial
Revolution and the swings of the trade cycle were creating sharp antagonism between masters and men, which had little to do with politics. A
strike was not a prelude to revolution. Employers thought they had no
option but to install modern machinery, lay off men and reduce wages if
they were to survive in the new competitive world. Workers thought that
if *they* were to survive they had to come together to resist and disrupt such
changes. Increasingly politicians began to believe that these were matters
which they should study and understand.

But it did not follow that they should intervene. If disorder was political and a threat to King, Parliament and Government it was the responsibility of Ministers to be active, even repressive in the interests of national
security. But if disorder was the result of industrial strife, then the
prevailing view was that the State should protect individual safety and
property from violence in accordance with the law, but not interfere with
the natural economic rules. The natural process would, they thought, over
time sort out industrial strife one way or the other.

This instinct grew strong among the Tory liberals whom Liverpool
brought into Government from 1822. Huskisson dominated economic
policy during this period as President of the Board of Trade. Peel had
already helped him over the Bullion Committee, and now worked with
him again from the Home Office. The two Ministers were led by this
doctrine into a remarkable decision in 1824 over trade union law.

On this subject, as on most, the law was a mess. At the height of the
danger from revolutionary France the Combination Acts of 1799 and
1800 had clamped down on any coming together of workers (or indeed

employers) to improve their bargaining position. The common law already punished combinations of workers. These were political laws designed to safeguard society, for Pitt and his colleagues saw trade unions as the harbingers of Jacobin revolution. Once the war was over these laws were widely evaded, and in practice workers began to come together to build their bargaining strength. Reformers like Bentham believed that all legislation on this subject was wrong. Working men and employers alike should bargain as individuals. Once the law intervened they believed it distorted economic freedom and one combination created another. In 1824 Huskisson persuaded Parliament to abolish the Combination Laws. Workers could combine to negotiate wages and hours of work, subject only to penalty for violence or intimidation.

But the Benthamites and the liberal Tory Ministers were confounded by the result. Freedom did not bring industrial harmony; so far from fading away, trade unions multiplied. With Peel's support Huskisson quickly modified the law to bring it in line with reality. Trade unionism continued to be legal, but it became easier to prosecute for violence or threats. Peel thought the amended law of 1825 'is founded upon just principles and I believe it will ultimately be as effectual as law can be. Men who have no property except their manual skill and strength, ought to be allowed to confer together, if they think fit, for the purpose of determining at what rate they will sell their property. But the possession of such a privilege justifies, while it renders more necessary, the severe punishment of any attempt to control the free will of others.'[4]

Disorder varied with the ups and downs of trade. A sudden slump hit the whole economy in 1825 and led to depression and disturbance in 1826. The downturn called into question the banking system, and in particular the cash payments restored by Peel's Act of 1819. Old Sir Robert at Drayton joined forces again with his friend Attwood in Birmingham to renew the call for looser credit and increased circulation of notes by the banks. Peel bent under this pressure, saw Attwood, and discussed adopting the Scottish system where the banks issued a generous abundance of one pound notes. In the end, however, Ministers rallied behind the liberal doctrine of non-interference. They required a reluctant Bank of England to advance loans on good security to firms and individuals, but otherwise relied on a revival of trade to right the economy and rebuild prosperity.

This happened but took time, and while they waited Ministers had to face widespread disorder. In April 1826 industrial Lancashire was convulsed with rioting and the breaking of machinery. Six workers were killed in a clash near Bolton, and another across the Pennines at Bradford. There was no unemployment benefit, no compensation for loss of jobs. Yet Peel could see that money was needed. He promised to persuade the King to contribute £500 from his own purse to relieve distress in Bolton if the town stayed quiet.

The reports of violence poured into the Home Office. It was Peel's responsibility to ensure, with the Duke of York as Commander-in-Chief at the Horse Guards, that troops were available (so far as they could guess) in the right places at the right time. This was not easy. There were complaints, for example, that there were no cavalry in Carlisle. Peel kept in particularly close touch with the military commander in Manchester, General Sir John Byng. But it was neither for the General nor for Peel to take the initiative and order troops into action. This could only happen at the request of the civil power put forward by magistrates on the spot. Magistrates had to accompany the troops. Britain was emphatically not under military rule. A frightened magistrate in Clitheroe tried to save time by entrusting this power in advance to General Byng. Peel administered a powerful rebuke. 'Mr Peel feels himself called on to acquaint you that the attempt to delegate to the military the authority which belong only to the civil power is altogether illegal, the military being only authorised to act in aid of and in the presence of a magistrate or of a peace officer.'[5] *

Part of the problem in Lancashire was that some magistrates were cotton manufacturers. Peel himself was the son of a cotton manufacturer and heir to a cotton fortune. But he saw the Government as committed to the rule of law rather than to the interests of the employers. Indeed as he gained experience he began to urge employers in particular disputes to show restraint and act justly. Peel did not doubt the real distress created by the slump, writing to his friend Henry Goulburn in Ireland on 22 July 1826, 'At home the prospects are gloomy enough. The great cause of

---

* This principle remains in force. For example the SAS in 1980 were only authorised to storm the Iranian Embassy in London when the Metropolitan Police Commissioner had formally decided that his men could do no more to rescue the hostages being held by terrorists.

apprehension is not in the disaffection, but in the real distress of the manufacturing districts. There is as much forbearance as it is possible to expect from so much suffering.'[6] He started to collect statistics about wages and prices which went beyond the usual range of the Home Office. It was the beginning of an interest which came to dominate his life.

Statistics might prepare minds for future action. The immediate need was for money. There were no funds from the taxpayer. Peel kept in close touch with such voluntary bodies as the Tavern Committee in London and the Spitalfields Fund who would provide large sums (£57,000 in 1826) for the relief of distress.

The Home Secretary sat in Whitehall contemplating a country seething with resentment, jealousies and restlessness of all kinds, but starved of accurate information from which he could anticipate and deal with danger. Large numbers of private individuals volunteered information to him, or answered his requests. Most of these had a viewpoint, or an interest to represent. It was hard to sort out the truth from varying accounts. For example, were the riots in Manchester in 1826 directed only at the new power looms in the cotton factories or did they aim at the owners themselves? Most informants said the looms were the only targets, but one reported that the rioters moved against calico printers even when the looms had been destroyed. Since that one informant was (almost certainly) old Sir Robert Peel, Under Secretary Hobhouse thought it sensible to report both views to General Byng.[7]

It was not possible to deploy troops quickly wherever there was trouble. Manufacturers must learn to defend themselves. 'Mr Peel concurs entirely in the opinion that the only effectual mode of defending the looms, which are the present object of popular vengeance is of the owners arming their men and defending the manufacturers till the military can arrive.'[8]

Peel, like all previous Home Secretaries, supplemented information from correspondents with news from paid spies. These agents were particularly directed at penetrating cells or societies which might have a political purpose. That system stretched back at least to Tudor times and the formidable apparatus of Francis Walsingham under Elizabeth I. The files are full of requests to Peel to authorise Post Masters to open letters; most of these letters were copied and sent on their way. Visiting foreigners were particularly subject to such attentions. Peel was naturally keen to follow up any suggestion of help or encouragement from abroad. He pressed for information about any ringleaders who might co-ordinate action in different places. None of this added up to anything like the systematic assembling of facts and figures or the sober measuring of opinion for which Peel must have longed.

Worse still was the absence of any buffer between disorderly citizens and the soldiers or yeomanry. Peel had defended the handling of the Peterloo Massacre in 1819, but he worked hard to prevent a repetition by insisting, as we have seen, on the responsibility of the magistrates to handle an outbreak before they called in the military. If a magistrate could rely only on the authority of his own loud voice reading the Riot Act, and a handful of decrepit constables alongside, there was a real danger of calling in the Army too soon, and then of the quick use of firearms by frightened men against a threatening crowd.

We at once see that an important piece was missing from the board. There was no Chief Constable, no police station, no bobby on the beat, no civilian force to investigate the crime or control the riot. Any Home Secretary today must find it hard to imagine how, without police, Peel could even begin to cope with his responsibilities.

Peel saw the remedy clearly enough; indeed he had already introduced it in parts of Ireland. The existence of an Irish constabulary had not solved the country's problems, but their professionalism had certainly made a difference. In March 1822, within a few weeks of becoming Home Secretary, he moved for a Select Committee on policing in London, which he hoped would obtain for the metropolis 'as perfect a system of police as was consistent with the character of a free country'. Peel became chairman of the Committee; but it did not work. On the contrary its report in June came down exactly where its predecessor had ended, with this negative conclusion: 'It is difficult to reconcile an effective system of police with that perfect freedom of action and exemption from interference, which are the great privileges and blessings of society in this country; and your committee think that the forfeiture or curtailment of such advantages would be too great a sacrifice for improvements in police, or facilities in detection of crime, however desirable in themselves if abstractedly considered.'[9]

So Peel was stymied. The very reformers like James Mackintosh who wished him to reform the criminal justice system blocked him from establishing a professional police force in London. We tend to believe in a self-satisfied way that reformers must inevitably have been pressing towards the state of affairs which we enjoy today, namely a reasonably liberal criminal justice system plus a professional police force. But the reformers of the 1820s did not instinctively think that way. They wanted to move towards greater freedom, in trade, in the currency, in speech, even in the organisation of trade unions. To them it was a backward step to create a police force, which they saw essentially as an instrument of government designed to watch the citizen and curb his freedom. A standing army was bad enough, and had to be reviewed every year by Act of Parliament. A standing police force smacked of Pitt's desperate wartime years, or George III's alleged nostalgia for Stuart tyranny.

Backbench Tories joined the argument. They prized the pre-eminence of magistrates and felt affection for the elderly watchmen and the traditions of the street. Nowadays we associate the Conservative Party with support for the police and scepticism about liberalising penal policy. Peel's experience was the reverse. The unreformed Parliament of 1822 was as Tory as you could get; it supported penal reform and blocked the creation of the Metropolitan Police. Peel retired from the debate but he did not give up. He waited in the growing turmoil of domestic politics for an opportunity to deploy what he believed was an unanswerable case.

In October 1822 Peel told the Prime Minister that he intended to tackle reform of the criminal law. From then on he spent much energy climbing that other face of the Home Office mountain, namely the protection of the individual citizen and the punishment of the criminal. To some extent the work was wished upon him. Peel's was not an original mind, but he was quick to assimilate and act on the ideas of others. The campaign for criminal reform had been under way for more than a decade. Whig politicians, Quakers, evangelical Christians and Benthamite Utilitarians had joined in pressing for change. The campaign achieved the necessary focus in a parliamentary Committee set up in 1819 under the chairmanship of James Mackintosh.

The Committee reported just as Peel took over as Home Secretary. They had taken a long journey into the chaotic jungle of the English criminal law. Paths through that jungle were hard to find. For centuries statutes had been piled upon statutes alongside the traditional common law. Penalties had multiplied; some two hundred offences were in theory punishable by death. The system looked in theory exceptionally severe, but in practice its cruelty was tempered by its incoherence. The result was a lottery. The outcome of a case would depend on the arguments of lawyers about contradictory statutes, and the mood of a jury. The Mackintosh Committee recommended in June 1822 among other things 'means of increasing the efficiency of the criminal laws by abating their undue rigour'.[10] Their specific proposals included repeal or amendment of obsolete statutes, revision of the forgery law, and the abolition of capital punishment for larceny in shops, houses and ships and for stealing horses, cattle and sheep.[11]

A slim majority in the Commons favoured this general approach, as a result of the long years of argument by the reformers. Nevertheless Peel could have continued the resistance to reform of his predecessor Lord Sidmouth. He could have relied on the House of Lords to block any except minor changes. He could have conjured up the dangers to public security of any softening of penalties. He could also with reason have pointed out that the Home Office was far from being a fit instrument for devising or implementing such reforms. On arrival Peel found a staff of fourteen clerks and various minor offices, substantially smaller than he had directed as Chief Secretary in Ireland. The offices were dark, crowded and smelly.[12] As we have seen, the Home Office concentrated not on crime against the individual but on public disorder. The facts and figures available to it on crime in general were hopelessly inadequate.[13]

Nevertheless, Peel did not hesitate. The interlocking tangle of statutes analysed in the Mackintosh report set him exactly the sort of problem which he relished. Staff were found; facts were demanded and advice sought from every quarter. He recruited a brilliant barrister called Gregson from the Northern Circuit. Peel relied heavily on his Under Secretary Hobhouse, but he himself carried the burden in the Cabinet and the Commons. Peel moved quickly, but never skimped detail. The immense process of reform lasted for eight years, with one break while Peel was out of office for a few months, and other pauses while he and everyone else concerned drew breath. A total of 278 statutes were repealed or consolidated. They covered more than three-quarters of all offences.

One or two examples will be enough. Before Peel, the law against forgery was contained in 120 statutes, sixty imposing capital punishment.

When he finished there was one Act running to six pages. About ninety statutes on theft were reduced to thirty pages. The scope of the death penalty for burglary was reduced by raising the limit from £2 to £5 for stealing from houses. The offence of grand larceny (which carried the death penalty) was abolished; so was capital punishment for arson or malicious shooting. The extent of the reforms was matched by their success in Parliament. Peel began to build up the record of which he could boast accurately at the end of his life, that he had carried into law every measure he had ever proposed.[14]

Peel explained the three main purposes of all this work. 'There is not a single law connected with my name which has not had as its object some mitigation of the severity of the criminal law, some prevention of abuse in the exercise of it, or some security of its impartial administration.'[15] Both then and later commentators have focused only on the first of these aims, namely the softening of the law and in particular the restriction of the death penalty. Advanced penal reformers at the time, such as Bentham, were disappointed and some modern critics have been scathing. Bentham, in one moment of disillusion, is reported to have said 'Peel is weak and feeble. He has done all the good he is capable of doing, and that is but little. He has given a slight impulse to law improvement in the right direction.'[16] The critics point out that the death penalty had already become a dead letter for many lesser offences; that Peel retained it for crimes such as forgery where it now seems wholly out of place; that the number of death sentences and even of actual executions during his time as Home Secretary showed little improvement; and that the crucial improvements were actually made by the Whigs in the 1830s, not by Peel in the 1820s.[17]

However, that is to refuse Peel a prize for which he was not competing. Peel was a Tory and a born administrator. The criminal justice system which he found was in his view unfair and indefensible, not because it was merciless but because it was a muddle. It was not a system at all. A man was, he thought, entitled to know what was likely to happen if he committed a particular offence, and was caught. There should be room for discretion, but this should be limited and clear.

The task of making the law clearer and simpler, when undertaken in 1820, was bound to lead to some mitigation. It would mean an end to confused statutes passed to deal with some forgotten crisis in earlier and more savage decades. The number of executions in Peel's time at the Home Office between 1822 and 1828 averaged 63 a year, compared with 67 a year in the war years 1805–12 and 105 between 1815 and 1821. Peel's reform took effect slowly. Moderation of punishment was part of the pressure for social change which he had pointed out to Croker in that thoughtful letter from Bognor in 1820. Peel created in the Home Office a machine, and (even in the unreformed Parliament) a mood which would lead to further softening of punishments. He recognised that this was likely, though he resisted some of the further changes when the time came. As a Tory he was concerned about timing. He called for 'no rash subversion of ancient institutions, no relinquishment of what is practically good for the chance of speculative and uncertain improvement'. He saw the gradual mitigation of punishment, including reductions in the death penalty, as a consequence of modernising the criminal justice system rather than its main aim.[18]

These were matters which brought Peel into close touch with the King. Peel was to see a great deal of George IV during his eight years as Home Secretary. Nowadays these duties are pleasant ceremonial occasions, which provide (though the Home Secretary should not phrase it like this to the Royal Household) a light-hearted interlude in a workload which in total can be crushing. In Peel's time the relationship was closer and more important. Peel and George IV shared an enthusiasm for collecting pictures, but had nothing else in common. They belonged to different generations at a moment when the difference between the manners and morals of generations was exceptionally marked. Peel was stiff in manner, hard-working because he loved work, truthful and devoted to his family. The King was emotional, idle, weak-willed, false in many of his statements and most of his relationships. Yet the King never railed against Peel as he did from time to time against most of his Ministers. Without ever entering or wanting to enter the circle of royal intimates Peel earned the King's respect.

In 1823 George IV wrote to Peel from the Brighton Pavilion on a theme close to his heart.

The King is obliged to observe that some steps should be taken with respect to Sunday papers. Why not treble the duty upon all Sunday newspapers? The King reads everything of this kind, and feels it a duty to do so; hence the King can judge of the mischief resulting from this absurd liberty of the press. These observations are equally applicable to obscene prints in the form of caricatures. There is scarcely a shop in London that deals in such trash in which the King is not exposed in some indecent ridiculous manner. This has now become constant practice, and it is high time that it should be put stop to.[19]

The King's observation was correct. His regency and then his reign marked the heyday of the cruel caricaturist. Gillray and Cruikshank were brilliant and merciless. Never before or since has a British monarch been so vilified. Peel played a straight bat. He warmly sympathised with the King by return of messenger, consulted the Attorney General twice, mentioned the matter in Cabinet, and advised the King that no prosecution was likely to succeed with a London jury.

But sometimes more than a straight bat was needed. The King possessed the power of clemency under the royal prerogative. In particular he was legally entitled to spare the lives of those sentenced to hang for one of the many offences which carried the death penalty. He exercised this power on advice from a body of senior Ministers and judges called the Grand or Nominal Cabinet, in effect a variant of the Privy Council. They met in the presence of the King and depended heavily on the view of the Home Secretary.

George IV himself had an occasional and wayward inclination to mercy. He was influenced less by the circumstances of the crime than by the youth and appearance of the offender — and the views of his mistress, Lady Conyngham. In these moods he found mercy 'a word more consoling to the King's mind than language can express'. Within weeks of Peel taking office the King induced Peel to alter the sentence of transportation on a young burglar, and send him instead to a house of correction. Encouraged by this success the King tried in May 1822 to secure mercy for four of a group of eight burglars convicted to hang. The argument swayed to and fro, and the executions were postponed. The King had written late on the evening before the fixed date that 'the executions of tomorrow, from their unusual numbers, weigh most heavily and painfully on his mind'. The King, who had already agreed that four of the men should hang, then desired Peel to find reason for reprieving the remaining four. Peel agreed that two should be spared, one because he had turned

King's evidence, the other because he was only seventeen. As a result of this unseemly bargaining, six of the eight were hanged.[20] Two years later, prompted by Lady Conyngham, the King urged mercy for a young forger named Miles. By now Peel was surer of his ground. He refused, there was no argument and the forger was hanged. Peel told his Under Secretary, Hobhouse, that he would have resigned if the King had persisted.

The King stayed quiet on the subject until the spring of 1830, when he himself was close to death. An Irish gentleman called Comyn had been sentenced to hang after conviction for perjury, forgery and arson. Without telling either Peel or the then Prime Minister, the Duke of Wellington, the King instructed the Lord-Lieutenant, the Duke of Northumberland, to commute the sentence. Northumberland protested to Peel and Wellington, arguing that it would be wrong to spare a gentleman when tenants had been hanged for the same offences. Ministers knew that once again Lady Conyngham had been at work. Peel told Wellington, 'This is quite intolerable.' The two of them wore the King down. The Duke went to Windsor on 14 April and found the King in good humour despite the huge doses of laudanum which he was taking. They did not directly discuss the Comyn case but Wellington came away believing that the King would give way. So it proved; Comyn was hanged; within six weeks the King too was dead.[21]

These episodes show that Peel was not to be swayed by liberal or humanitarian arguments in individual cases. That was not how his mind or his conscience worked. He was carrying through the most massive reform of the criminal justice system which had ever been conducted. As we have seen, part of that reform involved removing the death penalty from the statute for a large number of offences. He argued at great length in the Commons the case for change, and also the case for not changing more than he proposed. But to him these were legitimate arguments about the substance of the law. What Peel's orderly mind found intolerable was interference by the King to suit the caprices of the moment. 'The law should take its course' was to Peel not a cruel or baleful phrase but a statement of something that was obviously desirable. God would make his own judgements. Peel did not believe that the King or the Prime Minister or he himself was the right person to alter the decision of a properly constituted court of law.

The shrewder reformers noticed that the big difference between Peel's efforts and their own was that he got things done. It was one thing to write pamphlets, to hold well informed meetings, even to achieve a fragile majority in the House of Commons, as Mackintosh and his predecessors had done. It was another to pass Acts of Parliament and make them work. Peel achieved this by consulting, listening and eventually persuading the Lords, the judges and others who would have found no common ground with more zealous reformers. For instance, he went out of his way in 1823 to protect and defend the Lord Chancellor, Eldon, when he came under personal attack. Eldon had worked tirelessly to resist the kind of reform which Peel was putting in hand. But the critics were too harsh, the old man was honest and hard-working, and Eldon's gratitude was useful to Peel as he continued to hack through the thickets of the law.[22] Peel was not always to treat the hard, unyielding Ultra Tories with such understanding.

The advantages of reforming the letter of the law would be lost unless something was done about its enforcement. Peel found eighty-five Acts of Parliament dealing with juries; he reduced them to one, which clarified the way in which jurors were chosen and for special juries introduced the principle of the ballot. He tackled the law's delays by increasing the number of judges, establishing a third Assize court and lowering the level at which cases were heard. Many cases were transferred downwards from the Assizes to quarter sessions and from the quarter sessions to magistrates.

A public debate had begun about prisons in parallel with the debate about the criminal law. Led by the Quakers, reformers had been shocked by the untidiness and lack of purpose which they found in the system. Once again, indeed, system was the wrong word. Most prisons were locally run and standards varied hugely. As one Bedfordshire reformer noted, 'The occasional humanity of a sheriff remedies one abuse, relieves one misery, redresses one wrong, cleanses a sewer, whitewashes a wall; but the main evils of want of food, air, clothing, bedding, classification moral discipline, and consequently moral amendment, remain as before.'[23]

Peel had no difficulty in accepting this analysis and persuaded Parliament to enact the principles of a uniform system. The Gaol Act of 1823 proposed a system of classification. It forbade the use of alcohol in prison and called for the appointment of a surgeon and a chaplain. Education was to be provided, and magistrates were required to inspect prisons regularly. The outline of our modern prison system began to emerge. For the time being the new rules existed mainly on paper. The money for prisons had to be raised locally, and progress was slow. The Home Office had no means of enforcing the principles which Parliament had enacted. The first steps towards a prison inspectorate were taken by the Whigs in the 1830s. It was not until 1846 that Peel, in part as compensation for the repeal of the Corn Laws, agreed that central government should take over a small part of local prison costs.

Peel's practical mind found it easier to deal with these questions of statute and administration than with the principles of punishment. Everyone whom he consulted agreed that existing methods of punishment were confused and contradictory. The debate on what should follow ran on lines familiar to this day. Penalties should include an element of straightforward punishment, which was right in itself, and served as a deterrent to others. It should also provide an opportunity for the individual to reform himself, or as the Prayer Book said, 'time for amendment of life'. But how did the practical measures available fit these two principles? Where did whipping fit in, or solitary confinement, rules of silence, the treadmill, or the convict hulks and gangs of prisoners building forts and breakwaters? What was to be done about the system of transportation to Australia, already coming under pressure as reports of abuse and bad conditions reached home? Peel thought, listened and wrote but found no clear-cut answers.

He looked for good order and logic rather than mercy. This led him to cruel decisions. For example in 1829 he rejected a proposal that female vagrants with venereal diseases should be treated in prison hospitals. This would mean exempting them from the hard labour which he regarded as a just punishment.[24] Indeed, the reformers of his day did not advocate gentleness. They associated gentleness with the haphazard sentimentality of someone like George IV. Powerfully influenced by Bentham, they thought that a decent, well organised severity constituted the true mercy. It was this reforming spirit which when applied to poverty was soon to create the Poor Law of 1834, workhouses in every town, Oliver Twist and Mr Bumble.

Sydney Smith, Whig clergyman and wit, one of Peel's main correspondents, firmly believed in this doctrine of enlightened severity. In particular he thought that transportation was a soft option. In a letter to Peel in

1826 he parodied the passing of a sentence of transportation to Botany Bay:

> the sentence of the Court is that you shall no longer be burdened with the support of your wife and family. You shall be immediately removed from a very bad climate and a country over burdened with people to one of the finest regions of the earth, where the demand for human labour is every hour increasing, and where it is highly probable you may ultimately regain your character and improve your future. The Court has been induced to pass this sentence upon you in consequence of the many aggravating circumstances of your case, and they hope your fate will be a warning to others.

Peel was not good at badinage, except among close friends. He replied in full seriousness summarising the options before him and confessing bafflement. Yes, transportation was an inefficient method. The hulks held four or five thousand convicts doing public works, but there was a limit to this. Solitary imprisonment was, he thought, fine in theory, but its effect varied unpredictably with the individual; to some it made no difference, to others it was fatal. Public opinion would not tolerate seeing gangs of convict labourers with badges and chains. The question of food in prison was intractable. If prisoners were well fed, people outside complained, particularly in winter. (Sydney Smith favoured strict rations.) When rations were reduced, the result had been disease and death. 'The real truth is the number of convicts is too overwhelming for the means of proper and effectual punishment. I despair of any remedy but that which I wish I could hope for – a great reduction in the amount of crime.'[25]

Peel was not usually content with such an admission of despair and would certainly have returned to the subject of punishment had he remained at the Home Office, or indeed if his last years there had not been filled with matters which were more urgent if not more important.

Six

Partridges, Pictures, Parenthood

'I will certainly bring the humming top for Bobby. I have no
doubt it will amuse him, and it is a capital toy for him.'
Peel to Julia, 1823

'I do not understand how the house at Sudburn which you
used to describe to me as small and uncomfortable in
bedroom furniture can accommodate such a very large party
as the one now assembled within its adulterous walls'
Julia to Peel, 1824

'The Bishop of Oxford is still breathing; he shows no
symptoms of immediate dissolution'
Dr Lloyd to Peel, 1827, waiting for the bishopric

He was working harder than ever before. Julia was the mainspring
of his happiness, together with the babies whom she produced
year by year. Little Julia was born in 1821, Robert in 1822,
Frederick in 1823. The old Baronet still reigned at Drayton. Peel had no
responsibility for tenants or land, and enough money to indulge his own
pleasures including the renting of Lulworth Castle in Dorset, where Julia
and he could entertain and bring up the children far from the noise, stink
and disease of London. An early invitation went to his newest friend, Sir
Walter Scott, in September 1822. 'Come under the impression that
Lulworth never received a more welcome guest. I can promise you a castle,
two abbeys and a monastery, besides a Roman camp and tumuli without
end.'[1]

Later in his life Peel complained of the workload which wore him
down. But at the Home Office he was still on the upward curve of physical wellbeing. He thrived on the work and constantly added to it with

fresh initiatives of his own. A little earlier he had trouble with his sight. He endured an eye operation which more or less blinded him for some days and left him using spectacles for reading and writing for the rest of his life. It was probably during these years that a shooting explosion damaged one ear and stored up pain and worry for later. But the overwhelming impression from his private letters at this time is of a man healthy, strong and happy.

The happiness poured out in letters to Julia. While he worked in London she and the children were at Lulworth, then in several summer holiday homes in Kent, and later at Norris Castle which they rented on the Isle of Wight. Through the somewhat ponderous style of the age Peel's letters show the pent-up affection of a natural family man towards 'my own dearest love'. 'All your letters have come safe to me, and if it were possible every letter you write to me would make you more dear to me ... what shall I bring for Bobby, my little darling boy? The very mention of his name makes my heart warm towards the little fellow, and long to have him in my arms.' Then three days later, 'I will certainly bring the humming top for Bobby. I have no doubt it will amuse him, and it is a capital toy for him. God bless my little ones. I do hope they have not forgotten me. Has little Julia received any scratches in her wars with Bobby? She behaved very well when she received her last wounds.'

In their letters Peel and Julia both poked fun at Julia's stepmother, the dowager Lady Floyd. 'The Dow', as they called her, was not content with having made the match. She wanted to supervise it; in particular she kept watch on Peel's innocent comings and goings from their London house in Stanhope Street while Julia was in the country.

Not all Peel's letters were written from the Home Office or from Stanhope Street. He often spent weekends or most of a week away from his family at shooting parties in the grand country houses up and down England. These were in part political occasions where great men could confer, and little men pollinated the system with their gossip. But Peel excelled at the sport itself and Julia seemed to have accepted that it was best practised without her. She sent him gloves and asked him to give her details of the game bag. In return he described the houses which received him, their furniture as well as their inmates. The Duke of Wellington's house at Stratfield Saye was wretchedly furnished but warm and not uncomfortable. In the Baring house at Somerley he found enormous washing basins almost a yard across — very comfortable, and he thought Julia could get them at Wedgwood's.

Henry Baring bet in December 1823 that Peel would not in one day shoot one each of seven types of game bird* together with a rabbit and a hare. Peel won the match by one o'clock in the afternoon and Baring lost a hundred guineas. On a typical day in October 1825 at Somerley Peel shot thirty-eight pheasants, twenty hares, seven rabbits and two partridges. These were not huge figures compared to the massacres recorded on similar occasions eighty years later, but they marked him out as a first-class shot.

In the evenings there was music and whist, and everyone looked at everyone else. Peel had thought that Mrs Baring was a handsome woman, but 'I could scarcely believe my eyes when I saw a short and ugly stumpy woman ... an Italian singing master in concert with Mrs. B made a tremendous noise at the pianoforte after dinner'. Peel returned to the same poor lady when he wrote next day, 'she has a great power of acquiring languages, but that seems no very valuable quality at Somerley. She said she did not know how to make tea, and she told the truth.' The list of guests did not vary greatly from house to house. Wherever Peel found himself Croker was likely to be spinning his web and the Duke might yet again tell the story of Waterloo.

There was an awkwardness about these shooting parties which introduced a prickle into their happy marriage. Julia did not press to be included but she noticed that other ladies were present, and in particular ladies of a certain kind. We were at a crossing point between generations. George IV was still on the throne, but even before Victoria, strict attitudes were gaining ground, carried upwards by families like Peel's as they rose in the social scale. Elderly aristocrats thought little of consorting with the mistresses of their friends or providing their own in someone else's house. But that was not how Peel and Julia thought or behaved.

Until the final crisis of Peel's career Julia was cool to the Duke of Wellington because he was unkind and unfaithful to his wife. Peel was confronted week after week with country house carryings-on much more

---

* One pheasant, one red-legged partridge, one common partridge, one snipe, one Jack snipe, one woodcock, one wild duck.

aggressive than the Duke's. At first he tried to put a gloss on it. 'I must say I am pleased with the compliment which Lord Hertford paid to you by not asking you to this house.' He then listed the dubious ladies who were present at Sudburn, adding that Lord Hertford by omitting Julia 'paid homage to your virtue and good name'. He went on to stress how little he enjoyed the party apart from the shooting, how he had retired to his room two hours before the rest of them, and how he read there till he went to bed.

Predictably this stuff did not go well. Julia was no shrinking country girl. She had been out and about in London and Dublin. She knew perfectly well that Lord Hertford was a notorious rake. (He was caricatured in novels as the epitome of wickedness, by Disraeli in *Coningsby* as the Marquis of Monmouth and by Thackeray in *Vanity Fair* as the Marquis of Steyne.) He was sleeping at the time with Lady Strachan, who was indeed staying at Sudburn with her husband when Peel attempted his explanation. It was not enough for Peel to write 'I can behave to neither of them with common civility'. Julia was nettled. 'I do not understand how the house at Sudburn which you used to describe to me as small and uncomfortable in bedroom furniture can accommodate such a very large party as the one now assembled within its adulterous walls.'

The letters flew to and fro. It was the week before Christmas 1824. Peel assured Julia that he thought constantly of her, to which she replied, 'How will you bear to think of one compared to fifteen? I know it is nothing in the scale.' Peel remonstrated, but luckily before matters got worse he was safely back in Stanhope Street, and busy planning the christening of baby Frederick, to whom the King's brother the Duke of York was to stand godfather.

It is not easy to judge whether this friction was rough and serious or just the teasing of a young married couple deeply in love with each other. Whichever it was, they smoothed it out. A year later Peel was shooting at Teddesley near Lichfield with a local MP. Croker was as talkative as ever; the Duke played whist through the night. Peel shot more birds than anyone else, but once the shooting was over he longed to be away. 'There is nothing disagreeable here, but still I am away from you, and I am tired of the society of others ... I pray to God every night to bless you and our little ones. Kiss them for me, and tell them I do not forget them for a moment, though I have not a partridge to send them.'[2]

Although Peel and Julia for the most part brought up their family in the country, they needed a house in London big enough for them all. With Julia producing a baby every year, Peel's bachelor home in Stanhope Street was soon too small, and also inconveniently far from the House of Commons and the Home Office. Peel turned his energy to securing a Crown lease on a row of old buildings called Whitehall Gardens between Whitehall and the River Thames, only a quarter of a mile from the Commons. Once the lease was granted the old houses were pulled down. Peel and Sir Alexander Grant (nicknamed 'the Chin') agreed each to build a modern town house on the site.

Croker of course rallied round with ideas and sketches, but the task of design was entrusted to the fashionable Tory architect of the day, Robert Smirke. The Peels moved into their new home in the spring of 1825. Smirke favoured the Grecian Revival with plenty of pillars. He designed a great bow front which rose the whole three storeys of the building on one side. He included innovations such as concrete foundations and gas light-ing. The garden at the back ran down to the river, which in these years before the Embankment was built rose and fell closer to Whitehall than it does today. Peel spent £14,000 on the house (about £600,000 today), more than even he could afford, and had to borrow £5,000 from his brother William. He was delighted with the outcome. 'The view from the bedroom floor', he wrote to Julia, 'is superb. When the whole is finished and the distinction between our house and the Chin's next house is not visible, it will look like a palace.'

Peel's house is lost to us, having been pulled down in 1938 to make way for the new Ministry of Defence. This building, representing Britain's closest approach to fascist architecture, was not completed until well after the defeat of fascism in 1945. It still sits, heavy and soulless, surrounded by litter, grubby grass and inadequate statues, a reproach to the reputa-tion for intelligent design in England which Peel in his time did much to foster.

Peel was particularly pleased with his gallery on the first floor, which stretched sixty-six feet from the front to the back of the house. This was no mere fashionable ornament, but an opportunity for Peel to indulge what was becoming, after politics and family, the ruling passion of his life, the collection and display of pictures.[3] Old Sir Robert, the cotton manufacturer, had made the money; his son, well educated and widely travelled, had the luxury of spending it. His tastes veered strongly towards the visual arts. Peel became a serious patron, collecting for himself and ensuring that Government supported art projects for the public good. In today's parlance, he was a politician with hinterland.

Peel was a close friend and supporter of Thomas Lawrence; he served as a pall bearer at Lawrence's funeral in 1830. David Wilkie was also an adviser, and Peel bought contemporary works from both these two men. He used four leading art dealers to help him acquire the pictures he coveted: William Buchanan, John Smith, C. J. Nieuwenhuys and Samuel Woodburn. Such dealers were alert to the influx of art from the Continent, realising that the complications in Europe created by Napoleon opened purchasing opportunities, both from princely palaces and from the Church.

So it was that Peel acquired Rubens' 'Triumph of Silenus' and 'Le Chapeau de Paille' as well as Van Dyck's 'Crucifixion'. On Wilkie's advice he bought two Rembrandts, and Dutch and Flemish pictures by Gerard Dow, Hobbema, Teniers and van de Velde as well as Pieter de Hooch's 'Courtyard of a House in Delft'. One modern critic has called it the finest cabinet of Dutch pictures ever collected by an amateur.[4]

The galleries in Peel's houses were triumphant places to exhibit his pictures, giving him huge personal pleasure. Mrs Anne Jamieson, writing of a visit to Drayton in the 1840s, recorded Peel's telling remark made while he was showing her Ruysdael's landscape, 'A Pool surrounded by Trees': 'I cannot express to you the feeling of tranquillity, of restoration, with which in an interval of harassing official business I look around me here.'[5]

Jemima Wedderburn, the young niece of Peel's friend Sir George Clerk and a talented watercolourist herself, was also moved to describe her viewing of Peel's pictures, this time at Whitehall Gardens. 'Among other parties I went to with the Clerks was one at Sir Robert Peel's when he was at the height of his fame. He had a fine collection of Dutch paintings which he showed me round himself when the guests were gone. They were very fine, but I do not care much for Dutch pictures; they are beautifully done but of ugly subjects.'[6] Clearly Jemima thought the Prime Minister a better judge of politics than of pictures.

As we shall see, Peel built himself a second great house at Drayton in Staffordshire, complete with gallery. In this gallery he assembled a collection of portraits of the great men of the age. These were not just, in

Mordaunt Crook's words, 'The Tory Party preserved in oils', but men who were eminent in all parts of Victorian life. He asked Lawrence to paint Liverpool and Canning (both now in the National Portrait Gallery), Wellington and Aberdeen, Davy and Fuseli. These and many other portraits commissioned by Peel give us a vivid image of his contemporaries.

On his death in 1850, Peel's collection amounted to about a hundred and thirty pictures. In 1871 his son, the 3rd Baronet, decided to sell part of it, mainly the Dutch and Flemish pictures. After negotiation the National Gallery acquired seventy-eight of these for £75,000. In 1898, the 4th Baronet cashed in Lawrence's 'Julia' by selling her secretly to a Parisian picture dealer, Kleinberger. The Trustees of the Peel Estate, who were in the dark about the sale, were furious and sued for her return, without success. In 1904 Henry Clay Frick, the American industrialist, acquired her, and she now hangs gracefully in the Frick Museum, but sadly divorced from the Rubens companion picture. The profligacy and gambling debts of future baronets led to further sales, one in 1907 and another in 1917. The Peel collection is now spread about various galleries and museums. Peel's descendants have retained a few, but probably not as many as they would have wished.

His family, the Home Office, political activity, the new London home, the growing collection of pictures – these were not enough to exhaust Peel's energy. He entertained and corresponded with men of distinction and ingenuity across professions. The eminent scientist and inventor of the safety lamp, Sir Humphry Davy, shot at Lulworth in 1824; soon after he wrote to tell Peel that he had discovered a simple way of preventing the corrosion of the copper bottoms of the ships of the Royal Navy. Later that year Peel put to Sir Humphry the idea of a Natural History Museum like the Jardin des Plantes in Paris. Peel thought that Britain lagged behind: 'we ought to be ashamed of the beggarly account of boxes [in the British Museum] almost worse than empty, which comprise our specimens of animal life ... what with marbles, butterflies, statues, manuscripts, books and pictures, I think the Museum is a farrago that distracts attention'. Davy was enthusiastic, suggesting that the British Museum should be split up into three parts – a great Public Library, a Gallery of Art, a Gallery of Science. People would only then see 'what they liked'. But the Natural History Museum had to wait for the blossoming of Kensington a generation later.

Peel's most constant correspondent was his old tutor at Christ Church, Charles Lloyd. The two men were close friends, though a generation apart. They clothed the real friendship in elaborate language far from the colloquial jostling of today. They corresponded about the main political issues of the day, even about the bullion question on which one would not today expect competent advice from an Oxford cleric. Peel asked for personal advice about appointing a bishop in Ireland, and about a tutor for his children.

Because of the economic recession, the winter of 1825–6 was particularly fraught for the Government, and for the Home Secretary wrestling with public disorder. But Peel found time for theological concerns. Upon reading one of Lloyd's sermons, he wrote to Lloyd, 'I can hardly believe that a deathbed repentance though perfectly sincere after a life of continued transgression, will necessarily entitle a sinner to the whole measure of God's mercy.' Still less could he accept that every Church of England minister had the authority to absolve the sins of every repentant sinner.

Dr Lloyd replied briskly. 'I must needs tell you that in regard to the great doctrine of Christianity you are little better than a heretic.' Peel demurred: 'without being a heretic, I see some difficulties …'.[7] The correspondence swung to and fro over several months. Peel showed none of the theological subtlety of a Gladstone or a Newman. He belonged to no sect, and disliked the dogmatism with which one Christian attacked another. But that did not mean indifference to the intellectual problems of Christianity.

Other parts of this correspondence were distinctly worldly. In March 1822 Lloyd wrote that he wanted £500 more than he possessed. 'Do not put yourself to inconvenience, and I am sure that you are not too rich for your expenses.' Peel at once sent him an order for that sum, with a letter saying, 'I do, my dear Lloyd, consider your letter a real compliment to me, and a proof of sincere friendship.' Lloyd professed to be distressed, claiming that he had meant to say only that he might be short of that sum at the end of the year in making up his accounts.[8]

Five years later the climax of Dr Lloyd's clerical career approached. He was now Regius Professor of Divinity, but wanted desperately to be Bishop of Oxford. The present Bishop was dying but not dead. Lloyd sent Peel frequent bulletins. 'The Bishop of Oxford is still breathing: he shows no symptoms of immediate dissolution.' By 17 January 1827, there was daily drama: 'In the middle of the day he was not expected to live twelve hours, but is now a little better.' Nevertheless, it seemed sensible for Lloyd to draft a letter which Peel, should the sad event occur, might send to the Prime Minister, Lord Liverpool, recommending Lloyd as the next bishop. The tension was terrible; but on 28 January the Bishop died. Peel sent the letter to Lord Liverpool, and commented to Lloyd, 'this is the only letter of an applicant nature which I ever addressed to him in my life – he will not misunderstand it'. In an age where politics and patronage went hand in hand, Peel's abstinence from the pell-mell of job pushing is extraordinary.

Liverpool, coming to the end of a premiership of fifteen years, had a reputation for appointing bishops on merit. There was nothing against Lloyd, who had lectured eloquently at the University and was a respected theologian, but Peel's letter was not decisive. Lord Liverpool thought it too soon to make Lloyd a bishop and preferred Dr Gray, a learned prebendary from Durham. Lloyd abandoned, at least to Peel, any pretence of lofty detachment. On 30 January he let fly: 'He [Gray] has turned out the most absolute twaddle that the Church ever produced. There is not in the whole of the profession to be found a more miserable creature.' He urged Peel to remonstrate and if absolutely necessary propose a third candidate. But the same day he added a postscript. He had had second thoughts. 'I have determined that it is better policy that you should remain altogether quiet.'

Peel stayed calm. He told Liverpool that he had never heard of Dr Gray. It turned out that the King was behind the manoeuvre. By promoting Dr Gray he wanted to free his stall at Durham, probably for some clerical friend of Lady Conyngham. The King's whim evaporated. Peel worked behind the scenes for his respectable and well qualified friend. On 9 February Peel wrote to tell Lloyd that the Prime Minister had changed his mind and that Lloyd was to be Bishop after all.[9] He held the position for two stressful years, and died in 1829, still Peel's firm friend.

Seven

Police

——— ⟨signature⟩ ———

'He could hardly take tea without a stratagem'
Croker on Canning

'This country ought not and cannot be governed upon any
other principle than those of firmness no doubt, but
firmness combined with moderation'
Peel to Gregory, 1828

'[T]here never was such a good invention as that new police.
Peele [*sic*] ought to have a statue raised to him if for
nothing else.'
*Lady Palmerston to her brother during the disturbances over the Great
Reform Bill, 1832*

T he King's brother, the Duke of York, Commander-in-Chief of
the British Army, died in January 1827 after a long illness. His
patchy life had been marred by military failures in 1793 and 1794
which had caused Pitt to remove him from command. There was also the
scandal connecting his mistress, Mrs Clarke, with the sale of Army commissions. The passing years had pushed these discreditable dramas into
the background. By the low standard of George III's sons the Duke of
York had achieved a certain respect. He was good-natured, even jolly, and
had worked well with Peel during the disorders of 1825 and 1826. He had
created a momentary sensation in 1825 with a forthright speech defending
the existing restrictions on the Catholics; this stiffened his brother against
Catholic Emancipation. But otherwise he was neither particularly
admired nor detested.

The Duke of York's death need not have been a great event. There was an
obvious successor as Commander-in-Chief, and Peel helped to ensure that

the post was quickly offered to and accepted by the Duke of Wellington. It was the funeral rather than the death which would be remembered.

Peel had been shooting with Wellington at Stratfield Saye and the two men travelled together for the ceremony to St George's Chapel, Windsor. Peel wrote a detailed account to Julia. He approved of the impressive display of troops lining the streets of the town, but to his tidy mind everything else was a disaster. Those attending were kept hanging about for three hours on a January evening before anything happened. The chief mourner was the Duke of Clarence, later William IV, who while waiting for his brother's corpse chatted inconsequentially about totals of game shot at this or that weekend. St George's Chapel was in total darkness apart from a few small and grubby wooden chandeliers each holding three wax candles. The mourners, dressed in black, could see little of each other or the service, which was mumbled by the Dean without any attempt at solemnity.

Worst of all was the cold. There was no heating, no carpet, not even a mat or piece of green baize on the stone flags. Two celebrities present, the Duke of Wellington and Canning, were already ill. Peel advised old Lord Eldon, who had just recovered from an illness, to stand on his own cocked hat as some protection for his frail body from the lethal cold seeping up from the floor. Emerging from the funeral Canning remarked to Peel that such a performance in a theatre would have been hissed off the stage as contemptible. The casualties from the funeral were said to have totalled two bishops, five footmen and several soldiers.[1]

There was more to come. Wellington went straight home to bed, and was not seen next day. His poor neglected Duchess told Peel of her worries about his health. She thought he was dangerously pale. When Peel tried to reassure her she burst into tears, and her misery put Peel in mind of the various witty and glamorous ladies who distracted Wellington from his marriage. 'Such things make me still more hate the sight of those who can find it in their heart, even if they have no sense of virtue, to usurp her place ... It really seems something to her to have me to talk to. What wickedness and what folly to undervalue and to be insensible to the affection of a wife.'[2]

Wellington's natural stamina preserved him from the worst effects of the funeral. The same was not true of Canning, whose continuing poor health became a formidable political fact.

Lord Liverpool, who had not attended the funeral, was suddenly removed from public life. While reading his letters alone over breakfast on 17 February 1827 he suffered a stroke which disabled him. Liverpool had served as Prime Minister for fifteen years without interruption, a record in the nineteenth, twentieth and (so far) twenty-first century. In his last five years, with his own personal encouragement, the Cabinet had taken on a cautious, liberalising flavour. But when Lord Liverpool disappeared it was not his policies but his powers of conciliation which were most missed. So long as he was there he had the gift of preventing hostile elements in the political scene from colliding. In terms of policy this meant in particular the friends and opponents of Catholic Emancipation; in terms of personalities it meant the King and Mr Canning.

As soon as he heard of Liverpool's stroke, Peel gripped the situation. He drove down to Brighton that afternoon to see the King. George IV was the most volatile and unpredictable of the different elements now let loose. Peel would have remembered how five years earlier the King in Edinburgh had wanted at once to intervene when he heard of Castlereagh's suicide. Peel's aim was simply to prevent any rash royal decisions about the premiership.

As Home Secretary he had a standing in constitutional matters, and he was careful to keep in daily touch with the other two main players, Wellington and Canning. Nevertheless, it was a remarkable assertion of authority on his part, and would probably have been impossible if Canning himself has not been temporarily out of action. Peel, at the age of thirty-nine, was emphatically junior to Canning (fifty-seven) and Wellington (fifty-eight). In a way this was a help; he was not yet a realistic contender for the premiership. More important, by effort and steady judgement he had earned general trust. Anyway, it worked. The King agreed that no immediate steps should be taken. It was polite and just plausible to pretend that Lord Liverpool might recover. In reality time was gained for a considered debate about his successor.

The obvious candidate was Canning. No one ever doubted his ability; it shone through every speech he made and every article he wrote. Or his experience; it was twenty years since he had first become Foreign Secretary. Or his popularity; the press and public relished his quick wit and his robust way with foreigners. His place in the political spectrum fitted neatly into the patterns and mood of the country and of the House

of Commons just elected in 1826. He was a Tory with a staunch reputation as a disciple of Pitt – but a Tory rich in the liberal instincts now
coming to the fore.

Two obstacles to Canning's promotion were formidable. The first was
the King. Canning had mortally offended George IV by his support for
Queen Caroline. Perhaps the King no longer believed that Canning had
been the Queen's lover. Canning had recently worked hard on the relationship, and made good progress; but the problem was no longer purely personal. The King, like his father before him, was strongly opposed to
Catholic Emancipation, a cause of which Canning was now the best-
known supporter. It was one thing for George to accept and joke with
Canning as an amusing and successful Foreign Secretary, more tolerant of
his Sovereign's personal waywardness than Peel or Wellington. It was
another to accept as his Prime Minister a man who on the Catholic
question would press him to betray what he saw as his royal duty.

The other obstacle to Canning's promotion was Canning himself.
People did not trust him. Canning was not only clever; he blatantly
paraded the fact. If a man was clever and not ashamed of it, then it was
thought almost certain that he was using his cleverness for manoeuvres
and deceits from which decent men should recoil. This personal distrust
cropped up over and again. It was largely responsible for his failure to win
the Oxford University seat in 1817 before it passed to Peel. Ten years later
Bishop Lloyd continued to reflect the University's suspicions: 'The game
that Canning has been playing for the last two years could not escape the
observations even of a fool. He has been playing into the hands of the
Whigs and receiving their support and continual applause.'[3] Likewise the
Duke of Wellington, as his henchman Charles Arbuthnot reported,
'cannot bring himself to put trust in Canning. He thinks that in his own
department there is much of trickery; he sees that the sons and relations
of our most vehement opponents are taken into employ; and he cannot
divest himself of the idea that directly or indirectly, there has been an
understanding with some of the leaders of the opposition.'[4] Canning
himself was sensitive, too quick to imagine conspiracies and react against
those who he thought were ranged against him.

There is nothing definite or indeed morally disastrous in the accusations against Canning, but they reflected a strong feeling which did him
much harm. Croker thought that Canning should be Prime Minister, but

believed 'he could hardly take tea without a stratagem'.[5] A man with this reputation may fascinate and charm. He may draw to himself devoted followers and a great verdict from history; but he will find it more difficult to transact daily business than a man with fewer talents who has earned greater trust. This was a lesson which Disraeli learned and profited from learning. Disraeli had all Canning's brilliance, and in youth even more of his showmanship. But in his later years Disraeli could be as dull as necessary in the company of dull men; he tried not to meet dull women. Whether Canning ever learned the lesson is not clear; if he did he was not given time to put it into effect.

The King twisted and turned to avoid Canning. He played with several alternatives. The Duke of Wellington had no appetite for the premiership. Indeed he rashly said in public that he was not qualified for the job. Canning, tongue in cheek, advised the King that since the royal conscience felt so strongly against Catholic Emancipation he should choose a Prime Minister and Cabinet which agreed with him on the matter – an option which everyone knew was impossible. The King suggested that the Cabinet should choose the Prime Minister, but Wellington, Peel and Canning all told him that this was a task for the King alone.

The King could reasonably wonder about the nature of his authority when he was able neither to delegate this responsibility of choosing a Prime Minister nor exercise it in the way he wanted. The monarchy was entering a twilight zone, moving away from the age when the Prime Minister was, in fact as well as theory, the King's Minister, towards the present position of, in effect, an elected Prime Minister.

Eventually, driven into a corner, the King asked Canning to form a government. But who would serve under him? Although Wellington's instinct was always to serve, for once he declined. He had been irritated by the way Canning approached him and unwilling to overcome his distrust.

Attention turned to Peel, whose support in the Commons would be crucial. The King now saw in Peel his one hope of rescue from Catholic Emancipation. He wrote to Peel specifically proposing an odd alliance. The two men would prop each other up. He would rely on Peel to oppose Catholic Emancipation in Cabinet, and Peel could rely on him to block it by withholding his assent. 'The King on the one hand considers *himself* Mr Peel's *guarantee*, and on the other hand, Mr Peel is *the King's*. So that no means, let the Government be formed as it may, can be ever practised with a view of carrying the Catholic question, or of injuring the Protestant Constitution of the country.'[6] Peel's knowledge of his sovereign went too deep for him to trust any such arrangement. He was enjoying himself at the Home Office and had one project, the creation of a London police force, which he had not yet been able to launch. But he seems not to have hesitated. He at once told Canning that he intended to resign.

His refusal to serve under Canning was absolute. He explained it on grounds entirely related to his position at the Home Office. The Home Secretary was in effect responsible for the administration of Irish affairs. He had found it difficult enough to hold this position when he alone among Ministers in the House of Commons opposed Catholic Emancipation. But this had been tolerable because the Prime Minister had agreed with him. Now Liverpool had gone. 'Is it not obvious', he wrote to Canning, 'that my efficiency as a servant of the Crown must be materially impaired by an arrangement which transfers the highest and most powerful office from him with whom I entirely concurred to you for whom it is my misfortune on that question to differ?'[7] He emphasised that this was his only point of difference with Canning; if it had not existed he would have been glad to serve under him.

Afterwards Peel was able to show that there had been no conspiracy. He had not plotted against Canning; the arguments which swayed him did not apply to his other colleagues. Looking back a few months later he put the argument even more bluntly to Bishop Lloyd. If he had continued as Home Secretary under Canning he would

remain responsible for the administration of Irish affairs, with the whole Whig Party, half the Tory Party and the Prime Minister hostile to the principle on which they would have to be administered. The secret support of the King would be very like intrigue on my part against my colleagues. If decided and effectual, which it would not have been, it would initially lead to discourse. The proposal of office to me was in effect saying to me 'govern Ireland without support, discountenanced by all that is influential in the Government, and when we have discredited you, we will remove you'.[8]

It is worth pausing on this episode, since it resurfaced painfully at the end of Peel's political life. In the letters quoted above Peel somewhat exaggerated the role of the Home Secretary in the governance of Ireland, though he himself had built up that role by his close supervision of the Chief Secretary and Lord-Lieutenant. For, in truth, Peel was simply not willing to serve under Canning. Bishop Lloyd hoped that he would explain that he differed on a number of Canning's policies of which the University of Oxford disapproved, not just the Catholic question. But Peel would not do this. Canning paid tribute to his straightforward dealing and the two men exchanged stately letters of compliment and regret.

There is no need for colleagues to resemble each other like peas in a pod. Canning was quick, witty, a versifier, the son of an actress, sometimes in financial difficulty, a natural gambler. In all these respects he differed from Peel. However, the problem was not one of difference but one of trust. Peel shared the general view of the political establishment: Canning was too clever for his own good. Four years earlier Peel had told Arbuthnot that though he did not mind doing business with Canning in the Cabinet, and they were always very civil to each other in the Commons, yet Canning was the sort of person with whom he would be very sorry to have a tête-à-tête.[9] That was the point. A Home Secretary has to be able to hold a tête-à-tête with the Prime Minister. In April 1827 Peel left the Home Office.

But was the point strong enough? Peel was to make sacrifices of his own convenience much greater than would have been involved in serving under Canning in 1827. True, he was able to show later that there was no deceit. In 1827 he was still an opponent of Catholic Emancipation; there were doubts in his mind, but no conviction yet that the status quo was untenable. But he could have postponed the question. He might have secured some assurance that Catholic Emancipation would not be pursued against his wishes. He might have accepted a different post, for example the Foreign Office. The valid criticism of Peel is not that he betrayed Canning, but that he allowed personal dislike to take him out of a Government which badly needed his support.

The immediate casualty of this decision was his friendship with Croker. Croker did not aim for high office himself, but hated to feel that he was not at the heart of every intrigue. He had long worked to bring Peel and Canning together, and thought in 1827 that the moment had come. During the crisis he went for a walk in London with Peel. First they visited Somerset House to call on Huskisson in his office in the

Board of Trade. Then they crossed and re-crossed the river by the Westminster and Waterloo bridges. Pausing by Lord Eldon's house, Croker asked Peel if he thought Eldon would stay in the Government as Lord Chancellor. According to Croker Peel squeezed his arm and said, 'he will if I do'.[10] To men like Croker a squeeze was as good as a nod or a wink. He bustled on his way convinced that Peel had decided to serve under Canning. Reports reached Peel which convinced him that Croker was deep in Canning's confidence. He at once broke off their friendship, and returned curt answers in reply to Croker's long explanations and pledges of affection. Eventually, six months later, the breach was healed, though Peel still for a time refused to discuss politics with his oldest political friend.

Parliament rose early for the summer recess that year, and on 2 July, the last day of the session, Peel and Canning chanced to meet in Westminster Hall. Always courteous in their dealings with each other, the two men walked up and down for a quarter of an hour, the invalid Canning leaning on Peel's arm. Canning, worn out by hard work, retired to the Duke of Devonshire's famous villa at Chiswick in the hope that there he could recruit his strength. The opposite happened. Canning caught one chill after another. His liver and lungs were inflamed, he suffered spasms of intense pain, and the doctors were powerless. His mind remained lucid as ever while his body collapsed. He died on 8 August, worrying about a crisis in Portugal.[11]

For a few weeks it looked as if the structure of Canning's Government, composed of liberal Tories and a group of leading Whigs, might survive without Canning. As Prime Minister the King chose Lord Goderich, who as Frederick Robinson had been a competent Chancellor of the Exchequer. Goderich was a reformer in a mild sort of way and had in 1824 introduced the first of the liberal Tory Budgets, which concentrated on lifting burdens from trade. But the gifts required for the offices of Prime Minister and Chancellor are different. Goderich was a poor debater, not least because he was at all times convinced of his own inadequacies. Modesty is a virtue in a politician only up to a point, and in a Prime Minister can be almost as dangerous as arrogance. In Goderich self-criticism took the form of tears. He wept at every setback, so that even those who began by liking a likeable man soon became exasperated. He lasted five months, and threw in the towel in January 1828.

Peel had spent a happy autumn with Julia and the children at Maresfield, the house in Sussex which they had rented from Sir John Shelley. He was in no hurry to return to office, but cannot have been entirely surprised to hear from the Duke of Wellington on 9 January 1828. 'My dear Peel, I entreat you to come to town in order that I may consult with you.'[12] The King had overcome his resentment at the refusal of Wellington and Peel to help him by serving under Canning. George IV liked to have a grievance but his target varied from year to year. The royal resentment was now focused on Lord Grey, the leader of the Whig Party, who would certainly try to force Catholic Emancipation on him. His only hope of avoiding Grey was to forgive the Duke and Peel and summon them to run the country. Painful negotiations followed at Apsley House, the Duke's London home.

There were too many claimants for office. The Whigs would leave if Wellington was head of the Government but most of the liberal Tory Ministers expected to stay. The trouble was that other Tories who had left Government with Wellington and Peel expected to come back with them. There was just not room for everyone. The country gentlemen on the back benches, who had never trusted Canning, rejoiced at the prospect of a proper Tory government again, which would keep the reformers and the Catholics at bay. There was no doubt that the Duke would lead the new ministry and that Peel would return to the Home Office. But who would come in with them? And (more dangerous still) were these two men as resolute and unflinching Tories as they pretended? Doubts were already being expressed. The Duke of Rutland had a nose for weakness. Even in Lord Liverpool's time he was grumbling that the Government was composed of 'political theorists without a foot of land of their own'.[13] The Duke and Peel had acres of land enough; but had they the will to defend them properly against reform?

In January 1828 the argument broke out into the open. The critics provoked in Peel a response which shaped the rest of his political life. Up to then he had been content with a public position on the right of the Party.* Peel himself referred to the Tory Right as 'Ultras'. He could have

---

* The terms 'right' and 'left' were not current at the time, and their use at this point is an anachronism; but they are so convenient as a shorthand description that perhaps this may be forgiven.

become their acclaimed leader. True, as early as 1820 he had doubted to Croker whether reform could be indefinitely resisted. But that was in private. He had built his public reputation as a strong Chief Secretary in Ireland, and as the leading opponent of Catholic Emancipation. He had led the move back to honest money based on gold. His reform of the criminal justice system, though sweeping and thorough, had been argued and executed on a Tory basis. Most recently he had refused to serve under the devious Canning. To outward appearance Peel was well placed in 1828 at the age of forty to put himself at the head of Tories fully committed to upholding the Church, the monarchy, the unreformed Parliament and the system of agricultural protection.

The Ultras believed that these institutions should be preserved with the minimum of change as the only reliable bulwark against national decay and even revolution. Such would have been the hope and expectation of most of Peel's constituents in the University of Oxford. The Ultras did not throw up impressive leaders. But such were the instinctive views of a majority in the Lords, including the Dukes of Buckingham and Newcastle, and in the Commons of a fierce minority including Buckingham's son Lord Chandos, Edward Knatchbull and Charles Wetherell.

The Conservative Party will always include Ultras within its ranks. These are men and women who instinctively resist change and pine for a golden age that never was. Every Conservative Association has always contained such individuals, sometimes as its most energetic supporters. But the Ultras divide into two distinct types. There are those whose nostalgia is part of their charm. There is nothing ungenerous in their affection for the past; their backward look is warm-hearted, even delightful. They pick out selectively what was good during the lifetime of their grandparents and great-grandparents and lament its passing. Yet most of them live pretty comfortable lives. Anthony Trollope, himself a Liberal, creates some of his most attractive characters (Archdeacon Grantly, Dr Thorne, the Greshams) out of this attitude.

Ultras can be roused temporarily to great passion, as they were against Catholic Emancipation, for the Corn Laws, later against Home Rule for Ireland, later still in favour of Rhodesia, against European integration. But there are limits to their passion because in the end most of them are pessimistic about politics and in particular about their own chances of success.

The second and smaller group of Ultras are the sour Right. There is nothing warm or nostalgic about their politics. Many of them are intelligent and sincere; but their appeal is to the prejudices and cruelty which are part of human nature. The foreigner, the immigrant, the down and out, the Roman Catholic, the Jew, the Muslim – all of these have at different times become the focus of this sourness.

The difficulty of the Ultras, whether charming or sour, is that they cannot win and know it. Like everyone else, they want to win elections but theirs is not the way. A Conservative leader has to coax them towards reality. In this exercise Disraeli and Macmillan, holding no rooted views of their own, used wit and charm to great effect. Margaret Thatcher and Peel tried to impose their views by strong argument and displays of authority. Margaret Thatcher succeeded because although the Ultras disliked much of what she did (in Rhodesia, Ireland or Europe) they felt that at heart she remained 'one of us'. For a time Peel, too, succeeded. But he paid a heavy price for that success when the Ultras judged that his heart was no longer in the right place.

Peel was not at heart an Ultra. His mind moved through the study of facts to proposals for action. He worked to improve what he found, a desire based on general Christian sympathies rather than a precise evangelical or utilitarian creed. Certainly the aim of every proposal must be conservative, namely the preservation of the country's institutions and way of life. But the facts brought to him in Ireland and at the Home Office suggested dangers which could not be dealt with by simply holding to the status quo. Moderation, and when necessary reasonable change, were better conservative tools than repression. Peel was already fusing in his mind two concepts which in other minds were in conflict, namely the need to improve and the need to conserve. Ever since this time all Conservative policy-making has been an attempt to reshape and update that fusion.

The political crisis of 1828 made Peel straighten out his thoughts. He explained them at two levels, the strategic and the tactical, in letters to Gregory, his old colleague in Ireland. On 18 January he wrote that 'this country ought not and cannot be governed upon any other principle than those of firmness no doubt, but firmness combined with moderation'. A fortnight later he turned to the tactics. An Ultra Tory government would be 'supported by very warm friends no doubt, but the warm friends, being prosperous country gentlemen, fox-hunters etc. etc., most excellent men, who will attend one night, but will not leave their favourite pursuits to sit up till two or three o'clock fighting questions of detail on which, however, a government must have a majority. We could not have stood creditably for a fortnight.'[14] This notion of squires more reliable on the hunting field than in the division lobby, more concerned with their dinner than with the clauses of a Bill, became a staple of Peel's political correspondence.

He never saw the charm of the charming Ultras, only the sourness of the rest. Peel helped Wellington sort out the different claims to office, using his influence to insist that the liberal Tory Huskisson should be included (despite his unpopularity with the Ultras) because of his unrivalled knowledge of finance. The Duke was impatient with the intellectual chatter which complicated the formation of his Government. 'We hear a great deal of Whig principles and Tory principles, and Mr Canning's principles; but I confess that I have never seen a definition of any of them, and cannot make to myself a clear idea of what any of them mean.'[15]

In the end a Government was formed. It was a frail structure. The Duke was a shrewder politician than has been generally supposed, but he lacked the laid-back persuasive skills of Lord Liverpool. More important, the Canningite upheavals of 1827 had shaken the structure of Tory government, and sharpened personal antagonisms. The Wellington Government of 1828 never looked like lasting long.

Back at the Home Office, Peel wasted no time. He immediately resurrected his proposals for a professional London police force, determined now to see them through. Once again, as in 1822, he arranged for a parliamentary Committee to examine the problem, and he deluged the members with statistics about the rise of crime in London. The Committee worked quickly, and in July 1828 produced a report obediently reversing the stance of its predecessor in 1822. The new Committee believed that a better system could be produced, probably at less expense, and with no new restraints on the liberty of the subject.

Peel's plan was ready; the Committee's recommendations coincided with what he had in mind. This time the argument that a professional police force would be a threat to liberty failed to gather strength. Peel had no patience with such antique reasoning. 'I want to teach people', he wrote to the Duke, 'that liberty does not consist in having your home robbed by organised gangs of thieves and in leaving the principal streets of London in the nightly possession of drunken women and vagabonds.'[16] Introducing the Metropolitan Police Improvement Bill on 15 April 1829, Peel fastened on the example of the rapidly growing London borough of Kensington. Given its size it was not surprising that 'three drunken beadles should be no prevention of housebreaking and thieving in it. Indeed ... three angels, under such circumstances, would be a sorry protection.'[17]

The confusion and inefficiency of the existing system is illustrated by an actual case. In December 1811, eleven years before Peel became Home Secretary, a double murder was committed in the East End of London. Seven people were killed within twelve days. One shopkeeper was found bludgeoned to death along with his wife and his apprentice, then his baby was discovered with its throat cut. A few nights later a man and his wife were hacked to pieces with their maid at the Kings Arms, a pub which they kept in the next parish. The savagery of the crimes created huge anger and fear. There was no apparent motive; who was safe, who would be next? The excitement only died down after the chief suspect, who may well have been innocent, hanged himself in Cold Bath Prison before his trial. Not until the days of Jack the Ripper were London people so scared. But in 1887 Jack the Ripper was hunted in a city with 14,000 Metropolitan Police officers. They did not catch him, but their existence reassured the public. In 1811 London had no effective police force at all.

We are lucky that P.D. James and T.A. Critchley researched these Ratcliffe Highway murders for their dramatic book *The Maul and the Pear Tree*. They set out the state of policing in London in 1811. One small arrangement had been patched onto another, producing an incoherent series of inadequate devices. The main responsibility for countering crime in the East End parish of St George's, where the four murders were committed, lay with the church wardens, overseers and trustees of the parish. They appointed up to a dozen unpaid constables who had the job of setting and inspecting the night watch, charging prisoners and bringing them before the magistrates. The constables of St George's employed thirty-five night watchmen at two shillings a night, with a beadle to supervise them. The watchmen were supposed to patrol the streets, call the time every half-hour, and watch out for any suspicious characters. In practice they spent most of their time in small huts or watch-boxes. If the watchmen were young, they attracted prostitutes, who distracted them from their duties. If they were old they were not good at tackling burglars. St George's, like most parishes, plumped for elderly watchmen, and equipped them with a lantern and a rattle.

To this mainstay of order were added eight officers separately employed by the magistrates to cover six East End parishes, the Thames police force to control shipping, and the Bow Street Runners patrolling the main highways. These forces were all jealous of each other. One London magistrate, when asked in 1816 whether the different forces co-operated, replied 'certainly not ... different police officers keep their information to themselves and do not wish to communicate it to others, that they may have the credit and advantage of detecting offenders'. In these circumstances not much detection of offenders could be expected. The Home Secretary, who could ask all these bodies for reports, possessed no lever to convert the money spent on them into a useful instrument for dealing with crime.[18]

Peel by 1829 was prepared to tackle head-on the vested interests of the London parishes and magistrates. But this time there was no effective opposition. In June the Bill became law, and the world's leading capital was provided with the world's leading police force. Peel's Act set up a single police district covering, with the exception of the City, everything within a radius of ten miles from the centre of London. Two magistrates were to supervise a new police force, which was to be financed by a special police rate not exceeding eight pence in the pound on assessed rateable property. The Home Secretary was given wide powers over the recruitment and organisation of the force.

Peel understood that the success of the new force would depend not so much on its legal powers as on the quality of the men picked to staff it. He took great trouble over the choice of the two supervising magistrates. These soon became known as Commissioners, a more accurate title given that they were in effect the chief executives of a formidable new public body rather than traditional magistrates. He appointed as one of the first holders of the post Charles Rowan, a retired Army officer of forty-six who had served with Moore at Corunna and Wellington at Waterloo. The second was a young Irish barrister called Richard Mayne. The two men were recruited within a fortnight of Peel's Bill becoming law.

Peel ran into a typical difficulty when he came to appoint the third senior official of the new force. The Receiver was to take charge of its finances, and collect the rates from the (no doubt reluctant) parishes. Lord Chandos, a key Government supporter in the Commons and son of the Duke of Buckingham, had a friend whom he believed to be ideally suited for the job of Receiver. Peel resisted. This was not to be that kind of job. He wrote that the tasks of the new Receiver would be so heavy that he was absolutely bound to value the most efficient man he could find, who must have legal training and knowledge of accountancy. He found a solicitor called Wray whose qualifications were legal and commercial rather than political and aristocratic.

Peel chose men well: all three appointments were a great success. He took corresponding trouble over the recruitment of the bulk of the new force of just over 1,000 men – 8 superintendents, 20 inspectors, 88 sergeants and 895 constables. (The Metropolitan Police in 2005 had 47,000 men and women.)[19] Peel had to operate within a political system which still depended largely on patronage for many appointments. He had just relied on patronage to get himself a constituency. But, as in his similar enterprise in Ireland fifteen years earlier, he was determined that merit not patronage must from the outset govern the recruitment of his new police officers. Note in particular his charge in December 1829 to his two new Commissioners:

> All nominations for the police, as well as original nominations as promotions from inferior stations, should depend exclusively upon the character, qualifications and services of the persons selected; and I am satisfied that you have, on offering your recommendations to me, acted rigidly upon that suggestion in every instance. I am convinced that on the strict adherence to this principle, must entirely depend the efficiency and character of the new establishment.[20]

Eight years before Victoria came to the throne, long before the Northcote-Trevelyan changes in the Civil Service, let alone the later overhaul of the Army and Navy, we hear the authentic voice of the Victorian reformer proclaiming the supremacy of merit in the public service. Peel went on to deal with promotions, which must depend on a strict enquiry into the character and habits of life of each candidate. At the beginning some of those in authority would need to be recruited from outside the force; but Peel looked forward to the day when all promotions in the force would come from those who had served in the ranks. This merito-cratic principle was introduced and survives to this day. The fact that all senior officers come up through the ranks gives a distinctive flavour to the police service of this country.

Peel skilfully used the fear of crime as the main justification for his measure. Public opinion then, as now, was sure that crimes against indi-viduals were increasing and that the authorities were handling them with the utmost feebleness and incompetence. Affection for the ancient watch-men and traditional rights of parishes evaporated when tested against this concern. But there was another aspect of the creation of a large London police force. As we have seen, the main concern of the Home Office had traditionally been not individual crime, but public disorder. It was after all only eight years since London had been virtually in the hands of a mob stirred by sympathy for the absurd Queen Caroline; and that was just the last of a whole series of dangerous movements. Now there was to be a disciplined civilian force under the direction of a senior Government Minister empowered to give orders to the Commissioners whom he had appointed. This was a huge increase in the physical power of government at the centre of the political system.

Peel added a bonus for government in the provision that the force was to be financed from the parish rates rather than by the Chancellor of the Exchequer. This proved unrealistic, and four years later central govern-ment funding was introduced by the Whig Act of 1833.[21] In practice the powers of control given to the Home Secretary in Peel's Act were too wide and detailed for the tiny Home Office to exercise. Increasingly they were delegated to the Commissioners; in that sense the force outgrew its master. But whatever the method of finance and precise legal powers, the Peelers or Bobbies were there on the streets of London, uniformed, honest and polite. Peace-loving citizens slept easily in their beds.

Croker as usual had a view. He was back on friendly terms with Peel after their spat over Canning. Croker was sure that three shillings a day was far too low a wage for the new police officers. 'Your constable must live in a state of perpetual trouble, labour and disquiet so that other folks may enjoy their rest. Can this be expected from competent persons at three shillings a day?' Peel replied thoughtfully. It was too soon to be sure, but he was inclined so far to think that three shillings was about right. He had had more than 2,000 applications for the 1,000 jobs. 'No doubt three shillings a day will not give me all the virtues under heaven, but I do not want them. Angels would be far above my work. I have refused to employ gentlemen – commissioned officers, for instance – as superintendents and inspectors because I am certain they would be above their work.' As usual he had done some research. On this pay of a guinea a week he believed that a single man could feed, lodge and clothe himself, find a doctor if necessary, and still save ten shillings.[22]

In November 2005 the Commissioner of the Metropolitan Police, Sir Ian Blair, recalled Peel's decision on recruitment in his Dimbleby Lecture. Sir Ian said, 'Among the many directions he [Peel] gave to the service was that it was not to be an occupation for gentlemen. That has had the long-term effect of separating us from the established currents of British life, so that those who join the police are a bit of a puzzle to others.' He went on to say that 'the police service was consequently the preserve of the striving lower-middle class, predominantly white, predominantly male'. He appealed eloquently for an end to this discrimination.

Peel was dealing with a set of class attitudes which has disappeared today. First, he was determined to resist the lingering belief among the upper classes of his time that all parts of the public service could best be staffed by their own friends and relations. Second, he believed as he said later in the same letter to Croker that if he began to appoint gentlemen to the higher ranks of the police, 'they would refuse to associate with other persons who were not of equal [social] rank, and they would therefore degrade the latter in the eyes of the men'.

From time to time suggestions have been made that the quality of leadership in the police service could be raised by abandoning the rule that every senior police officer should rise from the ranks and replacing it with a cadet system similar to that in the Army. Margaret Thatcher used occasionally to urge this on me as Home Secretary. I tried to persuade her that whatever the theoretical merits of this system (which in one form was tried in the Metropolitan Police between the wars), it would simply not be acceptable to the modern police service or (I thought) to the general public.

In 1848, when thrones tottered across Europe and the Chartists marched on London, there were many reasons for the peaceful and orderly outcome in Britain; one was the existence of the Metropolitan Police. As early as 1832 Lady Palmerston, a staunch Whig, wrote to her brother that '[t]here never was such a good invention as that new police. Peele [*sic*] ought to have a statue raised to him if for nothing else.'[23]

One reason why Peel had so little difficulty with his Police Bill was the abundance of other controversy at the time. The Corn Laws, the struggle for Greek independence, and the first squalls over parliamentary reforms were enough to absorb public attention, give the Whigs ammunition against the Government and increase the strains inside the Cabinet.

The Corn Law of 1815, which imposed a total ban on imports until the price reached a high level, had proved too rigid to deal with the economic hardships of 1825 and 1826. It was generally agreed that a sliding scale of duty on imports was needed, so that the duty payable fell as the market price rose. Canning had not been able to complete his own proposals for this sliding scale. The Duke's Cabinet was bitterly divided on the detail and Peel had to negotiate a compromise between the Duke himself, whose instincts were throughout protectionist, and Huskisson who led the Ministers inclined to free trade. The 1828 Corn Law satisfied no one, but survived year after year for lack of an agreed alternative.

Peel as Home Secretary was responsible for handling an equally delicate issue, which, like the 1828 Corn Law, was pregnant with bigger changes to come. The Whigs were anxious to find a political cause on which they could unite, healing the division between those who had joined and those who had opposed Canning's Government. They chose the Test and Corporation Acts.

Since the reign of Charles II these Acts had in theory prevented Dissenters from holding government or municipal office. The Acts imposed on office holders an obligation to take the Sacrament according to the rites of the established Church of England. This was in theory only, because an annual indemnity relieved Dissenters from any penalties under the Acts. In practice there was little agitation on the matter, and Dissenters and Anglicans worked happily together in many public duties. The Test and Corporation Acts stood like crumbling memorials on an ancient battlefield, ineffective and largely forgotten. But theoretically they were indefensible, and by 1828 the country was developing a taste for theoretical examination.

In February, Lord John Russell on behalf of the Whigs moved that the

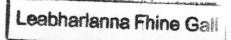

Acts be repealed. Peel consulted Bishop Lloyd at Oxford, who in reply paraded the theological arguments against repeal. Peel was not attracted by subtle points about the nature of the Sacrament. He told Lloyd that such argument would be lost on people 'who know very little about it, half of whom have dined or are about to dine, and are only forcibly struck by that which they instantly comprehend without trouble'.[24] After consulting Cabinet Peel rested his case against repeal on the familiar argument, 'if it ain't broke, don't fix it'. There was in practice no great grievance and no great agitation for repeal, so why bother? But this uncharacteristically lackadaisical approach did not convince and Lord John beat the Government by forty-four votes on his motion of principle.

Peel was momentarily cross, and Lloyd gently rebuked him for not having fought harder for the privileged status of the Church. But he accepted Lloyd's advice that he should consult the senior bishops about the Government's response to the wish of the Commons. The result was a skilful agreement reached by Peel with the bishops in March at Lambeth Palace. Instead of taking the Sacrament, office holders should make a declaration that they would not injure or subvert the established Church. Once he had reached a decision Peel recovered his parliamentary form and steered the compromise through the Commons. Lord Eldon was of course appalled. He recalled opposing similar measures proposed in 1787, 1789 and 1790 which he believed would have led, as in France, to the destruction of all union between Church and State. Alas, he wrote, 'the young men and lads in the House of Commons are too young to remember these things'.[25] But memory is not always the best guide in politics.

Peel had extricated the Government neatly from its dilemma. Nostalgic Anglicans noticed then and later that for the first time Parliament was unhinging the State from the Church of England. Lord John Russell remarked, 'Peel is a very pretty hand at hauling down his colours.'[26] The Dissenters were freed; the Tories and Whigs were at one in distinguishing the case of the Dissenters from that of Roman Catholics. The restrictions on Catholics remained. The Protestant fortress seemed well founded on its rock. Neither Peel nor Lord John guessed at the imminent storm which would bring it to the ground.

Eight

The Catholic Breakthrough

'The proceedings of yesterday were those of madness, but
the country is mad, and they have been allowed to proceed
in the career of revolution. It will not, cannot end well.'
Fitzgerald to Peel at the County Clare by-election, May 1828

'[I]t was a great shame that Mr Peel had so let the country
down as he had been such a kind gentleman when an
undergraduate'
The egg-cook at Christ Church on Catholic Emancipation, 1829

'It is not pro dignitate nostra to have a rat as our member'
John Henry Newman on Peel's election chances, February 1829

'Robin's the lad after all. No administration can stand in
this country without him. The Duke could do nothing
without him.'
*Sir Robert Peel, 1st Baronet, conversing about his son while playing whist,
1829*

I t ought to have been relatively easy. In May 1828 Peel's friend Vesey
Fitzgerald was appointed President of the Board of Trade in a
Government reshuffle. Under the rules of the day he had to resign
his seat in the Commons and stand for re-election in his Irish constituency of County Clare. Fitzgerald was a popular young man, a good landlord
in the County and well known as a supporter of Catholic Emancipation.
Nonetheless, O'Connell's political organisation, the Catholic Association,
decided to contest the election. They had some difficulty in finding a candidate. The prospect for a Catholic candidate was not entirely inviting.
He faced either losing, or winning and being unable to take his seat. The
Association responded to this dilemma by raising the stakes. They

decided to play their hand in such a way as to upset the table. On 24 June their leader, Daniel O'Connell, announced that he would stand for County Clare himself.

The scene entirely changed. Irish, like British, elections were famous for drunkenness, disorder and fraud. Worse, Ireland was full of murder and all manner of violent crime. By contrast in County Clare the Catholic Association deployed peaceful strength as a political machine, powerfully backed by the local priesthood. Fitzgerald, a pleasant fellow and competent administrator, was no fighting candidate. Even before O'Connell's announcement Peel had written to strengthen him against being upset by criticism. 'It really is quite unnecessary for a gentleman and a Minister of the Crown to notice the low slang of a county election.'[1]

Fitzgerald soon realised that the likely upset was not to his feelings but to his seat. He was going to lose. Polling lasted five days; by the end O'Connell's triumph was complete. He was elected to the Parliament in which he could not take his seat by 2,057 votes to 982. Fitzgerald wrote at once to Peel. 'The proceedings of yesterday were those of madness, but the country is mad, and they have been allowed to proceed in the career of revolution. It will not, cannot end well.'

Peel, clear-minded and practical, first tackled the immediate question: what should be done if O'Connell actually came in person to Westminster and claimed his seat? He took legal advice to buttress the willingness of the Speaker to enforce the law. If O'Connell forced his way into the Commons, the Speaker would declare him a stranger and if necessary instruct the Sergeant at Arms to throw him out.[2] But neither the Speaker nor the Sergeant at Arms could deal with the madness in Ireland which Fitzgerald had described.

It was more than ten years since Peel had decided that honest despotism would be the best form of government for the Irish. It became a common thought among those in charge of the nineteenth-century British Empire. A simple system of clear law and honest administration should be enforced on subject peoples for their own good. Somehow the ideal was never fully realised, or only fleetingly here and there. This was not just because of local resistance, though in Ireland such resistance was crucial. There was something amiss with the British themselves; they were not ruthless, full-hearted inheritors of the imperial mantle of Rome. There were never enough soldiers and administrators to impose effective direct rule on every area marked red on the map. But there was also in the British a certain reluctance to carry imperial rule to a logical conclusion. They could not in their hearts be happy with imposing on others absolute rule which they had themselves repudiated at home.

In Ireland one difficulty was the forty-shilling freeholder, who had been given the vote in 1793. So long as Catholic tenants voted as tenants rather than Catholics there was no problem. Landlords could organise their leases as pieces on the checkerboard of local politics. But in County Clare in 1828 the tenants were dramatically persuaded by the Catholic Association and their own priest to vote as Catholics. Fitzgerald polled his own tenants and some better-off electors in the small towns; the rest went to O'Connell.

Modern historians like to point out that single events rarely by themselves have the effect traditionally attributed to them. Attitudes, they point out, change over time, not suddenly; events are slow in preparation. Certainly the unreliability of the forty-shilling freeholder was becoming clear before the Clare by-election. There had been an ominous shift away from deference in the general election two years earlier. But the Clare result brought the danger into sudden focus. Peel wrote in his memoirs that the difficulty was not a violation of the law, but the exercise of the legal right to vote as a means of creating a force which would step by step encroach on government and paralyse its authority.[3]

Through the summer and autumn of 1828 Ireland simmered uneasily. As was his habit, O'Connell used his success to pile on the pressure up to but not past the point where it burst into organised rebellion. Likewise the Government made unsuccessful attempts to prevent public meetings of the Catholic Association, but hesitated to use the full panoply of coercion. O'Connell had achieved his objective. The British dilemma in Ireland was now in the sharpest possible focus. A Catholic had been elected to sit in a Parliament from which Catholics were barred – and not just any Catholic, but a celebrity known everywhere.

The absurdity and injustice of the system were exposed more abruptly by the Clare election than by thirty years of argument. What O'Connell had done could be done at just about every election or by-election in Ireland. The possibilities of disruption at Westminster were infinite. More serious was the question how Ireland could be governed. Of course there would always be enough British troops to put down an armed rebellion. But Ireland could not be run by British troops. The governance of Ireland needed not just a Lord-Lieutenant but magistrates, juries, local officials, with landlords and tenants broadly acquiescing in the way the place was run. O'Connell's success and the passionate agitation which grew round it put all this at risk.

That was the irresistible force; what about the immovable object? Were these difficulties so great as to overturn the deeply entrenched opposition in England to Catholic Emancipation? It took the political establishment eight months to answer that question. In the end the decisive voice was Peel's. As Home Secretary he had exercised a more dominant authority in Irish affairs than any of his predecessors. He was the most powerful member of the Government after the Prime Minister. Already in political cartoons Peel and the Duke of Wellington were regularly portrayed together as two partners roughly equal in power. Because of his dominance of the House of Commons Peel was indispensable.

On no subject were Peel's views better known than on Catholic Emancipation. He had set out the arguments in the letter already quoted to the Duke of Richmond in 1813. The allegiance of Roman Catholics to the Crown was still not clear. It was reasonable to exclude them 'from privileges for which they will not pay the price that all other subjects pay'. Since the great debate of 1817 he had established himself as the champion of the Protestant cause. He owed his seat in the University of Oxford and his reputation in Parliament and among the public to that unbending firmness. A few months earlier he had refused office in Canning's Government because Canning supported Emancipation. Nothing could be more certain than Peel's opposition.

Or so it seemed. But looking now at his speeches one can see gradually emerging the doubts and qualifications which were part of Peel's intellectual equipment. He was not a religious bigot, and his opposition to Emancipation had nothing to do with doctrinal belief or tribal prejudice. In his mind the question was political. The disaffection of Ireland was a threat to the security of Britain. As Home Secretary Peel received reports which suggested that the threat had not ended with the downfall of Napoleon; in 1823 a spy told of a plot to ship '50,000 stands of arms' to Ireland.[4] Ireland could best be protected by maintaining the Protestant ascendancy, which in turn was best secured by keeping Catholics out of high office and the House of Commons. The cost of keeping the restrictions on Catholics might become too high at the expense of that system of government which they were meant to preserve. Then obviously wise men would think again.

Indeed, foreseeing such a possible turn of events, wise men would begin to choose their words with care. In 1826 Peel had written, 'When I see it [Emancipation] as inevitable I shall (taking due care to free my motives from all suspicion) try to make the best terms for the security of the Protestant.'[5] In his letter to Canning refusing office in 1827 Peel did not argue against Catholic Emancipation, but merely said that he would be open to great criticism if he lent himself to advance a cause which he had strenuously resisted.[6]

In May 1828, just before the Clare by-election, Peel opposed Catholic Emancipation for the last time. 'He wished he could see a prospect of tranquillising Ireland, by the removal of the disabilities complained of – He would do all in his power, if he could once see that prospect, to effect the removal of those disabilities. But it was because he doubted – because he in no degree believed that measure would have the effect of restoring peace and harmony to Ireland that he gave it his strenuous opposition.'[7] There, in the middle of that passage, is the escape clause, followed by a repetition of his previous position. With benefit of hindsight we can see Peel's mind wrestling with unwelcome possibilities, but not yet decided on a new course. Croker, a shrewd observer, spotted at the time what was going on. A week after that debate in May 1828 Croker wrote of Peel that '[i]t is the turn of his mind to endeavour to get over adversaries by concession. He always gives more importance, and weight even, to a public enemy than to his own supporters.'[8]

The ambiguous phrases of politicians, sometimes described as weasel words, give the profession a lot of trouble. They are taken as signs of deviousness and a will to deceive – or at best proof of a feeble will. This is not necessarily true. A sincere and intelligent man may need time to make up his mind, or even more time to change it. While he is uncertain or moving from one opinion to another, he remains as silent as possible. But silence is not an option if he is daily in the public gaze, as Peel was in 1828. He constantly has to explain his views in private and in public. It is natural, and pardonable, that in these circumstances he should look for words which form a bridge between his past and future positions. Such uncertain words are unlikely to impress his audience or historians; but they may well work better than an unqualified statement of a view he no longer holds or a premature announcement of a conclusion he has not yet reached.

But now Peel moved. 'I am ready, at the hazard of any sacrifice, to maintain the opinion which I now deliberately give — that there is upon the whole less of evil in making a decided effort to settle the Catholic question than in leaving it, as it has been left, an open question.'[9] So there it was at last, in a long letter to the Duke, on 11 August. Before this crucial sentence Peel explained that he was still convinced of the dangers of Catholic Emancipation, but now even more convinced of the danger of resisting it any longer. He ended in his usual long-winded style by promising to support a proposal for Emancipation, but from outside government, since the task of putting it forward should be given to someone other than himself.

But that was not good enough. By then the Duke of Wellington needed no persuading of the need for Catholic Emancipation. His own processes of thought were less complicated than Peel's. As early as 1825 he had reconciled himself. Although he had been almost as deeply committed as Peel to the Protestant cause, he found it less difficult to change his mind. No opinion of the Duke's on a particular issue went so deep as his conviction that the King's Government must be carried on. The orderly continuity of government was more important than any particular policy. His own reputation was founded on the Peninsula victories and Waterloo, not on political consistency. He had come to expect criticism as a part of the sacrifice he had made in stepping down from his pedestal and taking part in party politics. For him the argument was essentially the same as Peel's. Ireland had to be governed, O'Connell's tactics had made it ungovernable without Catholic Emancipation, so Emancipation must be brought in. It should be brought in by those most competent to do it, namely himself and Peel. He could not do it without Peel. The first part of Peel's letter was therefore right, the second part wrong. The Duke set himself to keep Peel on board.

The Duke's concept of the King's Government did not depend on the particular monarch; he served four, a decidedly mixed bunch, with equal determination. He felt only exasperation for George IV as during the autumn and winter of 1828 he wrestled skilfully with the royal conscience. The King was occasionally swayed by a sentimental affection for the

Duke as the victor of Waterloo, but this was not enough to persuade him that Catholic Emancipation could be reconciled with his Coronation Oath. His sinister brother, the Duke of Cumberland, urged him to resist. The King was conscious of the tide of English public opinion swelling in the same Protestant direction. Peel was needed to change the King's mind, but Peel hung back. He believed he had done enough in changing his own position and felt no obligation to join in twisting his Sovereign's arm.

The King particularly disliked the Lord-Lieutenant in Dublin. Lord Anglesey gallantly lost a leg at Waterloo but his heroism did not translate into political wisdom.* He had long been convinced that Catholic Emancipation was inevitable. When Lord Anglesey held a strong view he revealed it to others. Under pressure from Peel he took half-hearted action against meetings organised by the Catholic Association. But neither Peel nor the Duke trusted his discretion. They kept him in the dark about their own maturing plans for Emancipation – wisely, since he was exchanging frank letters with one of the Whig leaders, Lord Holland. When the Lord-Lieutenant began writing in indiscreet detail to Irish Catholic ecclesiastics, the King insisted that he must go. Neither the Duke nor Peel tried to save him; they needed to checkmate the King on the main question, and in that game the Lord-Lieutenant was disposable. Lord Anglesey was dismissed at the beginning of January 1829.

Wellington had at first accepted Peel's proposal that he should resign and support Catholic Emancipation from outside government. But as the summer of 1828 wore into autumn it became clear that this would not work. Emancipation became more necessary as the situation in Ireland deteriorated. But public opinion in England began to rouse itself in opposition. George IV taunted Peel with enjoying the luxury of following his conscience while denying that luxury to the King. Wellington found that he could not put together a viable government without Peel. His acolytes the Arbuthnots gossiped to and fro about Peel's hesitation.

Eventually Peel made up his mind, and wrote to the Duke on 12 January, in typical vein: 'Not withstanding the constant and unreserved intercourse which I have had personally with you in regard to the state of Ireland, and

---

* At Waterloo, Anglesey was standing next to Wellington. After the explosion he famously remarked, 'By God, Sir, I've lost my leg,' to which the Duke replied, 'By God, Sir, so you have.'

the position of the government with reference to the Catholic question, I have thought it as well to commit to paper the general views which I have from time to time, expressed upon these most important subjects.'

The long-suffering Duke, having read this sentence which said absolutely nothing, might have been tempted to crumple the letter and throw it away. His own preferred style was crisp and military. But he knew Peel by now, and needed him badly. He had to read on. Peel again argued that it would be much better if someone other than himself proposed Catholic Emancipation in the Commons. Then, another portentous preliminary: 'You will do justice to the motives of the declaration which I am about to make, and you will take no advantage of it unless it be absolutely necessary.' Then, at last, to the point: 'If my retirement should prove in your opinion ... an insuperable obstacle to the adoption of the course which upon the whole I believe to be the least open to objection under all the circumstances of the time, in that case you shall command every service that I can render in any capacity.'[10]

So they had him at last; the Duke and his cronies rejoiced. Within four days the Duke confirmed to Peel that his resignation would indeed be an insuperable obstacle, and Peel stayed in government.

A politician, with great difficulty and after many declarations of unwillingness, had been persuaded to hold onto office. It is easy to smile and treat the unwillingness as hypocritical, part of a traditional mating dance. But Peel was serious in his reluctance. He saw clearly enough the crowds gathering outside and the faggots being piled up for his martyrdom. With a short interruption he had been Home Secretary for nearly seven years. Wellington's ministry was tottering and unlikely to last long. Even before his marriage Peel had shown when leaving Ireland that he was not one to cling to office. Now, with a beautiful wife, a growing family and a strong interest in building houses and buying pictures, he was genuinely tempted to prefer these to the political fire which would certainly disfigure if not destroy him.

Many years later Peel looked back in his memoirs on his decisions to go through the fire on Catholic Emancipation. He almost admitted that he had hung on too long to a hopeless Protestant cause. But he hotly denied that in abandoning it he had acted for unworthy motives. He argued that if he had been afraid he could have concealed his real opinion, rallied the King and the public, stayed with the Protestant cause and 'gained the hollow applause which is lavished upon those who inflexibly adhere to an opinion once pronounced, though altered circumstances may justify and demand the modification or abandonment of it'. He even made a formal affidavit: 'I can with truth affirm, as I do solemnly affirm in the presence of Almighty God to whom all hearts be open, all devices known, and from whom no secrets are hid that in advising and promoting the measures of 1829 I was swayed by no fear except of public calamity, and that I acted throughout on a deep conviction that these measures were ... conducive to the general welfare.'[11]

The final paragraph of the long self-justification is revealing: 'It may be that I was unconsciously influenced by motives less perfectly pure and disinterested – by the secret satisfaction of being,

> *... when the waves went high,*
> *A daring pilot in extremity.'*

The metaphor of the pilot (taken here from Dryden's *Absalom and Achitophel*) is common among politicians. It was particularly familiar to Peel's generation who remembered Pitt as, in Canning's phrase, the pilot who weathered the storm. The motives of politicians are neither more nor less straightforward than those of other human beings. We all operate on a compound of motives; the analysis is often impossible. Peel went through a double conversion, first to accept Catholic Emancipation, second to recognise that he would have to take it through the Commons himself. But mixed up in that genuine conversion was Peel's belief in Peel. The very heat of the coming fire gave satisfaction. He was singled out for exceptional punishment because he alone was capable of the necessary service to his country. Peel was preparing to taste for the first but not the last time the pleasure as well as the pain of martyrdom.

The greatest part of the difficulty lay with friends and family, particularly those who had stood alongside him in the Protestant cause. The staunchest official in Ireland was William Gregory. Peel was on close terms with him, and wrote fully and carefully to him with the news before it broke. Gregory replied at once:

Your letter has overwhelmed me with surprise and dismay. It is an event for which I was not prepared and I must have more time to collect my scattered senses, and weigh calmly all the difficulties you have stated ... that you have been influenced by the purest motives it is impossible to doubt; that you are making great sacrifices of everything dear to your honourable ambition is evident. Yet under the strong influence I do not think this is the time you should yield to the demands of menacing rebels; they should first be subdued ... But I will not venture to write more at present.[12]

Here is the authentic voice of the front-line public servant wrestling with the news that his superiors propose to give up the ground for which he has long fought. Gregory's dismay was tempered, as the rest of the letter shows, by genuine respect and admiration for Peel.

There was someone closer who was bound to share the same mix of feelings. Peel's letter to his father, now old and failing, at Drayton was formal, even awkward, concentrating on his decision to stay in office. 'At length, after various discussions, the question came to this. Would I abandon the King's service, refusing myself to take the course which I advised his Majesty to take? I answered that I would not abandon my post, be the consequences what they might.'[13] Sir Robert wrote back from his heart:

> My Dear Robert,
>   Though in the country we see through a glass darkly, I have not lately been blind to the difficulties of your unhappy situation, and have found myself but ill able, with an impaired constitution, to contemplate the peculiarity of your position without great uneasiness ... I fear your last concession will only embolden resistance and tend to widen the breach it is intended to close.

He hoped that his son's sincerity would help him to cherish new friendships without wounding old ones, and closed:

> I could say more, but am unwilling to withdraw your attention from subjects of more importance. With unabated attachment I am, my dear Robert
>   Your affectionate father,
>   Robert Peel[14]

As happens with retired politicians, old Sir Robert read too many newspapers for his own good, and in the weeks to come was much vexed by press attacks on his son. But the old Baronet rallied when Peel's speeches, printed overnight, reached him from Birmingham the day after delivery. As a speech was read to him in the intervals of his long rubbers of whist, Sir Robert would exclaim approvingly, 'Robin's the lad after all. No administration can stand in this country without him. The Duke could do nothing without him.'[15]

By now Peel was a good friend of Sir Walter Scott, whom he had persuaded to sit for Lawrence for his growing gallery of contemporary portraits at Whitehall Gardens. He was particularly glad when Sir Walter made public his strong support for Peel's change of heart, and thanked him in the informal style he kept for close friends:

> I wish you had been present at the Clare election, for no pen but yours could have done justice to that fearful exhibition of sobered and desperate enthusiasm ... I knew too much to make it possible for me to take any other course than that which I have taken. The time is past when either party can coquet any longer with the Catholic question ... Your name was of the utmost value, and had more weight than any other single name. The mention of it, as attached to the Edinburgh petition, was received with loud cheers ... What am I to do about your picture?[16]

But one obstacle could not be removed by skilful appeals to trust and old friendship. Peel had for nearly twelve years proudly represented the University of Oxford in the House of Commons. It had not been entirely clear in 1817 whether he had won because he was 'Orange Peel', the devoted defender of the Protestant cause, or because the electors distrusted Canning, his possible rival. Whatever the reasons it had been a notable triumph for a young man of twenty-nine. The University's dislike of Catholic Emancipation was certain. Moreover, the electors of the University believed that it was the job of their Member of Parliament to represent their opinions, a view which is now commonplace but would have appeared bizarre to the tiny and deferential electorate in Peel's previous seat at Chippenham. Once he had taken his decision Peel saw at once that he must offer to resign the seat, and wrote accordingly to the Dean of Christ Church on 31 January.

The unexpected letter burst upon Christ Church, detonating a trail of
secondary explosions in the College, throughout the University, and
among the many graduates who had kept the vote after leaving Oxford.
Our ancient universities are equipped by their constitution and intellectual habits to handle in the utmost disorder any great matter which is
suddenly laid before them. The Oxford University by-election of 1829 is a
locus classicus for students of such confusions. First of all came a dispute
about procedure. Peel was advised that he should have sent his letter to
the Vice Chancellor, not to his own college. He did this crossly, so that it
was read as a decision to resign rather than just an offer. The temperature
of discussion began to rise as learned men abused their Member of
Parliament and each other. Peel relied as usual for advice on his old tutor,
Dr Lloyd. Though like other friends deeply dismayed by Peel's decision,
Lloyd stuck by him. Christ Church, after much havering, came down in
favour of Peel and decided to nominate him for re-election. The College
Censor, Thomas Short, wrote: 'I should despise Oxford if they suffered
him [Peel] or any man to suffer for honestly doing what they knew he
deemed his duty.'[17] But by delaying Christ Church had lost its leadership
in the matter, and others had an opposite view of duty. Newman wrote to
a friend, in a sentence which combined two Oxford traditions, of the
classics and of uncharitableness, 'It is not pro dignitate nostra to have a
rat as our member.'[18] *

As the machinery for a by-election rolled forward, Peel's exasperation
grew. The dignity of his martyrdom was being lost among a pack of
squabbling dons. 'I care very little about the matter,' he wrote to Lloyd on
11 February. 'For God's sake take no step directly or indirectly that would
appear and intimate a wish to be returned.' Lloyd, irresolute and confused, interpreted this as a decision to retire from the contest. But it was
too late for dignity or coherence. The Warden of Merton formed a committee to re-elect Peel. On the same day the opposition found a
Protestant candidate, Sir Robert Inglis. Battle was joined, and emotions
rose even higher.[19] As the two days fixed for polling approached clergymen
on the list of voters flocked to join the fray. A Somerset rector found that

---

* This is the first example I can find (6 February 1829) of the rat image which was to dominate
hostile cartoons of Peel for years to come.

Old Sir Robert Peel, Peel's father, 1st Baronet, cotton manufacturer

Charles Lloyd, Peel's tutor at Christ Church, Oxford: for many years after that his closest confidant

Preparing the Double First: the library at Christ Church

(Top) Julia, Peel's wife, painted by
Lawrence, soon after Peel had
bought the original 'Chapeau de
Paille' by Rubens (left)

Regency Dublin, where Peel worked as Chief Secretary from 1812 to 1818

The reality of the Irish countryside

George IV, Wellington, Lady Conyngham (the King's mistress), Peel, 1829

The ghost of George III reminds his son of his Protestant Oath,
to the dismay of Wellington and Peel, 1829

Canning in his prime; but did Peel let him down?

Peel's new house on the Thames at Whitehall Gardens

Peel proudly shows off his pictures. A watercolour by Jemima Blackburn, who was present.

Peelers escorting their charges to Marlborough Street Police Court

The Duke's Cabinet, 1830: Wellington, Aberdeen, Ellenborough, Lyndhurst (with hand to ear) then Peel seated on the right

all places on the coach to Oxford were taken, and vented his indignation in his diary: 'I hope to my heart that he will be thrown out as a turncoat.'[20]

At the hustings Peel's proposer and seconder were both shouted down, and the crowd broke the windows of the Convocation House for air.[21] In each diocese the search for Oxford graduates gathered speed. 'Rouse all the bigotry in Kent,' wrote Newman to a friend.[22] The noise and emotion spread beyond the electorate. It must have been at this time that the words 'NO PEEL' were hammered in massive wooden nails onto the door leading up to Christ Church Hall.* The egg-cook at the College remarked, '[I]t was a great shame that Mr Peel had so let the country down as he had been such a kind gentleman when an undergraduate.' The sense of the University was, decidedly though not overwhelmingly, with the egg-cook. On 27 February Sir Robert Inglis was elected Member of Parliament for the University of Oxford with 755 votes as opposed to 609 cast for Sir Robert Peel.

By detaching himself from the actual contest at Oxford Peel rescued most of his own dignity. But as Home Secretary he had to follow carefully the commotions in the country as a whole. Demonstrations against Emancipation were organised up and down the land. Brunswick and Orange clubs were formed. Ancient memories of Popish plots and persecutions were painstakingly revived. Petitions poured into Parliament. There was no doubt that public opinion in England was still in favour of keeping Catholics out of Parliament. This fact had its effect on attitudes and votes in Parliament, but was no longer decisive. The argument had gone on so long; the emotions it aroused were familiar; the two trusted men at the head of affairs had changed their minds; there was no one competent to take their place and rally the Protestant cause. The public reaction against Popery, though strong, did not last. Apart from a few lesser revivals in Victoria's reign, it was the final, almost ritual rendering of an old song.

But Peel had an immediate and very practical problem. On 27 February he lost his seat in Parliament; on 5 March he was due to present the

---

* The College archives have no trace of this event. The work is too solid to be the result of a drunken undergraduate prank. The College authorities must have connived at what in other contexts they would have regarded as an outrage.

Catholic Relief Bill to the House of Commons. Postponement would spoil the chances of success. In the Commons Peel was indispensable, but Peel was no longer in the Commons. A seat had to be found very fast. The old unreformed system went to work with speed and efficiency.

Sir Manasseh Lopes is a man forgotten by history. He sat in Parliament for the Wiltshire borough of Westbury. This humdrum fact suddenly blazed with importance. Westbury was close to Peel's old seat at Chippenham, both on the map and in corrupt reputation. Three years earlier Cobbett had ridden through the town and awarded it one of his characteristic insults: 'A nasty odious borough, a really rotten place. It has cloth factories in it, and they seem ready to tumble down, as well as many of the houses. God's curse seems to be on most of these rotten boroughs.'

What was odious to Cobbett, and in Cobbett's view to God, was precious to Sir Manasseh, and invaluable at this critical moment to Peel. Sir Manasseh had a nephew who was Mayor of Westbury, and another nephew who needed a job. Sir Manasseh was an old hand at the game, and had already been twice fined and imprisoned for electoral bribery.[23] The deal was done through intermediaries; Sir Manasseh resigned his seat and offered it to Peel. He and Peel set out for Westbury together. They were in a hurry, and wisely so. Catholic Emancipation was no more popular in Westbury than elsewhere. Most of the inhabitants had no vote, but they liked to express themselves at election time. Missiles were thrown, and one of them hit Sir Manasseh on the hustings at the town hall. It was lucky that this rumpus caused no delay, for a chaise and four was on its way from London carrying a Protestant candidate keen to put up against Peel. By the time the chaise and four arrived the Mayor had completed his duties and declared Peel elected.[24] On 3 March Peel took his seat in the Commons as Member for Westbury with two days in hand.*

Those two days turned out to be crucial. The Cabinet had spent February thrashing out the details of the Catholic Relief Bill to be pre-

---

* The last trace of Sir Manasseh vanished from Westbury when the Lopes Arms, the town's main hotel, was recently renamed. Peel had difficulty in persuading the Foreign Secretary, Lord Aberdeen, to find a job for Sir Manasseh's nephew, whose other merits were not clear. He was eventually appointed His Majesty's Consul in Pernambuco.

sented to the Commons. By this stage they were working in the belief that the King, however sulkily, had told them that he was resigned to the change. But George IV's conscience too had been at work, prompted by his brother the Duke of Cumberland. The King persuaded himself that all he had agreed was that the Cabinet should *discuss* Emancipation. He sent for the Duke, the Lord Chancellor, Lord Lyndhurst, and Peel, who arrived together at Windsor early on 3 March. The King said he was still deeply uneasy and asked Peel to set out the Government's proposals in detail. Among these was a modification of the Oath of Supremacy. The King said that he blamed no one, but there had been a misunderstanding, and he could not possibly accept any alteration in the Oath of Supremacy. There was a pause, after which the King asked what the three Ministers intended to do now that they knew his views. 'Now Mr Peel, tell me what course you propose to take tomorrow.'[25] Peel replied at once that he would tell the Commons that he had resigned as Home Secretary. The Duke and Lyndhurst spoke on the same lines. The King accepted their resignations, kissed them each on the cheek, and thanked them for their services. The meeting had lasted five hours. The three Ministers told the Cabinet that evening that everything was over, and the Government was out.

Except that no one quite believed this. In one way or another most of them had worked for George IV as Prince Regent and King for nearly twenty years. They knew that his naturally keen intelligence had no foundation in settled convictions. His mistresses, his brothers, his fondness for brandy and laudanum, caused him to sway to and fro in search of an easy life. On 3 March he believed that he could at the last minute deter his Ministers by pleading the royal conscience on the question of the Oath. On 4 March he realised that his Ministers were immovable in all senses of the word – he could not change their minds, and he could not find new Ministers who would carry out his views. So he wrote to the Duke asking him to withdraw his resignation and to proceed on the basis which Peel had outlined at Windsor. News of these comings and goings with the King leaked, and so it was in an atmosphere of drama that Peel rose in the Commons on 5 March. He at once asserted his authority: 'I rise as a Minister of the King, and sustained by the just authority which belongs to that character, to vindicate the advice given to His Majesty by a united Cabinet.'[26]

The Bill owed everything to Peel's hard work with his colleagues. This is particularly evident in the treatment of the question of securities. This was the name given to a whole series of proposals designed to reassure Protestants about the results of Catholic Emancipation. They included different plans to harness the Catholic Church in Ireland to the State, for example by paying priests a salary or asserting a veto by the Crown over the appointment of Catholic bishops, or insisting that priests take an oath of loyalty. These proposals in different forms had gone the rounds since the days of Pitt. They still attracted some members of the Cabinet, including Wellington, who hoped they would damp down opposition to the Bill. But the more Peel studied these ideas, the less he liked them. He used against them when proposing Emancipation in 1829 much the same arguments as he had used against them when opposing Emancipation in 1817. He declared that most of these so-called securities were unworkable. They would uselessly prolong the debate. They would alienate Catholics without satisfying Protestants. Peel had been slower than Wellington to embrace Emancipation, but once he changed his mind his embrace was more complete.

The one specific safeguard which he accepted had no direct connection with the Church. The crisis had been brought about by O'Connell's victory in the Clare by-election. That victory had been caused by the success of the Catholic Association, which had mobilised the forty-shilling freeholder to vote at the bidding of his priest rather than of his landlord. Peel and opponents of his Bill agreed that the infection, left unchecked, would spread to all elections and to juries. The qualification for voting was raised to £10, namely to a level which would leave the vote with the kind of prosperous tenant or town dweller who had voted for Fitzgerald in County Clare while excluding most of those who had voted for O'Connell. Eighty thousand Catholic voters lost the vote in Ireland under the measure which enabled Catholics to sit in Parliament.

Peel spoke for four hours on 5 March 1829, moving that a committee be set up to consider the laws imposing disabilities on Roman Catholics. It was one of the defining speeches of his career. Having established his authority as the King's Minister, he dealt with his own previous opposition to Emancipation. It had not been an unreasonable struggle, he said, but it could no longer be maintained. 'I yield therefore to a moral necessity which I cannot control, unwilling to push resistance to a point which might endanger the Establishment that I wish to defend.'[27] He went through the long history of the argument. He analysed the consequence of the Clare election. He showed that coercion would not work without a deployment of troops, which would be impracticable and intolerable. Concession was therefore necessary. He went through the detail of the Government's proposals. Peel ended with an appeal for an Ireland at ease with itself.

> Surely government, civil government, means something more than the rigid enforcement of penal law ... there is a willing moral obedience, founded on the sense of equal justice, without which the terrors of the law would be vain ... God grant that ... by the admission of the Roman Catholics to a full and equal participation in civil rights, and by the establishment of a free and cordial intercourse between all classes of His Majesty's subjects, mutual jealousies may be removed – the moral storm may be appeased ... that the turbid waters of strife may be settled and compassed ... and that having found their just level, they may be mingled with equal flow, in one clear and common stream.

So a new note was struck. Hitherto Peel had tended to speak of the Catholics in Ireland as a dangerous majority, to be treated justly but firmly, but not to be trusted as partners in governance. But the logic of Catholic Emancipation was to Peel inescapable. The Government had not simply abandoned an outwork of their rule in Ireland in order to fortify the citadel more strongly. On the contrary, they were inviting the Catholics into the citadel. This would only work if the Catholics responded to Peel's invitation to 'free and cordial intercourse'. The appeal was therefore more than a platitudinous peroration; it was meant to mark a new chapter in the Government's policies. The reasoning was still in large part political. O'Connell and the Association had created a link between the denial of civil rights to Catholics and the Union of Ireland with Britain. Catholic Emancipation broke that link. 'We shall have dissolved the great moral alliance that has given strength to the cause of the Roman Catholics. We shall range on our side the illustrious authorities which have heretofore been enlisted upon theirs: the rallying cry of "civil liberty" will then be all our own. We shall enter the field with the full assurance of victory.'[28]

The flaw was that the denial of the right of Catholics to enter

Parliament or hold other offices was only one, and not the greatest, of the Irish grievances. Its removal did not transform the political scene except in the short term. But Peel had changed his views on how the union with Ireland might survive. Two years earlier Peel had been one of the congregation when the Reverend Thomas Chalmers, celebrated Scottish philosopher and divine, had opened the Scottish National Church in London. In his sermon Chalmers had argued that laws discriminating against Popery gave it 'that moral strength which persecution always gives to every cause that is at once honoured and sustained by it'. The friends of religious liberty had made a big mistake when 'they hurled aside argument and brandished the ensigns of authority'.[29] Peel was not by temperament a liberal, but was wide open to liberal arguments when practical circumstances gave them force. Dr Chalmers' argument in 1827 against restricting Catholics may have made no immediate impact on him. But by 1829 County Clare had returned O'Connell and Ireland was spinning out of control; Peel made Dr Chalmers' argument his own. From 1829 on, as Peel thought endlessly about the many-headed problems of Ireland, he never lost that sense of their moral dimension.

The debates in Parliament in 1829 were furious, but the outcome not in doubt. The Commons had for years been in rough balance on the principle of Catholic Emancipation, with the Whigs and plenty of Tories in favour. Once the central Tory group led by Peel shifted ground there were big majorities in favour of each part of the Bill, even the disenfranchisement of the forty-shilling freeholders which the Whigs were at first reluctant to support. The fury of the Ultras was the outstanding characteristic of the debates. As usual they had difficulty in producing leaders with natural reputation or appeal. In ferocity they were led by the Attorney General, Sir Charles Wetherell, who resigned on the issue. While still in office he piled on the adjectives of abuse, accusing his colleagues of 'miserable contemptible apostasy'.[30] To give freer rein to his passion Sir Charles unbuttoned his braces, so that his waistcoat rode up and his breeches fell down as he developed his argument.[31]

Peel mastered the difficult debate. He displayed in public the tendency which Croker had already privately noticed, praising those such as Fox, Grattan and Canning whom he had formerly opposed, and reserving his scorn for those who had not followed him in his change of mind. There was a paradox here. Just at the moment when Peel was shifting towards a new and morally based approach to Ireland, he felt bound to defend the shift by promoting expediency to one of the principles of government. Bishop Lloyd had rallied round after the fumbling embarrassment of the Oxford election. He sent Peel copious quotations from Virgil and Shakespeare on the theme that timing is everything in human affairs, and that wise men notice and act on the need to change. Without using these quotations Peel called in aid the eternal right of politicians to alter their course according to changing needs. 'This has been the opinion of all former statesmen at all times and in all countries. My defence is the same, with that of all others in similar circumstances.'[32] Peel was not pleading expediency against morality, but preferring expediency to party political consistency when circumstances change. 'Concede nothing to agitation', he wrote, 'is the ready cry of those who are not responsible – the vigour of whose decisions is often proportionate to their own personal immunity from danger, and to their imperfect knowledge of the true state of affairs.'[33]

The Duke had full control of the Lords, though the fury there was as violent as in the Commons. Lord Winchilsea accused the Duke of planning to introduce Popery into every department of state, in terms so bizarre that Wellington felt bound to issue a challenge. The two men fought a duel in Battersea Fields on 21 March; neither was hurt. Within a month more modern methods of settling an argument had prevailed. The Bill finally passed the Commons on 30 March with a majority of 178, and the Lords on 10 April. On 13 April the King gave his assent. The argument on Catholic Emancipation which had vexed and fragmented the political system for nearly thirty years was finally settled.

Peel came near to spoiling the effect by preventing O'Connell from immediately taking his seat as MP for County Clare. Of course this was technically correct; he had been elected at a time when Catholics were disqualified from sitting, and therefore should wait to be re-elected under the new law. But the delay upset O'Connell and made it difficult for him in the future to accept Peel's good intentions.

The effect of Catholic Emancipation was not as great as either its friends or enemies had foretold. It did not open the floodgates to Popery; nor did it usher in a new era of partnership in Ireland. It removed one indefensible grievance, and so eased the immediate political situation; but it did not settle the underlying contradiction between Irish nationalism and Ireland's Union with Britain.

Peel emerged from the debate as the leading political figure in the country. It was his change of mind which had changed the law. It was he who had stood up to the King's objections. It was his mastery of the subject which persuaded his colleagues to propose a simple dramatic measure which went to the heart of the subject without a clutter of unworkable securities. It was his skill in the Commons which had seen the measure through. He was pre-eminent, but as Professor Gash wrote, 'it was a lonely and dangerous eminence'.[34]

Those who supported Catholic Emancipation were hugely relieved that the argument was over. Their thanks were tempered by criticisms that Peel had hung on too long to a thoroughly bad set of arguments in defence of the status quo. But this criticism was as nothing to the bitterness of his former supporters. The young man who had inspired them, who had stood out against political correctness and the spirit of the age, who had led them to believe that there was nothing inevitable about the dismantling of their ancient fortress, had not only admitted defeat but led the forces of destruction. One magazine summed it up. 'Mr Peel's public life [has been] one continuing course of despicable grovelling, unnecessary faithlessness to principles and party.'[35] He had betrayed them with firmness and force, with a minimum of regret, neglecting even the search for securities which could have softened the blow. He had reserved his full scorn for those whom he had led, striking them at the points where they were most vulnerable.

There was no great outburst of public bitterness. In April Peel was presented with the Freedom of the City of London in a gold box, in a clear rebuke to the University of Oxford. But the image of Peel as a turncoat and a rat became familiar, not as a verdict of public opinion in general, but as the conviction of an embittered minority. At Ascot the King was rude to all Ministers who went to his stand, remarking to Peel that he would sooner have expected to see a pig in church as Peel at a race.[36] The Duchess of Richmond decorated her dining table with stuffed rats under a glass cover depicting Wellington and Peel. 'Some joker let loose a live rat in the House of Lords during one of their debates.'[37] Such images can lie dormant for years in the public mind, but they are still there, and the wise politician does nothing to stir them to life. Churchill knew the truth of this. After Gallipoli the general view that this rash man could not be trusted with handling a war prevented him being persuasive when attacking appeasement in the 1930s. Churchill, unlike Peel, survived, indeed reversed this reputation.

Catholic Emancipation remains one of the great reforms of British history – because of its effect not just in Ireland but on the politics of the nation. For the first time a pressure group from outside Parliament had forced Parliament to alter the Constitution. The Catholic Association had achieved this not by violence but by the peaceful and shrewd use of a legal power, the right of the forty-shilling freeholder in Ireland to vote. The next example of such pressure would reach its successful climax four years later with the abolition of slavery in the colonies. That was a triumph over a powerful economic interest; Catholic Emancipation was an assault on the very institutions of the State. If such pressure could alter the sacred 1688 Constitution, could persuade Peel and defeat the Duke of Wellington, then other movements could gather strength for other purposes, and use that strength to besiege and convince Parliament. Within months the movement for parliamentary reform was under way.

Of course there were cross-currents. It would be wrong to imagine a solid mass of progressive opinion which moved from pressing for Catholic Emancipation to pressing for parliamentary reform. Indeed disgust at the way the representatives of rotten boroughs had been seduced into supporting the first cause, helped to create support for the second. Peel continued to believe for many years that pressure on Parliament from outside was in principle illegitimate and to be resisted. It was for the qualified electorate to choose fit and proper persons to serve in Parliament, and for those persons to use their judgement undeterred by mobs or mass meetings. But, legitimate or not, the power of such outside pressure was now apparent; it was a lesson that all could learn.

Nine

Reform or Revolution?

'[I]s it presumed then that I am not to do what I will with
my own?'
*The Duke of Newcastle, when criticised for evicting tenants who voted the
wrong way, October 1829*

'My dearest love, I have been all morning occupied about
your cloak. I mean to give you one of my own choosing,
and made to please my fancy. I do not like what they call
merino cloth.'
Peel to Julia, October 1829

'Neither Lord Grey nor any nobleman of his order, nor any
gentleman of his cast, will govern the country six weeks
after the reformed Parliament will meet, and the race of
English gentlemen will not last long afterwards'
Wellington, writing to Lord Wharncliffe about the Reform Bill, 1831

'There's that fellow in the Commons, one can't go on
without him; but he's so vacillating and crotchety that
there's no getting on with him'
Wellington on Peel, November 1831

*T*he Duke of Wellington, not a man easily flustered, was still in
charge. Having survived the crisis of Catholic Emancipation, he
saw no reason for alarm. He now had the full confidence of King
George IV, and in theory his Tory Party had a good majority in the
Commons. The Duke took no particular pleasure in being Prime
Minister; so far as his own reputation was concerned he knew that after
Waterloo everything was downhill. His political allies showed even less
discipline than the Spaniards and Portuguese in the old days in the
Peninsula. But he owed service to the Crown, and after 1828 believed that

his best service was to use his unique personal authority to keep a Tory government in power.

The Duke was straightforward in word and deed. He analysed a problem clearly and was shrewd in his judgement of men. Though his instincts were strongly conservative, he was no diehard; in political as in military difficulties he showed himself perfectly ready to sound the retreat. But in 1830 he misjudged both the tactical and strategic weaknesses of his Government.

Sitting in the Lords and already hampered by growing deafness, Wellington relied heavily on Peel, his only strong Minister in the Commons. Peel did his best to inform and guide his chief. The two men were at the beginning of a close political relationship which lasted seventeen years. During this time they changed places and the junior man became the senior. Each respected the other, and knew that the other was an indispensable colleague. The partnership was not easy; it never broke down, but it often creaked and groaned. The two men came from different backgrounds, had different friends, and found no particular pleasure in each other's company. In the first and last few years of the partnership they met regularly in Cabinet. But neither then nor in opposition did they attempt to establish an informal late-night relationship of brandy and soda with one another. This left plenty of space for gossips and go-betweens, including those like Croker for whom the role had become a way of life.

In Mr and Mrs Arbuthnot the Duke had two close political henchmen. Harriet was, so Peel and many others thought, his mistress, and certainly over many years his faithful friend. Her husband Charles was a junior Minister, a poor speaker who was never promoted to the Cabinet; but like his wife he was trusted with the Duke's confidence. In her journal Mrs Arbuthnot wrote copiously about Peel and his relationship with the Duke, her comments going up and down with changing events. In January 1829 she recorded that the Duke disliked Peel for his ill temper and the difficulties he made on every subject. A month later, she noted, Peel had behaved very handsomely. By late 1830 Peel was 'sour and dissatisfied. He is a strange person; he is anxious for popularity and instead of seeking it by courteous manners, by good humour and frankness he is morose and austere and proposes the most liberal measures in order to please our enemies.'[1]

Peel had growing reason to be morose. He pointed out to the Duke
how savagely the Government's position had deteriorated in the
Commons. This was partly the Duke's fault. Wellington had always been
irritated by the reforming Trade Minister, William Huskisson. He took
advantage of a rash letter of resignation written by Huskisson at two
o'clock one morning in 1828, and refused to let him retract it. Palmerston
and the other close disciples of Canning resigned with Huskisson. The
Government's centre of gravity shifted to the right.

But it was precisely the Right which was outraged by Catholic
Emancipation. Politicians are often in a state of outrage. They find it a
convenient condition for a day or two. They usually recover quickly and
get on with the other pleasures of life. Outrage becomes important only
when it is so fierce and lasts so long that it generates an unappeasable
appetite for revenge. This self-destructive tendency seems particularly
strong on the sour Right of the Conservative Party. The outrage and
hope of revenge which followed the dismissal of Margaret Thatcher in
1990 helped to undermine her successor John Major. The same emotions
of betrayal after Catholic Emancipation undermined the Duke and Peel.
In the Commons Peel could only count on the solid centre of the Tory
Party, and they were not enough.

As Peel had noted in that letter to Croker ten years earlier, the underlying reason for the decay of the Government lay outside the Commons.
The spirit of the age, articulated by the rising middle class, was questioning. In some ways this was a sign of health. People no longer felt that it
was dangerous to question the institutions of the country. Society was
strong enough to stand examination and survive change without disintegration. Old men might disagree as they re-read Burke on the French
Revolution. When Eldon and Sidmouth heard reformers talk they also
heard the tumbrils rattle over the cobbles and saw the guillotine fall, this
time on them and on all they respected. But that generation was passing.
Catholic Emancipation had shown that change was possible without revolution, and that change could be forced on Parliament by outside pressures. The question after 1829 was not whether there would be further
change, but which institution would be the next for attack.

There was no shortage of targets. The monarchy under George IV was
at its lowest ebb since Charles I. The House of Lords was out of sympathy with the rising middle class. The abuses of the Church of England

were attracting strong criticism, particularly from within its own ranks. The Corn Laws had just been moderated, but in a way which satisfied no one. Slavery still existed in Britain's colonies. All these institutions were the product of history. None of them could be defended in the pure light of nineteenth-century reason. The appetite for reasoned argument grew stronger than respect for the past. As the pamphlets, newspapers and public meetings multiplied, all these institutions and policies were at risk. In that letter of 1820 to Croker Peel had singled out Parliament as particularly vulnerable. But he could not then have foreseen the circumstances which ten years later proved him right. The next great cause was to be parliamentary reform. The way in which the House of Commons was elected was challenged and, after a bitter fight, transformed.

The electoral system of 1830 had hardly changed for sixty years. Time had increased its absurdities. There was no uniform system. All voting was in public. The electorate varied from as few as one or two in a pocket borough to 16,000 in the constituency of Westminster. The combined population of Manchester, Birmingham and Leeds was approaching half a million, having doubled since 1800; yet these cities were not represented at all in the Commons. If you added Wiltshire to the eleven seaboard counties between the Wash and the Severn they contained more than half the English borough seats. Most of the boroughs were treated as political assets in the pocket of a patron or group of patrons. The key part of this mechanism was often the town corporation, usually self-electing, often without even a residence qualification. The corporation welcomed a patron who could help the town. The patron used the corporation to acquire political influence in the Commons. Wiltshire was particularly rich in such arrangements. We have seen how it worked for Peel and Sir Manasseh Lopes at Westbury. Old Sarum became a tourist attraction because, there being no resident electors, a field and the ancient earthworks returned two Members of Parliament. In Marlborough the corporation usually consisted of the steward, butler, footmen and other dependants of the Marquess of Ailesbury. The corporation could organise votes by granting the status of freemen to individuals from outside the borough. The laws against corruption were largely ignored. Often the traditional arrangement was so solid that there was no contest; but where there was a contest plenty of money would be spent buying votes.

The English county seats enjoyed higher prestige than the boroughs because in the counties there was at least a standard voting qualification. This had been fixed in 1430 at the ownership of freehold land or property worth forty shillings a year. But this qualification did not mean independence; most freeholders were also tenants and under the influence of the landowner. Each county had two seats, and the main local landowners would try to agree on how they should be divided. A county contest could be very expensive; several thousand voters expected at least travel and accommodation expenses for their journey to the single place of polling at the county town. The Yorkshire election of 1807 was said to have cost the candidates and their supporters £250,000, more than £10 million today.

All that need be said about the electoral system in Wales, Scotland and Ireland is that borough by borough, county by county, it was more closed than and as corrupt as its English equivalent.[2]

The system began to decay visibly in the 1820s. This was not because it was undemocratic. Only a handful of the leading reformers were democrats. Their voice was not entirely silent. Cobbett and Hunt, the Radical leaders with the largest following, issued a joint manifesto in July 1829, calling for annual parliaments, universal suffrage, and the vote by secret ballot. These formed the basis of Chartist demands which reached their climax in 1848. In 1830 there was no chance of a democratic reform which would give the vote to every adult man, let alone adult woman. Most of the reformers accepted that parliamentary representation should take account of property. They thought it reasonable that men with a stake in the country, men of standing in their town or county, men who spent money and gave employment, should have a greater say in choosing Members of Parliament than others. After all, such men had more to lose from wasteful, corrupt or tyrannical government. But the claims of property, not in themselves unreasonable, were increasingly asserted in a disreputable, controversial and therefore ineffective way. The system began to feel the first tremors of an earthquake. Peel might make a joke in the Commons about his respectable electors in Westbury, but by 1830 the joke was no longer funny.

The general election of 1826 had made matters worse. Local misdeeds were more notorious than ever. At Northampton the corporation's candidate was shown to have been paid £1,000 out of the corporation funds. At Leicester the Tories in control of the corporation enrolled 800 new

freemen with the right to vote, and paid one of their candidates £7,000
for election expenses. The town's charitable funds were reserved almost
exclusively for voters of sound views. The number of contests rose
sharply. The cost of maintaining the old system began to alarm even
those who benefited from it.

There was no rush to reform. Canning as Prime Minister dazzled
reformers with a liberal foreign policy and support for Catholic
Emancipation. He proposed to handle parliamentary reform, not by a
general change, but by dealing severely with particular examples of abuse.
Coleridge wrote that Canning 'flashed such a light round the constitution
that it was difficult to see the ruins of the fabric through it'.[3] The leading
Whig enthusiast for reform was Lord John Russell. But faced with the
dazzlement of Canning even Lord John for the moment abandoned the
cause of parliamentary reform, arguing that so long as people saw that
the general affairs of the country were conducted in a spirit of improvement, they would not look too narrowly into the constitution of the
House of Commons.[4]

Lord John and the Whigs were crucial. The only way parliamentary
reform could be achieved without a revolution lay through persuading the
Whig Party that reform was necessary, and then recruiting enough Tory
support to force change through the unreformed Parliament. Yet the
Whigs were divided. After all the Whigs were just as adept as the Tories
at keeping the old show on the road in the counties and boroughs. There
were Whig as well as Tory dukes, and many of them would have agreed
with the Duke of Newcastle who in October 1829 was reproached for
evicting tenants who had voted against one of his candidates. The Duke
retorted '[i]s it presumed then that I am not to do what I will with my
own?'[5]

This particular Duke was indirectly responsible for lighting the fuse
which exposed one outstanding scandal of the system. The borough of
East Retford in Nottinghamshire had through many elections continued
a comfortable system by which the freemen were paid twenty guineas for
each of their votes for the two borough Members. Forty guineas was a
sizeable sum for the freemen. Both patrons, candidates and freemen, preferred this arrangement to the uncertainty of a contest, and the seat was
peacefully divided between the nominees of the Whig Lord Fitzwilliam
and a group based on the corporation. This agreement came adrift in

1826. The Duke of Newcastle, who had an interest which he had allowed
to go to sleep, woke up and put forward a third candidate of his own. The
fierce contest which followed exposed the corruption of East Retford so
conclusively that almost everyone, including Peel, agreed that the borough
should lose its franchise.

There was no parliamentary corruption in nearby Birmingham because
there was no seat to buy or sell. Birmingham was entirely unrepresented.
It was in Birmingham that the pressure for reform took its clearest shape.
It was Thomas Attwood who led the charge, the public-spirited
Birmingham banker who was well known to the Peels, father and son,
because of his opposition to a tight monetary policy and the return to
gold. Attwood was a staunch Tory who had been Master of the Pytchley
Hunt and kept a fine herd of shorthorn cattle. Like many businessmen
past and present, he combined Tory views on most matters with a desire
to see plenty of money sloshing about in the system. He turned to
parliamentary reform because the unreformed Parliament had been
induced by Ministers to support Peel's Currency Act of 1819 and
had refused to relax it despite the economic hardships of 1825 and
1826. He believed that a reformed Parliament would be more progressive,
by which he meant inflationary, on currency matters. With Attwood
belief was quickly translated into action. In December 1829 he
founded in Birmingham 'a general political union between the lower and
middle classes' to work for parliamentary reform. After a slow start
the political union's membership reached 6,000. It was no longer
disreputable for businessmen to join tradesmen in a pressure group to
influence Parliament from outside. O'Connell had shown the way to
succeed on Catholic Emancipation; within months his example was
followed. There was still no single reform movement, but different bodies
quickly sprang up across the country, each with their own schemes.
The strong anti-slavery movement, disgusted at the delay in abolishing
slavery in British colonies, linked itself to the cause of parliamentary
reform.

Peel was reluctant to enter the argument. He was busy setting up the
new police force in London. The bruises of the struggle on Catholic
Emancipation were still painful. The pleasures and problems of family
life were time-consuming. A new baby son was born in August 1829; he
was successfully vaccinated and christened with the name of his godfather

the Duke.* Even when hard at work in London Peel enjoyed taking time off for little projects which reminded him of Julia.

On 8 October he wrote:

My dearest love,

I have been all morning occupied about your cloak. I mean to give you one of my own choosing, and made to please my fancy. I do not like what they call merino cloth at the dressmakers! It is exactly like the cashmere cloth of which gentlemen's summer coats are made. It would not sit well and would not be warm enough … We are to have another Cabinet today, and shall probably fill up the interval between this and Monday with Cabinets every day.[6]

It was a bitterly cold winter. Once again Peel at the Home Office began to receive reports of distress which led to violence, particularly in Wales, the Midlands and the North. Under the pressure of hunger and resentment workers were coming together to picket the mills in a way forbidden by the 1825 Act; but the authorities were reluctant to prosecute. Peel involved himself more closely than before in the merits of industrial disputes. He had no sympathy with the action of embryo trade unions in trying to force up wages in a way which would ruin businesses. But he had no doubt that poverty was the root cause of the troubles.

There were still no police forces outside London and the Home Secretary had to make sure that troops were available to deal with disorder. This gave local commanders a standing in local disputes which would be inconceivable today. Peel was clear how this influence should be used. For example, he advised General Bouverie to go himself to Manchester in the hope that he could 'inculcate upon the masters and the magistrates the necessity of combining with firmness great moderation and discretion'.[7]

At the national level Peel began to worry away at the same problem of poverty. The Liverpool Government had started in 1824 to lift some of the indirect taxes on consumption which raised the cost of living, particularly for the poor. But the scope for this was limited by the present state of public finances. Orthodox politicians like Peel would not contemplate

---

* His early promise was maintained. Arthur Peel served as Speaker of the House of Commons from 1884 to 1895, and was made a Viscount.

a deliberate policy of government deficits financed by borrowing; they still hankered after surpluses which would enable them to reduce the existing National Debt. The only remedy would be a return to the wartime income tax, introduced by Pitt to help beat the French, but abandoned in 1816 once the war was over. In March 1830 Peel and a few of his colleagues began to argue in Cabinet for a revival of income tax, but were unsuccessful. The Duke and most Ministers believed that income tax was in principle dangerous and indeed disreputable. An opportunity for fiscal reform was thus lost in 1830: the public finances languished in the Whig decade which followed.

That spring the Duke of Wellington fell into an uncharacteristic fit of depression. He had been severely criticised for continuing on his usual round of country house visits during the public hardship of the winter. He was not feeling well; in particular he found himself going to sleep in his carriage. He decided that it was time to resign the premiership and hand over to Peel. He composed a letter to this effect. Mrs Arbuthnot was appalled. She was genuinely attached both to the Duke and to her own role as principal gossip to the Prime Minister. 'It will be felt by the whole country as an unfair abandonment of his post in a moment of great difficulty.'[8] What would become of the Arbuthnots or indeed of the Tory Party under the leadership of gloomy, austere Peel? He would certainly want to broaden the Government by bringing back that suspect reformer Huskisson and even a few of the dreaded Whigs. The Duke hesitated under this pressure, changed his mind and the proposed letter of resignation was never sent.

If the Duke had persisted, his letter would have reached Peel at a particularly difficult moment. The old Baronet at Drayton was gradually fading out of life. He became seriously ill in April. Peel visited him on 6 April and wrote to Julia, 'He cried and kissed me two or three times. He was very feeble, and his voice very faint, but he was sitting in his dressing gown in his sitting room upstairs ... He is much thinner and feebler than when we were here in the autumn.'[9] He continued to play whist, until the time came when his hands shook so much that he could not deal the cards. He refused to let his nephew deal for him, and gave up the game. At the beginning of May Sir Robert had a relapse. He sat dozing in his armchair at Drayton, and died without anyone noticing until hours later. Peel arrived too late to take a final farewell.

The old man was eighty. It had been a good life, well sustained by family pleasures, worldly success, orthodox Christian faith and a strong practical mind. Peel had inherited most of his father's instincts. They never quarrelled, though Peel by education had developed an interest in ideas which impressed the old man but which he could not share. They had differed over Catholic Emancipation the year before the Baronet died. Julia seems to have felt that this disagreement in some way went deeper and might even have affected the provisions of his will. But this was not so. Peel burned all his father's family letters without looking at them, but that seems to have been done on principle rather than because of any particular scandal or unpleasantness. The will was read in the library at Drayton after the funeral, which had been attended by the whole corporation of Tamworth and sixty tenants on horseback. Sir Robert left his eldest son all his lands in Staffordshire, Warwickshire and Lancashire, and total assets worth four times the amount given to each younger son.

Old Sir Robert had given Peel an excellent start in life and taken great pride in his son's success. Peel recognised this and was grateful. The two men's minds worked in different ways. One could not imagine Peel writing to his father as he wrote to Bishop Lloyd or indeed to Croker. Their correspondence was formal in the style of the age. But behind the mutual courtesies, which sound stilted today, there was a strong affection and respect.

That summer another old gentleman was moving towards his close. On 16 May Peel called on George IV at Windsor. The King sat huddled, untidy and unshaven, in a wheelchair. To some extent he redeemed his lack of any great quality with a multitude of small ones. Included in these was a memory of detail characteristic of the Hanoverian dynasty. (Perhaps this is true of most crowned heads, for whom an appetite for detail can redeem the inevitable tedium of each royal day.) The King talked at length about old Sir Robert's life and death, with a sympathy which touched Peel the more because it came from a man who was himself visibly struggling with death.

The struggle continued for a few more weeks; George IV died on 26 June. His natural intelligence and sense of style, allied to a wayward kindliness, have not been enough to tip the scales of history in his favour. The King's search for pleasure and an easy life became in the end vexatious to himself and a nightmare for others. It was often possible to spend an amusing evening with George as Prince of Wales, Prince Regent or King; it was impossible to rely on him in any substantial enterprise. 'No monarch', commented *The Times*, 'will be less generally remembered.'[10]

His brother, King William IV, was greeted as a welcome refreshment. It was not supposed that at the age of sixty-five he would bring to the throne any special gifts of wisdom or heroism. As Prince William and as Duke of Clarence he had followed a haphazard naval career and bred ten illegitimate children with the actress Mrs Jordan. He married Princess Adelaide of Saxe-Meiningen once it became clear that a legitimate child might inherit the British throne. William was excited and happy at becoming King. His cheerful naval vocabulary and informal manners brought him quick popularity. His speeches were long, rambling and unpredictable. He cut back on his brother's yachts and horses and sacked an army of French cooks. But on his birthday he gave a banquet at Windsor for 3,000 of its poorest inhabitants.[11] William was no politician, and no one could have foreseen that in his short reign he would make decisions which in their outcome fundamentally shifted the balance of the British Constitution.

William's sympathies had always been Whig, but these were less strong than his awe and affection for the Duke of Wellington. He at once made it clear that he intended to keep the Duke as Prime Minister. That might be the King's intention, but by 1830 the King's intention was only one factor (though still important) in deciding on a government. Under the rules there had to be a general election after the death of a king and the election of summer 1830 brought to a head the discontent which had already seriously weakened the Wellington Government.

The Duke hoped that he would be able to strengthen his position. He believed that the traditional techniques of managing elections, particularly in the boroughs, would enable the Tory magnates and corporations to get rid of the rebel MPs, followers of Canning and Huskisson, who had begun to vote against his Government. It did not work out that way. It was hard in 1830 to be certain about the mathematical outcome of an election, because party loyalties and the likely behaviour of new Members were not always clearly defined. But there was no doubt that the Government lost ground. More serious, the target of the electorate, and of politically conscious citizens without a vote, had become not only the Government, but the whole political system.

There were many more contests than usual, and every contest meant expenditure, which dismayed the usual beneficiaries of the system. This was particularly true in the prestigious county seats. One of the county seats in Yorkshire was won by the brilliant reformer Henry Brougham at the expense mainly of the local Whig magnates. In some of the rotten boroughs, the old placemen were re-elected but there was unprecedented noise and trouble. In Marlborough, for example, the corporation, composed as usual of Lord Ailesbury's servants, duly elected his nominees; but this time there was a riot, and the venal electors had their shirts ripped from their backs by the crowd.[12] Peel wisely removed himself from the similar and neighbouring borough of Westbury. This had been a welcome port in the Protestant storm of 1829, but it was no safe haven a year later once the wind blew for parliamentary reform. On his father's death Peel became the squire of Drayton. He moved quickly to neighbouring Tamworth, which he represented for the rest of his life. The arrangements at Tamworth were traditional rather than democratic: the two borough seats were held by men of good standing with extensive property in the area. Peel, who liked to trace the underlying currents below the surface of politics, would have endorsed a modern historian's verdict on the 1830 election. The target 'was the whole parliamentary and electoral apparatus. Everywhere the men of the establishment found themselves naked to the wind.'[13]

While the British electorate pondered its choices, the French were again making more dramatic changes. At the end of July the authoritarian rule of Charles X was swept away. He was replaced by his cousin King Louis Philippe, who symbolised the change by calling himself 'King of the French' rather than 'King of France'. There is no strong evidence that the new revolution in France altered the election results in Britain, but the outcome had a more subtle effect in months to come. Among hardline Tories the old fears briefly revived. There they were again, the French, with their riots, barricades and loud-mouthed empty slogans; anarchy and terror could not be far behind. But before long a different French lesson emerged. When the noise subsided the French were being governed by a constitutional monarch, amiable and pear-shaped, advised by intelligent, soberly dressed middle-class Ministers like Guizot. These men carried umbrellas, not swords; in temperament and views they were not a million miles from Huskisson or Peel. No Robespierre, no Napoleon was in sight; the nightmare of the old revolution had been banished. If the flighty French could get rid of an unpopular system without bloodshed perhaps, it might be thought, so could solid John Bull in Britain.

Peel felt increasingly weary. The departmental workload was heavy and he carried an extra burden as the only effective spokesman for the Government as a whole in the Commons. He would have liked to persuade the Duke to bring Huskisson back into the Government and might eventually have succeeded, but fate intervened. On 15 September Huskisson was knocked down and crushed by one of the new steam engines at the opening of the Liverpool–Manchester railway. Though a more prosaic politician than Canning, Huskisson had a clear brain and enquiring, modern spirit. He and Peel were not personally close, but their minds moved in the same direction. Had he proved more agile in avoiding the steam engine, Huskisson would have proved an able lieutenant to Peel in handling and guiding the pressures for change.

Peel could not afford to wait indefinitely for extra support in the Commons. He persuaded the Duke to make an offer to Palmerston, who had been Huskisson's principal ally. The negotiation was clumsily handled, and broke down. Peel soldiered on, opposed by the Whigs, by the followers of Canning and Huskisson, and by a band of vengeful Tory Ultras. The situation in the country outside Westminster was deteriorating. Sporadic disorder continued in the North. More relevant to the personal wellbeing of most Ministers was the burning of ricks and smashing of threshing machines in the countryside. It is not surprising that the Arbuthnots and others found Peel morose.

Political debate now focused sharply on parliamentary reform. The Whigs healed their differences, at least on the question of principle. Even the Whig grandees who managed a large part of the old system now recognised that it could not last. The Whig leaders argued among themselves about tactics and the contents of their proposal, but the Party had swung firmly in favour of reform. The lines were set for a massive political confrontation.

The Duke of Wellington fired the first shot of battle by accident. On 2 November both Houses of Parliament debated the King's speech at the opening of the new session. In the Commons Peel did not exclude an eventual moderate reform, but saw no prospect at present of an acceptable proposal. Wisely he spent most of his speech talking about the crisis in Belgium. Following the revolution in France the Belgians were also in tumult, wresting control from the Dutch rulers who had been wished on them sixteen years earlier by the Congress of Vienna. But in the Lords the Duke was totally clear; his views on reform could not be more absolute. All was for the best in the best of all possible worlds. Not only had his Government no plan for reform, 'he had never ... heard of any measure which could in any degree satisfy his mind that the state of the representation could be improved ... He was fully convinced that the country possessed at the present moment a legislature which answered all the good purposes of legislation.' The Duke charged even further down this dangerous road. 'If he were asked to advise another country on forming a legislature, he would not try to suggest the British system immediately for the nature of man was incapable of reaching such excellence at once.' In case any doubt remained after this salvo, he concluded that as long as he held any station in government he would resist any reform measures proposed by others.[14]

When the Duke sat down, their Lordships reacted with prolonged murmurs, which remains the normal method in their House of expressing strong excitement. The Duke asked the Foreign Secretary sitting beside him why the Lords were so stirred up. We do not know exactly how Lord Aberdeen replied. In fact the Duke had started his last big battle; it was a battle he could not win.

Disorder multiplied in the country as the campaign for reform intensified. In London, King William and his Ministers were due to dine at the Guildhall in the City on 9 November to celebrate Lord Mayor's Day. There was talk of violence, of an attack on the Tower to seize weapons, of assassination attempts on Peel and Wellington. The new police force was being harassed by unruly crowds. The Duke and Peel met on 7 November, and decided to advise the King to cancel his visit to the City. It was a sensational climbdown.

November 9 would still be a tense day. Peel as Home Secretary kept the King informed with several notes. A crowd round the House of Lords was dispersed at six in the evening. Bands of one or two hundred men were moving through London, followed by police. Peel had arranged for a magistrate to attend a likely meeting of 2,000 citizens in the Rotunda. If the police could not manage the crowd, the magistrate would read the Riot Act and call on two detachments of cavalry who would be at hand.

At twenty to eight the Duke wrote to Peel, 'I am at home and have dined, and will go down [to] the Home Office as soon as I shall learn that you are there. I don't think that this mob in Catherine Street can be ten thousand, or that it is going to attack the police office in Whitehall Place. We are all quiet hereabouts, but there are a great many people in the street.' At nine, Peel reported to the King that there were said to be a considerable mob of many thousands beyond Temple Bar, though he thought this was probably an exaggeration. The new police were holding the mob in check, but several of them had been hurt by stones. By eleven-thirty the mob was dispersing and public peace had been restored.[15]

Peel's police had handled their baptism with honour, but the blow to the Government's prestige was severe. Since in the end nothing serious had happened, the Radicals argued next day that the Government had panicked and that the police and cavalry had never been needed.

The next test of strength came in the Commons. The Government had proposed the new Civil List, providing for the expenditure of the new sovereign. There were substantial savings on the King's own spending, but there was now a Queen where there had previously been mistresses; the Queen, unlike the mistresses, had a legitimate claim on the public purse. The new King was still popular and there was no strong argument about the figures. The vote was a test of confidence in the Government as a whole, on an issue when all its opponents would combine against them. The Government was likely to lose, but Peel, exhausted and cross, was adamant that there should be no concessions to win doubtful votes. On 15 November the Government lost by twenty-nine votes, having been opposed by the Whigs, the Huskisson group, twenty-three Ultra Tories and forty-nine of the sixty-six county Members who were present.

Peel at once drove to Apsley House to report to the Duke. On arrival he was sweating profusely and called for tea and soda water in high emotion. He insisted that the Government should at once resign. Mrs Arbuthnot wrote in her journal, 'I never saw a man so delighted as Peel. He said when the opposition cheered at the division ... he did not join in but it was with difficulty he refrained.'[16]

Defeat and resignation brought a welcome respite to Peel, but not an answer to the problems which were frustrating him. This was the dead point of Peel's political career. Unusually, he felt unable to act on his own analysis. He saw the need for parliamentary reform. The old system was defensible to a Tory like Peel so long as it worked, but by the autumn of 1830 it was no longer working. It had run out of time. Unlike the Duke Peel did not believe that the old system was part of a constitutional establishment so fragile that if you touched any part of it the whole would collapse. Yet he felt bound to counter any substantial reform put forward by opponents, and refused to put anything forward himself. The furthest he went was to agree that a corrupt borough liked East Retford should give up its seat to others, but even then he argued that the new representation should go to neighbouring Bassetlaw rather than to huge, unrepresented Birmingham.

This obduracy was an uneasy choice for Peel, but he stuck to it throughout the argument. The reason was clear and personal. Peel had just paid a heavy price for changing his view on Catholic Emancipation. He had abandoned those who had supported him most strongly in resisting the Catholic claims. It was ironical that before his change of mind he had been more vehement in defending the Protestant monopoly of power than he had ever been in defending rotten boroughs like Old Sarum, Marlborough or Westbury. A change of view on parliamentary reform would actually have been easier for him intellectually and emotionally than the one he had already made. But in 1830 the bruises from his first change of mind on Catholic Emancipation were too recent and too sore. He was not willing to be called a rat all over again. He felt that he could not set his pragmatic common sense free to work out a moderate compromise on reform. That would set off again the accusations of betrayal which still echoed around him. Others could do it; he could not join them. Indeed he felt he must oppose them, though not with great conviction.

Bound up in this personal problem was his attitude to the Ultras in his own party. They were divided on parliamentary reform. Their passions ran high, but flowed in different directions. Some, as we have seen, regarded the rotten boroughs as responsible for their defeat on Catholic Emancipation. The corrupt Members and their patrons who had betrayed their Protestant birthright should be swept away. If Peel and Wellington were destroyed in the process, that was the just fate of traitors. But for other Ultras the old parliamentary system was as important as the Protestant establishment. Because the one had gone, it would make even less sense to abandon the other. They liked the old boroughs and the easy route for their sons or cousins to follow them into Parliament. These Ultras, particularly strong in the Lords, prepared to resist parliamentary reform in the last ditch.

Peel had no time for either type of Ultra. His dislike went deeper than a difference of opinion. He despised what he saw as their amateur and selfish approach to politics. He rejected their refusal to look beyond their park gates to the interests of the nation as a whole and consult the greater good. He was uncomfortable to find himself voting with them, just as they disliked his leadership; but for the moment neither saw an alternative.

So Peel passed through a phase of bad temper. He had plenty else to think about and act on – his wife and children, his pictures, his interest in science and literature, the new home he was planning at Drayton. To the irritation of his followers he often detached himself from daily politics. At this time his judgement on tactical matters was inept because his attention wandered. But the detachment was not fundamental. In a bad temper he would mishandle an immediate tactical situation; but he was brooding over a long-term future for his party. He knew that parliamentary reform was inevitable.

Before that point was reached the country lived through a political melodrama with several acts. Never, in modern terms (except perhaps in the years just before 1914 when Commons and Lords struggled over Lloyd George's Budget and then Ireland) have the Houses of Parliament been so convulsed night after night with passionate argument. The nation outside was fully roused. In these excitements there were for the moment several heroes and a few villains. Peel figures on neither list.

Following the electoral defeat and subsequent resignation of Wellington's Government in November 1830, the King sent for the Whig leader Lord Grey. At the age of sixty-six Grey, proud, handsome and aristocratic, judged that only an immediate and radical reform would save from destruction the social order in which he believed. That order began with the miners, farm workers and tenants on his Northumberland estates and included now the industrial workers in cities such as nearby Newcastle. It stretched upwards through the new middle class and men like Peel till it reached his colleagues and himself in the House of Lords. The system was historically linked with the Church of England, and culminated in a King whose personal oddities could not alter his necessary position at the top of the pyramid. The difference between most Tories and a Whig like Grey was his belief that this social order depended on a willingness to make timely and sometimes sweeping changes of a kind that most Tories detested. Grey had been a cool reformer of this kind all his political life. For him timing was everything and he judged in 1830 that the time for a drastic parliamentary reform had arrived.

Grey's Government began to prepare its Bill. Peel retired to Drayton. Croker wondered if the Duke would be able to 'warm the cold caution of Peel into some degree of party heat; but if he will not lead us there are others who will at least make the attempt'.[17] Julia was not well over Christmas, but in the New Year the Peels filled Drayton with guests. Instead of old Sir Robert's Staffordshire squires and rubbers of whist, the house now welcomed Peel's close political friends. Croker of course came, and shot a bittern, though it is not clear whether this exploit pleased or shamed him. He found Peel in better spirits, and busy with plans for building a new house at Drayton. When Croker asked Peel to follow the Duke in pledging himself against all parliamentary reform, he replied cheerfully that he was sick of eating pledges and would avoid them in future. This was not encouraging for the Party. Nor was Peel's refusal to accept the Duke's invitation to a gathering of Tory grandees at Stratfield Saye which met in deep snow at the end of January. Peel said that he was too busy looking after Julia and conferring with his architect and gardener. 'Everyone seems to mistrust him,' wrote Croker – 'I do not; but I am convinced that he wishes to stand alone.'[18] Quite so; and in 1831 there was no formal post of Leader of the Opposition to constrain him, and no such thing as a Shadow Cabinet.

In any case there was not much the Tories could do until the Government produced its plans. Lord John Russell, small and persistent, sharp-faced, thin-voiced, was never a great orator. But on 1 March 1831 in his speech introducing the Bill, he made a reputation which lasted him for the rest of his long political career. The content of Russell's speech, not the eloquence of the speaker, astounded the House. Peel and many others had miscalculated. They looked at the Cabinet of Lord Grey, Lord John Russell, Lord Palmerston and other Whig magnates, in wealth and background far more magnificent than Canning or Huskisson or Peel. They supposed that the Whigs would propose a minimum measure. They would doubtless get rid of the more disreputable rotten boroughs, enfranchise some of the industrial cities, speak a good deal about the good old cause, the 1688 revolution and Charles James Fox, and leave it at that. But in one respect Peel was out of touch. He had never fought a contested election outside Oxford University. He had little first-hand knowledge of the pressures which had changed political life in the county constituencies and many boroughs in the elections of 1826 and 1830. Those who had for the first time contested a county seat at great expense or watched their borough slip away from them had a clearer grasp of reality than Peel, who had moved dexterously from Oxford to Westbury and from Westbury to Tamworth. Ministers had decided that only with a deeply radical Bill would they be able to assert their control of the political system and preserve its traditional institutions.

Lord John announced the abolition of sixty boroughs (Schedule A) and the reduction of forty-seven from two Members to one (Schedule B). One hundred and sixty-eight MPs were to lose their seats; the electorate was to be increased by half a million. As Lord John read out the historic names of the doomed boroughs, most Tories opposite reacted noisily, at first in shock then in elation. The Government had gone mad; neither Parliament nor people would stomach such a massacre, such an overturning of history. In that first excitement they thought it would be easy to kill the Bill and bring the Duke back to his proper place at the head of affairs. Peel by contrast sat silent. His expression darkened and towards the end of Lord John's speech he covered his face with his hands. He made no attempt at an immediate reply. His followers were deeply disappointed. He was criticised by Croker and others for not forcing a vote at once, and it is conceivable that in the passion of the immediate moment that challenge might have been successful.

Peel was a quick tactician who made and seized parliamentary opportunities with skill. But he must have seen that an immediate vote would not have killed the Bill. A government with the boldness to produce such a Bill would have the boldness to keep it alive – as indeed was quickly proved. The real point for Peel was different. The Government had destroyed the centre ground on which Peel liked to work. The Bill was too extreme. There was no room for manoeuvre and a compromise such as he had achieved over the Test and Corporation Act in 1828. He was left with no choice but to fall back and make common cause with all those who opposed the Bill, and in particular the Ultras whom he now despised.

The immense popularity of the Bill in its different versions became from that point the determining fact in its success. The great majority of those who at different stages mustered petitions, illuminated buildings, gathered crowds, shouted, threw stones and broke windows in support of the Bill would have no vote in the reformed Parliament. Some indeed in big constituencies like Westminster would lose the vote they now had, once Lord John's standard threshold of £10 householders was established.

The Great Reform Bill would leave the propertied classes firmly in control of the political system. It only increased the electorate by about 45 per cent, from 3.2 to 4.7 per cent of the population.[19] But the symbolism of the struggle was different. The middle and working classes were showing by different methods their rejection of the present way their country was run. The message was heard by those for whom it was meant. It was acted on by the Whigs to an extent which disappointed the minority of true democrats, appalled most Tories, but satisfied most of the nation. If reform could happen once it could happen again.

Two days later Peel spoke against the Bill. He opposed not all reform but the Government's particular plan. He foretold that this widening of the franchise would be followed by others. He criticised the Government for stirring up dangerous excitement: 'They have sent through the land the firebrand of agitation and no one can now recall it.'[20]

Despite the popular pressures the Tories still hoped to defeat the Bill when it came to Second Reading in the Commons on 21 March. A strong tide was flowing against them. Much turned on the attitude of King William. He was known to favour a moderate parliamentary reform. If the Commons threw out the Bill on second reading would the Government advise the King to dissolve Parliament and would the King agree? Few Tories and not many Whigs relished the thought of another expensive election eight or nine months after the last one. The Ultras in particular went different ways. When it came to the point twenty-five of them who had voted against Catholic Emancipation voted in favour of parliamentary reform; the Duke, Peel and the whole system had to be punished for letting down the Protestant cause. But thirty other Tory opponents of Catholic Emancipation turned out against the Reform Bill. In scenes of great excitement a record number of MPs voted, and the Second Reading was carried by 302 votes to 301.

As the popular agitation grew, the Bill settled into detailed examination clause by clause in Committee. In particular General Gascoyne, a Tory Ultra from Liverpool, proposed an amendment which would have prevented any reduction in the number of seats allotted to England and Wales. There was much manoeuvring. The Government made concessions, but they were not enough. Peel, forced again to align himself with the Ultras, still refused to work closely with them, behaving, so Mrs Arbuthnot recorded, 'with annoyance and insolence', and repeating twenty times over 'these are the fellows who turned us out three months ago'.[21] In the end, on 20 April, the Gascoyne amendment was carried by eight votes. The Government was too far committed to draw back. They could not accept the amendment. They advised the King to dissolve Parliament. But would he agree? William IV tossed and turned. Contradictory rumours abounded. On 22 April the Commons discussed the situation, the Tories passionately opposing dissolution. But through the noisy debate Members began to hear the boom of the guns in the Park saluting the King's carriage as he drove towards them to make the announcement they dreaded. The King had given way, despite the poem which he himself composed:

> *I consider dissolution*
> *Tantamount to revolution*[*]

Peel lost his temper and shouted. Once again the Whig Government had shown the boldness which would bring them success. Once again he was forced into angry impotence. The Commons trooped to hear the King pronounce their fate. Many Tories believed that this was the end of the world as they knew it. One told Greville that 'as he looked at the King upon the throne with the crown loose on his head, and the tall figure of Lord Grey close beside him with the sword of state in his hand, it was as if the King had got his executioner by his side; and the whole picture looked strikingly typical of his and our destinies'.[22]

---

[*] There had been technical problems in rushing the King into this ceremony. The Crown had to be fetched from the Tower. This was in itself irregular since there had not yet been a coronation. The Master of the Horse was dragged protesting from his breakfast. When the King was told that it would take five hours to plait the manes of the horses, he is supposed to have said that he would if necessary go in a hackney carriage.

No one found it difficult to predict the result of the general election of 1831. The unreformed Parliament was swept by public opinion to vote for its own transformation. Ultras like Sir Edward Knatchbull in Kent declared for reform. The old interests crumbled one by one. Lord Lowther, who had controlled Cumberland and its boroughs for as long as anyone could remember, found relative after relative facing defeat. Even Westbury returned two reformers. Gascoyne was beaten in Liverpool. Members who had voted against the Bill pulled out of many contests to avoid humiliation. The Whig Government ended with a majority of more than 130 seats.

The Government quickly produced a new Bill for the Commons. Immediately after the election, Peel dismayed his supporters by hinting at compromise. At Tamworth on 18 May he told his constituents, 'If necessities were so pressing as to demand it, there was no dishonour ... in relinquishing opinions or measures and adopting others more suited to the altered circumstances of the country.'[23] This was the old argument which he had used to justify his about-turn on Catholic Emancipation. Times had changed and wise men changed with them. In fact he was far from ready to act on that old analysis a second time. Yet he saw little point in tediously opposing in the Commons a Bill which was bound to succeed. He stayed at Drayton until June. Then perforce he began to take part in the sham debates on detail in the Commons.

Julia and the children went to Drayton for the summer. Peel stayed alone in London and complained bitterly to Julia from the new house in Whitehall Gardens:

24/8/31

My own dearest love

I cannot much longer bear this separation from you. I get a sort of lassitude and languor here which quite depresses me. The coming home at 2 or 3 o'clock in the morning to a desolate house with the prospect of the same thing the next night, the bedroom with your table and glass and all the outward marks of habitation, the lonely nursery and the drawing room all silent and unoccupied – are sometimes too much for me ... Tell little Julia that I have got her watch at home and that I will wind it up every night and see how it goes.[24]

The sessions dragged on through August and September, but that was too much for Peel. He told his colleagues that if they wished to go on debating the Bill clause by clause they were free to do so, but he was leaving London. Colleagues might be cross, but the partridges could not wait. Peel came back to London only for the final Third Reading of the Bill on 21 September, then as quickly as possible returned to Drayton. The birds were good that autumn; one day he shot thirty-six partridges with his single gun.

The final phase of battle of the Reform Bill began when the House of Lords rejected it on 8 October by a majority of forty-one. There were two ways in which the Government could overcome this obstacle. They could water down the Bill by doing a deal with a group of wavering Tory peers, or they could persuade the King to create enough new Whig peers to swamp the Tory opposition. But a creation of more than forty peers was more than the King had ever contemplated. He favoured reform, but not reform achieved through one hereditary institution (himself) under-mining the authority of another (the Lords).

Ministers operated against a background of steadily growing public feeling — which now spilled into large-scale violence. In one sense public opinion was the Government's ally, but it was now taking a sinister form. In October Nottingham Castle, the property of the Duke of Newcastle, was burned to the ground. Drayton lay only thirty miles from Nottingham, and only fifteen from Birmingham. Peel left London again to make sure that his family was properly protected. Writing to invite a friend to see the progress of his new house, he added, 'I am just import-ing carbines, as I mean to defend my old one as long as I can.'[25] The vio-lence led Peel to use traditional Tory language. He wrote to Croker, 'I read the progress of our moral contagion with the utmost disgust and indignation ... the inevitable consequence of a King and government hallooing a ten pound mob against the House of Commons in the stupid belief that they could have the hunt to themselves.'[26] Later in October a mob seized Bristol and ruled that city for three days, burning the Mansion House and the Bishop's Palace.

The nation's leaders tried to interpret what was happening to suit their own preconceptions. To the Duke, most Tories, and in some moods the King, events in Nottingham and Bristol were simply a foretaste of what they had foretold. Reform was a preliminary to revolution. Every bishop's palace, every duke's castle, would be at risk if the Bill went through.

Wellington told Lord Wharncliffe (leader of those Tory peers who favoured compromise), 'neither Lord Grey nor any nobleman of his order, nor any gentleman of his cast, will govern the country six weeks after the reformed Parliament will meet, and the race of English gentlemen will not last long afterwards'.[27]

The Whig Government needed no prompting to deal harshly with disorder; Lord Melbourne was as tough a Home Secretary as any Tory. But Ministers had no intention of retreating from reform. They were too deep in for that; they felt even more sure that reform was necessary to save castles and palaces and much else besides from mob rule.

So yet another Reform Bill, the third, was introduced into the Commons to replace the one the Lords had thrown out at the beginning of October. Once again Peel had to go through the motions, mounting an opposition which he knew to be futile with colleagues he found uncongenial. This time the Government had made concessions in advance, designed to wheedle the waverers when the Bill should reach the Lords. General Gascoyne had lost his seat, but the Government now included his amendment in their Bill. The number of English and Welsh seats was not to be reduced. Lord Chandos led an alliance of Tories and Radicals in an amendment which enfranchised better-off tenants who had no security of tenure and so were likely to vote with their landlord. But these changes were not enough to give Peel a way out of his dilemma. He continued to oppose the Bill. He stood aloof both from the waverers who were trying to fashion further compromise, and from the Ultras who wanted full-blooded opposition to the Government. Yet even in this half-hearted state Peel was indispensable to his party. The Duke summed it up to Lady Salisbury in November. 'There's that fellow in the Commons, one can't go on without him; but he's so vacillating and crotchety that there's no getting on with him. I did pretty well with him when we were in office; but I can't manage him now at all. He is a wonderful fellow – has a most correct judgement – talents almost equal to those of Pitt; but he spoils all by his timidity and indecision.'[28]

Peel was unused to being in opposition, and in 1831 he was at a personal disadvantage to the Government's choice as main champion of the Bill, Lord Althorp. Like Peel, Althorp was a master of detail, but unlike Peel he was keenly interested in the Reform Bill. Peel (unusually for him) left the detail of the debates to men like Croker, who mastered the minutiae and bored the Houses. Althorp knew it all, but carried his knowledge lightly. Most important, everyone in the Commons trusted him and respected his fair-mindedness. Clause by clause he set a genial lead, and the House lost the edge of its passion on a most passionate subject.[29] *

At the end of March 1832 the Commons sent the Third Reform Bill to the Lords. The drama reached its final act. The Cabinet was divided on whether to advise the King to create peers if the Lords rejected or amended the Bill. The Tories in the Lords were divided between the waverers and the stalwarts led by the Duke and backed by Peel. The King was divided in his mind as to whether he should agree to create peers. On 14 April the Lords passed the Bill on Second Reading by nine votes. The arguments of the waverers and the pressure from outside Parliament had turned the Lords round that far. But everyone knew, as the Commons had shown a year earlier, that the test for the Bill lay in detailed discussion in Committee.

On 7 May Lord Lyndhurst carried by thirty-five votes an amendment postponing discussion of the famous Schedules A and B which disfranchised the rotten boroughs. The Prime Minister, Lord Grey, lost patience, believing that the Lords were after all out to destroy, not amend, the Bill. He persuaded the Cabinet, drove to Windsor and asked the King to agree to the creation of at least fifty peers.

The King, annoyed and perplexed, thought he could find another way. Queen Adelaide, through the rest of her life a blameless lady, had already been in touch quite improperly with the Duke of Wellington. Her Lord Chamberlain, Lord Howe, had an appetite but not an aptitude for intrigue. Between them they had put into the King's head that he should ask Wellington to form a government to pass a moderate Reform Bill. This was a welcome thought for William. He desperately wanted to avoid creating peers and had always hoped that a compromise Bill could be worked out by all the main actors. Grey and the waverers had failed to

---

* The closest we have come to Althorp in recent years was Margaret Thatcher's Deputy Prime Minister, Willie Whitelaw. On one occasion Althorp replied to an able speech from Croker by saying that he had made some calculations which clearly showed that Croker was wrong; but somehow he had mislaid these calculations and could only ask the House to accept that he had made them and reject Croker's amendment. The Commons took his advice. In my time only Willie Whitelaw could have produced this argument with success.

achieve this; Wellington with Peel might after all do it. So the King refused Grey's request for the creation of peers and accepted the Government's resignation. Lord Lyndhurst, as a former Lord Chancellor, was asked to sound out the Duke and Peel to see if they could form a government. It was a misguided choice. Lyndhurst combined brilliant oratory, high intelligence and deviousness to an extent which bewitched the young Disraeli but repelled most of those with whom he had serious dealings.

However, the defects of the messenger did not really matter; the message itself was wrong. The way chosen in desperation by the King was soon blocked – though not by the Duke, to whom the main appeal was made. Wellington had opposed the Reform Bills more stridently than Peel, ever since his defiant speech to the Lords as Prime Minister in November 1830. But for Wellington consistency was no great matter, compared to his absolute duty to serve the King. He sprang to attention yet again at his Sovereign's call. He was willing to make the attempt to pass a Reform Bill. But he could not succeed without Peel, and Peel's response was immediate, absolute and negative. He had foreseen this moment. Croker believed that the Whig reform meant revolutionary government but maybe, just maybe, a Tory Reform Bill could square the circle with public opinion and bring the Duke, Peel, Croker and his friends back to office. He urged Peel to help the Duke pass a Tory Bill. On 12 May Peel wrote calmly explaining why he could not do this. It would be a personal degradation. Something like the present Whig Bill would have to pass. 'One of the greatest calamities that could befall the country would be that utter want of confidence in the declarations of public men which must follow the adoption of the Bill of Reform by me as a Minister of the Crown.'

The pressures from the public were by now overwhelming. Britain was nearer to a violent outburst of popular feeling in these famous Days of May than at any time in the last three centuries. The middle and working classes were in general commotion. Meetings, processions and petitions were organised across the nation; factories and shops closed; there was a run on the banks; citizens declared they would withhold taxes; the King was hissed; men of the Scots Greys in Birmingham said they would not act against a constitutional protest.[30] Manoeuvres between Lords and Commons might fascinate men like Croker. The King's muddled appeal might sway the Duke. But parliamentary reform was inevitable on Whig lines, and no Tory halfway house stood a chance.

After Peel's refusal, the end came quickly. The Duke told the King he could not form a Government. The King reluctantly called Grey back, agreed to create peers, but in the end there was no need. The Tories knew the game was up and on 4 June only twenty-two diehards opposed the final stage in the Lords. At the third attempt the Great Reform Bill became law.

Peel did not in his heart believe that Whig parliamentary reform as proposed by Lord Grey meant the end of the kind of Britain in which he had grown up. Croker had put the extreme prophecy succinctly to Sir Walter Scott in April 1831. There would be 'no King, no Lords, no inequalities in the social system; all will be levelled to the plane of the petty shopkeepers and small farmers; this perhaps not without blood-shed; but certainly by confiscations and persecutions'.[31] Croker acted on his belief: he refused to stand for the reformed Parliament. Wellington's view was the same as Croker's, except that he could not understand Croker's reluctance to soldier on in dutiful pessimism.

Peel thought differently. He had been genuine in his opposition to the Reform Bill. He was not play-acting when he held his head in his hands as Lord John read out the list of doomed boroughs. The Whigs had gone too far too fast. They had to be opposed to show them the difficulties of rushing headlong into change. Parliamentary reform would be followed by attempts to change other institutions, including further efforts to expand the franchise. Some change was inevitable, as he had written to Croker in 1820. But there should be nothing automatic about each step. It should be measured; it should respect the past, it should seek consensus; change should be led by men of substance with a stake in the country, the new professional and mercantile classes, lawyers, the squires and aristo-crats. Princess Lieven, listening to these differing views of the Duke and Peel on the future after reform, explained this as the difference between seventy and forty. She somewhat exaggerated the Duke's age, but other-wise she was right. The Great Reform Bill of 1832 resulted in many polit-ical, economic and social changes which Peel, the forty-year-old at Princess Lieven's table, strongly opposed; but it led into a period of national prosperity and greatness on lines which he was beginning to glimpse and to which he would notably contribute.

Ten

The Hundred Days

'We are making the Reform Bill work; we are falsifying our
own predictions ... we are protecting the authors of the
evil from the work of their own hands'
Peel to Croker, March 1833

'Monday 8 Dec. [1834] ... reached Calais at 5 o'clock. Sailed
that evening at 6, reached Dover at eleven. Julia and Julia
staid all night at Dover. I left it in a hack chaise at 20 min
to 12, reached London at ½ past 8. Tuesday morning 9 Dec.
Saw the King at ½ past ten, accepted the office of First
Lord of the Treasury and proceeded forthwith in the
formation of the Government.'
Peel's notes, December 1834

'In all his ways, his dress, his manner, he looks more like a
dapper shopkeeper than a Prime Minister. He eats
voraciously and cuts creams and jellies with his knife.'
Greville, February 1835

*I*n most parliaments a handful of fervent activists are spurred on by
the belief, however unreal, that their party is likely to win the next
election. Without such blind enthusiasm the action of the party
falters. In this spirit the Tories, including Peel, met for dinner in festive
mood at the newly founded Carlton Club in November 1832. True, they
had just failed to defeat the highly popular Reform Bill. True, they were
now about to face for the first time the new electors whose right to vote
they had so vigorously resisted. Yet their experts foretold a decent result.
They held that a popular reaction against the violence which had accompanied reform and a fear of more attacks on property in all its forms
would produce maybe 250 seats out of just over 650.

Peel himself had an easy time at Tamworth, being unopposed. But even for him in rural Staffordshire it was a new world. Peel carefully canvassed more than 600 Tamworth electors, undertaking to accept the Reform Act which he had opposed, and to vote for the abolition of slavery.

As the results came in it became clear that the Tories were smashed; the electorate (now one in seven of the male population) showed that it wanted more, not less reform. It was still not possible to be exact about the allegiance of every Member; but it looked as if the Tories would muster only 150, compared with 320 Whigs and not less than 190 Radicals and Irish. The Tories were now effectively in third place, and correspondingly depressed.* Indeed one up-and-coming Member, Lord Mahon, wrote to suggest that they should not sit on the traditional opposition front bench opposite Ministers in the House of Commons, but should retire to modest seats below the gangway. This would, he thought, acknowledge that they would be umpires rather than parties to the coming political struggle.[1]

Peel had no intention of retiring from the main fray. In electoral terms the worst had happened, but the misfortunes of the Party had cleared his mind. While the Reform Bill was passing he had shown himself bad-tempered, hard to work with, unsure of his tactics. Now the fog cleared, and he saw how to proceed. The Tory establishment around him were deep in gloom once the false flicker of an election revival had faded. They believed that O'Connell, the Radicals and the mob now had the whip hand. The King, the Lords, even the Duke had been unable to stave off disaster; nothing was now safe. No doubt Peel nodded sympathetically as friends and colleagues mourned around him; but his own mind was stimulated.

Peel gained strength by not allowing political work to dominate his whole life. Because he thought and wrote so fast his political output was at all times formidable. Looking at this vast store of material one can easily suppose that he had room for little else. But this would be wrong. Peel was devoted to Julia and the children and full of schemes for their

---

* The later Tory crashes in 1906, 1945 and 1997 were equally depressing. But at least those concerned knew about the swing of the pendulum and could hope to be back in power one day. In 1832 many Tories thought that the new system would exclude them for ever.

welfare. As we have seen he spent much time and money forming his collection of pictures. In 1832 and 1833 he was building his second big home
to replace at Drayton the old house in which his father had lived and
died. By 1832 the garden had already been laid out by Gilpin, and that
summer the roof went on the new house. Peel was in constant conference
with Smirke, the fashionable architect whom he had chosen for a second
time following the success of the house at Whitehall Gardens. The mix of
styles which the two men chose for Drayton left plenty of room for argument, a game which as usual attracted many players. Croker had left
Parliament knowing that civilisation was doomed, but he still had views
on architecture. He favoured battlements and labels on windows. Peel's
reviving confidence carried over into architecture. 'I am not going to have
battlements and I am not going to have labels to protect the windows of
the main body of the house; and I am confident that I am right. The
parapet or ornamental balustrade was in use in the time of Elizabeth and
James, and not the battlement. The battlement was of an earlier date.'
Croker retorted that battlements were more beautiful and less expensive
than balustrades. He regrouped his forces before returning to the charge,
this time on the question of the tower; it should have a belfry, and square
base rising into an octagon, as at St James's Palace.[2] Peel was more concerned with plumbing, heating and comfortable furniture.

Nor did politics prevent Peel from continuing the winter round of
shooting parties in country houses. Comfort in these houses was a matter
of pot luck. There was rather less adultery on these occasions than when
Peel first did the rounds twenty years earlier, but Julia, though firmly left
at home, continued to receive lively accounts of houses and guests. Of
Lord Westmorland's seat at Apthorpe Peel wrote 'its equal in discomfort
cannot be produced'. He had to pass through three dark rooms to his
bedroom, in one of which his candle blew out, so that he was forced to
start again. When found his bedroom contained a closet full of spiders
and rats; the rats scampered all night round the head of his bed. Next day
was stormy. Lord Westmorland, worried that the fires in the house
would smoke, gave prudent instructions to servants. Escaping just before
midnight from the two whist tables (Croker was present, playing whist
with his host), Peel 'felt my way for a quarter of a mile through cold
blowy galleries and passages' to his bedroom. 'The moment I opened the
door out went the candle again, and well it might, for both the windows

were wide open, and not a coal live or dead left in the grate, every one
having been carefully raked out either on the hearth or on the floor.' The
shooting at Apthorpe was exceedingly bad. 'The attempt of the whole day
was to prevent us from killing the very little game there was to kill.'³ His
hosts, the Fane family, were rude and hardly bothered with their guests.
Dinner included two newborn pigs on one dish, and another of pickled
herring and apples.

Later in the month he was entertained by the Duke of Rutland at
Belvoir, where by contrast everything was magnificent and in excellent
taste. Cannon were fired to greet the arrival of the royal Duke of
Gloucester, the splendid dinner reminded Peel of George IV at Windsor,
and the gold carving in the drawing room had come from Marie
Antoinette's apartment at Versailles.⁴

Peel's weekends were not entirely swallowed up in sport. He always
enjoyed historical debate and speculation. At the end of 1833 he had a
long talk at Hatfield with Lord Mahon, who was writing about Sir
Robert Walpole, Britain's first Prime Minister. The two men disagreed,
and Peel invited Mahon to Drayton to look at the new house rising
alongside the old Hall, but also to finish the argument. They continued to
differ, Lord Mahon being particularly severe against the corruption for
which Walpole had been notorious. On 23 December Peel wrote at length
with a more tolerant view:

> There must surely have been something very extraordinary in the char-
> acter and powers of that man to bring the son of a private gentleman,
> without any advantage from a distinguished name or the services of
> illustrious ancestors to be Prime Minister of England amid great
> public difficulties for a period of twenty years, who mainly by his per-
> sonal exertions contributed to establish and confirm, without severity,
> without bloodshed, a new and unpopular dynasty, who tolerated no
> competition for power, was emphatically the Minister of England, and
> who seems to have rebuked the genius of every adversary.⁵

That said something about Walpole, something also about Peel's own
idea of leadership.

In preparing his first speech to the new Parliament, Peel had already
spelt out his underlying approach in a letter to Henry Goulburn, his

natural confidant on parliamentary affairs now that Croker had left that scene. There was an urgent tactical choice to be made. Should the Tories make the defeat of the Whig Government their main objective? If so, then they should seek out occasions when they could vote in the same lobby as the Irish and Radicals. This did not mean pooling their views with men whose fundamental philosophy seemed to Tories wrong and dangerous. It meant finding issues when Tories, Irish and Radicals were all against the Government, albeit for different reasons. It might not be difficult by this tactic to win early victories in the short term, even to force the Government out. But Peel was determined not to think in the short term. 'There is no use in defeating, no use in excluding a Government, unless you can replace it by one formed on principle more consonant to your own – our policy ought to be rather to conciliate the goodwill of the sober-minded and well disposed portion of the community, and thus lay the foundation of future strength, than to urge an opposition on mere party grounds, and for the purpose of more temporary triumph.'[6] So within days of realising the scale of the Tory election defeat, Peel set out the strategy of constructive opposition which would bring his party to terms with the new political world.

As I studied Peel leading the opposition after the Great Reform Bill, I read of David Cameron's first encounter with Tony Blair in the Commons. Cameron's offer to help the Government carry the good parts of the education reform and defeat its own backbenchers compared exactly with Peel's concept of opposition. Peel aimed tactically to embarrass Ministers by occasionally siding with them against their supporters, while strategically he built a reputation as a commonsense moderate leader who put the merits of an issue before party advantage. The Conservative Party in 2005 adopted for reversing the defeat of 1997 Peel's recipe for reversing the defeat of 1832.

It is always difficult to hold back party enthusiasm from taking a quick trick. Many of the Ultras already distrusted Peel's instincts. He had ratted on Catholic Emancipation; he had pinned the country down into a tough currency policy which was hard on farmers and businessmen; he had just failed to support the Duke in the Days of May. There was no doubt about the talent in his head, but if Peel had a heart where did it lie?

An early test came over the first Whig Budget. The malt tax was deeply unpopular because it hurt farmers and raised the price of beer. The

Chancellor of the Exchequer, Althorp, proposed to keep it. In a thin House the Commons voted to halve the tax, which would lose the Exchequer £2.5 million. The Government could not afford this concession – but could not get it reversed unless Peel helped. In his heart Peel already disliked taxes which raised the cost of living and would have preferred an income tax. But that was no more feasible in 1833 than when he and Huskisson had flirted with it in the Duke's Government in 1829. The Whig Government was in a hole. If they lost the Budget political chaos would return. Peel persuaded his followers to help them out of the hole and reverse the Commons vote. The malt tax, Althorp's Budget, and the Whig Government were saved. Peel wrote to Croker that he could have trampled Althorp in the dust, but 'we are making the Reform Bill work; we are falsifying our own predictions, which would be realised without our active interference; we are protecting the authors of the evil from the work of their own hands'.[7]

But the Commons was not the only House of Parliament; nor was Peel the only leader of the Tory Party. Peel and the Duke of Wellington were in 1833 roughly equal in political reputation, Peel rising and the Duke sinking in the esteem of most commentators. Each was indispensable to the other. Peel was the only possible leader of the Tories in the Commons, but his strategy could not succeed if the Lords took a different line and used their undoubted power to defeat the Government. The two men had to work together, but to the despair of their close adherents they found this difficult. This was not because the Duke disagreed with Peel's strategy. He did not reason in the same way as Peel, but he reached the same conclusion by a direct military route. As the Duke saw it the country was in continuing disorder, only Grey, Melbourne and the Whigs could keep control, the King had entrusted the task of government to them, so the Tories had a duty to serve the King and keep the Radicals at bay. But the fact that the two men were basically agreed did not make for an easy partnership. They were not at ease with each other. Neither sought the other's company, and when they found themselves in the same room they spoke with formal courtesy. After dinner at the Carlton Club in February 1833 Peel sat reading a book by the fireplace, while the Duke conversed with the rest of the guests.[8]

They had fundamentally different attitudes to women. Peel was devoted to Julia, and longed for her company; but he never sought her advice on politics. Julia neither shone nor aimed to shine in such matters. The Duke, when asked whether Lady Peel influenced her husband, replied 'No. She is not a clever woman. Peel did not wish to marry a clever woman.'[9] For political discussion Peel relied on an informal group of friends, all men, who came and shot and talked at Drayton, and a wider group of acquaintances who dined at Whitehall Gardens. The Duke by contrast neglected his wife, but enjoyed gossiping on politics with other women. Peel was not averse to a chat with women like Princess Lieven or Lady Shelley, but he thought the Duke's women were a mediocre lot. 'The foolish ones envelop him with incense, and he has fallen a victim to this weakness and to his own vanity.'[10]

Small matters rubbed the relationship the wrong way. The Duke was apt to defend vehemently his vain effort to help the King by forming a government in the Days of May of 1832 to pass a moderate Reform Bill. He was in the habit of saying that he would have been ashamed to show his face in the street if he had turned the King down. Peel heard this and interpreted it as a criticism of himself for having in those same days refused to help the King. Peel should not have been so sensitive. He had taken the rational decision in the Days of May and been proved right. He should have realised that the Duke was bound to thrash around, without thinking of Peel at all, for arguments to justify his own quixotic interpretation of loyal duty.

On the second matter it was the Duke who showed himself insensitive. In November 1833 Lord Grenville, Chancellor of Oxford University, lay dying. He lingered for several months while around him the University worked itself into chaotic frenzy about his successor. The High Church Ultra Tories in the University asked the Duke of Wellington to put himself forward. It was an astonishing idea, as the Duke himself argued when writing to Lord Bathurst: 'I answered that I had not received a University education; that I knew no more of Greek or Latin than an Eton boy in the remove; that these facts were perfectly well known and that I must be considered incapable and unfit.'[11] But the University Tories persisted and wore the Duke down. Lord Grenville died, and other possible candidates withdrew. Entertained and flattered by the unexpected compliment the Duke accepted, and was elected unopposed.

But another possible candidate was acutely conscious of his own claims, which were stronger than the Duke's. Peel had taken an Oxford

degree with the highest possible distinction. He had represented the
University in Parliament for twelve years. He was a man of wide intellectual interests, already a noted patron of the arts, literature and science.
No one could have been better suited to be Chancellor. This was indeed
the view of at least two heads of Oxford colleges, the Warden of Merton
and the Principal of New Inn Hall. But with mistaken punctiliousness
these gentlemen took no action until the breath was out of Lord
Grenville's body. They then asked Peel to stand, but by then he knew of
the Duke's decision. He turned them down with the frostiness which
came naturally to him at moments of embarrassment. His vexation
became public knowledge.

Both parties had behaved correctly, but each felt that the other had
been insensitive. The Duke knew that he had at first been genuinely reluctant and would have yielded to Peel if Peel had come forward. Peel felt
that the Duke should have talked to him informally while there was time.

In the background was the political history. Peel had in effect been
turned out of the University seat in 1829 because he had ratted on
Catholic Emancipation. The orthodox Tories were certainly not prepared
to accept the same rat as their Chancellor. Yet Peel had changed his mind
in 1829 in order to help Wellington. It was bitter that the Duke should
gain a prize from Tory resentment at Oxford against an act by Peel in
which the Duke had himself joined and of which he was the chief benefi-
ciary. Peel's chagrin can only have been increased when he read in June
1834 of the Duke's triumphant installation as Chancellor. For three days
Tory Oxford held high carnival. The Ultras turned out in force, old Lord
Eldon being greeted with particular enthusiasm because he had voted
against every conceivable reform of anything. The Duke got through his
Latin speech with only two false quantities. Young Lord Maidstone of
Christ Church was interrupted by thunderous applause as he declared
heroes succeeded heroes, year by year. 'We have one only, and that one is
here.'[12]

So the two Tory chieftains, joined by necessity, brooded in silence over
each other's shortcomings. Their acolytes, alarmed out of their usual love
of divisive gossip, tried to bring them together. Charles Arbuthnot invited
both men to dinner on 1 May 1834, the Duke's birthday; but they hardly
exchanged a word.[13] He wrote at length to Lord Aberdeen, now one of
Peel's most trusted friends, and Aberdeen showed the letter to Peel.

Gradually Peel and the Duke came together. Politics made that necessary. They were like two batsmen sharing an innings who, without any personal bonding on other matters, learn precisely how their partner will deal with a ball, call a run or stay in his crease.

It is not too difficult for us today to understand some of the issues of nineteenth-century politics. We can grasp the arguments about taxation and a balanced Budget, about parliamentary reform or free trade versus protection. But it is hard now to conceive how much effort and passion during the 1830s went into debating the established Protestant Church of Ireland. The number of Irish bishops, the collecting of Irish tithes, the allocation of Irish Church revenues are questions so distant from us today that it is easy for us to turn the pages wearily until we reach a more congenial, comprehensible topic. Yet this was the subject which at that time preoccupied the King, his Ministers and the Tory Party – and which provided the pressures which held Peel and Wellington together.

The fundamentals were clear. Out of eight million Irishmen, less than a million belonged to the established Church of Ireland, which was in structure and doctrine a weak sister of the Church of England. The Church of Ireland maintained 1,385 benefices across the country, and twenty-two bishops and archbishops. But this imposing superstructure was not mainly paid for by the members of the Church. The tithe system meant that the Catholic peasant, often in addition to supporting his own priest, had to pay much of the income of the local Anglican parson. Sydney Smith put it kindly. 'The bell of a neat parish church often summons to worship only the parson, and an occasional conforming clerk, while two hundred yards off a thousand Catholics are huddled together in a miserable house, and pelted by all the storms of heaven.'[14]

To most observers the Church of Ireland required drastic reform. But in 1833 any Whig attempt at reform was suspect to most Tories. Some were Irish landlords with church livings in their gift. But most were not interested in the detail. They had just lived through a political whirlwind which had transformed the House of Commons. They had all predicted that this was only a preliminary to further massive assaults on the other institutions of the Kingdom one by one. Here within months of the Reform Act was the next attack. Naturally the Whigs were choosing the weakest target, and it was sinister that they were supported by the Irish demagogue O'Connell. But if the Church in Ireland was undermined, few doubted that the Church in England and Wales would be next in line. The subversion they had predicted was under way. It was possible to believe as Peel did – that a moderate reform was justified but also that some Whigs, and all Radicals, favoured this as part of a wide assault on the country's institutions which Tories must resist. Peel did not accept that the whole fortress of British institutions. including this weak outlying tower, had to be defended if all was not to crumble. On the contrary he judged that by accepting compromise on the Irish Church, Tories could strengthen their chances of resisting the wider Radical assault. This judgement collided with the simpler view of most Tory peers that the Lords should use their power to defend the whole fortress. It was on this point that the Duke of Wellington held the key.

The Government's Bill proposed a radical overhaul of the tithe system and the abolition of ten bishoprics and a crop of sinecures. Peel eloquently supported the Government in its defence of powers needed to repress disorder in Ireland, but at the same time criticised the detail of their Church Bill. The argument began to turn on the complicated question of the appropriation of funds. The Bill reorganised the administration of Irish Church estates, and this was expected to yield more income than the Church needed. Should this surplus be kept by the Church, or could funds be diverted to other worthy purposes? The Bill said they should be so diverted; Peel said they should not. This secondary argument about appropriation aroused primary passions, and rumbled on year after year.

For the moment in 1834 the Whig Government dropped this controversial clause. There had been a subterranean explosion within the Cabinet: Lord Stanley, Irish Chief Secretary, had successfully objected to any appropriation of revenues. With great difficulty Peel and the Duke then persuaded enough Tory peers to let the Bill in this milder form pass into law.

But a new actor had thus appeared at the front of the political stage whose fortunes for the next thirteen years were to be closely intertwined with those of Peel. Lord Stanley, eleven years younger than Peel, heir to the earldom of Derby, was born like Peel in Lancashire, but from a very different background. The Earls of Derby had abandoned their rule over the Isle of Man but not their grip over the politics of Lancashire. Stanley's grandfather, the 13th Earl, had combined strong Whig convictions with the pursuit of gambling, game shooting and horse racing. Stanley remembered learning as a young boy a family catechism beginning, 'What does A stand for?' 'An Axe.' 'What is an Axe for?' 'To chop off Kings' Heads.'[15] No such revolutionary thought infected Stanley's own thinking. He inherited his grandfather's love of racing and passion for politics, but also the devoted Anglicanism of his mother. To this were added the rigours of a classical education at Eton. Stanley thrived on a diet of the ancient historians Herodotus and Livy, and at the age of eighteen was writing extensive notes on the Hindu and Muslim history of India. At Oxford he contrived in a thoroughly Etonian way both to win the Chancellor's Prize for Latin composition and to lead a group of drunken undergraduates who pulled the statue of Mercury from its plinth in the centre of Christ Church. He entered Parliament as a Whig because the Stanleys were Whigs, but without any taint of radicalism. Throughout his life he disdained popular agitation and the national press. Progress, he believed, came through Parliament, preferably under the supervision of an enlightened Whig aristocracy.

His abilities and connections brought Stanley into Parliament at the age of twenty-three. His first Cabinet post was the same as Peel's had been eighteen years earlier: in 1830 Grey appointed him Chief Secretary for Ireland. Like Peel he was appalled by the cruelty and disorder of the Irish scene; again like the young Peel he reacted by putting the restoration of the rule of law at the head of his priorities, well ahead of any political or social reform. This brought him, once more like Peel, into bitter conflict with O'Connell, after Catholic Emancipation now legally elected as the Member for County Clare, and thus an opponent across the floor of the House. Stanley, tall and handsome, looked right and sounded splendid; he quickly established himself as a master of fiery debate. It was to support Stanley's request for extra powers in Ireland that Peel delved back into his memory and gave the Commons the story already quoted of the woman throwing turf on the fire to light the faces of her murderers. Stanley bickered with his colleagues in Cabinet over the Irish Church. He thought that he had killed the clause in the original Bill allowing Irish Church revenues to be appropriated to secular purposes. But that irrepressible reformer Lord John Russell bobbed up with a speech repeating his own personal support for this diversion. Stanley, fed up, resigned from the Government in May 1834 and, with a tiny handful of independent supporters, tried to build up a balancing position between Tories and Whigs.

This first crack in the Whig Government was quickly followed by others. Peel exposed the continuing confusion of their Irish policy. Grey, fed up in his turn, resigned as Prime Minister in July. The Government, re-elected triumphantly to power eighteen months earlier, collapsed. William IV, like most monarchs, yearned for a coming together of all his sensible centre-minded subjects. He asked the Home Secretary, Lord Melbourne, if he could form a coalition with Peel and Wellington. The idea collapsed because Melbourne insisted that the legislation on the Irish Church must be pursued in a form which the Tory leader could not accept. So Melbourne became Prime Minister at the head of a weakened Whig Government. The House of Lords accepted the Government's Irish coercion Bill but threw out their Bill on Irish tithes.

It was obvious that though Wellington accepted in principle Peel's general strategy of constructive opposition, he tended to apply it in a more warlike way than Peel. But there was little doubt which of them was now the more important political figure. Peel's increased reputation did not bring universal praise. There were observers who found something faintly ridiculous about Peel which they attributed to his lack of breeding. He was putting on weight and slightly overdressed – certainly not a dandy, but with a watch and chain just too large for elegance. Because of a riding accident in which he had lost a thumb his coats were made to open up the wrong way for a man, the buttons fastening right on left. This could hardly be held against Peel, but he could have taken more trouble with his table manners. 'I never was so struck as yesterday by the vulgarity of Peel. In all his ways, his dress, his manner, he looks more like a dapper shopkeeper than a Prime Minister. He eats voraciously and cuts creams and jellies with his knife.'[16] So wrote the diarist Greville. Greville was a thoroughgoing Whig snob, but he had shrewd political judgement and from this angle found Peel more and more interesting despite the unfortunate jellies. In this summer of 1834 he wrote: 'Peel's is an enviable position; in the prime of life, with an immense fortune, *facile princeps* in the House of Commons ... No matter how unruly the House, low, impatient or fatigued, the moment he rises all is silence and he is sure of being heard with profound attention and respect.'[17] Greville went on to analyse the reasons for this success. 'His great merit consists in his judgement, tact and discretion, his facilitude, promptitude, thorough knowledge of the assembly he addresses, familiarity with the details of every sort of parliamentary business and the great command he has over himself.'[18]

At the end of the 1834 session Peel needed a holiday. This meant what he described as a small conspiracy against the partridges at Drayton in September. Then followed something new. Neither he nor Julia had ever visited Italy. Taking with them Julia, their eldest daughter, they set out on a meticulous version of the Grand Tour with the accent on serious sight-seeing. It took them a month to reach Rome, where there were galleries to be seen, sculptures to be bought, and the Pope to be visited. There was no reason why politics should need his attention until Parliament returned in the usual way after Christmas.

The next event was only a small pebble, but enough to set off an avalanche. Earl Spencer was an old man, and his death on 10 November 1834 can have come as no surprise. But the predictable, coming at a difficult moment, sometimes catches professionals unprepared. They have gazed at the obvious so long that they no longer notice it. Earl Spencer's earldom would be inherited by his son Lord Althorp, Leader of the House of Commons. Since the renunciation of hereditary peerages lay more than a century in the future, Althorp with his new title would have to move from the Commons to the House of Lords.[*] The Prime Minister, Lord Melbourne, acknowledged to the King in a detached sort of way that the Government had been gravely weakened by Earl Spencer's death. Melbourne showed none of the tenacity in hanging onto office which was so apparent in him five years later. He was deeply irritated by his own party's squabbling. So was the King. The separate exasperation of these two elderly gentlemen produced a constitutional crisis.

Melbourne made things worse by proposing Lord John Russell as the

---

[*] The son of an English peer could be elected to the Commons while his father was alive and in the House of Lords, even if he himself carried a title. Thus the Duke of Buckingham's son Lord Chandos sat in the Commons until his father died. In special circumstances an eldest son could if he wished move up to the Lords even while his father was still there. This happened to Lord Stanley, who moved to the Lords before he succeeded his father as Earl of Derby. What the eldest son could not do in those days was renounce his peerage and so dodge elevation to the Lords when his father was dead. Needless to say, the rules for the Scottish and Irish peerages were different.

new Leader of the House of Commons to replace Althorp. The King and Lord John could never be on cosy terms. William until recently had favoured the Whigs in a bluff, imprecise way, believing like many Whigs that progress could be achieved without changing anything very much or upsetting anyone who was sensible. Lord John by contrast nursed a passion for detailed reform. Small, honourable but fussy, he was often to be found picking away at this institution or that, with scant regard for those who felt genuine affection for it.

Lord John's present target was the Irish Church. William IV, like his brother before him, was hardly a model of Christian living; but both Kings followed their father George III in believing there was something mystical, though hard to define, in the Coronation-Oath which they had taken to defend the Church. The thought of Lord John, in alliance with O'Connell and the Radicals, siphoning off the revenues of the Irish Church for purposes of their own choosing filled the King with dismay. He decided to seize the opportunity offered him by Melbourne's frankness about the Government's chances of survival. On 14 November he dismissed the Government, using the argument that by Melbourne's admission it was in a precarious state. Melbourne accepted the decision cheerfully. Of the outgoing Ministers only the Lord Chancellor, Brougham, showed real anger. He leaked the story to *The Times*, blaming it on Queen Adelaide, and sent the Great Seal back to the King wrapped up in a bag 'exactly as a fishmonger might have sent a salmon for the King's dinner'.[19] The great Whig hostess, Lady Holland, complained of bad manners and inconvenience.[20] But there was no tumult, no rioting; no windows were broken, no castle was burned. The Whigs went quietly. Nothing exceptional marked the last occasion on which a King of England dismissed his Ministers of his own accord.

The King at once sent for the Duke of Wellington and asked him to form a government. Probably in his heart William hoped that the Duke might agree, impossible though the odds were, given the huge majority of Whigs and Radicals in the Commons. Neither man thought of government in terms of legislation. The King's Government should not be measured by Bills passed, but by the good order and security of the country. The Commons were necessary for the voting of money, as the Stuart kings had discovered. But under this old-fashioned approach, provided a government had the confidence of the King and enough support in the

Commons to raise money, it did not need votes day by day, for the simple reason that it did not need to legislate.

But the Duke had learned the limits of his simple, unadorned doctrine that the King's Government must be carried on. This was arguably the finest hour of Wellington's political career. It took the form of renunciation combined with practical help. He did not leave himself time to be tempted by the flattering advice which he would doubtless have received from his intimates, that he was indispensable as Prime Minister. Anyway Mrs Arbuthnot, to his great sadness, had died that summer. The Duke told the King that the Prime Minister must be in the Commons, and this meant Peel. But Peel was – where? No one knew. It was thought that he was in Italy with his wife and daughter, but nothing was certain. Yet the King was in a hurry. He had created a void, and knew it would be dangerous to leave it empty. The Duke supplied the practical answer. He was willing to serve as caretaker, occupying simultaneously the Treasury, Foreign Office, Home Office and War Office, without any colleagues except Lord Lyndhurst as Lord Chancellor. 'At last we have a united Government,' said one wit.[21] The Duke ranged through Whitehall as occasion required, taking only immediately necessary decisions. In later days he talked happily about his brief period as dictator.

James Hudson, aged twenty-four, a young official in the Queen's Household, was told to go and find Peel. He received little information and no practical help. It was Sunday, the banks were closed, but he managed somehow to rustle up £500 for travel expenses. Hudson reached Dover that evening, to find that the last steamboat had sailed. He hired a rowing boat and oarsmen, who landed him at Boulogne four hours later. No one at the Embassy in Paris knew where Peel was. Hudson headed south, whisked round the hotels in Turin, then Milan – still no news. The suspicious police (Lombardy was restless under Austrian rule) held him up for eighteen hours by impounding his passport. At Bologna he heard that Peel was in Florence, in Florence that Peel had left for Rome. Floods forced him to abandon his luggage and Hudson travelled to Rome in an ox-wagon, after that an ancient rattletrap. He arrived at Peel's hotel wet and spattered with mud on the evening of 25 November. Peel returned from a ball given by the Duchess of Torlonia; he sat down to read the King's summons and the Duke's brief account of events. It is said that he greeted Hudson coolly, cross-examined him on his itinerary, and established that he could have managed the journey in eight days rather than nine. But that would only have been conceivable if Peel had left in London particulars of his own movements. In fact Hudson had done very well; he left Rome (and the history books) the next day carrying Peel's brief replies to the King and the Duke accepting office.

The Peels were already on the road. They travelled together; Julia and her daughter refused to remain in comfort in Italy or to return at leisure. The roads were bad and the snow deep in the Alpine passes; the Peels spent four nights in bed and eight in the coach. At Macon a letter from the Duke gave further news and suggested a possible list of Ministers; other letters already asked for Government jobs. The steam packet *Ferret* was waiting for them at Calais. Peel in his little brown pocketbook noted, 'Monday 8 December: [Breakfasted] at Montreuil, reached Calais at 5 o'clock. Sailed that evening at 6, reached Dover at eleven. Julia and Julia staid all night at Dover. I left it in a hack chaise at 20 min to 12, reached London at ½ past 8. Tuesday morning Dec 9. Saw the King at ½ past ten, accepted the office of First Lord of the Treasury and proceeded forthwith in the formation of the Government.'[22]

Peel had had plenty of time to think as his carriage rolled through the wintry landscapes of Europe. From the guarded phrases of the Duke's letter it was clear that the King had acted rashly and without full justification. He was entrusting government to a party which at present was neither first nor second but only third in parliamentary strength in the Commons. Whether or not Peel's strategy in opposition would work in the long term, it had certainly not had time to do so yet. The moderate men of property to whom he had begun to appeal had not had time to recognise in him, let alone in the battered old Tory Party, their true safeguard against radicalism and violence. The King had offered him the precious gift of office, but too soon, before he was politically strong enough to turn it into power.

Peel's only hope was to arrange for a new election at once. It was just possible that he might be able to broadcast his message widely to the new electorate and create a Parliament in which his Government could survive. It was a faint hope, but he mustered his full determination to give it reality. Physically tired and mentally tense, he was in a hurry to unleash the plans which he had pondered during the journey.

The King asked Peel if he needed more time to reflect on his decision to accept office. Peel brushed this aside; he was ready, though he warned the King that success was doubtful. He was not content to choose Ministers only from the relics of Wellington's Government of 1830. He tried first to persuade Stanley and his chief lieutenant Sir James Graham to join the Cabinet. He wrote to both that first afternoon of his return from Rome, 9 December 1834. These two able men were poised with a handful of supporters between the Whigs they had just left and the Tories they were not yet ready to join. If they came aboard the Government would at once look quite different from the Duke's old Tory team. But Stanley was not willing and Graham followed Stanley. In a letter expressing much personal esteem Stanley reminded Peel that they had been recently opposed on every subject except the Irish Church. Stanley believed (wrongly) that the Duke would be the dominant force in the new Government; he disliked the Duke's reactionary tendencies and most recently the way he had run the whole Government as a virtual dictator.

Behind these arguments there was personal rivalry. Stanley, strong-minded and high-spirited, fancied his own ability to construct a brilliant platform of intellectual moderation, led of course by aristocrats such as himself. The young Disraeli told Lord Melbourne about this time that he wanted one day to be Prime Minister. 'No chance of that in our time. It is all arranged and settled', was Melbourne's reply. 'Nobody can compete with Stanley.'[23] That was also Stanley's view. It did not suit him to attach himself to what looked like a particularly frail vehicle driven by Peel, who was his main rival for the position in politics which he had marked out for himself.

Peel was forced after all to put together an updated version of the Duke's last Tory Government He brought in his close friend Henry Hardinge as Chief Secretary for Ireland. The list of Ministers included in junior positions young men who were to become important colleagues and remain Peel's devoted disciples – Gladstone, Sidney Herbert and Lord Lincoln. Other faces were familiar – Goulburn at the Home Office, Wellington at the Foreign Office and Aberdeen at Colonies. Croker, now back on close terms with Peel, still refused to enter the reformed Commons and so was not available as a colleague; but he was useful as a sounding board. Peel complained to Croker after Stanley's refusal that his would be only 'the Duke's old Cabinet'. With gritted teeth he had reached an accommodation with some of the Ultras, including the most sensible of them, Sir Edward Knatchbull, as Paymaster of the Forces. He agreed politely to differ with the pretentious Duke of Buckingham and his son Lord Chandos. Lord Lyndhurst, unreliable and brilliant, played his own game as Lord Chancellor. It was not an ideal Government, but it was presentable.

The new Cabinet dined together on 13 December. They at once began to plan for the dissolution of Parliament and a general election. They agreed without difficulty that Peel should at once put out a statement explaining the principles on which the Government would act. Since under the rules of the time Peel would have to be re-elected at Tamworth on accepting office even before a general dissolution of Parliament, there was no reason why he should not immediately address his own electors. Peel worked on his text. The Cabinet met again four days later on 17 December. Peel's draft was approved by Ministers. There was no dissent. It was copied at midnight, and sent round by messenger to *The Times*, *Morning Herald* and *Morning Post* for insertion in the waiting presses. The Tamworth Manifesto was published across the country on 18 December.

To anyone familiar with the party procedures of today (ponderous despite the march of modern technology) the speed of Peel's manoeuvre is impressive. On 8 December, not yet Prime Minister, he had landed wearily at Dover. Within ten days he had formed a Government, arranged a dissolution and launched the first national election manifesto in British history.

The Tamworth Manifesto begins with a statement in the formal language which came naturally to Peel, designed here to reassure the electorate that everything was being done in a proper manner:

Gentlemen,

On the 26 November last, being then at Rome, I received from His Majesty a summons, wholly unforeseen and unexpected by me, to return to England without delay, for the purpose of assisting His Majesty in the formation of a new Government. I instantly obliged the command for my return, and on my arrival I did not hesitate, after an anxious review of the position of public affairs, to place at the disposal of my Sovereign any services which I might be thought capable of rendering.

Peel then moved to the heart of the political debate – the considered reaction of his party to the Great Reform Act which he and they had done their best to frustrate: 'I consider the Reform Bill a final and irrevocable settlement of a great constitutional question – a settlement which no friend to the peace and welfare of this country would attempt to disturb, either by direct or by invidious means.' But what would follow the Bill? That to Peel was the crux, not just of the election which he was calling, but of the new Conservative Party he was creating:

> If by adopting the spirit of the Reform Bill it be meant that we are to live in a perpetual vortex of agitation; that public men can only support themselves in public estimation by adopting every popular impression of the day – by promising the instant redress of anything which anybody may call an abuse – by abandoning altogether that great aid of government – more powerful than either law or reason – the respect for ancient rights and the deference to prescriptive authority; if this be the spirit of the Reform Bill, I will not undertake to adopt it. But if the spirit of the Reform Bill implies merely a careful review of institutions, civil and ecclesiastical, undertaken in a friendly temper, combining, with the firm maintenance of established rights, the correction of proved abuses and the redress of real grievances – in that case, I can for myself and colleagues undertake to act in such a spirit and with such institutions.[24]

The Manifesto went on to deal with topical policy points such as have appeared in election manifestos ever since. Municipal corporations, the rights of Dissenters, the position of the churches, a peaceful foreign policy, strict governmental economy – on all these Peel set out his stall carefully, that is without too much precision.

Peel's aim in the Tamworth Manifesto was practical and immediate. He was in a hurry. An election was imminent; he wanted to win seats. He needed to convey to as wide a public as possible what he and his colleagues stood for. He had set out the general approach in his first speech to the reformed Parliament nearly two years earlier. But part of the art of the new politics was (and remains) repetition. Before reform there were a few constituencies (the larger counties and some boroughs which by historical fluke had a big electorate) where contests could be swayed by the movement of opinion on particular issues. But in most places the result was decided by allegiance to particular families or interests, tempered by negotiation between these interests and lubricated by money. These arrangements were not abolished by reform, as any reader of Dickens or Trollope can see; but the element of argument and persuasion became much more important with the larger electorate. The growth of the national and local press provided the means of persuasion. A consistent message could now be emphasised and repeated until it became familiar in the further corners of the Kingdom. That was the purpose of the Tamworth Manifesto.

The Manifesto was, Greville wrote, a prodigious sensation. 'Nobody talks of anything else.' It flummoxed Stanley who at Knowsley had been hatching something similar. The King hoped it would be widely circulated. The Bishop of Exeter, a man given to exaggeration, thought it one of the best documents ever issued from the pen of man. In the ensuing weeks it was quoted from innumerable election hustings.[25]

The Tamworth Manifesto will never be read as great political literature. Peel's public style was long-winded and portentous; only in private letters and minutes was he concise and sardonic. Nor is it a flash of lightning containing blinding revelation of a new message. The document succeeded because of its timing, its wide distribution, and its shrewd appeal to the mood of the moment. Politics is partly about choosing opponents with care. In the Manifesto, endorsed by the whole Cabinet, Peel's party set itself against radicalism, both the fiery version of O'Connell, Cobbett and Hunt and the detailed reform of institutions dear to Lord John Russell. But it also set itself against automatic opposition to reasonable change.

The Manifesto coincided with the growing use of the name 'Conservative' to describe the Tory Party. The name had been used for the first time four years earlier in the *Quarterly Review*. It passed gradually into the political vocabulary of the time. Peel was at ease with the new name, which signified change but not too much of it. The Ultras grumbled, pining for a leader who would put the clock back and restore an age of gold which they associated strangely with the younger Pitt and Burke. But at this stage the Ultras had no leader and no convincing battle cry. Catholic Emancipation and the Reform Bill were past recall, and the malt tax was hardly a cause to set hearts afire. The Ultras came in all shapes and sizes, but in 1835 most of them would reluctantly have agreed with Lord Monmouth in Disraeli's novel *Coningsby*: 'Peel is the only man suited to the times and all that; at least we must say so and try to believe so; we can't go back.'[26]

Peel had grasped the essence of what had actually happened in 1832. The enlargement of the electorate had by itself a limited effect. The House of Commons was still securely in the hands of men of property. The way in which the Great Reform Bill was carried had more signifi-cance than the Bill itself. Public opinion had mobilised itself to influence the political class, and the political class had decided to listen. The stage was now set for a new kind of politics based on an increasingly coherent party system, on manifestos, party platforms and an ever widening range of appeals to public opinion.

Benjamin Disraeli was, at thirty, still rather young. He knew he intended to be Prime Minister, but was not sure yet whether he was a Radical or a Tory. He fought the 1835 election at Wycombe as an Independent.[*] Ten years later he coined in the same novel a phrase aimed at the heart of Peel's thinking: 'A sound Conservative government,' said Taper, musingly. 'I understand, Tory men and Whig measures.' There was truth in the gibe. The most perceptive political novelist of the century, Anthony Trollope, carried the critique into a metaphor of gods and giants.[27] The gods were the Whigs, dwelling on high, the natural possessors of power and organis-ers of change; the giants were the Conservatives, who occasionally fought their way up to Olympus. The Tory giants dislodged the Whig gods for a time, but then found they were compelled to act much as the gods had done, to the disgust of their faithful diehard followers down below.

Peel's concept of a moderate conservatism has usually prevailed, appealing to the sensible centre, resisting violent change but also restrain-ing the romantic or brutal instincts of its keenest supporters. Disraeli when he at last reached the top of the greasy pole tested a different model but found himself, despite his earlier dreams, leading a rather dull, sensible, middle-class free trade Conservative Party.

---

[*] Because he was fighting against Whig candidates his patron, Lord Lyndhurst, persuaded the Tory managers to contribute £500 to Disraeli's election expenses. He later claimed to have stood at Peel's instigation, but there is no supporting evidence for this.

This Conservative Party is forced to define itself afresh after each catastrophe. After the Great War, faced with the rise of the Labour Party, the Conservatives turned to Baldwin. Peel would have handled the General Strike of 1926 and its aftermath exactly as Baldwin did, insistent on public order, but in industrial matters conciliatory from a position of strength. After the Second World War and the electoral catastrophe of 1945 the Party kept Churchill as its leader but beneath the surface Rab Butler and the One Nation Conservatives revived the Party with the same instincts as Peel showed in his reconstruction after the defeat of 1832.

Margaret Thatcher was the most radical Conservative Prime Minister after Peel, given that Disraeli jettisoned his early radicalism and Joseph Chamberlain never got to the top. She was radical in both style and substance, Peel only in substance. Margaret Thatcher responded to the desperate needs of the time. Her medicine was necessary, and it worked. But she did not change the fundamental instincts of the Party.

In December 1834, thanks to the King, Peel was no longer in opposition, but had been thrust prematurely to the edge of power. Prematurely, because in the circumstances of the time it was impossible to conceive an election result which would give Peel a working majority. Many seats were uncontested; many local arrangements were still strong and impervious to national argument. Moreover, the force had by no means gone out of the general enthusiasm for reform and for the Whigs who had successfully ridden that wave. But Peel was determined to make the strongest possible effort.

The Tamworth Manifesto was part of that effort; so was an unprecedented exercise in Party organisation. The Carlton Club came into its own; the first constituency associations were formed. Neither was entirely new in the 1835 election, and neither was Peel's own handiwork. The Carlton Club had been founded in 1832 to replace an unsuccessful effort at Party co-ordination based at the Chief Whip's house in Charles Street. Peel had no hand in the Charles Street venture. He subscribed to the Carlton Club, but its rapid development as a centre of Party communication was organised by lesser colleagues, including the Duke's man Arbuthnot and a remarkable newcomer, Francis Bonham, who was fighting to enter Parliament after losing his seat in 1831.[28] Bonham was content to remain in the shadows throughout his career, and it is difficult to construct his character let alone his views. But already he acted as Peel's right hand in all matters of Party management and organisation. There was no official list of Government candidates; but Bonham sat quietly at the Carlton Club seeing people, writing letters, collecting and disbursing money, always keeping Peel informed. One of Peel's early actions in December 1834 was to tie Bonham into his new Government: 'I never could have accepted office without seeking your aid and offering you some appointment or other which might give me the frequent opportunity of communicating with you.' He made Bonham Storekeeper to the Ordnance with a salary of £1,200 a year.[29]

The last weeks of 1834 and the early part of 1835 saw the quite separate growth of Conservative organisation in the constituencies. Over the next few years several hundred Conservative Associations were formed. They were not organised from the centre, either by Peel or by Bonham at the Carlton Club. They did not choose candidates, though they could arrange negotiations between individuals and local interests. They acted as a buttress rather than a replacement for traditional methods of organising an election. The Associations certainly expected no say in Party policy. They responded to the technical needs created by the Reform Bill. In order to cast his vote an elector now had to register in advance. An Association could encourage and organise the registration of likely Conservative voters. As elections involved and interested more people, arguments about the purity of elections became more common. Deals behind closed doors were not so easy. The Reform Bill did not do away with fraud or corruption at election time — far from it. But such illegal practices were now more likely to be challenged — both at the stage of registration and at the election itself, when a petition was often lodged to displace the successful candidate. These challenges needed money, and they needed lawyers; the new local Associations set themselves to produce both. Thus in *Coningsby* Disraeli portrayed 'a Conservative Association with a banker for its chairman and a brewer for its vice-chairman, and four lawyers knibbing their pens and assuring their neighbours that Property will tell in the long run'.[30]

The Conservative Party (and indeed its rivals) changed shape more slowly than the new situation required. It is much easier to see this with hindsight. We know now that the power of the Crown to choose a Prime Minister had ebbed rapidly, and would not return; but this was not clear in the weeks after William IV dismissed Melbourne. We know now that the Crown's authority would pass during the nineteenth century to a House of Commons chosen on political grounds by a steadily increasing electorate; this too was far from certain in the 1830s.

Peel, so clear-minded on many subjects, remained confused on one implication of this change. He gauged brilliantly the appeal which the new Conservative Party should make to the new electorate. He helped, though he did not originate, these changes in the Party organisation at the centre and in the constituencies. But he did not fully understand that the changes would also require a new relationship between a Conservative Prime Minister and his followers in the Commons. If the Prime Minister was now to be more than the King's Minister, so his supporters were to be more than the Ministry's obedient friends.[31] Peel welcomed, indeed relished, the first change, which was to give the Prime Minister great power, but never came to terms with the second change, which made that power dependent on his parliamentary supporters.

At the start of 1835 Peel, in high spirits, did not allow the premiership or the election to crowd out the pleasures of life. On one weekend in January he went to bed in London at two on the Friday morning, rose at four, and travelled to Drayton for a ball with the two Julias that evening. Next day he shot eleven wild ducks and twelve pheasants, and then wrote to Croker criticising Stanley's indecisiveness.[32] The election results began to arrive. Peel and the Conservatives had hoped for a score of 315 Government supporters in a House of 658 Members – not a working majority, but enough for a sporting chance, given the divisions in the opposition. By the end of January the final result showed 290 Conservatives, with 218 Whigs and Stanleyites and 150 Radicals. This was disappointing, but by no means disastrous. The Conservatives had nearly doubled their numbers; in the English counties with their large electorates they had gained twenty-nine seats and lost none. The odds were against the Government's survival for more than a month or two; but they might manage it provided that they could keep the opposition divided by attracting some moderate votes.

Peel had already decided his priority for Government. He was determined to tackle the Church of England. To many, perhaps the majority, of his supporters this was the most important of the institutions which the Party existed to protect. It was bold to choose the Church of England to test the central philosophy of the Tamworth Manifesto, that the best way to conserve was to reform. But Peel was already deep in the subject. He knew that reform was needed. He knew that if he did not undertake it, others would. As he wrote to Herries on 11 January: 'I feel that I can do more than any other man who means his reforms to work practically and who respects and wishes to preserve the British Constitution.'[33]

There were two parts to this enterprise – the dominance which the Church of England still claimed over English social life and the structure of the Church itself. On the first point, Peel had already taken the lead in allowing Catholics into the House of Commons, and in removing the requirement on Dissenters to receive the Anglican Sacrament before taking public office. The controversy of the moment was about the marriage of Dissenters. Was a Christian marriage only acceptable if conducted with the rites of the Church of England? In a complicated uncertain way Lord John Russell had already been nibbling at the subject during the Whig Government. Peel gripped it firmly. His conclusion came in the form of a letter dated 7 January to Hobhouse in the Home Office. Gone from this document are the roundabout phrases and portentous justifications with which Peel filled out most of his public pronouncements. Here is a Prime Minister cutting to the heart of a subject and setting out concisely what he requires. These four brief paragraphs might be a model for all Prime Ministers:

> Retain the laws as to marriage, and the registration of marriage as they now stand without alteration for members of the Church of England.
>
> For all who do object, not being members of the Church, require a civil ceremony, superadded to any religious rite which the Dissenting party may choose to adopt.
>
> Encourage the religious rite, but do not make the performance of it essential to the validity of the marriage contract. Make the civil ceremony absolutely essential.
>
> Let the civil ceremony be of the simplest kind – an acknowledgement before a magistrate by each party in the presence of witnesses, according to a form supplied by authority.
>
> The difficulties in the way are difficulties of detail.[34]

So Peel wrote; so it happened; so until recently with minor changes it remained.

Peel approached the bigger question of the structure of the Church of England as a loyal Anglican. He worshipped regularly and generously supported the local church at Drayton Bassett. As we have seen, he had been in the habit of consulting his old tutor Dr Lloyd on theological questions. After Lloyd's death he jotted down similar questions in the little brown notebooks which he kept about him. We found one such jotting in the Surrey archive in Woking of his executor, Henry Goulburn. Peel scribbled: 'If mere secular knowledge leads to equally valid moral convictions, what is the use of revelation?'[35] No answer is recorded.

From his lectures and speeches it is clear that Peel believed strongly in an all-powerful Providence whose designs we must trace and follow as best we can. But he was not interested in the arguments and divisions of churchmen, believing that the divisions were a scandal, and the arguments often pointless. This trait came as a disappointment to those of his friends who took a vigorous part in Church controversies. Lord Ashley (later Lord Shaftesbury) described Peel in his diary: 'He has abundance of human honesty and not much of Divine faith; he will never do a dishonourable thing; he will be ashamed of doing a religious one.'

Gladstone, sensitive about his own first book on Church and State, saw that Peel was puzzled and bored by it. 'Sir Robert Peel', said Gladstone, 'who was a religious man was wholly anti-church and unclerical, and largely undogmatic – quite incapable of comprehending the movement in the church, the strength it would reach, and the exigencies it would entail.'[36]

Gladstone went on to describe Peel as languishing 'under the Erastian yoke', by which he meant the subordination of the Church to the authority of the State. There was a parting of the ways among those who agreed that the Church of England was in poor shape. Newman, Keble and indeed Gladstone looked for a revival of the spirit, for enthusiastic doctrines reaffirming the authority of the Church over the State, as a kindly light amid the encircling gloom. Peel approached the Church as a public institution founded and guided by God, but in drastic need of change by men. It was in this brisk spirit that in January 1835 he set about the task of loyal reform.

The Church of England was deeply unpopular. Its leaders were identified as determined opponents of reform. Twenty-one bishops had voted against the Reform Bill, only two in favour. The senior clergy tried not to be conspicuous. Mr Johnson, supplier of clerical hats to the clergy, was selling them off at thirty shillings a dozen. It was quite widely supposed that disestablishment of the Church was inevitable. Lord Grey when Prime Minister had already set up a Commission of Enquiry.

Peel acted decisively and with speed to head this off. He identified two reforming bishops, Howley, Archbishop of Canterbury, and Blomfield, Bishop of London. On 4 January 1835 he wrote to them proposing an Ecclesiastical Commission. On 9 February the Commission held its first meeting in Peel's house in Whitehall Gardens. Peel had by then included Members of all shades of opinion including the deep-dyed Tories Lyndhurst and Goulburn. Peel's impetus carried them all with him. He attended every full meeting himself. The Bishop of London was his main ally; Owen Chadwick described Blomfield as the clerical Peel, 'Though Peel was more capable and less amusing, they resembled each other in practical energy and remoteness from the common man.'[37] The same historian described the Commission as, like Peel, 'bureaucratic, capable, and cold'.*

But remote or not it saved the Church of England from disestablishment and spoliation. As with the police, the criminal justice system and prisons Peel started a reforming process in the Church of England which was later extended and developed by his Whig successors. The essential problem was money. Not, as now, because the Church of England had too little but because it had too much, conspicuously deployed in the wrong places. Cathedral closes and sinecures, fat livings, uncared-for slums, rich bishops and impoverished curates were equivalent in this field to the rotten boroughs and unrepresented cities before the Reform Bill.

The new Ecclesiastical Commission did not simply investigate and report. It obtained the power to direct revenue from bad to good purposes. It reorganised the boundaries of bishoprics, shifted money to new cities, and began to reduce the differences between stipends. None of this was on a heroic scale. The revenues diverted amounted to only £360,000 a year. On particular issues Peel favoured a conservative route to reform.

---

* Disraeli in *Tancred* sketched Blomfield as possessing 'great talent for acting together with very limited powers of thought. All his quandaries terminated in the same catastrophe, a compromise.' But this was also Disraeli's verdict on Peel.

For example it was argued that there were too many canons of Westminster Abbey with not enough to do. Peel's Ecclesiastical Commission preserved the number, but provided one of them with the task of running the nearby parish of St Margaret's, which then possessed a sizeable working population as well as the heavy burden of tending the souls of Members of Parliament. The specific changes might be modest, but they had the effect of galvanising other decision-takers, in the Church itself and elsewhere.

This was a long-drawn process. In the first of his Barchester novels Trollope lovingly describes a sinecure in that city and the struggle which developed round it. But *The Warden* was published in 1855, twenty years after Peel's Commission began work. The battles dragged on diocese by diocese, year by year. The hottest opponents of the Ecclesiastical Commission came not from the Church's enemies but its friends. The ever active Croker became one channel for the discontented. He had already written Peel a letter of twenty-four pages criticising the Government's commonsense solution on Dissenters' marriages. Now he reported a complaint of 'some of our Tories' against the work of the Ecclesiastical Commission. Peel was never more vehement than when rebutting attacks from the Ultras, who persisted, as he saw it, in fouling their own nest. 'It is a very harmless occupation', he replied, 'for some of our Tories to keep themselves in wind by attacking windmills of their own creation. Who ever dreamed of "equalisation of livings"? I am sure I never did.' Then he turned to the serious argument. The critics argued that the Church had to provide adequate men of birth and learning to enter its ranks. Well and good; but if that became the main objective, 'you have left hundreds of thousands to become Dissenters, or more likely infidels, because you would not divert one farthing of ecclesiastical revenue from this deanery or that great sinecure'. The pretended friends of the Church would provoke disestablishment if they were not careful. Peel ended his riposte with an example. 'Is this right, that in a parish of 10,000 acres overrun with Dissent, the whole tithes go to an ecclesiastical corporation to the amount of £2,000 a year; that there is only one service in the church, and cannot be two because the said corporation will only allow £24 a year as a stipend to the vicar?'

Sadly the 'ecclesiastical corporation' referred to here was Trinity College, Cambridge. Henry VIII gave to Trinity in 1546 the rectory of

Monks Kirby in Warwickshire, having dissolved the Carthusian priory which was the previous owner. Monks Kirby was indeed sizeable, containing eleven hamlets. The College Archivist courteously confirms that Peel was right about the vicar's annual stipend of £24. He cannot, however, trace annual income to the College of more than £615 during the years around 1835. Even if Peel was given an inflated figure for income, the gap remains formidable. Action was considered by the College, but deferred, the Fellows evidently judging that the needs of the College must prevail over those of Monks Kirby.[38] I am not sure whether Trinity was then, as now, the richest college in Cambridge.

Peel was obviously warming to this work, but the political scene began to shift against him. Peel could still hope for help in Commons votes from the group of moderates in the centre even if Stanley and Graham would not join the Government. Moreover the opposition was divided; the Whigs and the Irish had little in common. But both these favourable hopes began to evaporate. Stanley's group dwindled to a handful, justifying O'Connell's earlier gibe that they could fit into the nineteenth-century equivalent of a taxi, 'the Derby Dilly with his six insides'. More ominously, Lord John Russell and O'Connell, two very different men, came together in a compact agreed at Lichfield House. They agreed to work with each other against Peel's Government. This Lichfield House compact delivered a setback for the Conservatives over the Speakership of the Commons at the start of the session and forced a steady run of defeats in later votes.

The Government for its part made mistakes. The Duke for example thought it clever as Foreign Secretary to get rid of the tiresome Ultra Lord Londonderry by appointing him Ambassador in St Petersburg. Londonderry had not grasped that an Ambassador is supposed to express the views of his government on foreign policy. Believing that the Russians were entitled to attack Turkey and slaughter rebellious Poles, he said so. The Whigs made a row. Greville wrote in his diary, 'Peel spoke clearly as usual, but fighting under difficulties and dodging about and shifting his ground with every mark of weakness. The result is that Londonderry cannot go and must either resign or his appointment be cancelled.'[39] Londonderry stepped down; the Government staggered on.

Conservative backbenchers were not good at turning up for votes. Peel's room for manoeuvre became more and more restricted. The majority against him in the Commons became daily more compact. Peel began to look for the right ground on which to resign. In early March the Duke and most of the Cabinet were ready to soldier on. So too was the King. They called in aid the memory of the young Pitt, who with the old King's support had battled his way through 1784 against many defeats in the Commons, until the skies cleared and he became Prime Minister with one interruption for more than twenty years. But 1835 was not 1784. The Whigs were more popular in the country than Pitt's opponents Fox and Lord North had ever been. More important, William IV had none of his father's influence over Members of Parliament. Indeed the whole balance of power in the Constitution had changed since the Reform Bill. The losers had been the King and the House of Lords; the gainers were the Commons, and to a lesser extent the new electorate which had begun, still partially and imperfectly, to influence through the Commons the whole course of politics.

At the end of March the Commons returned to the weary issues of the Irish Church. Peel spoke often, and on the whole well; but the defeats multiplied. On 7 April the Government was beaten by twenty-seven votes on Irish tithes. The Cabinet had agreed that if this happened they would give up; they resigned next day. There was no possibility of a coalition, and no point in asking the King to dissolve Parliament and hold an election only four months after the last one. So the King had to swallow his pride and send for Melbourne. Peel returned to opposition and his long-term strategy.[40] Peel's first premiership was over after one hundred days.

A final flourish showed how his interests spread beyond the range of most politicians. In leaving office he wanted to recognise literary and scientific merit. The poet Robert Southey was given a pension and William Wordsworth encouraged to ask for a position for his son. Peel told the Professor of Astronomy at Cambridge that he had heard that his salary was painfully low: his wife, Mrs Airy, received a pension from the Civil List. The poetess Mrs Hemans was ill and in poverty: Peel sent her £100 and offered her son of seventeen 'a clerkship in a respectable public department'. He rediscovered James Hogg, the Ettrick Shepherd, whose literary worth had been originally revealed by Sir Walter Scott. Peel wrote on 31 March 1835 that he heard that 'you have not turned your intellectual labours to any great account in a pecuniary point of view'. This was putting it mildly, and the Ettrick Shepherd leapt at the offer. 'Greatly was

I astonished when I received yours with the liberal enclosure,' he wrote from Altriven Lake by Falkirk, 'wondering how it should have come into your head to think of the old shepherd in the wilderness ... As for my refusing his Majesty's bounty, you need not have had any scruples about that, for I have a particular facility in accepting of money ... common-sense seems to have been withheld from me, for I am always poor but almost always happy.'[41]

The Conservatives were gloomy at losing office. The Ultras by now distrusted Peel, and there was even some talk of soldiering on with the Duke, as if the House of Commons did not exist. But even the Ultras would rather have a Conservative Government with Peel at the top than find the country launched again into uncharted seas of reform steered by Lord John Russell and O'Connell. The Duke of Newcastle felt particularly strongly. This was the Duke who had, in relation to rotten boroughs, asked if he might not do what he would with his own, who had stirred up the East Retford question by asserting such a right, and whose castle at Nottingham had in 1831 been burned by the mob. On 29 March he wrote excitedly to Peel: 'I am not a reformer at all. My satisfaction in seeing you at the head of affairs is not pure and unmixed. It is because in my view of the case, concession leads to revolution that I would, directly or indirectly, concede nothing.' But Peel must stick at it, argued this Duke and stay in office. 'The salvation of every interest of the country depends on it ... should this be your determination, call for the sacrifice of life itself and you shall have it from me. Require that I shall share the scaffold with you – if it should even come to that, and depend upon it I will adhere to the condition without flinching.'[42]

Neither Peel nor the Duke of Newcastle was required to go to the scaffold. Newcastle survived to be a nuisance on another occasion. Lord Melbourne resumed his unrevolutionary premiership – but with a difference. Whatever the views of the Ultras, the reputation of Peel in the country as a whole had enormously increased as a result of the Hundred Days. He had become a national figure, different from the 'Orange Peel' of the 1820s and also from the partisan uncertain figure who had opposed the Reform Bill. The verdict of diarists and letter-writers at this time was overwhelming. The Grosvenors were Whigs but Lady Elizabeth wrote to her mother in April, '[a]s to Sir Robert Peel he deserves all possible gratitude at what he has done, and I heartily wish he will still be pressed to do so still more with fairer opportunities. He is the only person in whom one can feel real confidence, and with whom one feels that honour and talents go together and that he is unshackled, unprejudiced and unguided by any party and set of people.'[43]

This was precisely the endorsement which Peel had aimed at when he launched the Tamworth Manifesto four months earlier. Now he had to multiply such endorsements until they gave him effective power.

Eleven

Constructive Opposition

'What was the grand charge against myself – that the King
had sent for the son of a cotton spinner to Rome in order
to make him Prime Minister of England'
Peel, at the Merchant Taylors' Hall, 1835

'He is such a cold odd man, she can't make out
what he means'
Queen Victoria writing to Lord Melbourne about Peel, May 1839

'The walls were panelled with mahogany, the ceilings with
oak ornamented with carved ribs and bosses; the galleries
were lit by coloured skylights set in coffered surrounds; the
door cases were crenulated, the floors covered with inlaid
parquet, and everywhere antique busts, candelabra and
potted palms'
Drayton Manor as described by the historian Mordaunt Crook

'[The aim of the Party was] the preservation and defence of
that combination of laws, of institutions, of usages, of
images, of habits and manners, which have contributed to
mould and form the character of Englishmen'
Peel, at the Merchant Taylors' Hall, 1838

Peel had held briefly the highest office in the land, but without the
political power to use it as he wanted. For many politicians in his
day (and in ours) office was all that mattered. There was much that
they could do without a majority in the Commons. The Prime Minister
and Foreign Secretary by virtue of their offices directed the foreign policy
of the country. The Prime Minister and his colleagues through the Royal
Prerogative controlled the Armed Forces of the Crown. The Prime
Minister needed no parliamentary majority to create bishops, deans and

lord-lieutenants of counties. Although the patronage of the Crown had
been reduced since its heyday in the eighteenth century, by 1835 what
remained was more under the control of the Prime Minister than of the
monarch acting alone. The Prime Minister decided who should be a
Knight of the Garter; the Prime Minister rewarded his followers with
official positions high and low; the Prime Minister bestowed pensions on
men and women of literature, the arts and science according to his whim.

As Trollope repeatedly shows in his political novels, the idea that these
activities were the essence of government lingered long into the nineteenth century, particularly among Tories. The Duke of Wellington never
believed that the test of a government's power was its ability to change the
law. For him legislating was a different process from governing the
country and it was governing the country that mattered. A government in
which the King had confidence, provided that it did not insist on controversial legislation, might carry on pretty well month after month, raising
money as best it could, picking support from different places on different
issues, exploiting the fact that party discipline was weak and individual
views strong in both Houses of Parliament.

But this would not do for Peel. He had enjoyed his hundred days as
Prime Minister. He knew that as a result he had gained greatly in public
prestige. But he also knew that this had come too soon. He would not
accept the premiership again without the power to make it effective. He
did not itch to legislate on every subject in the same way as, for example,
Lord John Russell. But he needed control over the Budget; and where
action was needed he needed the power to carry it through.

The experience of his Hundred Days confirmed to Peel the wisdom of
his Tamworth Manifesto. It was a sign of his new authority that the merchant bankers and traders of the City of London gave a massive dinner in
his honour at the Merchant Taylors' Hall a month after his resignation.
Peel spelt out the message again. It was now the House of Commons
which counted; it was now the middle class which had to be persuaded.
Peel always enjoyed illustrating an argument by reference to himself.
Dealing with recent events: 'What was the grand charge against myself –
that the King had sent for the son of a cotton spinner to Rome in order
to make him Prime Minister of England.' He exhorted his audience to 'do
all you can to reserve to other sons of other cotton spinners the same
opportunities'.[1] What did this mean in terms of parliamentary strategy?

The Conservative Party should avoid opposition for opposition's sake. They should resist the temptation to snatch at quick tactical success even if this could bring them another episode of office without power. In particular the Party should support the Whig Government when it acted sensibly and not side with the Radicals to embarrass it. It should try to improve rather than reject the reforms which the Government proposed. This was not in Peel's mind a languid policy, rather an active strategy of moderation.

It was certainly compatible with spending less time in the Commons than had been Peel's custom in the 1820s. This suited him. During these years Peel could be active and happy in his family and private life without sacrificing his political ambitions.

By definition, the Whig Government which had carried the Great Reform Bill was dedicated to reform. Its followers though not all its leaders knew that the impetus had to be maintained. This fact was regretted by Lord Melbourne when he took back office from Peel in the summer of 1835. The Prime Minister's appetite for change, never strong, had been sated. He had been a determined and energetic Home Secretary, and was clear that administration rather than legislation was the essence of government. But he was beset by restless colleagues such as Lord John Russell, supported by the growing weight of intellectual opinion outside Parliament. Such men saw the Great Reform Bill as having opened the door for further necessary change in Britain and in Ireland. They were not revolutionaries, most of them were not even Radicals; but they believed that the country was still full of absurdities and abuses. More change was needed before the country would feel at ease and its propertied classes safe. They should not hesitate to work with the Radicals and the Irish under O'Connell to bring about such change.

What would the Government choose for its next target? The most catastrophic predictions of the Tory Ultras were already looking absurd. True, the Whigs would not let go of the weary arguments about the Irish Church; they brought forward new proposals to deal with its tithes and other revenues. But the Irish Church was for many Tories a battered and barely defensible outwork of the institutions they existed to defend. The Church of England was a different matter, an inner fortress. Criticism of the Church of England had been blunted by the creation of Peel's Ecclesiastical Commission which the Whigs carried forward with enthusiasm – just as they carried forward his initiatives on prisons and the police. There was no Whig attack on the monarchy, the House of Lords, the Corn Laws, or the general ability of men like the Duke of Newcastle to do what they would with their own. In theory he and others had now lost their pocket boroughs, but even there the change was often more apparent than real.

The Government soon let it be known that the keystone of their programme was reform of local government. To Peel this was welcome news. It would have been strange to leave in the hands of ancient and often corrupt oligarchs the governance of boroughs now that their parliamentary representation had been rationalised and extended to £10 householders. A Commission of Enquiry on town and city government had been sitting since 1833. Peel himself was convinced of the need for reform. It was the kind of subject which he loved, for it needed the mastery of detail and clear exposition at which he excelled. The Government proposed a municipal electorate of all permanent rate-payers who would elect representatives for a three-year term. Peel welcomed the general thrust of this Municipal Corporations Bill, and set about drafting constructive amendments. They were voted down, but this did not greatly matter. He had shown how he intended to lead the opposition.

He had also helped forward his main tactical objective, which was to attract into his ranks Stanley and the small group of moderates who had left the Whig Government on the question of the Irish Church. Stanley was not an easy man for the son of the cotton spinner to catch. He and his colleagues had refused to join Peel in Government during the Hundred Days. Peel found James Graham, Member for Cumberland, more biddable. Prolonged consultation on the rights of freemen and on property qualifications for the local franchise offered fertile soil for a long and fruitful friendship between these two deeply serious men.

So far, so good. But whatever Peel might say in political speeches, the House of Commons was not the same as Parliament. There was another House. The Municipal Corporations Bill passed to the House of Lords. As usual the Duke of Wellington invited Conservative peers to confer at Apsley House. At first all seemed well; they agreed not to oppose the Bill's Second Reading. But this was the limit of their reasonableness. It became clear that if compelled to sit through August considering the Bill the Tory Lords were likely to enjoy smashing it up. Their reasons were

various. Some peers were genuinely attached to the old city and town corporations with their deep roots in history – just as they had been sad to
see the old London watchmen replaced by Peel's smart new policemen.
For others the corporations were a source of power and income. The
Duke of Newcastle was at it again. He never touched an argument
without pushing it to the extreme. A year before he had offered to go to
the scaffold with Peel if only Peel would hang on as Tory Prime Minister.
Now he demanded that Lord John Russell be sent to the Tower.[2]

Other peers were resolute, however, not so much for the old corporations as against the Government. They had little patience with Peel, his
strategy of moderation, or the Tamworth Manifesto. They wanted to
attack and defeat the Whig Government on every possible occasion. The
most extreme of these Ultra peers was the King's brother. The Duke of
Cumberland, though without any noticeable talent, used his royal position with such forceful brutality that Lord Grey once remarked that no
government could survive that had the Duke of Cumberland either as its
friend or its enemy. More intelligent, more devious and much more eloquent was Lord Lyndhurst, patron of the young Disraeli, and until
recently Lord Chancellor. Lyndhurst believed in office for the sake of
office, and had no time for Peel.

The Duke of Wellington, increasingly deaf and distinctly uninterested
in municipal government, proved unable to keep the Tory Lords in check.
He agreed with Peel's strategy when they discussed the subject, but in his
heart he disliked the Bill and worried about 'a little Republic in every
town'.[3] He suffered at close quarters the assaults of the Duke of
Cumberland. 'There is no person who feels more than I do the inconvenience of the Duke of Cumberland. I feel it every day and all day. Others
feel it only occasionally. But I can't see a remedy. His amusement is mischief, preparing for it, hearing parties talking about each other and
talking of it afterwards. But I never could discover that he felt any real
interest in any question or entertained any serious opinion.'[4] The young
Gladstone noticed at this time the technique which Wellington used when
others expressed their views. 'He receives remarks made to him very frequently with no more than "Ha", a convenient suspensive expression,
which acknowledges the arrival of the observation and no more.'[5]

The rebellious Tory peers nourished at the back of their minds the
notion that the King was on their side. William IV had lost the last

shreds of his old Whig sympathies. What he felt in private he said in public, often and at length. Peel was embarrassed when, at the dinner of Trinity House elders on 7 August, the King 'was by no means courteous towards his Ministers. He drank wine with me about ten times, and on the last occasion said I shall now drink to the health of Lady Peel and all those that are dear to you, whom you have left at home. He made a vast number of speeches, some very long.'[6]

But the smiles and toasts of a King by 1835 weighed little more than a bundle of feathers in the scales of power. Peel knew this from his own recent experience. The Tory peers had learned nothing; once more they were launching themselves blindly towards the edge of a cliff. Peel watched their indiscipline with cold anger. Lyndhurst's brilliant attacks in the Lords were slashing at the principle of municipal reform, not the details of the Bill. This was contrary to the policy which he had laid down and agreed with the Duke. Peel made clear to everyone that he would take no responsibility for their acts or the consequences. At a dinner party he clashed with the Duke of Cumberland, who talked violently of honour and conscience. The Tory peers began to carry amendments going well beyond what Peel had attempted in the Commons. 'I suppose the King and the Court will be in ecstasies with the division of last night, in my opinion with little reason. No good will come for what has happened.'[7]

Peel had had enough. He wrote to Julia at Drayton every day in that first week of August about his plan for escape. On 3 August he told his supporters in the Commons that he would leave London for Drayton at the end of the week, even though the Commons, like the Lords, was still in session. They were dismayed, saying this would lead to a general exodus. Peel said this did not matter. The Lords had the right to make what amendments they chose. There was no obligation on Conservatives in the Commons to take responsibility for the results and he certainly would not do so. He refused to change his mind. 'I defy all attempts to detain me after Friday night, and shall expire if I do not dine with my own Love on Saturday.'[8]

Peel spent the rest of August at Drayton, while Lord Lyndhurst hacked indiscriminately at the Municipal Corporations Bill. Peel shot with the Duke of Rutland near Bakewell, and kept himself fully informed. The crunch would come at the end of the month, when the mutilated Bill must come back to the Commons. The Lords had introduced some changes, for example preserving the position of aldermen for life to make up a quarter of each corporation, which went well beyond what Peel, let alone the Government, thought reasonable. Peel returned to London. No one knew what he would do. No one knew how the Government would react. There was of course in 1835 no mechanism by which the Commons could overrule the Lords. Would the Government resign and force yet another general election, this time directed against the House of Lords? That was Peel's worry and he acted to head off the destruction of his strategy and the long-term hopes of the Conservatives.

Luckily Lord John Russell reintroduced the Bill in the Commons in conciliatory vein, accepting some of the Lords' amendments, explaining why others should be rejected. Peel responded in a similar spirit. The two men never liked each other, and never worked warmly together. But on this occasion they behaved like adults clearing up after a stormy children's tea party. A compromise Bill was agreed in the Commons. Attention turned back to the Lords. Yet another meeting was held at Apsley House. As on the Reform Bill in 1832, the Ultras collapsed. Lyndhurst gracefully changed course and accepted the compromise which Peel and Lord John had worked out. The Municipal Corporations Bill became law, and Peel returned to Drayton. His authority had been re-established; his objective was unchanged; but he saw more clearly than before the fragility and occasional incoherence of the materials which he had to use.

Peel was cross with the Lords. He was also genuinely tired, and had been earnestly advised to rest by his doctor, Sir Henry Halford.[9] He always longed for the company of Julia and the children. But there was another reason why it was particularly attractive to spend time at Drayton that summer and autumn. His great new house was almost ready. He had been building it for four years, within a stone's throw of the plain seventeenth-century home which his father had bought. There was nothing plain about the new Drayton Manor or its gardens. By the summer of 1835 the trees had been planted under the supervision of Gilpin; the ornamental lake and bridge were in place. The old house came down in February 1835, and during his disgruntled stay that summer Peel camped in his steward's house while the stonework was pointed and the painting and papering completed.[10] He gave his first formal dinner party in the new Drayton Manor in December, though the heating was not working properly. It was not till the autumn of 1836 that most of his pictures were transferred from Whitehall Gardens to the new gallery at Drayton; but by then Julia and the children were firmly established in what was to prove a happy and successful home.

Successful for the Peels, but not in the eyes of architectural critics. Drayton Manor was built in the last years of William IV. Professor Gash describes it aptly as 'one of the first great examples of the disintegration of taste commonly associated with the reign of his successor Queen Victoria'.[11] During Victoria's reign the Gothic style reasserted itself, in churches and public buildings, the new Houses of Parliament designed by Barry being the most sensational example. But the Gothic style was never supreme; it never gained a monopoly of taste. Peel was as unlikely to build a purely Gothic house as Palmerston was later to choose a purely Gothic Foreign Office. Both men derived from a classical education a dislike of dogmatism in such matters. Clients of this type had been brought up with a wide range of tastes which they wished to display; architects like Smirke learned how to please them. Having borrowed examples from all over the world, they plumped the results down side by side without respect for harmony.

We have seen how Peel resisted Croker's case for battlements, but it is hard to name another architectural feature which did not find a place at Drayton. J. Mordaunt Crook gave a notable description of this magnificent jumble:

> dull cupolas and Dutch gables, a Gothic porte cochère, and a classical arcade, a 'Swiss lodge' and 'French' gates, and an Italian campanile ... The gardens included a gaslit conservatory copied from Frogmore, an Italian garden, an American pool, an avenue of monkey-puzzle trees and balustraded terraces festooned with winged cherubs and 209 marble urns. The interior was equally eclectic. Smirke's elaborate marble chimney-pieces were decorated with ogee arches, quatrefoil bands, miniature cupolas and battlements. [Croker must have rejoiced at this small concession.] The walls were panelled with mahogany, the ceilings with oak ornamented with carved ribs and bosses; the galleries were lit by coloured skylights set in coffered surrounds; the door cases were crenellated, the floors covered with inlaid parquet, and everywhere antique busts, candelabra and potted palms.[12]

Such profusion would have been thought incompatible with good taste in the eighteenth century – and our own. But to Peel, and to many Victorian home-builders after him, it signified not just wealth (though there was no harm in that) but also learning and an understanding of the rich variety of European and indeed Asian civilisations.

Above all the house was comfortable. Even its critics conceded that. Most of us take for granted a high degree of domestic comfort, and comment only if it is not provided. But for Peel's generation central heating, decent plumbing and upholstered furniture were the exception, to be warmly welcomed in the new Drayton Manor. Lord Talbot found there 'every convenience' as well as magnificence. Haydon the painter thought it 'splendidly comfortable, and a noble consequence of integrity and trade'. This praise was echoed at the highest level. After her visit in 1843 Queen Victoria told Lord Aberdeen that 'Drayton is certainly the most comfortable house I ever saw'.[13]

Despite its size, Drayton Manor was not isolated from its surroundings. It was not a palace which a town dweller had planted in Staffordshire to entertain his family and grand urban acquaintances. Drayton became a much loved country home. Peel reared his own partridges and on a summer morning fed them with corn from the French windows of the breakfast room. He entertained the neighbourhood, presided over the local farmers' club and acted as steward of Lichfield races. When he was in London Julia sent down violets, strawberries and new potatoes from Drayton, and he constantly longed to be there. 'My heart is far away,' he wrote from Whitehall, 'basking with you in the bright sun on the terrace or dawdling about on your walks.'[14]

The glory and comfort of Drayton Manor have departed. His successors to the baronetcy needed only seventy-five years to run through all Peel's money. They found themselves compelled in the 1920s to pull the place down. In 1988 I went there as Home Secretary in autumn darkness to celebrate at a Peel Society dinner the bicentenary of his birth. It was not until I began preparing this book in 2004 that I saw modern Drayton in daylight. It is an amazing sight. A far-sighted Midlands businessman bought the desolate site in 1949 and turned it into a highly successful theme park. George Bryan has owned Drayton longer than Peel. All that remains of the magnificence which Peel and Smirke devised are the estate office and the clock tower, from which the machinery has been removed for fear of vandals. A small plaque on the estate office wall recalls the past. George Bryan sends a cheque to help preserve Peel's parish church at Drayton Bassett. But he is too shrewd to ram history down the throats of his customers.

On the day I first visited, 7,000 Midlanders piled into Drayton Park. It has a zoo, a tram and traditional merry-go-rounds, but the insatiable demand is for modern rides and slides. To stay competitive Drayton Park has to import every year or two some new dramatic machine which carries its customers to soar above Sir Robert's trees, then plunge them squeaking and shuddering into Sir Robert's lake. On that visit I wandered past the Haunting Pirate Adventure, the Knight's Eatery, the Old Lighthouse Inn and the Buccaneer Burger Bar. Visitors still use the bridge built for the visit of Victoria and Albert in 1843. What would the Queen, Albert and Peel have made of this bustle and commotion? But the son of the cotton spinner and the creator of the Great Exhibition of 1851 did not believe that the world would stand still after they had gone. After overcoming his initial shock, Peel might even have welcomed the proof around him that spectacular prosperity had reached so many people of all classes.

By 1836 Peel had built two large houses. All his life he lived and spent as a rich man. Old Sir Robert had settled large sums on all his children during his lifetime. Peel had received £230,000 in this way, and a further £100,000 when he married. When the old Baronet died, Peel's share of his father's remaining wealth amounted to £154,000. So when he built Drayton Manor his invested wealth was around £500,000, in modern terms about £22 million. On top of that he owned about 9,000 acres in Warwickshire and Staffordshire with a rent roll of about £25,000. His total annual income after 1830 touched £40,000, that is around £1.75 million of our money.

There had been a time of some anxiety between his marriage in 1820 and his father's death in 1830, when he bought pictures, built Whitehall Gardens and outspent his income. His salary as Home Secretary had been £6,000 a year, roughly £250,000 today. He never ceased to entertain lavishly and to give generously, particularly to local causes in Staffordshire after 1830. His investments were worth rather less at his death than when he inherited the baronetcy, but part of this money had gone into buying more land to round off the boundaries of his estate. Without being a spendthrift Peel thoroughly enjoyed spending. He found this a welcome recreation from his main work. In 1832 for example he paid £2,363 for a diamond necklace and earrings for Julia, with an emerald and diamond clasp.[15] He expended a lot of time and energy on these shopping activities and always discouraged Julia from worrying about money.

Back at Westminster the session of 1836 passed quietly. After the commotion between Lords and Commons over municipal reform, some repair work was needed within the Conservative Party. Once again the followers nearest to Peel and to Wellington busied themselves with the relationship between the two Conservative leaders. Arbuthnot wrote to Hardinge that the Whig Government was relying for survival on the supposed want of cordiality between them. Hardinge showed the letter to Peel. Once again the wheels turned. The two men, who never seriously disagreed but did not naturally seek each other's company, were brought to realise that this was not good enough. Peel invited the Duke to Drayton, the Duke accepted, brought his red coat for a day's hunting at the age of sixty-six, and took part there in a cordial conference with other leading Conservatives. Neither Peel nor the Duke wanted to harass the Government to the point where they could credibly resign and force a general election. Peel was reluctant to move amendments to the King's Speech in the Commons just in order to keep up the spirits of Conservative MPs. He declined to 'look on a party as a pack of hounds which must have blood ... I do not disregard altogether their views; but in these times the points on which amendments as indication of principle must turn, are too important to be treated ... like wild foxes.'[16]

The Melbourne Government was slowly running out of steam. It tried to reform Irish municipal corporations and to deal at last with Irish tithes. Both measures were blocked in the Lords, but neither provided the Whigs with a rousing battle cry for the electorate. In the Commons Peel and Stanley edged cautiously towards each other.

Peel did not spend that August and September at Drayton. Instead he rented Norris Castle on the Isle of Wight, and wrote happily to Goulburn 'from a circular room with windows embracing the whole sea view from the Needles to Spithead, with trees in perfect foliage down to the water's edge and, as it happens today, a hundred boats pursuing four yachts which are sailing for the King's Cup all close under the castle'.[17] At this time Peel read many French histories and memoirs of the Revolution. His spoken French was less accomplished. When he and Julia visited Paris that October they dined with the King and Queen of the French. The Queen, sitting next to Peel, was reduced to a device usually attributed to Englishmen faced with an ignorant foreigner. She talked very slowly and loudly in her own language, 'J'espère que vous – vous plais – ez – à – Pa – ris.'[18]

Politics at Westminster continued in the doldrums, but Peel realised increasingly that not all worthwhile political events occurred there. In the autumn of 1836 the students of Glasgow University nominated and elected him as their Lord Rector. Sir James Graham wrote at once urging him to accept. Graham knew Scottish politics well. Though still a Stanleyite, independent of both Whigs and Conservatives, he saw a strong opportunity for Peel to rally support in Scotland for his new kind of politics. Many Scots had welcomed the Reform Bill and traditionally regarded themselves as Whigs;[19] but now they looked for a bulwark against excessive further change.

Peel had enthused about Scotland ever since his holidays there as a young man. He was a friend of Sir Walter Scott. He admired the simple, hard-working piety which he supposed to be dominant in the Scottish character. At a more intellectual level he had absorbed the arguments of Adam Smith. He was in touch with Dr Chalmers, the vehement, complicated Scottish theologian who was later to help break up the Church of Scotland. In January 1837 his address at the ceremony of installation in Glasgow University gave him the chance to draw all these threads together. The address contained nothing original. At some length Peel praised the steam engine and the railroad for speeding the intercourse between men's minds.[20] * He set out his lofty yet conservative view of government as a 'great machine in the discharge of its proper function beating with a healthful and regular motion – animating industry, rewarding toil, correcting what is irregular, purifying what is stagnant or corrupt ... But let me tell you that in the social and material machine ... the movements cannot be regular until the foundations of the edifice are stable and secure, and the main springs and organs of action are free from perpetual disturbance.'[21] He drew attention to the examples of history, and endorsed the consoling power of religion. Peel had given much thought

---

* It may have been a recollection of this speech which led Disraeli in 1845 to tease Peel for his laborious style of argument – 'he traces the steam engine always back to the tea kettle'.

to this uplifting discourse, which was widely circulated. Lord Londonderry, who had somehow managed to get to Russia after all, reported that nothing else was talked of in St Petersburg; Tsar Nicholas himself was full of admiration. The novelist Maria Edgeworth admired the elegance of the language and the knowledge which the speech displayed, but more particularly 'the high and pure tone of moral principle and the freshness of mind' too rare among experienced politicians.[22]

Two days later a great banquet was held in Glasgow for Conservative supporters at twenty-five shillings a head. No building in the city was big enough for the purpose. A temporary hall of wood and tarpaulin was put up in twenty-six days. The tables were grouped round a set piece of solid rock, which symbolised the British Constitution, inscribed with the words, 'King, Lords, Commons'. Three thousand four hundred guests attended. Turtle soup and venison were served on the platform, cold meat, chicken and lobster in the body of the hall, and sandwiches and biscuits in the gallery. There was unlimited port and sherry for all.[23] Peel spoke for two hours. The balance of his message was unchanged. The Conservative Party was the enemy of corruption and abuse, but also of perpetual meddling with the institutions of the country. In particular he defended the rights of the House of Lords and the established Churches of Scotland and England. After him speech followed enthusiastic speech. The dinner began at five in the evening and continued until half past one in the morning, nineteen toasts having been drunk between ovations. Glasgow had never seen the like. Peel as ever impressed his audience with his mastery of facts, but outside Westminster a wider impression was taking root. He was becoming known as a man courteous to his opponents and honest in his dealings with all men.[24]

On 19 June 1837 King William IV died, full of aches and discomfort, having achieved his last wish and lived through the anniversary of Waterloo. In his tribute to William in the Commons, Peel said that it would be impossible to find a man 'who felt more pleasure in witnessing and promoting the happiness of others'.[25] This was generous but also true, spoken of a King about whom there was not much else to praise. Peel was among the Privy Counsellors who thronged Kensington Palace on 20 June to pay homage to Queen Victoria. She was eighteen, plain, with good eyes and a pleasant voice. No one knew anything about her. She had been brought up in seclusion by her ambitious, ever complaining mother the Duchess of Kent. The new Queen was different in every way from her uncles, who had dominated the royal scene since her grandfather George III finally lost his reason. For that difference the nation gave thanks; everything else was to play for.

As usual the immediate result of a monarch's death was the dissolution of Parliament and a general election. This was the last time the rule came into effect. Both the main parties had had time since the last election in early 1835 to improve their constituency organisation. As expected the Conservatives lost ground in Ireland, and there was not much change either in Scotland or in the English boroughs. The Whigs defeated the defector Graham in Cumberland, but the Conservatives won twenty-three other English county seats and in total elected 313 Members compared to a strength of 295 before the election, leaving the Whig Government with a majority of 32 instead of 58. The figures were not precise for there were still Members whose independence made them hard to allot to a party, though these uncertainties grew less at each election as the party systems strengthened.

Once again events had forced an election before Peel had completed the strengthening of his party. But the public began to feel that although Peel was in opposition it was he in practice who decided what the Government could and could not do. The phrase 'government through opposition' was used. The Whigs clung onto office because of support from O'Connell and the Irish; but they had lost their majority in England and Scotland and had no way of outflanking the Conservative control of the House of Lords. The flow of the tide towards the Conservatives was unmistakable; success could only be a matter of time.

Meanwhile Peel had to deal with a local difficulty of a kind which particularly troubled him. There had, unusually, been a contest at Tamworth, a borough with two parliamentary seats. Peel had been returned and for the second seat another Conservative defeated Captain Townshend, who fought as a Whig representing the interests of Tamworth Castle (as opposed to the Manor, i.e. Drayton). Townshend was a bad loser. He publicly accused Peel of breaking a promise not to use his influence to decide the outcome of the second seat. This touched Peel on the nerve, always raw, of his personal integrity. There was talk of a duel. Hardinge sorted the matter out, and secured an apology from Townshend, though not before Peel had sent to London for his pistols.

The new Parliament was not to meet until November 1837. Peel was troubled with sciatica. Friends suggested various remedies, including acupuncture, wearing leather drawers or taking the waters at Buxton in Derbyshire or in Germany.[26] There was a consensus in favour of rest, which Peel defied by shooting game at Bakewell:

> With the aid of a pony which Sir Richard Sutton lent me I killed thirteen and a half brace of grouse, got twice wet through in a deluge of rain, went to bed quite lame, and awoke more free from lameness than I have been the last three months. So puzzling are speculations about disorders and their remedies. I am certain Brodie would have pronounced me insane if he had seen me wet through, stumbling over great stones concealed by heather three or four feet high.[27]

Peel took his wife and their eldest daughter Julia on holiday to Germany. He was plagued by an approach from his old opponent the Duke of Cumberland. The Duke became King of Hanover under the strange working of the Salic Law, which prevented Victoria from succeeding her uncle William as Queen of Hanover as well as Queen of England. This noiseless separation of Hanover from the Hanoverian dynasty in England turned out to be a great blessing for both countries. But in the short run the new King was anxious about the constitution of Hanover and sought Peel's advice. Peel refused to enter into detail and blandly recommended prudence and moderation, qualities to which his correspondent had always been a stranger.

Peel kept a neat travel diary in a little brown notebook, jotting down days spent and places visited. As in Italy two years earlier the emphasis is on museums and galleries – and occasionally a meal. On 20 October he and his daughter dined at a restaurant in Würzburg:

> Served as different courses, with an interval of ten minutes between each:
>
> FIRST   Soup
> SECOND   1 Tench
>   1 Boiled salmon
>   3 Pickled anchovies
>   4 Potatoes au naturale

THIRD	1 Boiled Beef
	2 a curious preparation of horse radish in oil and vinegar
FOURTH	1 Beefsteak in oil or butter and
	2 Potatoes fried
FIFTH	1 Cotelette de mouton
	2 an omelette and
	3 cauliflower
SIXTH	a <u>Pike</u>
	2 fricandaise of veal and potatoes in a new form
SEVENTH	a plum pudding with two sauces of wine cinnamon etc.
EIGHTH	1 a leg of chevreuil
	2 a Woodcock
	3 a salad dressed

I am writing this at the table, putting down each course as it arrives, after an interval which nothing can curtail. What I have written is literally true without the slightest exaggeration – all this is for Julia my child and me, Lady Peel having had her tea and gone to bed – what may be coming I know not: we said half an hour since that we had quite done.

| NINTH | It is over – concluding with peas, 2 dishes of cakes and filberts |

Mem. Each course was really a separate one – one totally removed before the other made its appearance.[28]

That year Parliament returned to work before Christmas. The Queen's Speech in November 1837 contained no surprises. The Whig Government proposed no further sweeping reforms. They and Peel were locked in a political stalemate. The Conservatives had a majority in the Lords. The Lords could frustrate legislation, but could not overthrow the Government. But this stalemate could not last for ever. There were dynamic forces at work. One was the growing pressure on Peel and the Duke of Wellington to force the pace. Both Conservative leaders by temperament despised weak government. Up to this point that instinct had led them to prop up the Whigs when they came under pressure from the

Radicals. But after 1837 they reached a tipping point. From then on they had to consider whether the Government was so irredeemably weak that a strong effort should be made to overthrow it, even though this might mean another Conservative Government too weak to survive more than a few months.

The Conservative position in and outside the Commons grew steadily stronger. The long-drawn flirtation with Stanley and his small band of ex-Whigs finally succeeded. After losing his seat in Cumberland, Sir James Graham wrote a letter to Peel which marked the start of a remark-able political friendship – remarkable because of the humble basis which Graham proposed. 'I do not believe there now exists between us one shade of difference of opinion on public matters and my confidence in you is such, founded on personal regard and respect, that my inclination will be strong to prefer your judgement to my own.'[29] Graham found a new con-stituency at Dorchester. Through many troubled years he held to the self-effacing principle set out in this letter. When some 300 hundred Conservative Members of Parliament met at Peel's house in Whitehall Gardens on the morning of the Queen's Speech, Stanley and Graham attended. This was an open declaration; from that moment they acted as Conservatives.

The next crisis for the Government in 1838 came from overseas. Both Upper and Lower Canada were in revolt. The Government proposed to suspend the constitution of Lower Canada and send out Lord Durham to work out a new constitutional settlement. Peel and Wellington felt bound to support the Government in suppressing the unrest in Canada. But they distrusted Durham, and came under pressure to attack the Government for its laxity in allowing the crisis to develop so far. Peel and Lord John Russell manoeuvred against each other in the Commons like experienced professionals. Peel resisted the temptation to ally with the Radicals against the Government's colonial policy and the Government survived the crucial vote by twenty-nine votes. Soon afterwards the same two men reached a compromise on the ancient question of Irish tithes.[30]

Peel broadened his campaign outside the chamber of the Commons. Three hundred and fifteen Conservatives, almost all Members of Parliament, gathered once more on 12 May at the Merchant Taylors' Hall. Lord Chandos, a leading Ultra, took the chair; Julia and seventy ladies watched from the gallery. Peel spoke directly and with striking confidence. He set out why the Conservatives, now a great and powerful party, had to act patiently and responsibly, even when this meant rescuing the Government from its own supporters. But this was a unifying speech. The aim of the Party was 'the preservation and defence of that combination of laws, of institutions, of usages, of images, of habits and manners, which have contributed to mould and form the character of Englishmen'.[31] This was congenial stuff for his audience, and the applause echoed through the medieval hall.

These were high years for political dinners. For the two political parties they were an ideal means of building local support with the new middle-class electorate. Not everyone approved. In 1834 William IV's private secretary had written to the Prime Minister, 'His Majesty has not ceased to deprecate the practice ... of giving grand dinners, which are a sort of political assembly at which topics are introduced, which necessarily lead to crimination and recrimination when parties are split as at present.' But that was the whole point. Whatever the King might wish the split between parties was not temporary, but from now on a permanent and necessary part of the political system. Political dinners with their many speeches and toasts were a useful way of defining party differences. The local newspaper relished them, particularly in the autumn when Parliament was not sitting and political news was scarce. Julia Peel once complained at Tamworth that ladies were not invited, but ladies had no vote; their presence would have diluted the political as well as the alcoholic impact of the occasion.

Parties measured their political progress by the size of their dinners. Lord Londonderry wrote in high spirits to Peel after the Durham Conservative dinner in February 1838: 'Our cause is making great and really most unexpected progress in the North. We Conservatives have had a more glorious muster than ever was known of before.' In some places the organisers linked the dinners with the new process of registering to vote. Professor Kitson Clark put it vividly and with evident sympathy: 'The last months of 1836 ... resounded with the noise of Conservative dinners, with the clink of glasses, the clatter of knives and forks, the hubbub of dinner table conversation now and again to be hushed for fiery denunciation of O'Connell and the Ministry and praise of the peerage. Such sounds drummed the great party on to political victory.'[32]

In the market towns of England one toast at such dinners would certainly have been to the health of Agriculture, coupled in the minds of all present with the continuation of the Corn Laws. They would have noticed the foundation in 1838 of the Anti Corn Law League. Few would have spotted the cumbersome but all-important nuance with which their leader now defended protection. In a debate in the Commons in March 1839 Peel stated that 'unless the existence of the Corn Laws can be shown to be consistent not only with the prosperity of agriculture and the maintenance of the landlord's interest, but also with the protection and the maintenance of the general interests of the country, and especially with the improvement in the condition of the labouring class, the Corn Law is practically at an end'.[33]

Overseas events continued to vex the Government – after Canada, Jamaica. The local Assembly had quarrelled with the Governor. Slavery in the British colonies had been abolished in 1833, but the former slave-owners in the Assembly were reluctant to end the system of Negro apprenticeship which had been introduced as a transitional measure. The Government in London proposed to suspend the constitution and impose direct rule to protect the anti-slavery measures. The Conservatives thought this was precipitate; Peel argued for delay. The Government, exhausted and depressed, saw its majority sink unexpectedly to five. The Government could have survived this moment of weakness, as it had survived others. Ministers had after all not been actually defeated. This Jamaica issue was not one on which the Conservatives would be happy to fight an election in which they would have been accused of sympathising with the former slave-owners. But Lord Melbourne had had enough. On 7 May 1839 he resigned and advised the Queen to send for the Duke of Wellington. It seemed clear to everyone that for the Conservatives the long period of waiting was over.

Or almost everyone. But political actors and commentators alike had missed one character newly present on the stage, who now stepped into the limelight. It was known that the Queen's sympathies were with the Whigs. After the vote on Jamaica she wrote 'we had a majority of five' as if Queen and Government were the same thing.[34] Everyone knew that she was particularly close to her Prime Minister, Lord Melbourne. No one realised that this partisanship would carry her and the country into a constitutional crisis.

Much has been written of the intimate friendship between the Queen

and Melbourne. But reading at length the Queen's own journal in the
Royal Archives at Windsor is something again. Not that there is anything
improper in a sexual sense about what the nineteen-year-old wrote about
her sixty-year-old Prime Minister. To read the journal for these years is
like dipping a rod into a boundless ocean of affectionate triviality.

There seems to be no subject which the two did not explore in conversation. The tone does not vary – bantering affection on the part of the
instructor, unquestioning admiration from the pupil. I take at random a
tiny example which I have not seen mentioned elsewhere. On 5 April 1839
the Queen exchanged views with her Prime Minister on their respective
sleeping habits. 'I talked of my sleeping so long. Lord M. thought 9 hours
not too much. He said he was very sleepy of a morning and unwilling to
get up. Talked of my sleeping with my head so very low, almost as low if
not quite as my feet. "I have it a little higher", he said.'[35] And so on,
subject after subject, day after day. Lord Melbourne refreshed the discussion with anecdotes from the past, and always remembered to pat Islay,
the Queen's favourite dog. He taught the Queen while amusing her. She
had never talked to a man for any length of time before she came to the
throne. Sir John Conroy, her mother's lover and keeper of her Household,
was the only man prominent in her life, and she detested him. Free from
the constraints of Kensington Palace, Victoria fell at once under the spell
of the witty, highly experienced cynic who was her Prime Minister.

Melbourne's benevolence towards the human race was the more
impressive because of the hint of wild days behind him. He would not
have been human if he had not grasped at these happy, carefree hours,
sitting, riding, driving, talking and talking with the breathless girl who
happened to be Queen. He did not abuse her trust for Party purposes.
He always spoke respectfully of Peel, whom she did not know and hardly
ever met. 'For God's sake go and speak to the Queen,' he once whispered
to Peel as he stood awkwardly in a corner at a Buckingham Palace ball;
and to the Queen he said 'you must try to get over your dislike of Peel,
he's a close stiff man'.[36] But, though he was not excessively partisan,
Melbourne was a curious teacher for the Queen who was to give her name
to a deeply serious age. He was sceptical about the value of education:
'none of the Pagets can read or write and they get on well enough'. He
said he was afraid to go to church 'for fear of hearing something very
extraordinary'. It probably did the Queen good to spend time with an

educated sense of humour such as neither she nor any of her relatives possessed. Any chance that it might create cynicism in her own character was soon obliterated. She noted all Lord Melbourne's sayings as she noted everything, but then brushed any cynicism aside, assuring herself that her Prime Minister was 'truly excellent and moral, and has such a strong feeling against immorality and wickedness'.[37]

Victoria detested the idea of having to break this spell. A month before Melbourne resigned she described Peel as 'in my opinion a cold unfeeling disagreeable man. Lord M. says he didn't think he meant to be cross.' She did not see how she would get on with a Tory ministry, 'since her feelings' were 'completely opposed to them'.[38] Note the word 'feelings' rather than 'views' or 'opinions'. The young Queen had no fixed political views; she dealt almost entirely in personalities and emotions.

At this particular moment Victoria had another reason for fearing the Conservatives. One of her ladies-in-waiting, Lady Flora Hastings, unmarried at thirty-two, developed stomach pains and a noticeable swelling. The Queen and Melbourne joined in tittle-tattle about a possible pregnancy. The Queen's doctor, Sir James Clark, admitted that he had suspicions. Lady Flora was outraged, but agreed to a medical examination, which found her innocent. But the pains and swelling continued, as did the gossip. The Queen was reluctant to believe the result of the examination. Lady Flora died in July 1839. The post-mortem showed that she was a virgin and had suffered from a tumour of the liver. The Queen was hissed at Ascot.[39] The Hastings family, staunch Tories, were indignant at the behaviour of the Court, and at Melbourne's failure to check it. The press took up the story and at the time of the political crisis the Queen found herself suddenly unpopular. Victoria needed Melbourne, not just for gossip about their sleeping posture, but for support in her first personal drama as Queen.

As Melbourne advised when he resigned on 7 May she at once sent for Wellington who, as was expected, said that he was too old and deaf for the premiership. He advised her, as he had advised her uncle five years earlier, to send for Peel. The Queen stayed calm in front of others, but in private gave way to storms of weeping. 'The state of agony grief and despair into which this placed me may be easier imagined than described.' She went on to describe it nonetheless: 'All, all my happiness gone. That happy peaceful life destroyed — that dearest kind Lord Melbourne no more my Minister.'[40]

Peel was uniquely unsuited to deal with this situation. On 8 May he had a first stiff but civil meeting with the Queen at Buckingham Palace. She made no pretence of pleasure at having to ask him to form a Government. She hoped that there would be no dissolution of Parliament and that the Duke would be a member of the Government; she added that she wished to continue to see Lord Melbourne. Peel saw no difficulty in any of this; the Duke was indispensable, he would certainly give the present Parliament a trial, and there was no reason why she should not see Melbourne. He promised to submit the names of Ministers next day and added that he hoped the Queen would show confidence in her new Ministers by making some changes in her own Household.

The Queen scribbled away. 'He is such a cold odd man, she can't make out what he means', so 'dreadfully different' from Melbourne's 'frank open and natural' manner.[41] The Queen at once fastened her alarm and displeasure on Peel's remark about her own Household. Suddenly her ladies became all precious to her, a refuge in the hateful storm which was overwhelming her happiness. This hard man and the wicked Tories were bent on destroying that happiness. But Peel had a strong point. The Royal Household was quite a different creature from anything we know today. Melbourne, lax rather than mischievous, had allowed six of the twenty-five posts of ladies-in-waiting to pass into the hands of relatives of his own Whig colleagues. Two were sisters of Lord Morpeth, the Irish Secretary, one the wife of the Secretary at War, another the daughter of the Chancellor of the Exchequer and so on down the list.

The Queen argued that she never talked politics with her ladies, but that was not the point. The Household had an ostentatiously Whig flavour and it was reasonable to ask the Queen to make changes. Another point lurked in the background which Peel could never have even hinted to the Queen. The courtiers who were gossiping against the virtue of Lady Flora Hastings were hypocrites. Lord Conyngham, the Lord Chamberlain, and Lord Uxbridge, his successor, both installed mistresses in the Palace. The Queen was very young and still unmarried. Peel and those who advised him thought it important that she should have round her people of moral standing who would help keep the Court free from the scandals which had beset in turn all the sons of King George III.

Peel called again at Buckingham Palace on 9 May. He began to discuss the names of senior Ministers. 'Now, about the Ladies,' said Peel. The Queen cut him short. She would not give up any of her ladies. Peel asked if she meant to keep them all. 'All,' she replied. 'I never saw a man so frightened,' she wrote afterwards. Peel was not so much frightened as baffled. He asked her to reflect, to make some concessions; she refused; he left. Peel called up reinforcements. The Duke of Wellington came to reason with the Queen, but in vain. Peel told the Queen he would have to consult his colleagues. Both men were clear that they needed some change in the Household as a sign of confidence. If the Queen continued to be surrounded by Whig ladies, it would look as if she expected Peel's Government to fall quickly. Peel and Wellington together saw the Queen with this message, but once again failed.

Meanwhile the Queen was in excited correspondence with Lord Melbourne. He had already advised her to hold her ground on the ladies, but not to let the discussion with Peel fail on this issue. Once again he tried to explain Peel to the Queen. 'I've been brought up with Kings and Princes which gives me that ease ... now he has not that ease, and probably you were not at your ease.'[42] Now despite his advice negotiations had broken down on the sensitive point, and the Queen appealed to him for help. He and his Whig colleagues met and the Queen received a note from him at two o'clock in the morning of 10 May saying that they would stand by her. He drafted a message for the Queen to send to Peel which she immediately signed and sent off. In it she wrote that she had considered Peel's proposal to remove the ladies of her Bedchamber, but she could not consent to a course contrary to usage and repugnant to her feelings. Peel sent a considered reply that morning, recalling the whole series of events, and repeating that he felt it essential that there should be some changes in her Household.[43]

The triumphant Queen at once sent for Melbourne and asked him to continue as Prime Minister. Artlessly she showed him Peel's last letter. Melbourne started visibly at the phrase 'some changes'. He saw at once that his dealings with the Queen, and the chivalrous decision of the Whig Cabinet to stand by her, rested on a complete misunderstanding. The Queen had implied that Peel was asking her to change all twenty-five ladies of the Bedchamber. Now it was clear that he only wanted some changes, quite a different proposition. When Melbourne pointed this out the Queen swept him aside; she did not see the difference between some and all. She was impatient with this minor detail. A principle was at stake and she had successfully defended it – and restored Melbourne to his proper place as her Prime Minister.

On the following Sunday the anthem sung at the Chapel Royal in the Queen's presence had the title 'They of the household divided the spoil'; there was much tittering in the pews. But the Queen was wholly unrepentant.[44] She wrote repeatedly of her dislike of Peel, and his followers. 'The Tories do all in their power to make themselves odious to me.'[45] She swore that she would never send for Peel again.

It had been an astonishing performance of courage moving into effrontery. The nineteen-year-old Queen had single-handed defied both the victor of Waterloo and the effective master of the House of Commons. In her passionate anxiety she had given Melbourne and his colleagues an account of what was happening which was misleading on the crucial point. By this means she breathed life back into a dying Government. And all this because on personal grounds she could not bear to be parted from Melbourne. Victoria got away with it because she was new and young, and because Peel, the Duke and the Conservatives would never raise a cry against the Crown. The Conservatives, like the old Tories before them, were thoroughgoing monarchists. Sir James Graham wrote to Peel that he would never regret the stand he had taken: 'Though queens may frown and courtiers intrigue, yet if the monarchy is to be defended yours is the only hand which can combine and wield the weapons of defence.'[46] But if Victoria believed she had regained without damage her happy, carefree partnership with Melbourne she was mistaken. The political position continued to be as precarious as ever; the battle of the Bedchamber was not one she could win again.

The Government remained inactive in using the power which the Queen had restored to them. The Cabinet was divided. Lord Howick (Lord Grey's son and heir) accurately described what he called Melbourne's 'stationary system, which cannot bear adopting any new measures unless he is absolutely compelled to do so, and thinks it quite enough to deal with the difficulties which immediately press upon him without looking forward to those which are likely to arise thereafter'.[47] Howick resigned from this stationary vehicle soon after the Bedchamber crisis. The Radicals pressed hard to get the vehicle moving again. A divided Cabinet felt obliged to allow a free vote on the annual motion put forward by the Radical Member (and historian) Grote in favour of a secret ballot at elections; this was only defeated by Conservative votes.

Peel too had his difficulties, no easier to handle because they were by now familiar. Some of his party, for example the lively new Member for Maidstone, Benjamin Disraeli, wanted an all-out parliamentary attack on the Government. Peel was clear that these hotheads did not understand the nature of the party in which they belonged. It was not well designed for partisan warfare:

> When gentlemen complain, as they do now, that the division does not take place precisely at the hour which enables them to dine comfortably and be down by half past ten, they would soon get tired of a plan of operation which, to be successfully acted upon, must require incessant and general attendance. After you had deducted the idle, the shuffling, the diners-out, the country gentlemen with country occupations, and above all the moderate and quiet men disliking the principle of a factious Opposition, we should find the Conservative ranks pretty well thinned.[48]

This was a valid description, which he had given before; this time he left out his usual reference to fox-hunting. But beneath it lay a deeper division. The troops behind Peel were hungry for the fruits of office. By contrast Peel and the Duke were well-to-do men with full private lives. They already had the power to check the Government from doing mischief. They felt no great personal hunger to hold office again, and above all they disliked the idea of leading another weak Conservative government. For the moment they preferred power without responsibility to responsibility without power.

Not that Peel and the Duke were at ease together. Once again the stories went round that the two men never met. Once again Arbuthnot wrote to Peel's confidant, this time Graham rather than Hardinge. Once again the letter was shown to Peel. The disagreement this time was over the Government's Bill to unite Upper and Lower Canada as Lord Durham had recommended. Peel wanted to delay the measure, the Duke would have liked to vote it down. The Duke was older and deafer now. Though still active on the hunting field, he did not always catch what was said at Party meetings. But his hold over the Lords remained absolute, as did his loyalty. Once he grasped Peel's reasoning he organised the Lords accordingly, and himself abstained on the Canada Bill. Both men had to explain the facts all over again to their anxious disciples. It was true that they did not live in each other's pockets, their tastes and their country houses being far apart; but they trusted each other and they found that whenever they met they agreed.

One side of the relationship was pleasantly illustrated in 1840. Peel's second son William, aged fifteen, had joined the Navy and was serving as a midshipman in the *Princess Charlotte*. He wrote often and fondly to his parents, trying to work out from the known movement of ships when he might get the next letter from home, always asking about his brother and sisters. William's handwriting is easier to read than his father's, except when he writes up and down as well as across the paper, trying in the manner of the time to cram as much news as possible onto one sheet. At the age of sixteen he found himself off the coast of Syria, taking part in Palmerston's brief war against Mehemet Ali, who had seized that province of the Ottoman Empire. The note of schoolboy pride sounds through William's account of his first naval action:

> My dearest Papa and Mama,
>
> I hope you are well. I am. You will be glad to hear that the fortress of Acre is ours. It did not however become so without a good resistance, and I will now give you an account of it.[49]

Peel showed the letters to two naval captains of his acquaintance. With their encouragement he sent them to the Duke. He was immensely pleased with the Duke's reply. Wellington described William's letters as 'very interesting', encouraged him to go on writing accurate accounts of naval happenings, and said that he was 'most likely to direct and carry on great operations'.[50] On 18 October 1854 Captain Peel, serving in the Naval Brigade at the siege of Sevastopol, picked up a live 42-pound Russian shell with a burning fuse which had landed among several cases of powder in the English trench. Clasping the shell to his chest Captain Peel carried it to the parapet and threw it out. For this he was awarded one of the first Victoria Crosses. He died of smallpox in 1858 during the Indian Mutiny. His letters to his parents and his brother Frederick reveal a remarkable and sensitive man.

Wellington, like Winston Churchill, carried into post-war political life

a unique wartime reputation. Like Churchill, when peace came he deliberately put his reputation at the service of the Conservative Party. Like
Churchill, he continued his political career despite ill health beyond the
point at which that reputation began to suffer. Like Anthony Eden, Peel
waited many years as heir apparent. Like Eden, he combined occasional
impatience with a fundamental respect for the older man, which came
through in this episode of William's letters. The differences between the
two situations were nonetheless great. Authority passed gradually into
Peel's hands, because unlike Churchill Wellington had no remaining ambition and no political ideas which he was determined to pursue. Above all,
Peel enjoyed the good health which enabled him to make full use of the
power which finally passed into his hands.

Peel's children were now reaching the age when problems mingle with
the pride and pleasures of parenthood. Johnny was sent to Eton at the age
of thirteen in May 1840:

> My own dearest dearest Mamma,
>
> I hope you are quite well. I am quite well, but so very unhappy, that
> I wish you would come and see me. It is very short distance and it will
> be a nice drive. It only takes half an hour. We have had some rain. I
> hope dearest Papa got back quite safe, for I am so unhappy. Do come.
> Love to all.
> Your most affectionate son,
> John Peel.

Peel scribbled on this 'My dearest, you must write and comfort the little
fellow'. Julia did better. She went to Eton, took Johnny to dine at
Windsor and walked him up and down the Castle terrace. Johnny felt
better and his next letter was mainly a vivid account of the drowning of a
schoolmate. 'His face was quite pale with some foam over his mouth. It is
a very shocken [*sic*] story.' But he added, 'I am nearly quite happy ... I will
do as well as I can.'[51]

Peel had the task of looking after his daughter Julia (whose nickname
was Tooti) as she was launched into a London season. This meant escorting her to balls. He described to Julia 'her amusement – and my penance
– at the Duchess of Somerset's yesterday. I dare say she was pleased, but I
thought it insufferably dull, lasting from five to twelve as far as we were

concerned.' Julia had her mother's beauty and charm. She never lacked for
dancing partners and soon attracted the attention of Lord Villiers, son
and heir to the Earl of Jersey. The Jerseys were at the Duchess of
Somerset's ball, and Peel was not quite sure how to handle them. They
were a grand family; how would they react to a connection with the
granddaughter of a cotton spinner? 'I think our object should be to keep
on good terms just as usual, but to show, very decisively if it be necessary,
that we are thinking of no closer connection.'[52] But all went well. Lord
Villiers proposed and the two were married in the summer of 1841.

Another happy wedding at this time had a powerful effect on Peel's
future. Queen Victoria married Prince Albert of Saxe-Coburg in January
1840. The arrangements for the marriage deepened the gulf between the
Queen and the Conservatives. In particular the opposition, with the help
of the Radicals and some Whigs, cut the Civil List allowance for the
Prince from £50,000 to £30,000 by a majority of 104. The Queen recorded her fury. 'Sir Robert Peel spoke against it! It is too bad. I shall
never forgive him.'[53] Peel was quietly pleased. He believed wrongly that
the Queen herself had insisted on £50,000 against the advice of her
Ministers. 'The division will inform the Queen that she must not place
too much reliance on the forbearance of the Conservative Party ... There
was a wonderful degree of spontaneous uniformity of opinion in favour
of £30,000 among our party.'[54]

Opinions varied about the new Prince. 'Albert has been selected, I hear,'
Peel wrote to Ashley, 'as a young gentleman who will not busy himself in
politics or affairs of State, who will rather pursue hunting, shooting,
dancing and other amiable distractions. I am informed however by the
Duchess of Cambridge, who knows him well, that he is the reverse of
this, and entertains very stirring and ambitious views.' Peel had got it
right, but could not be sure yet whether the result would suit him.[55]

The Government sputtered on. They had their good days, winning a
vote of confidence by twenty-one votes. Melbourne had run out of
energy but his more ambitious colleagues looked for a scheme which
might rekindle the Party's enthusiasm for their leaders. The nation's
finances were in a bad way. The Whigs had run a deficit in 1838, and a
larger one in 1839 because of the unexpected expense of introducing the
Penny Post. They had to cope with a deficit of £2 million in 1840. The
Chancellor of the Exchequer, Francis Baring, increased taxes that year but

After changing his mind on
Catholic Emancipation Peel is still
in disgrace at Christ Church, 1829

Peel succeeds his father as Sir Robert in
1830 but is still remembered for ratting
on Catholic Emancipation

He brought her round: Peel reading to Queen Victoria

Peel with Victoria and Albert in Scotland, 1842 – but is he enjoying himself?

PUBLIC MEETING.

In consequence of the measures adopted for the support of the families of the Unemployed, at the Meeting on Tuesday last, of the Gentlemen, having the superintendence of the "Operative relief Fund." A General Meeting of the Inhabitants of Paisley, are requested THIS DAY, at 3 o'clock afternoon, in the Gaelic Chapel; when the result of that meeting, and the Hon. Mr. Peel's letter, respecting the plan; which he suggests to alleviate the distress existing among the Unemployed, will be laid before them,

By order of the Committee.

A Collection will be made at the doors, to defray necessary expences.

☞ Please send this Bill down the Street.

Paisley, 23rd April 1829.

G. Caldwell, Printer.

The other face of Scotland: distress in Paisley

The reformed House of Commons in 1833: Peel is seated on the front row (third to the right of the Speaker); Wellington is standing in the foreground on the right of the picture (facing to the right).

FRIENDS

Liverpool

Croker

Goulburn

Gladstone

Disraeli

O'Connell

Stanley

Bentinck

A ragbag of architectural styles. Peel's new house at Drayton Manor,
Staffordshire, with the grand gallery (below) for his portraits.

this was not enough. In 1841 Baring looked for rescue to a report on import duties, which suggested that by reducing them the Exchequer would actually gain revenue because more goods would come in. He proposed accordingly to reduce the duties on sugar and timber. At this point Lord John Russell took a hand. It was ten years since Lord John's great moment when he had stood up and astounded the Commons with the audacity of the Great Reform Bill. He was always looking for a new occasion of greatness. He now proposed to reduce the levy on wheat from the sliding scale of 1828 to a fixed duty of eight shillings a quarter. But the Whigs had left their burst of free trade radicalism too late. Melbourne was opposed to his colleague, and the Budget was clumsily handled. The proposals offended the domestic sugar and timber interests, and above all the farmers and landlords, without being credible to a wider public.

Nevertheless, Peel had to think carefully. It was certainly not for him, the former colleague of Huskisson and Robinson, to argue in principle against reducing import duties. But wheat was different. The Whigs were moving against the Corn Laws, which for many of his own supporters were as precious a British institution as the House of Lords and even the Church of England. He replied in only the most general terms to questions about his own financial policy. He argued that the Whigs in a mood of desperation were bringing forward haphazard proposals which had not been thought through. He mocked Baring: 'Can there be a more lamentable picture than that of a Chancellor of the Exchequer, seated on an empty chest, by the pool of bottomless deficiency, fishing for a budget? ... I won't bite; the right honourable gentleman will return with his pannier as empty as his chest.'

On 18 May 1841 the Government was badly beaten on the sugar duties after a discussion lasting eight days. At first it was assumed that they would resign at once, but Ministers had second thoughts. They pushed forward as if nothing had happened, and ran straight into a challenge of no confidence from Peel. The debate lasted from 27 May until 4 June, with an interruption for the Whitsun holidays. Peel renewed his attack. The result was unpredictable. Whigs who had voted against the Government on sugar would return to cast loyal votes against a motion of no confidence on the Government. The Whips on both sides exerted themselves with full force. The Whigs carried through the lobby Lord Hallyburton, the Member for Forfar, who was unconscious and said to be out of his mind. Every single Conservative either voted or was paired; for once the country gentlemen refuted what Peel had said about their dinners and lack of discipline. 'When the tellers forced their way through the crowd on the floor of the House towards the Speaker's chair, and the black hair and immense whiskers of Fremantle [Conservative Chief Whip] were seen to be on the right hand side, a great roar went up. The Conservatives shouted and stamped and clapped, and when the result was announced – for the resolution 312, against 311 – they shouted and stamped again.'[56]

One vote was enough. The Government was finished. The Queen was desperate. She wrote to Melbourne that she was sure he would do all he could 'to save the Queen from having to have recourse to those hated Tories'.[57] Melbourne himself was willing to soldier on, though in a mood of total pessimism. But his colleagues overwhelmingly argued that they must fight a general election – which the more eager such as Palmerston believed they could win. On the following Monday Lord John Russell announced the dissolution of Parliament. This would be the third election which Peel would fight as leader of his Conservative Party.

Twelve

Victory

'West Riding manufacturers the Pride of England', 'The
Altar, the Throne and the Cottage', 'If agriculture decays
trade will not flourish'
Conservative posters in Yorkshire, 1841

'Tis the first time that I remember in our history that the
people have chosen the first Minister for the Sovereign'
Croker to Peel, 1841

'I confess, to be unrecognised at this moment by you
appears to me to be overwhelming and I appeal to your own
heart ... to save me from an intolerable humiliation'
Disraeli begs Peel for a job, 1841

The supremacy of television has changed the nature of a British general election. The party campaigns have become centralised, noisy and dull. Everyone over eighteen has the vote but only about half of us bother to use it. In Peel's time elections were still overwhelmingly local. The general election of 1841 stands roughly halfway in style and spirit between its successors in the twenty-first century and its predecessors before the Great Reform Bill. The pace of change was quickening. By 1841 the parties were year by year increasing their grip on the constituencies. There were fewer independent or incalculable candidates. In the eighteenth century the persuasive power and patronage of the Crown had helped at elections to provide the King's First Minister with a coherent majority. By 1841 the Conservative and Whig parties, though still immature, were slowly replacing the Crown in that role.

The new Conservative constituency Associations did not at this time choose candidates, let alone decide policy. There was no Conservative

Central Office. Conservative candidates emerged from the traditional local influences, now helped occasionally by judicious suggestions from the central team at the Carlton Club under Bonham. The local Associations had two main tasks. They organised the annual registration of voters which was necessary under the 1832 Act, as it is today. As now, if you did not register you could not vote. Peel did not take a close personal interest in Party organisation, but on the importance of this process he was emphatic. In 1837 he had told his supporters at Tamworth that whereas some of their opponents said 'agitate, agitate, agitate', his advice to Conservatives was 'register, register, register'.[1]

The second task of the Associations was to help the candidate to canvass the electors. With the electorate still modest in size this was a highly personal business. In 1841 Sir James Graham was still nervous after his defeat last time in Cumberland. On 22 June he wrote to Bonham from the battlefield in Dorchester: 'I have canvassed for 6 hours, and have called on 180 voters; the number on the register is 342; my promises are 105 ... I think tomorrow I shall make myself safe, if there be faith in promises.' Next day he thought he had clinched it. 'I have amended matters since yesterday very decidedly. I have now called on every voter and have seen personally a large majority. I doubt whether there will be a contest.'[2] The last point is important. Less than half the constituencies were contested in 1841, but this was not a sign of apathy. Today parties aim to fight just about every seat. They are interested in the total number of votes cast in the nation; they do not want to allow their leading opponents a free run in their home constituency which gives them time to campaign elsewhere. By contrast in 1841 the parties were only interested in winnable seats; they put forward candidates only where they saw a good chance. If Graham had not bothered with his canvass a candidate might well have popped up against him late in the campaign. As it was he was returned unopposed.

The role of the party leader in the election is now central and compelling. For much of the modern media no one else counts; they treat the candidates as nonentities, even though it is for the local candidate that the elector actually votes. In 1841 such centralisation was impossible. Before the age of photography few people outside Tamworth and Westminster would have had any idea what Peel looked like, unless they saw a sketch in one of the new illustrated papers. They were more and more likely to have heard of him, and read summaries of his speeches. The tax on newspapers had been reduced in 1836, and they grew rapidly. By 1841 it would be normal for a sizeable town to have both a Conservative and a Whig newspaper. These newspapers could at once pass on to their readers accurate texts of parliamentary debates. The London papers now circulating through the country competed for the same readership. This was the way in which Peel could work for the attention of the British people and he used it to the full. There is something rather moving in the thought of the new fast trains, speeding north and west through the night, conveying to thousands of breakfast tables and reading rooms detailed accounts of what had been said and done in Parliament in the name of those who read them.

Despite the trains it did not occur to Peel as Party leader to campaign personally up and down the country. Election contests were still so local in character that he would have thought this notion odd and intrusive. It was natural to give a hand to neighbouring Conservative candidates, but that was all. He had no problem with his own seat in Tamworth, but as in 1837 there was a sharp contest for the second seat in that borough, and Peel campaigned hard. He reported to Goulburn, 'Having carried Tamworth, am now doing what I can in North Warwickshire for Dugdale, in South Staffordshire for Ingestre and Dyotte and in North Staffordshire for W. Baring.' This included entertaining a large party of county voters to an early breakfast before setting out on the election trail. 'We had today groans in abundance, our opponents having the advantage of a Lichfield mob. But I still think our prospects are pretty good.' This local campaign kept Peel out of the general gaze and after listing these efforts he found it necessary to write to Goulburn on 29 July from Drayton. 'I need say no more, in answer to your kind enquiries, to convince you that I am not dead, according to one report which I read in the newspapers, nor have undergone a severe operation for a lumbar abscess, as I read in another.' In most constituencies this degree of activity was still a novelty, but Peel justified it in the same letter to Goulburn. 'It is vain to ask tradesmen and farmers to go to the poll and leave their business, and tell them that important interests are at stake, unless gentlemen will themselves set the example and make some sacrifice of time and comfort.'[3]

Today the content of each party's campaign is ruthlessly and absurdly centralised. Infinite care is taken to make sure that the smallest candidate says nothing out of line, in case the media should create a general embarrassment out of his or her indiscretion. Hour by hour the candidates are bombarded from headquarters with briefs and texts designed to pen them into orthodoxy and reduce to the minimum the possibilities of original thought. Candidates still produce a manifesto, but are lucky if it has any individual content apart from a smiling picture of themselves and, if attractive, their family. By 1841 the concept of the constituency manifesto was taking hold, including definite pledges on policy, but these were still emphatically individual productions. They gave the candidate full scope for unorthodox pronouncements tailored to their own views and particular electorate. Indeed, since there was no national manifesto and of course no national broadcasts, the only definition of Conservative Party orthodoxy came in Peel's speeches. His cautious and oft-repeated pronouncements more or less dried up once Parliament was dissolved. The candidates were out on their own, enjoying city by city, county by county a festival of political debate amid considerable intellectual anarchy.[4] They picked those quotations from Peel which fitted their own opinions. This was particularly true in 1841 on the main election issue, which was the Whig Budget and its effects on the Corn Laws and sugar duties.

Yorkshire was a notable battlefield and can stand as an illustration of the whole. Of its thirty-seven seats, twenty-four were held by the Whigs. Each of the three Yorkshire Ridings was in electoral terms a separate county, with two Members each and relatively big electorates (11,716 in the North Riding, 7,180 in the East, 31,020 in the West). The rest were borough seats in all shapes and sizes, including the big port of Hull and new industrial cities such as Leeds and Bradford. The Conservative Associations calculated where the dominant Whigs were most vulnerable and as a result put forward just twenty-eight candidates. As challengers they were quicker than the Whigs in organising registration and in making use of tracts and newspapers to promote their arguments. They circulated Peel's speeches and repeated his phrases, for example his criticism (easily translated into a cartoon) of Baring, the Chancellor of the Exchequer, 'fishing for a budget'. But each candidate put what gloss he liked on Peel's utterances, and there was no one to bring all these interpretations into some sort of consistency. The Conservatives could be more flexible than the Whigs; the latter, being in government, had specific reforms and proposals which their candidates (more or less) had to defend.

The most conspicuous contest in Yorkshire was for the two West Riding seats, both held by the Whigs. One of these, Lord Morpeth, was in the Cabinet as Irish Secretary. He carried forward the recent Whig movement towards free trade, arguing for the total repeal of the Corn Laws. He defended the 1834 Poor Law and vigorously attacked the radical Chartists. The Whigs made a bad mistake in choosing their second candidate. The old-fashioned argument in favour of young Lord Milton was that he was the son and heir of the great local landowner Earl Fitzwilliam. This was an argument which Lord Milton himself used repeatedly. It had little effect, not least because he was rarely audible. Lord Milton had a poor, thin voice which was easily drowned by hecklers. The leading Conservative candidate, John Stuart Wortley, had fought the seat before and knew it backwards. On the economic question he offered a little bit to everyone. He spoke for tariff reduction, recalling the days of the Tory liberal Huskisson, but was moderate on the Corn Laws, supporting the Tory sliding scale of 1828. He opposed repeal and accused the Whigs of corruption and bribery. Contrary to Peel's policy he strongly attacked the inhumanity of the Poor Law. The Conservatives organised processions, for example of 4,000 supporters through Halifax, behind the music of the Yorkshire Hussar Band. They had clement weather for their canvass (always a good sign), whereas the rain poured down on Whig meetings. Their banners read: 'West Riding manufacturers the Pride of England', 'The Altar, the Throne and the Cottage', 'If agriculture decays trade will not flourish'.

Strong campaigns develop their own impetus which affects the atmosphere and the result. The Conservatives in the West Riding were on a whirl, the two Whig grandees in trouble. In other parts of Yorkshire the pattern was similar, though with wider eccentricities. While Conservative views on the Corn Laws varied widely each candidate claimed Peel's views as his own. Side issues flared up, then disappeared. The Conservatives in the Commons had criticised the Whig Budget for lowering sugar duties and thus favouring imports from West Indian plantations which until recently had been run by slaves. In York, an African Tory was found to walk up and down with a billboard bearing the slogan 'No Slave Labour Sugar'. In a confused way free trade versus protection continued as the main issue of the campaign; but the candidates were all over the place. An elector would have to listen carefully at the hustings or read his local paper thoroughly to discover where the candidates in his particular constituency stood on the issue. At Knaresborough the Conservative candidate, Ferrand Busfield, canvassed for four days and then decided to change his own campaign to the ancient cry 'No Popery'. He was triumphantly elected. Yet not far away in York his Conservative counterpart was praising Peel and Wellington as religious libertarians.

Some Conservatives had no compunction in allying themselves with the radical Chartists, thus contradicting at local level Peel's fundamental decision through the years of opposition that Conservatives should forswear opportunist tactics and back the Whig Government against every kind of radicalism. The working-class Chartists could not elect candidates of their own in the restricted middle-class electorate but they were useful in rallying crowds to harass Whig candidates like poor inarticulate Lord Milton. Yorkshiremen too poor to have the vote could thus take an exciting part in the campaign, and the general atmosphere was one of turbulent jollity.

The Yorkshire election was generally held to be less corrupt and more orderly than usual. This did not prevent each side from producing lurid accusations against the other. All voting of course took place in public on the hustings. In Bradford the Conservatives were said to have kidnapped a few Whig voters on polling day, while in York their procession to the polls was led by 'Tory lambs', energetic men armed with bludgeons to persuade any waverers to hold to their promises. The Conservative charge against the Whigs, particularly the landowning grandees, was of bribery and corruption. But there was something slightly routine and half-hearted about all the accusations.

In the end the unpopularity of the Government and the superior Conservative campaign did the trick in Yorkshire. Of the twenty-eight Conservative candidates in the county for the thirty-seven seats, twenty-one were successful. Nine seats were won from the Whigs and one lost. Seats were gained in industrial Leeds and Bradford. The Lords Morpeth and Milton were soundly beaten; for the first and only time in the nineteenth century the Conservative candidates won both West Riding seats with majorities of 1,000 and 700.

England as a whole went the same way. In the big urban constituencies the Conservatives made a net gain of nine seats despite the Whig initiative to modify the Corn Laws. In the English counties Conservative success was more emphatic, with a net gain of twenty-two seats. In Scotland Peel had become engulfed in the bad-tempered dispute which led to the defection of dissenting ministers from the Church of Scotland. The influence of the Kirk was exerted against him, and though the Conservatives held their ground, they could not match in Scotland their gain in England. In Ireland, where the 1832 Act had actually reduced the number of tenants who could vote, the Conservatives made eight gains. By the third week of July it was clear that overall they had a majority of between seventy-six and eighty in the United Kingdom – a working majority at last.[5]

For the first time in British history a government had been overturned, not by the King, not by a vote in Parliament, but by a vote of the British electorate. There was no doubt about the long-term significance of this change, nor about its main architect. This dramatic assertion of the new power of the electorate was achieved by the leader of the party dedicated to the preservation of ancient institutions.

'The elections are wonderful, and the curiosity is that all turns on the name of Sir Robert Peel,' wrote Croker to Peel on 20 July. ''Tis the first time that I remember in our history that the people have chosen the first Minister for the Sovereign ... every Conservative candidate professed himself in plain words to be Sir Robert Peel's man, and on that ground was elected.'[6] This verdict was broadly true. Peel's cautious strategy, stubbornly pursued over nine years through endless difficulties, had won its reward. He had confuted the Ultras who thought that Catholic Emancipation and the Great Reform Bill together spelled the ruin of everything the Tories had stood for. Equally wrong were the progressives who thought that in their modern world the party of Throne, Altar and Cottage was unelectable. From the ruins of 1832 Peel had gathered round him individuals of outstanding talent, and formed a new party stretching from dukes to small farmers and tradesmen. He had somehow kept that party together when the instruments of party discipline barely existed, and marched it to success on the centre ground where British elections are usually won.

But Croker's compliment to Peel was more limited than he perhaps supposed. The Conservatives now forming the majority in the Commons might well be 'Sir Robert Peel's men'; but as the Yorkshire story showed, they held very different ideas about what that meant. They used the name of Peel because he had established through the country a reputation for personal honesty and intelligence. But what Peel stood for and what as Prime Minister Peel was likely to do were questions to which 'Sir Robert Peel's men' had given very different answers on the hustings. Their own conviction and the promises they had made varied greatly, particularly on the central question of the economy. There had been no way of bringing these different views into the same room and reconciling them – and no immediate need to do so. Later some of these promises were remembered; but for the moment Peel saw no problem. He was their leader, he would soon be the Queen's Minister, and now they had been elected it was their duty to follow him. The country needed strong government. Peel, always overflowing with facts, figures and convincing argument, could never in his heart accept that it would be the duty of his Government to consult, let alone follow, the views of backbenchers who by definition knew less than he and his colleagues on any subject under discussion.

Perhaps we can take one last, almost nostalgic look back at the 1841 election. It is easy to stress the narrow electorate, the inconsistency of the argument, the noisy confusion of the hustings, and the strong grip which traditional influences still held on much of the reformed electorate. But these were genuine local contests which produced robust argument and definite results. Events showed that those elected were very conscious of the particular pledges which they had given. These men were elected as individuals to a Parliament composed of individuals. They carried a party badge, but thought of party discipline as secondary to local interests and their own views. In the last century and a half this local and individual character of a Member of Parliament has been largely squeezed out of elections. Those of us who care to do so wearily elect a homogenised House of Commons, voting for candidates who are trained and equipped to say the same things wherever they stand, as if Cornwall was the same as Carlisle, Wigan identical with Witney. The individual canvass is now usually a token affair, designed to produce a photograph or a local story. The excitement of the hustings has gone. The habit of holding village and ward meetings has in most places evaporated. Political colour has vanished from gardens and windows. We are now encouraged to vote inertly by post. These are the politics of obesity. We can sit at home without being required to visit a polling station, let alone trundle in a coach or on horseback across half a county to cast a public vote in front of a cheering or jeering crowd.

In the summer of 1841 Peel could look back with satisfaction on his years of tilling the political soil. Now at last there was a harvest. But a big element was missing. A gap had developed in Peel's perceptions of the country he wished to lead. During the 1830s he did not focus on crucial events which lay outside the narrow parliamentary politics which absorbed him.

For ten years after he became Home Secretary in 1822 Peel had been in close touch with the realities of daily life in England. True, as a wealthy man he looked down on that daily life from a great height, but he knew what was going on. For most of that time he had been Home Secretary, dealing with a flood of reports about disorder and distress in virtually every part of the Kingdom. He turned away from the traditional Tory fear that disorder was the result of conspiracy and a prelude to revolution. He saw that the breaking of looms and the burning of ricks were the result of genuine distress. This understanding did not lead him – a firm Tory – to condone public violence, but in the 1820s he began to take an interest in trade unions and the settlement of industrial disputes.

After 1832 Peel's attention had wandered away from the subject. The division in society and the poverty of the great majority were no longer day by day before his eyes – precisely when they were beginning to dominate the minds of intelligent and imaginative people outside politics. They called this the Condition of England question. Peel was preoccupied with great constitutional arguments, first Catholic Emancipation, then parliamentary reform, then the struggle to run a minority government during the Hundred Days, then the Tamworth Manifesto and the creation and handling of a new political party. None of these issues was insignificant; each required huge swathes of his personal time.

There was little in Peel's personal life to remind him of the Condition of England. During these years Peel established himself as squire of Drayton. He understood and dealt generously with local views and problems in Tamworth and in Staffordshire. But Tamworth was not Manchester or Liverpool; nor were the new problems of industrial Scotland best understood by addressing 3,000 enthusiastic businessmen in a Glasgow marquee. Others began to think through these problems, form views and found organisations to further those views. A mass of reports and articles resulted. To take one example, the German Friedrich Engels, friend and ally of Karl Marx, spent twenty months in and around Manchester, and concluded, '340,000 workers in Manchester and the surrounding districts nearly all live in inferior, damp and dirty cottages; the streets are generally in a disgraceful state of filth and disrepair. The layout of the dwellings reflects the greed of the builders for profits from the way in which ventilation is lacking. In such houses only inhuman, degraded and unhealthy creatures would feel at home.'[7] Peel did not lack sympathy for the poor. He told the French statesman Guizot in 1840, '[t]here is too much suffering and too much perplexity in the condition of the working classes: it is a disgrace as well as a danger to our civilisation, it is absolutely necessary to render the condition less hard and less precarious'.[8] But he was not yet ready to say how this should be done.

The Condition of England as a theme embraced a tangle of different arguments about poverty. The Whig Government had tackled the consequences of poverty with the Poor Law of 1834. Edwin Chadwick, a ruthless reformer, was the leading influence in producing the new plan. The Poor Law set up the famous or infamous workhouses to replace the haphazard system of outdoor relief at the discretion of local magistrates. This was typical of the rationalised severity adopted by progressive thinkers. (We noticed another example when discussing prisons and the ethics of punishment.) Out went expensive and ill-conceived charity, in came harsh and efficient benevolence. At least, that was the intention; but it soon became clear that the harshness prevailed over the benevolence. There was a strong popular reaction against the workhouses, immortalised by Dickens in *Oliver Twist*, which appeared in instalments in 1837. In 1839 the young Disraeli was one of a group of Conservatives who attacked the Poor Law. We have seen it as a cross-current in the Yorkshire election of 1841. At a by-election in April 1841 John Walter, owner of *The Times* newspaper, stood as a Conservative in the Liberal seat of Nottingham, and won it because of his individual opposition to the Poor Law.

This was not the position of his leader, however. By temperament Peel the administrator was attracted to the neat orderly theory of the Poor Law and to the financial saving. He was as usual anxious not to ally himself with the Radicals and Chartists. The Poor Law saved many of his agricultural supporters money on their parish rate. The workhouse, particularly if run by a Mr Bumble, was more economical than the old outdoor relief. Indeed at the end of 1838 Peel angrily rebutted the accusation that he had made trouble for Ministers over the Poor Law. In a letter to Croker he described this as a shameful falsehood. In the recent general election he had been taunted at the hustings in Tamworth because he had supported the Poor Law. 'It was our support of the Poor Law that enabled the Government to pass it without fearful resistance. It was our co-operation in practically wording the Law; in becoming Guardians, Chairmen of Unions etc. that has reconciled, where it is reconciled, the rural population to it.'9 The reconciliation, if it ever existed, turned to anger. As the indignation against the Poor Law grew, Peel had to trim his sails and qualify his support. He fell back on the tactic of continuing to support the principle of the 1834 Act but criticising the way it was administered. In 1841 he successfully pressed the Government to renew the Poor Law Commission for only five years instead of the ten they had proposed.10 But this was something less than a battle cry.

Equally tepid was Peel's response to the fervent and persistent pressure on him from Lord Ashley to support the restriction of factory hours. Ashley, a strong Tory and an evangelical Anglican, was one of Peel's most regular correspondents. Ashley strove mightily at each important turn of events to transform Peel into the passionate champion of God's will in England. Factory hours for children were regulated by the Whig Government's 1833 Act, which marked a big step forward from old Sir Robert Peel's Act of 1802 but fell far short of Ashley's own proposals in his Ten Hour Bill. Peel respected Ashley and tried to keep him close at hand; but he could not agree to a measure which would have disrupted the way in which mills were run for adult as well as child labour and (so Peel feared) made them dangerously uncompetitive.

In May 1838 a group of working-class men published the People's Charter. The Chartists acted at a time of economic depression, but the demands in their Charter were purely political: annual parliaments, universal male suffrage, equal electoral districts, no prosperity qualification for Members of Parliament, the payment of MPs and a secret ballot. All of these demands except the annual parliament have now been granted. None of them was acceptable to the political establishment during the years from 1838 to 1848 when the Chartists knocked most insistently upon the door. The Chartists aimed in effect at giving the working classes a

controlling influence over the government of the country. The movement
grew quickly and achieved mass support. But for Peel these were out-
landish claims. The former Home Secretary regarded the Chartists mainly
as a political threat to public order. He saw no meaning in the romantic
dream concocted by Disraeli of a chivalrous alliance between Tory aristocrats and working-class Chartists. Disraeli had not yet written his best
novels, *Coningsby* and *Sybil*, in which this dream is expounded with a
mixture of wit and contrived passion. Peel knew indeed that there were,
as Disraeli was soon to write in *Sybil*, two nations, the rich and the poor,
and that when pushed to extreme in times of distress this difference was
dangerous and wrong. But Peel sought his remedy in official reports and
statistics, far removed from the soaring fantasy of Disraeli's Young
England.

More significant in Peel's life was the foundation in Manchester in the
same year, 1838, of the Anti Corn Law League. The League pressed for
the total abolition of the Corn Laws. The League's campaign began
slowly, but gained impetus. Unlike the Chartists this was a movement
with a foot inside the House of Commons and an appeal to thousands of
middle-class voters in the industrial north. Its first leader, Charles Villiers,
used his position as a Member of Parliament to launch annual debates
and present huge petitions for repeal, using all the moral and economic
arguments for free trade.

Peel thoroughly disliked the idea of pressure groups from outside
exerting influence on Parliament. The inspirers of the League came from
the same social background as his father; some had achieved the same sort
of financial success. They were manufacturers and employers, outstanding
beneficiaries of the Industrial Revolution. But the son of Sir Robert the
cotton spinner had become a country squire. He had no particular social
or personal sympathy with this new generation of manufacturers or with
their champions, Cobden and Bright. He himself had been one of the
team of liberal Tories who had supported Huskisson and Robinson in
the first reduction of tariffs under Lord Liverpool. His own mind was
revolving on the question of corn but not yet decided. As we have seen,
Peel was beginning to use cautious phrases in his own convoluted style.
But his phrases lay hidden in the general Conservative support for a
system of agricultural protection which the Party had introduced in 1825,
reshaped in 1828 and largely defended in 1841. Indeed when Lord John

Russell persuaded the desperate Whigs to promise reform of the Corn Laws on the edge of the 1841 election, Peel went for him as a lamentable opportunist. The backbenchers were reassured. Any Conservative candidates devoted to the Corn Laws had plenty of Peel's quotations to use in his campaign, and saw no need to remember the qualifying sentences. The Anti Corn Law League was high on their list of enemies.

These varied stirrings of opinion outside Parliament on the Condition of England were gradually coming to a head. They might not have absorbed Peel's attention in opposition, but from now on he neither wished nor was able to ignore them.

Lord Melbourne's Whig Government had lost the election, but did not immediately resign. There was a rumour that they might have the audacity to hang on, trying to regain popularity by pursuing their last-minute initiative to reform the Corn Laws. The Conservatives moved quickly to scotch this possibility. This was their hour; they had waited long enough. Their victorious hero of the West Riding, John Stuart Wortley, was chosen to move a motion of no confidence in the Government. The debate lasted four nights but the only remarkable speech was made by Peel. On the eve of becoming Prime Minister he gave two messages to his supporters, one particular, one general. He went out of his way to link the question of poverty to the question of the Corn Laws, warning that if it could ever be shown that a sacrifice by the agricultural interest could prevent social distress, 'I would earnestly advise a relaxation, an alteration, nay if necessary a repeal of the Corn Law'. Once again the words were carefully chosen; he had not made up his mind; he did not argue that the link was yet in place. He was warning that he would never be willing to consider the Corn Laws as an agricultural matter in isolation from their effect on the nation as a whole.

The general message was even clearer. The mood of exaltation was unmistakable:

> If I accept office, it shall be by no unnatural factious combination with men – honest I believe them to be – entertaining extreme opinions from whom I dissent. If I exercise power, it shall be upon my conception – perhaps imperfect, perhaps mistaken, but my sincere conception – of public duty. That power I will not hold, unless I can hold it consistently with the maintenance of my own opinions; and that power I

will relinquish the moment that I am not supported in the maintenance of them by the confidence of this House, and of the people of
this country.'[11]

This could be read as a rebuke to the Whigs for struggling on in forced
alliance with the Radicals. But it was also a warning to the Ultras in his
own Party. Yes, the good times had come again for the party of the
Throne, Altar and Cottage. Yes, if they carried the vote of no confidence
they could have a Conservative government and enjoy the pleasures of
office. But this would not be a government of internal intrigues and compromises. If they wanted Peel as Prime Minister, it must be on Peel's
terms. There would be, in his words, 'no servile tenure'. The Conservatives
cheered loudly and without foreboding. On the evening of 27 August
they made their choice; the Whig Government was defeated by ninety-
one votes, and next day Lord Melbourne told the Queen that his ministry
was at an end.[12] They stood together under the stars on the terrace at
Windsor, talking over old times, and he told her 'for four years I have seen
you daily and liked it better every day'.[13]

     This was hardly an ideal background for Peel as Melbourne's successor.
Indeed the Queen had for weeks made no effort to conceal her forebod-
ings. She wrote every few days to her uncle Leopold, King of the
Belgians. She suspected him of being sympathetic to the Conservatives.
Indeed like most leaders on the Continent Leopold disliked Palmerston's
noisy foreign policy; but he confined himself to sententious advice to his
niece that a parliamentary constitution did from time to time mean
changes of government. This was not good enough. 'You don't say that
you sympathise with me in my present heavy trial,' wrote Victoria on 24
August, 'the heaviest I have ever had to endure, and which will be a sad
heart-breaking time for me, but I know you do feel for me. I am quiet and
prepared, but still I feel very sad, and God knows very wretched at times,
for myself and my country, that such a change must take place. But God
in his mercy will support and guide me through all. Yet I feel that my
constant headaches are caused by annoyance and vexation! Adieu dearest
Uncle! God bless you.'[14]

     The Queen's headaches were not the result of any detailed study of
Conservative policies. She thought in general that they were wretched,
negative people, but her misery was at the prospect of losing dear Lord

M, and having to deal with Peel, that awkward, incomprehensible man who had been so wrong to harass her over her ladies two years earlier. But by August 1841 she knew that these indignant conversations could not be repeated. A new actor had appeared on the scene. The young German prince whom she married in 1840 had already a clearer grasp of the needs of the British Constitution than Queen Victoria or her first British Prime Minister. Prince Albert had been horrified to learn the story of the Bedchamber Crisis of 1839. Within eighteen months of their marriage he set himself to make sure that it could not happen again. He was encouraged by his main adviser and former tutor Baron Stockmar, who had made a close study of Britain, her Constitution and her eccentric royal family for more than twenty years. Although Prince Albert was still a stranger in Britain, his Constitutional position obscure and his wife by no means yet ready to accept his advice, he did not hesitate. He moved at once into action.

On Sunday morning, 9 May 1841, when it looked as if the Government would fall over the sugar duties, a young man called George Anson called on Peel at Whitehall Gardens. Anson was only twenty-nine and had until recently been a Private Secretary to Lord Melbourne. But he explained to Peel that he was now serving Prince Albert and was calling at the Prince's request. The Prince wanted to find a way of preventing a new crisis over court appointments if, as seemed likely, the Government fell in the next few days and the Queen was once again advised to send for Peel. The Prince's solution was simple. Three leading Whig ladies, the Duchess of Sutherland, Lady Normanby and the Duchess of Bedford, would in these circumstances announce their resignation without any request from Peel – together with any other ladies whom Peel might request.

Peel's reaction was characteristic. First, he cautiously asked if the Prime Minister and the Queen both knew of this approach. The answer was yes, although there is some doubt whether at this first stage Albert had been at all specific with his wife. Then Peel launched into a long defensive account of his handling of the problem in 1839 and his anxiety not to offend or embarrass the Queen. But the two men came to the heart of the matter when Peel said that if in 1839 he had been told that these three ladies intended to resign he would have been entirely satisfied. There were further meetings and difficulties over detail. The Duchess of Bedford was not enthusiastic about being shunted into the sidelines. The Queen argued that the new ladies must be appointed by her, though approved by Peel, but Anson, Stockmar and Peel smoothed over these points. As it happened the Government did not fall in May 1841, but stuttered on through the general election until the end of August. But the deal had been done.[15]

When Peel was summoned to Windsor on 30 August he did not need to raise the matter. The Queen was heavily pregnant and sad, but civil. The first interview lasted only twenty minutes. They talked about Wellington, and Peel explained that the Duke was now so deaf and apt to go to sleep at meetings that he would not want to run a government department again; but they agreed that he should be in the Cabinet. At another meeting two days later they discussed other appointments. Peel showed himself anxious to oblige the Queen over her personal preferences for several minor offices. He asked and was told exactly which official papers the Queen wished to see in advance of decisions. They were stiff and awkward together; but a new start had been made. Within hours of Peel's first audience the Queen wrote an account of it (in the third person as always) to Melbourne, ending with the usual lament, 'It is very very sad, and she cannot quite believe it yet ... We do, and shall miss you so dreadfully.' She obviously hoped that Peel would not last long. 'Happier and brighter times will come again.'[16]

During the next few weeks the Queen and Melbourne corresponded almost every day, she asking for and he giving advice on points which Peel raised. This would have developed into a real danger if not checked. The problem was the Queen's devotion not to her ladies, but to Melbourne. She had seen him every day for four years, with few exceptions. 'Eleven days was the longest I ever was without seeing him, and this time will be elapsed on Saturday, so you may imagine what the change must be.' The Queen was angry when her aunt, old Queen Adelaide, wrote with singular lack of tact to express her hope 'that you will have perfect confidence in the able men who form your Council. Our beloved late King's anxious wish to see Wellington and Peel again at the head of the Administration is now fulfilled.'[17]

Melbourne was of course flattered that the Queen was so intent on keeping their friendship alive. He must have seen the dangers. He could argue that he used his position to ease the Queen's relationship with Peel. He correctly assured her that Peel was anxious to please her. He thought that the new Government's policies would not be all that different from his own. When some of the new Ministers showed ignorance of Court protocol he told her that this was not surprising given that the Conservatives had been out of office for so long. He found ways of getting advice to Peel about his handling of the Queen. He asked Greville to tell him, '[s]he likes to have them [government proposals] explained to her elementarily, not at length and in detail, but shortly and clearly, neither does she like long audiences'. Through Anson, he advised Peel not to irritate the Queen 'by talking at her about religion as she particularly disliked what she terms a Sunday face'.[18] This harmless, indeed helpful advice was outweighed by the flow of letters on political matters between Melbourne and the Queen behind Peel's back. Canada was proving difficult again. Peel proposed to send out Sir Henry Bulmer. Melbourne wrote to the Queen: 'He is clear, keen, active: somewhat bitter and caustic and rather suspicious. A man of a more straightforward character would have done better, but it would be easy to have found many who would have done worse.' The Duke of Beaufort was hardly equal to the job of Ambassador to St Petersburg, though he would be good at chatting to the Emperor at military parades.[19]

This kind of stuff did not include direct attacks on Peel or Government policy, but would nonetheless have done the Queen much harm if the letters had leaked. That at any rate was the view of Albert. In the letter to King Leopold in which the Queen lamented the departure of Melbourne she added about her husband, 'I cannot say what a comfort and support my beloved Angel is to me and how well and kindly he behaves.'[20] The beloved Angel had no quarrel with Lord Melbourne, but he was using his growing power to get rid of Melbourne's strongest supporter at Court, the Queen's governess Baroness Lehzen, who had actually given financial support to the Whigs in the election. Albert was determined to protect the Queen's political impartiality. It was no good tackling the Queen direct. He used his two main allies, Stockmar and Anson, to lean on Melbourne. Stockmar was heavy and German, Anson more supple.

It took them several months to shake Melbourne. Stockmar wrote a memorandum advising Melbourne to decline an invitation from the Queen to stay at Windsor. Anson showed it to Melbourne, saying that the difficulty was increased by an attack which he had just made on the

Government in the Lords. Melbourne exploded. He walked up and down his room in a frenzy: 'God eternally damn it ... Flesh and blood cannot stand that ... I cannot be expected to give up my position in the country.'[21] That was not the point; it was his position alongside the Queen which was at issue. Their correspondence continued; worse, it became generally known. Melbourne could hardly have chosen a more foolish confidante than his former mistress, Caroline Norton, a lady renowned for her powers of conversation. She chattered and Peel must have heard something. During a talk with Stockmar in November Peel changed the tone of the conversation and said with sudden emphasis that he would resign at once if he ever knew for a fact that the Queen was taking advice on public affairs from someone else.[22] Stockmar seized this new weapon, and loosed off another memorandum to Melbourne. He received only a cold acknowledgement, but gradually Melbourne's correspondence with the Queen lost its political edge, reducing itself to the witty gossip about the ways of the world which had always made up a large part of Melbourne's charm.

On 3 September 1841 the Queen received her new Ministers at Claremont (King Leopold's house near Esher in Surrey) and formally said goodbye to the old. It was another difficult day for her. Melbourne wrote the day before that 'he hopes and trusts that when tomorrow is over Your Majesty will recover from that depression of spirits under which Your Majesty now labours', or in other words, 'Cheer up, Ma'am, and pull yourself together.' Greville, in his dual capacity as Clerk of the Council and the most famous gossip of the day, watched her closely. 'She looked much flushed and her heart was evidently brim full ... Though no courtier, and not disposed to be particularly indulgent to her, I did feel a strong mixture of pity and admiration at such a display of firmness. Peel told me that she had behaved perfectly to him. He was more than satisfied; he was charmed by her.'[23]

Peel rapidly developed an alliance, growing into friendship, with Prince Albert. In a master stroke he suggested to the Queen that Albert should chair the Royal Commission on Fine Arts which he wished to set up. Queen and Prince were delighted, and Albert was the right man for the job. But Peel's journey was still uphill. On 2 October Anson sat next to the Queen at dinner at Windsor. She still talked about Peel's awkward manner, which she felt she could not get over. 'I asked if Her Majesty had yet made any effort, which I was good humouredly assured Her Majesty thought she really had done.'[24]

It took Peel a fortnight, working between sixteen and eighteen hours a day, to complete all the appointments to his Government. This was a more arduous task in 1841 than today, even though the number of Ministers was much smaller. Now the Prime Minister acts at once. The Cabinet is complete within hours of his or her appointment with the Queen and the rest of the government is shaped within three or four days. In our media-driven world the situation would run out of control if the key decisions were not quickly taken and announced in a way which precluded further argument. The vehicle for consultation is the telephone or now e-mail. In a world without telephone or e-mail Peel was deluged each day with a mass of letters, some of his correspondents giving advice, others applying for jobs. In 1841 he came to the conclusion that no one who asked for a job was fit for it.* Peel had been working on his plans for several months. Wellington had written on 17 May to say that he would like to sit in the Cabinet and lead for the Government in the Lords but without a department. His sensible and unselfish decision had enabled Peel to sort this point out quickly at his first audience with the Queen.[25]

He worked closely at the task of forming a government with two men whom he had come to trust. Sir Thomas Fremantle had been Chief Whip of the Conservative Party since the election of 1835. Peel noted at the time that this was 'a place which required a gentleman to fill it and which no gentleman would take'.[26] In modern times this difficulty has been overcome by finding Chief Whips with a special skill and zest for the peculiar job of managing fellow politicians. Fremantle must have had that skill. He survived in the job and Peel found him discreet, straightforward and popular. Peel's other confidant, Francis Bonham, operated from his private desk at the Carlton Club. His field of action was wider than Fremantle's, covering the constituencies as well as the parliamentary Party. For Bonham, knowledge was everything; he knew everyone and tracked every ripple of opinion. But Bonham was careful with the hoard of facts

---

* This rule of thumb indeed worked fairly well until recently. Now many public positions are given only to those who apply, so that silent merit no longer finds reward. This is thought to be a great advance.

and gossip which he accumulated. Peel, but no one else, had access to what Bonham knew. Disraeli described him as 'one gentleman who by his knowledge of human nature, fine observation of opinion, indefatigable activity, universal prudence and feasibility of resource, mainly contributed to the triumph [of 1841] though he was spoken of only with whispers and moved only behind the scenes'. Lord John Manners was more specific, remembering sixty years later 'an elderly man, dressed in a long brown coat and carrying a large strapped book full of electioneering facts, figures and calculations ... rough, faithful, honest, indefatigable, the depositary of a thousand secrets and the betrayer of none'.[27]

There were, and are, two possible principles to guide a Prime Minister in choosing a Cabinet, which may conflict with each other. Prime Ministers may select colleagues on the grounds of fitness for running a department and carrying out government policy; or (particularly if their personal position is weak) they may need to balance within the Cabinet the different strands of opinion in their party. Peel did not concern himself greatly with the second principle. His personal position was very strong. He had no respect for the Ultras in his party, but just enough prudence to see that they should be represented in the Cabinet. Sir Edward Knatchbull had been a harmless Paymaster General in Peel's Government of the Hundred Days and now returned to that position. More problematic was the future of the Duke of Buckingham, a self-important champion of the agricultural interest. This Duke, whose vanity led him into repeated disappointment, wanted to be First Lord of the Admiralty. He was persuaded to accept the post of Lord Privy Seal, without specific duties but with a place in the Cabinet.

Peel certainly needed to accommodate Stanley and Graham, who had proved the success of the Tamworth strategy by crossing the floor of the House to join the Conservatives. Stanley accepted the Colonial Office and the headaches of Canada and Jamaica. His ability and debating skills were not in doubt, and he was never slow to state a view. But he was not as close to Peel as Sir James Graham, who was appointed Home Secretary and became Peel's closest supporter. Peel brought into the Cabinet three other able men on whom he had come to depend for loyalty and good sense – Lord Aberdeen as Foreign Secretary, Goulburn as Chancellor of the Exchequer, and Henry Hardinge as Secretary at War. Lord Lyndhurst and Lord Ripon were there at the top table because they had been at the top table since anyone could remember. That more or less made up the list. Into ministerial posts below Cabinet Peel brought his clever younger disciples, Lord Lincoln, Sidney Herbert and an absurdly articulate young man called William Gladstone.

Gladstone treated Peel's simple proposal that he should go as a junior Minister to the Board of Trade under Lord Ripon* as a matter of huge complexity requiring lengthy correspondence with the hard-pressed Prime Minister. He pointed out first that he knew little about trade; second, Macaulay and others had criticised him in the press; third, he and Peel were not at one on issues of Church and State. Peel dealt as briefly with Gladstone's many pages as was compatible with courtesy. He must have suspected that behind them lay disappointment that the offer did not include a seat in Cabinet. But Gladstone's appointment turned out highly successful both for Peel and himself.

Of course there were difficulties. Lord Ashley was a particular problem. For him every political decision, including his own promotion or exclusion, was first of all a matter of high Christian morality, and then connected with his passionate crusade for the Ten Hour Factory Bill restricting hours of work. At the end of July he had written to tell Peel: 'You are about to be summoned to the highest and most responsible of all earthly situations. No crowned head has a tenth part of the dignity and moral power that accompany the Prime Minister of the Sovereign of these realms.' He went on to urge on Peel 'in these days of speciousness, of peril and of perplexity, ... a vigorous and dauntless faith which shall utterly disregard the praise of men'. There was nothing insincere in Ashley's exhortation, and nothing cynical in Peel's different approach to his coming premiership. The two men operated on different wavelengths. In a separate correspondence about Church controversies, Peel was driven to snub Ashley: 'it frequently happens that these zealous controversialists on religious matters leave on the mind of their readers one conviction stronger than any other, namely that Christian charity is consumed in their burning zeal for their own opinions'. Peel was anxious to have men

---

* Even close students of the peerage may be puzzled that Frederick Robinson who had been Chancellor of the Exchequer under Lord Liverpool, was Viscount Goderich when he became a tearful Prime Minister in 1827, and now Earl of Ripon when Peel sent him to the Board of Trade. They are all the same man.

of Christian probity around the Queen and offered Ashley a post in the Royal Household. Ashley was indignant at the idea of 'a department in which I could have exhibited nothing good but my legs in white shorts'.[28] He refused to consider any position with the Queen or with Prince Albert unless the Government accepted his Factory Bill. Peel was not ready to do this. Ashley retired to brood pessimistically over Peel and his spiritual shortcomings.[29]

Letters poured in from Members of Parliament proving their own case for appointments or honours. As in Ireland nearly thirty years earlier, Peel's underlying puritanism found caustic expression. 'The distinction of being without an honour is becoming a rare and valuable one', he wrote to Graham, 'and should not become extinct.'[30] He enlarged on this theme to Croker in a mood of pompous but sincere indignation. The reward of the Prime Minister 'is not patronage, which imposes nothing but a curse, which enables him to do little more than make *dix mécontents et un ingrat*; not ribbons or hopes of peerage or such trumpery distinction but the means of rendering service to the country and the hope of honourable fame'.[31]

Each applicant believed that he was a special case. None was more convinced of this than the Member of Parliament for Maidstone. By 5 September Benjamin Disraeli had still heard nothing from the Prime Minister. 'I am not going to trouble you with claims similar to those with which you must be wearied,' he wrote on 5 September, before doing precisely that. Of course there were special circumstances. Disraeli argued that by enrolling under Peel's banner he had had 'to struggle against a storm of political hate and malice which few men ever experienced … I confess, to be unrecognised at this moment by you appears to me to be overwhelming and I appeal to your own heart, to that justice and that magnanimity which I feel are your characteristics to save me from an intolerable humiliation.'[32] A nice try, but hopeless. It was not a letter which would strike any sort of chord with Peel, even (or particularly) when backed up by a similar letter from Mrs Disraeli reminding Peel that she had helped to spend £40,000 in Maidstone in the good cause. Peel replied to Disraeli with cool courtesy, misunderstanding a reference which Disraeli had made to encouragement from a Minister, and regretting that there were so many able qualified people whom he was bound to disappoint. There was nothing in Disraeli's achievements to date which required Peel to consider him as a Minister, and plenty in his manner and reputation to keep them apart.

So Peel completed his first task as Prime Minister. There was no questioning the talent which he had brought together in Government. His own reputation for intelligence and integrity had been rebuilt in the years of opposition after the personal setbacks of Catholic Emancipation and the Reform Bill. He had given no precise policy pledges. His general purpose of conservative reform had been proclaimed at Tamworth in 1834 and defended ever since. He took over a country in financial difficulty and industrial distress. Curiosity about his intentions was intense. Those who followed policies were familiar with Peel in opposition or an earlier Peel who served under others. In September 1841 they were faced with a different Peel, a proud, awkward, intelligent man who dominated the political scene and now at last possessed real power.

Thirteen

The Welfare of the People

'It would be next to insupportable to live in a country
where such a tax were permanent'
*Lord Ashburton, head of the house of Baring, to Peel on proposals for
income tax at six pence in the pound, 1841*

'I think the income tax a very disagreeable thing, but so I
do blue pills, rhubarb or castor oil, and it does appear that
a strong dose of help is needed for the finances of the
country'
Lady Stanley of Alderley, 1842

'The accounts from various parts of the country are very
bad ... there has been much violence and great
confusion ... I have requested some new arms in perfect
order and ammunition to be sent to Drayton'
Peel to Julia, August 1842

'The danger is not low price from the tariff, but low price
from inability to consume, from the poor man giving up his
pint of beer and the man in middling station giving up his
joint of meat'
Peel to Croker, July 1842

Government is the art of matching what you want to do with what
you have to do. Happy Prime Ministers find on arriving in office
that events of the moment are propelling them in the direction
which they want to take anyway. But that was certainly not Peel's position
in the summer of 1841. Before and during the election he had set out in
general terms his approach to government. This had hardly varied since he
issued the Tamworth Manifesto seven years earlier. There was no specific
programme, but on economic matters there could be no doubt about

Peel's sense of direction. He wanted to take up the liberalising policy begun by Huskisson with his support under Lord Liverpool and Canning before 1827. This meant in particular lowering tariffs on imports so that trade could flourish. The question was whether he could afford to do it.

The liberalisation of trade and the maintenance of a strong currency based on gold were the two pillars of Peel's economic thinking throughout his life. They rested on a moral base. Peel reached his conclusions by an intellectual process. He considered the facts of a subject against the background of the ideas which his mind had weighed and approved. Because he was a Christian who took his faith seriously his conclusions had to fit into Christian teaching as he understood it, including the concept of a divine Providence presiding over human affairs. But his mind rather than his faith was the driving force. His mind as taught by experience led him to distrust attempted manipulations whether of the currency or of trade. Politicians, he thought, would always find tempting arguments for issuing insecure paper currency or for distorting the normal working of demand and supply in trade. Bankers would always be busy up the back stairs. Peel was not by temperament dogmatic and acknowledged that there would often be valid exceptions to a general rule; for example it was often right to respect established interests. But the wisdom of that general rule against manipulation seemed clear.

By 1841 the argument for tariff reduction was not just theoretical or commercial. A new and compelling reason had joined those which had persuaded Huskisson and Canning. The Condition of England, that is to say the poverty of so many of its people, was forcing its way to the top of the political agenda. Peel with his other interests and preoccupations had been slow to grasp this, and even in 1841 his analysis was not yet driven by a sense of overwhelming necessity. But his chosen remedy for widespread poverty was already apparent. It did not lie in changing the Poor Law, or reducing factory hours through a Ten Hour Bill, or in accepting the irrelevant political demands of the Chartists. Still less did it consist in commissioning that engine of public welfare and State guidance of the economy to which we became accustomed in the twentieth century. Peel and most of his contemporaries would have regarded our giant complex of State machinery as a destructive restraint on individual freedom.

He now began to connect his intellectual support for liberalising trade with the humanitarian case for reducing poverty. The poor could best be

helped by cutting the burden of tariffs on the imports on which they and
their employers increasingly relied. But the Budget figures were against any
bold move. According to the orthodoxy of the time a government should
only cut tariffs if it could do so without running into deficit. The
modern concept of financing a deficit year after year by huge borrowing
would have been regarded by all Peel's generation as indecent, to be contemplated only in a mortal crisis such as the war against Napoleon.
Cautious men argued that Peel needed a surplus for his plans. But the
Whig Government had left behind no surplus, quite the reverse. The
Grey and Melbourne Governments had been notable reformers in several
fields, but taxation was not one of them. Since 1837 the revenue had failed
to meet costs. For the year ending April 1842 there was an estimated
deficit of over £2 million, creating an accumulated deficit of some £7.5
million. Palmerston's foreign policy had produced bad relations with both
France and the United States. War with either was possible, so naval and
military spending would be hard to cut. The introduction of the Penny
Post in 1840 had proved unexpectedly expensive. The scope for economy
in government spending seemed small.

As we have seen, one school of thought was already arguing that tariffs
could safely be reduced even in such bleak circumstances; under this new
argument reduced rates would increase trade to such an extent so that the
yield to the Exchequer would grow even at the reduced rate. Lower tariffs
would thus mean higher Customs revenue. The Whigs in their desperate
political plight had grasped at the argument when Baring went fishing for
his Budget before the election. But Peel and his colleagues were cautious
men, not easily persuaded by an abstract doctrine. Even if the argument
had merit, how long would it take to work? They were prepared to experiment, but not to place their whole future on this gamble. Ministers
needed to consider how other forms of taxation might be increased to
finance not only the Whig deficit but also the substantial cut in tariffs on
which Peel was resolved.[1]

Peel knew that the answer was income tax. He had argued in favour of
reviving the income tax when Herries had proposed it in Wellington's
Cabinet twelve years earlier. But they had been a minority in the Cabinet,
and nothing had happened. As soon as the election results of 1841 were
clear, even before the Whigs resigned, Peel began a careful consultation
about income tax. He started with Goulburn, who had backed an income

tax back in 1830. Goulburn's reply on 22 July was brief and workmanlike. His letter shows us both why he was useful to Peel and why he would not rise to the very top. In a few paragraphs Goulburn summed up the arguments for and against. The income tax was introduced by Pitt to win the war against France and had been peremptorily abolished by the House of Commons in 1816 as soon as peace returned. Goulburn doubted 'whether there is virtue enough in a Reformed House of Commons to admit of such a measure being carried, except under the pressure of war expenditure'.[2] The necessary Bill would be complicated, and easy to frustrate in detailed debate. If Ireland was included there would be one sort of outcry; if it was excluded, another. Income tax would hardly be worth doing for a rate of less than sixpence in the pound, which would yield between £4 million and £5 million. It could be devised to bear almost entirely on the wealthy, but they would resent having the Government poke about in their personal finances. Goulburn drew no conclusion, but in his analysis the doubts prevailed.

Peel replied within a week, telling Goulburn in confidence that in his view they would have to revive the tax, and should begin to lay the foundations. He then began a careful process of further consultation. The Duke of Wellington agreed without difficulty; it was not his subject, and Peel's lead was clear. Graham was for delay and a thorough search for economies in spending before a decision was taken on income tax; Stanley was doubtful, but saw that Peel might be driven to attempt it. By October Peel had extended, though still cautiously, the ring of those consulted. Lord Ashburton, head of the great house of Baring, was brought into his confidence. As a true conservative financier Ashburton was still indignant at the Whig idea of curing the deficit without raising taxes. Not for him the painless seduction of Hume's Select Committee. 'I am not aware that mountebankery on so bold a scale was ever attempted by any party.' After reviewing the options Ashburton was ready to overcome his strong objections to a temporary income tax. Nevertheless this would be 'a most hazardous experiment', and 'it would be next to insupportable to live in a country where such a tax were permanent'.[3] Lord Ashburton was commenting on a proposal for income tax at sixpence in the pound, or 2.5 per cent. His successors in the Baring family have just about managed to scrape a living in a country which at one stage levied the income tax at 80 per cent, and 98 on rent, interest and dividends.

Despite the reservation this was a reassuring endorsement for Peel. Gladstone, as a junior Minister at the Board of Trade, was also consulted. Being Gladstone he replied at length. He welcomed the principle of direct taxation, but found six objections to income tax. He would prefer to revive the tax on houses, which the Whigs had abolished in 1834. Peel responded courteously to his junior colleague with counter-arguments. He had a devious motive for circulating Gladstone's paper to other Ministers, believing that a house tax would be so unpopular that income tax would seem attractive by comparison.[4] Finally on 24 January the Cabinet approved a proposal for income tax pitched at a slightly higher threshold than Goulburn had suggested in July with exemption for those earning less than £150 a year. This was calculated to yield £3.7 million at a rate of seven pence instead of sixpence in the pound. Ireland was exempted but in compensation had to pay higher duties. In all these proposals would bring in £4 million. Peel had taken a great step, but only the first. The rest of the Budget had to be agreed and the whole Budget with the tariff changes carried through Parliament.

Peel had chosen an able Cabinet, but they were new, and he felt they needed constant supervision. The burden of work on the Prime Minister was already formidable. Sir James Graham told Gladstone in February 1842, 'the pressure upon him is immense. We never had a Minister who was so truly a first Minister as he is. He makes himself felt in every department, and is really cognisant of the affairs of each. Lord Grey could not master such an amount of business. Canning could not do it. Now he is an actual minister, and is indeed capax imperii.'[5] That same month Peel wrote to Croker, 'I suppose it must have been beautiful weather by this glimpse of the sun which I sometimes catch. I wish they would give me a ten-hour Bill.'[6]

Peel did not shoot much game during these months and sometimes the opportunity was unexpected. In January 'in thin shoes, pepper and salt pantaloons and a long blue frock coat, with borrowed gun and apparatus of all kinds, I had the honour of accompanying Prince Albert at a *chasse*, which lasted an hour and a half, in Windsor Park.'[7] That morning they shot eighteen pheasants, sixteen hares, fifty-one rabbits and one partridge. Albert had invited Peel to come down the night before precisely for this purpose. He liked to snatch a precious hour or two in the morning before the Queen began her calls on his time. Peel and he had quickly come together. The Queen's pregnancy in the autumn had provided a reason for Peel to discuss State matters with Albert and show him papers. The habit developed into a firm alliance. Peel never enjoyed Court life. He did not dance, and the pleasure of playing solemn rubbers of whist with the Queen's mother, the Duchess of Kent, quickly faded.[8] The French states-man Guizot noticed how awkward Peel seemed on Court occasions at Windsor; he was the most important man in the room, but never looked it.[9] But in Albert, nearly thirty years his junior, Peel found an intellectual companion to whom he could explain his views frankly, and through whom he could achieve the much needed sympathy of the Queen. The Prince Consort and the Prime Minister by reason of their different posi-tions could not become intimate friends, but they worked together with a shared view of the general good. Under their influence the Queen turned from passionate Whig to a firm admirer, if not of the Conservative Party, at least of its leader.

Peel needed all the support he could get, for his Budget did not stand alone. There was little doubt that the Corn Law needed reform. Lord John Russell had reopened the debate before the election and plenty had been said on the hustings. But even without Lord John's stillborn initia-tive the system was ripe for change. The 1828 Corn Law was not working properly. In theory imported wheat paid duty on a sliding scale, the rate rising as the home price fell. In theory there was a high level of protec-tion; but the calculation of the home price was open to fraud, and con-trary to the purpose of the Law, prices fluctuated sharply. Everyone was dissatisfied. The Anti Corn Law League raged with increasing insistence against the whole system. The agricultural interest were suspicious of any change, only asking that the Law be applied efficiently. Peel had never pledged himself specifically to maintain the 1828 Corn Law. As we have seen he had begun to slip into his speeches saving clauses pointing out that the Corn Laws depended on the general interest. But he was well aware that he and the Conservative Party were seen as champions of agri-cultural protection. He might be scornful of many of his supporters and the priority they gave to fox-hunting in the countryside and punctual dinners in London, but he was not blind. He knew that the Corn Laws could arouse quite as much passion in the cities and shires as Catholic Emancipation or the Great Reform Bill.

At the same time as Peel was digging with Goulburn into the details of a new income tax, he did the same with Lord Ripon at the Board of Trade on a new Corn Law. If nothing were done the stiff duties sometimes applied on wheat under the sliding scale would stand in absurd contrast to the tariff cuts on other imports. The junior Minister in that Department, Gladstone, was encouraged to take a hand, and submitted three separate papers on the subject. Peel made sure that the agricultural interests were not left out. Their leader, the Duke of Buckingham, was included in the ministerial committee considering the subject. Peel corresponded at length with R.A. Christopher, the knowledgeable farming Member for North Lincolnshire.[10] Lord Ashburton was once more asked for his views. Once again, as on income tax, he laid down a definite principle which Peel was beginning to doubt. 'Our Conservative Party is a party pledged to the support of the land, and if that principle is abandoned, the party is dissolved. I am also convinced that protection is the true honest policy for the country, and all its interests.'[11] But again, as over income tax, Ashburton qualified this generalisation by admitting that the level of protection under the 1828 Law was too high. This was enough for Peel. His correspondence with the ministerial team at the Board of Trade multiplied. He pressed Ripon and Gladstone for more and yet more details about the wheat price at which the British farmer could make a profit, and the price at which wheat would be available from Hamburg, the Baltic ports or North America. He persuaded them to propose a lower level of protection than they had originally favoured.

On 22 January 1842, after this intensive discussion, Peel proposed to Cabinet a new sliding scale providing a duty of twenty shillings a quarter on wheat when the home price was fifty shillings, which would drop to a nominal one shilling duty if the price rose to seventy-three shillings. This was a considerably lower sliding scale than previously existed, but not far from what Christopher, the backbench farmer, had suggested. Indeed it was more protectionist than expected by Gladstone, whose own views had shifted sharply towards free trade as he studied the figures which Peel had demanded. But he was struck by the way in which Peel clung to as much of the familiar detail of the old arrangements as was compatible with his aims, thus reducing the points of disagreement to a minimum. 'Until we were actually in the midst of the struggle', he wrote on 26 February, 'I did not appreciate the extraordinary sagacity of his parliamentary instinct in this particular.' Peel told Ripon and Gladstone that in principle he would have liked to propose a lower level of protection, but this was not practicable in the present state of opinion in the Cabinet and Parliament. He was still taking a cool politician's view of the possibilities.

The new Corn Bill of 1842 was a political compromise. It would please no one. It was carefully crafted to navigate a tight channel between the free traders and the agriculturalists. But did that channel actually exist or was shipwreck inevitable? The first test was in the Cabinet. The new Bill was too much for the Duke of Buckingham, who resigned from the Government. As Lord Chandos before he succeeded to the dukedom, he had gained a high though narrow reputation among the Ultras, first by successfully moving an amendment to the Great Reform Bill which gave added weight to the agricultural interest, then by trying unsuccessfully to abolish the malt tax. Because of this reputation Peel had given him the Cabinet seat of Lord Privy Seal; Buckingham's abilities were not such that Peel would trust him with running a specific department.

Peel found a device which minimised the political damage of his resignation. He was able to write on 6 February, 'The Duke of Buckingham remained to the last on cordial terms with us, professed the greatest gratitude for the consideration with which he had been treated, and ultimately retired, not in my opinion because he differed from us, but because he was haunted by the recollection of pledges given at farmers' dinners, in the capacity he assumed of being especially the farmers' friend.'[12] That description 'the farmers' friend' appears on the Duke's tombstone in the Grenville mausoleum at Wootton Underwood.

The device which Peel found for emasculating the Duke of Buckingham is not available to modern Prime Ministers. The Order of the Garter, the prime title of English chivalry, rests now in the personal gift of the Queen. In Peel's time the Sovereign acted on the Prime Minister's advice over this as on most decisions of patronage. The total number of Knights of the Garter, each with a stall in St George's Chapel, Windsor, is strictly limited. As can be seen by its appearance in contemporary portraits, the blue ribbon was coveted beyond all others among the aristocrats for whom it was in practice reserved.[*] Other honours could be

---

[*] In Trollope's novel *The Prime Minister*, the Duke of Omnium's growing eccentricity in that office becomes apparent to all when he awards the Garter, not to a duke of his own Whig

scattered around by a Prime Minister like Pitt in need of political support; the Garter was special. The Duke of Buckingham, who had not concealed his ambition in this direction, at once accepted Peel's offer of the Garter when he resigned. His opposition of principle to Peel was thus neutralised at a stroke. In Wellington's view he became 'the ridicule of the whole nation'.[13] Julia was equally scornful. 'No one is sorry but himself. He found himself unfit for office and was glad of some pretext to cut and run.'[14] Disraeli, having been refused a place in the Government, was already looking around for someone who could help him overthrow it. But even Disraeli, despite his romantic passion for the aristocracy, drew the line at the Duke of Buckingham. 'If he had only brains', Disraeli wrote in August 1842, 'he might be premier ... but then I don't think he ever read a book in his life on any subject.'[15] Peel was anxious to keep Knatchbull, a more reliable Ultra, in the Cabinet and in this for the time being he succeeded.

On 9 February 1842 Peel presented the Corn Bill to the House of Commons in a detailed defensive speech. As was his habit, he used a mass of statistical detail to smother criticism. Outside the House delegates of the Anti Corn Law League were shouting free trade slogans at individual Members as they entered inside. Peel, pointing to the proposed reduction of duties by at least half, argued that complete abolition of the Corn Laws would merely add poverty in the countryside to poverty in the towns. Outside the Commons the agriculturists were anxious and grumbling, inside Peel stressed to them the importance of greater price stability under the new scale. He found his way down the narrow channel between the rocks, and the Commons rejected by big majorities three alternative proposals by the official Whig opposition, the spokesman of the Anti Corn Law League and the agriculturists. But Peel was consciously speaking for the short term only, and stressed once more that agricultural protection could only be defended so long as it was in the interest of all classes. Privately he began to doubt if he had gone far enough; he did not contradict Sir James Graham who wrote a few months later that the

Party, but to a Tory peer whose only qualification is that he helped the unfortunate in society. In 1946 the Prime Minister Clement Attlee agreed to the request of King George VI that the Garter should in future be given on the Sovereign's personal decision without political advice, as when the Order was originally founded by Edward III. This must be the only power which has moved against the tide into the personal discretion of the Sovereign.

next change in the Corn Law, if there had to be one, must be to open trade.[16] The fuse was lit; it had a few years yet to splutter.

Meanwhile Peel fell into a small trap devised by the League. The phrase 'public relations' had not been invented, but the profession and its techniques were flourishing. A Manchester free trade manufacturer called Barlow sent Peel two pieces of velveteen of the highest quality. He accepted with thanks, writing that his wife would convert one into a cloak, and he would use the other himself. He did not notice that the elegant design of the cloth of a stalk and ear of wheat had the word FREE on a scroll beneath it. The velveteen was a political manifesto. The press was told, the *Manchester Guardian* picked up the story, *The Times* followed, speculation grew. *Punch* enjoyed itself. 'Great, indeed, would have been the triumph of the League, if the Minister had donned the insidious trousers and taking his seat in the House of Commons had, without knowing it, based his Ministry upon "free" corn.' There was no neat way out of this. Peel returned the velveteen, writing clumsily that he had not noticed its 'allusion to matters that are the subject of public controversy'.[17] The 'velveteen plot' was long remembered.

Having personally launched the new Corn Law, Peel did the same for the Budget. There was no question of leaving the task to the Chancellor of the Exchequer. Goulburn was proving himself an able lieutenant, but it was Peel's Budget and only Peel had the necessary mastery of the Commons to get it through. His speech lasted three and a half hours on the evening of 11 March; it was not the most eloquent of his life, but one of the most constructive. He followed a structure familiar to professional politicians. First, the bad news about the fiscal position, which at this stage could credibly be blamed on the recent Whig Government. Without any change in policy there would be a deficit of £2.5 million in 1843, contributing to an aggregate deficit of over £10 million in six years, or about one fifth of the annual revenue of the country. The country could not drift on in this way; a decisive change was needed.

Next came the painful surprise, the less painful because it was a surprise. Surprises well presented have a persuasive force of their own. There had been no leaks about the return of income tax, and such boldness was not expected. Peel clothed the proposal in the language of a patriotic appeal. Rather than raise taxes on consumption which fell mainly on the poor, he called on the possessors of property to help repair the mighty evil of the Whig deficit which he had just outlined. He described the proposed income tax to a House now thoroughly stirred and attentive.

Finally, the good news. Money was needed for India and China; the Whig deficit had to be met. But after all these outgoings there would be a surplus of £1.8 million. That would enable him to finance a vast remodelling of the tariff system. For some goods the prohibition of imports would be removed; for raw materials the tariff would be down to 5 per cent or less; for foreign manufactured goods to 20 per cent or less. Seven hundred and fifty different tariffs would be reduced out of the cumbersome total of 1,200. Export duties would also be reduced. At the end of this the prudent Government should still have a surplus of half a million pounds.[18]

Peel with his appetite for detailed reform had, as Prime Minister, accomplished for the trade tariffs what he had achieved for the Criminal Justice System as Home Secretary fifteen years earlier. On both occasions he proposed a comprehensive overhaul of a kind inconceivable for any previous Minister except Pitt. But the 1842 Budget was a greater leap than the criminal justice reforms. It dealt with matters at the heart of political controversy. It solved the immediate fiscal problem of the deficit by introducing a remedy which made possible much wider benefits. Peel thus raised and widened the whole quality of debate. The routine discussion of depressing statistics was suspended by a simple act of political courage. The revival of income tax might have defeated Peel as surely as the proposal for a tariff defeated Baldwin in 1923. It might even have ruined him as the poll tax helped to ruin Margaret Thatcher in 1990. But Peel's sense of timing and mastery of detail saw him through. Even more important was the self-confidence, the intellectual and moral certainty which he had gradually built up over the years of opposition.

Peel's letters to Croker are of particular interest at this time. He was briefing his friend for articles which he hoped Croker would write supporting the Government in the *Quarterly Review*. The arguments are put with a simplicity rare in Peel's official papers. On 22 July he wrote Croker a letter which went to the heart of this thinking. The essential aim must be to revive trade and manufacturing:

If you had to constitute new societies, you might on moral and social grounds prefer cornfields to cotton factories, an agricultural to a manufacturing population. But our lot is cast, and we cannot recede ... We must make this country a cheap country for living and thus induce parties to remain and settle here – enable them to consume more by having more to spend ... It is a fallacy to urge that the loss falls on the agriculturist. They too are consumers. They lose almost as much in increased poor rates alone as they gain by increased price. Lower the price of wheat; not only poor rates but the cost of everything is lowered. We do not push this argument to its logical consequences ... we take into account vested interests, enjoyed capital, the importance of independent supply [i.e. independence of foreign wheat] the social benefits of flourishing agriculture.

But 'the danger is not low price from the tariff, but low price from inability to consume, from the poor man giving up his pint of beer and the man in middling station giving up his joint of meat'.[19]

The immediate sensation after Peel's Budget speech was the income tax. Greville described 'a masterpiece of a financial statement ... A few people had expected an income tax, but the majority did not ... This great measure, so lofty in conception, right in direction and able in execution, places him at once on a pinnacle of power and establishes his government on such a foundation as accident alone can shake.'[20] Yet Greville was a Whig. So too was the Member of Parliament who went into the Travellers Club that evening and remarked 'one felt all the time he was speaking "Thank God Peel is Minister"'.[21] Of course there were critics. Cobden and Bright on behalf of the Anti Corn Law League were violently hostile. Their members wanted the abolition, not amendment, of the Corn Laws, were suspicious of tariff reduction on manufacturers, and certainly had no desire to pay income tax.

The last word on income tax might go to Lady Stanley of Alderley. She was not a political lady but she read *The Times* eagerly each day and confided to a cousin on 18 March: 'I think the income tax a very disagreeable thing, but so I do blue pills, rhubarb or castor oil, and it does appear that a strong dose of help is needed for the finances of the country, and that it cannot go on with half measures and experiments any longer. I would like to ask those who object to this tax to point out another that would certainly answer as well; and if they cannot I should like them not to stir up a factious and useless opposition.'[22] So said most articulate people at the time; and so with occasional exasperated variations have we continued to say ever since.

Peel met greater parliamentary difficulty over the part of the Budget which from his standpoint contained the good news. He might have expected a storm of objections to the income tax and to the new Corn Law, but neither blew at full force. Conservatives and Whigs could not object in principle to tariff reduction, since governments of both parties had practised it. But once the details of the new rates emerged the interests affected, and particularly the agriculturists, began to protest. At the outset Peel once again argued the case in the Commons himself. He showed how smuggling frustrated some of the protection which farmers thought they enjoyed. Unplaited straw was admitted with only a nominal duty, whereas once it was plaited it attracted seventeen shillings and sixpence a hundredweight. Peel held up a bundle of unplaited straw in which was concealed a small parcel of the plaited article which had certainly not paid duty. The list of tariffs contained a mass of such detailed distinctions which in practice meant nothing.

Politicians in general are divided between those who by nature complicate and those who simplify. Peel, though a master of detail, was by nature a simplifier. He liked to sweep away the cobwebs; it was not the least of his political virtues. Peel was particularly pleased to have reduced the duty on timber – 'the best thing we have done without exception'. Free access to Baltic timber would benefit everyone concerned with ship building, fisheries, all public buildings such as piers and harbours, and anyone repairing a farmhouse, who would find savings on timber to offset his income tax.[23]

Gladstone took over from Peel the handling of the detailed tariff debates in the Commons, and earned high praise from the Prime Minister for his skill. The Cabinet decided to leave the sugar duties untouched for the moment. They had caused a lot of trouble for the Whig Government in its last days and the argument was still simmering. To the usual contest between commercial interests was added in the case of sugar particular emotions about slavery, now abolished in British colonies but not yet in other sugar-producing countries like Brazil.

Cattle turned out to be the main problem. In an age before refrigeration the best way of importing meat into Britain was on the hoof from the Continent. The import of live cattle or of carcass meat had been totally prohibited, though the demand for meat was growing. Peel thought that as a result the price to the consumer was extravagantly high. He proposed to allow in live and carcass imports, paying a duty of £1 a head for live cattle and eight shillings a hundredweight for carcasses. The alarmed agriculturists protested; Peel assured them that the duty would give them adequate protection. He easily beat off a protectionist amendment in the Commons, but the Government's majority contained a good number of opposition votes, while eighty-five Conservatives voted against the tariff cuts. It was the awakening of backbench distrust.

Peel watched the markets keenly. As usual Arbuthnot expressed the anxieties of the Ultras, but Peel batted him down. It was said that disease among cattle was adding to the distress of British farmers: 'Could that', asked Peel, 'be a serious argument for refusing to import wholesome meat from abroad?' Cattle imports would be a tiny proportion of the whole. 'There were 174,000 head of cattle sold in Smithfield alone last year. If 10,000 head of cattle should cross the sea from foreign parts, I shall be very much surprised, but I must fairly say I hope they may. I think the price of meat unduly high.'[24]

As 1842 wore on, a new and deeper note began to sound in this debate. Peel's convictions became firmer and his language harsher and more defiant. For outside the confines of Westminster the Condition of England was no longer just a matter for intellectual analysis or abstract humanitarian concern. The trade cycle and the failure of successive harvests were creating hardship which quickly turned to disorder. Men remembered the tumult at the time of the Great Reform Bill. Then there had been plenty of observers who feared a violent revolution in the French style. That fear had gone. True, in 1841 the Chartists were in full cry with their political demands. But Peel and his Home Secretary, Sir James Graham, were clear that at the heart of the discontents lay not politics but poverty. This did not make Peel lenient when faced with violence. In such matters he remained a Tory, for whom the first duty of government was to maintain public order. He thoroughly disliked any attempt to put pressure either on Parliament from outside or to intimidate employees or workers. But he grasped the link between the economic state of the country and the proposals which he had put before Parliament. To relieve poverty by cutting the cost of living was not only morally right and intellectually sound; it was now a condition of restoring a stable society. Conservatives above all should see this; Peel's harshest contempt was addressed to those of his supporters who preferred to stay blind.

Unrest came to a head in August 1842. Rising unemployment and low wages created a general mood in the cities which was inflamed for their different purposes by the Chartists and the Anti Corn Law League. The Chartists had failed in May 1842 to persuade the Commons to receive a mammoth petition, six miles in length with (it was claimed) three million signatures. They gained no sympathy even from Radicals in the Commons. The Chartists made the mistake of neglecting the tradition of incremental change in Britain. Peaceful evolution was certainly possible in Britain; violent revolution was still just conceivable; but the quick, peaceful revolution at which the Chartists aimed was never on the cards. As Peel pointed out, they were in effect proposing a different Constitution. This had no appeal for Queen, Lords or Commons, and would bring no help to those who were hungry or out of work in the summer of 1842. Discouraged at the centre, the Chartists fell back on organising marches and industrial action in the cities.

By contrast, the Anti Corn Law League was noisy where it mattered politically, in the Commons and among the middle-class electorate. Ministers and the Conservative Party were enraged at the way in which Cobden and Bright stirred up the trouble for which members of their own League were partly responsible. Such employers threw men out of work, introduced short time, and tried to cut wages. Cobden strongly opposed the income tax designed to finance the tariff reductions which would reduce the cost of living for the poor. Yet the League appointed lecturers who went round the industrial areas exploiting grievances as if they were brought about solely by a selfish aristocracy who cared only for the Corn Laws. The vocabulary of the League implied that physical force was justified to achieve its ends. Ministers were accused of murder, and one speaker said that few tears would be shed at Peel's funeral.[25] Many Conservatives (and some Chartists) believed that the League was actually organising violence. Peel and Graham decided against prosecution, but set about compiling a damaging dossier on the League's agitation which eventually appeared, thanks to Croker, in the *Quarterly Review* in December 1842.

For Peel the growing violence presented a close personal danger. He wrote from Whitehall to Julia on 12 August: 'Secret. The accounts from various parts of the country are very bad. In Scotland as well as the north of England there has been much violence and great confusion.'[26] He kept her more closely informed than usual in the next few days, during which he had to cancel a plan to join her in the Midlands. Birmingham, fifteen miles from Drayton, was quiet but uneasy, and the countryside was full of rumours. On 20 August: 'I have requested some new arms in perfect order and ammunition to be sent to Drayton. We had better say nothing about it. I think one of the rooms in the Tower would be the safest place of deposit. The ammunition should be carefully kept near the arms and in a dry and safe place.'[27]

This arming of Drayton was organised by Bonham, in his general capacity as handler of delicate matters for Peel. But Julia was a General's daughter. There had been a report that agitators would march on Drayton after attacking Lord Anglesey's home in Staffordshire. Julia was ready for them, and replied to Peel the next day, 21 August:

> My dearest love,
>   During the whole of this late tumultuous scene and expected attack I felt anxious only to save you from an alarm for us, lest you might think things exaggerated. You will know that I was never guilty of a sentimental or ignoble fear. Our arrangements were quickly and vigorously made, and should have been equal to an attack from two or three hundred until assistance had come – but then we expected three or four thousand. I am confident however that no men actually attacking doors and windows here would have left this place alive. I sent for Mr Grundy and desired him to see to the preparation for the supply of water. You see we were armed at all points![28]

Lord Melbourne thought that politicians (except himself) were to blame for these outbreaks. They had allowed political debate to become dangerously heated. He wrote to the Queen:

> The Tories and Conservatives (not the Leaders, but the larger portion of the party) have done what they could to inflame the public mind upon that most inflammable topic of the Poor Laws. The *Times* newspaper has been the most forward in this. The Whigs and Radicals have

done what they could in the same direction upon the Corn Laws. Mr Attwood and another set have worked the question of the currency and the whole career of Mr O'Connell in Ireland has been too manifest to be mistaken. It is no wonder if working in this manner altogether they have at last succeeded in driving the country like this which is certainly very near, if not actually, a rebellion.[29]

The violence reached the nearest approach to rebellion in the middle of August 1842, when Melbourne wrote that letter, and the secret carbines reached Drayton. By this time coal miners were on strike in the potteries. Crowds many thousands strong roamed through Shropshire and Cheshire trying to spread trouble. At the same time mill-owners in the north-west began to cut wages. The crowds attacked pits and mills, public buildings and private houses. Two policemen were killed in Manchester. Disorder spread from the north-west of England to the north-east, Wales and Scotland. The Chartists joined in, adding their political slogans to the agitation caused by economic hardship.[30]

In such tense situations the authorities need to watch for anniversaries. The bitter memory of a date can be used to bring emotions to a head. 16 August was the anniversary of Peterloo, when in 1819 the yeomanry and the Hussars had attacked a huge crowd outside Manchester, killing eleven and wounding several hundred. The Government began to receive alarming reports from Manchester of plans on the anniversary for what Peel characteristically described as 'a great assemblage of persons riotously disposed'. With Graham he decided on firm action. As compared with the time of Peterloo, indeed since Peel's time as Home Secretary in the 1820s, the authorities disposed of two new and crucial assets. First, though it was a slow process and with many gaps, police forces had been formed in northern cities following the success of Peel's Metropolitan Police in London. Second, trains could now carry large numbers of troops quickly to places of danger. These two facts altered the balance in favour of the Government.

On 13 August three magistrates arrived from Manchester with a gloomy account of its situation. The Cabinet decided at once to send a battalion of Guards to the city by train that evening. They also resolved on an immediate proclamation to warn citizens against attending riotous meetings. The proclamation needed a meeting of the Privy Council at

Windsor that evening. Peel organised this before warning the Queen, a sign already of his greater confidence in handling her, though he carefully timed the Council for six-thirty in the evening before she needed to dress for dinner.

The effect of this show of military force was reassuring. The magistrates and the police in Manchester recovered their nerve. Riots occurred, and in Preston four people were killed, but there was no Peterloo. The worst was over in the north. On 18 August Peel wrote:

My dearest love,

I have gone through all the accounts from the country this morning with Sir James Graham. I think, upon the whole, they are satisfactory. Manchester, Wigan and Preston are quiet and Birmingham seems never to have been disturbed except by strangers entering the town. In Yorkshire there is still uneasiness, but if we can put out the fire at Manchester, which we shall do, it will soon cease to blaze at a distance.[31]

Trouble, though not so threatening, came to London the next day. Graham dined late with Peel that evening; they were interrupted by a report from Mayne, the Metropolitan Police Commissioner, of a big crowd in Lincoln's Inn Fields. The two men went together to the Home Office, where Peel remained into the small hours of the morning, organising police and troops to head the crowd off from moving from the City into Westminster.[32]

Peel and Graham worked closely together without dispute or rivalry through these anxious weeks. They trusted each other's good faith and good judgement. Graham was more likely than Peel to make moral judgements and bring Providence and the Almighty into his correspondence. He was not witty like Croker, nor learned like Gladstone, not as politically obedient as Goulburn, not as personally close as Hardinge. But his work with Peel was unmatched in quality over the years of government and produced a friendship of steel.

Peel suffered that month from overwork and headaches. The disorder in England died down, but for him there was no rest. The Queen had long planned a visit to Scotland at the end of August 1842. Her Ministers were worried about her safety; Peel in particular had been deeply alarmed at an attempt on her life in May by a lunatic with a pistol. A similar attack followed in July. But, looking coolly at the danger, Ministers judged that she was no more at risk in Scotland than in England, and the visit went ahead. As Prime Minister, Peel was required to attend. He went ahead by train as far as Darlington, then by post-chaise to Edinburgh. No one knew exactly when the Queen would arrive on her yacht, the *Royal George*; to be on the safe side Peel made sure he was at the pier between three and four in the morning and waited for hours in the dawn. The planning of the visit was confused and in the circumstances dangerous. The big crowds came very close to the Queen's own carriage. On the drive into Edinburgh some Chartists hooted and groaned, but Peel thought the massed onlookers were 99 per cent favourable. The hectic enthusiasm continued throughout the tour. 'Radical Town Councillors bursting with loyalty, enormous crowds all in good humour.'[33] As on Peel's visit with George IV in 1822, there was plenty of Scottish summer rain, and this time cases of scarlet fever in Holyrood Palace. The Queen processed from one grand house to another as far north as Taymouth, enjoying the bonfires on the hills and much Highland dancing.

The Queen was more entranced by all this than her Prime Minister. Peel might be Rector of Glasgow University but at heart he was deep, deep English. He wrote to Julia: 'There is a certain novelty and familiarity about the Highland customs that is striking for a time, but it soon becomes very tiresome. I wish most heartily I was relieved from witnessing them. I have just left a new room below stairs in which a singer of Scotch songs from Perth is performing, full of smoke, the room being just furnished and a fire lighted for the first time.'[34] Peel noticed that the caterers for the immense meals came from London and that most of the houses smelt strongly of new paint. At Scone the Queen's bed arrived shortly before herself. Peel's hands became swollen and bruised with shaking hands on both sides of the carriage, but he observed that it was better than receiving stones. Peel advised the Queen not to venture as far north as Sutherland, but she stayed on in Scotland after he returned, exhausted but relieved, to his desk in Whitehall.

Out of this experience Peel at once set in hand one necessary change. Remembering the hours of waiting at the pier on the Firth of Forth and the resulting confusion of the Queen's entry into Edinburgh, he decided that royal visits should no longer depend on the vagaries of the wind.

'The first act of Sir Robert Peel on his return from Scotland was to write to Lord Haddington and strongly urge upon the Admiralty the necessity of providing a steam yacht for your Majesty's accommodation.' This would be ready by the following summer. It would be driven by a revolving screw, not a paddle:

> Sir John Barrow assures Sir Robert Peel that he has been on board a steamboat moved by the screw, and that the working of the engine is scarcely perceptible – that there is none of the tremulous motion which accompanied the beats of the paddles and that it will be possible to apply an apparatus by means of which the smoke can be consumed and the disagreeable smell in great measure prevented. Sir Robert Peel will leave nothing undone to ensure Your Majesty's comfort and safety.[35]

His commitment to the Queen's safety was soon tested. A year later, before the Queen had actually sailed on her, Peel was told that the new royal yacht did not answer the helm correctly and was unsafe. Experts were arguing for and against her. Peel suggested to the First Lord of the Admiralty that those on both sides of the argument should be sent on board to the Bay of Biscay in December to establish which was right. Apparently without such a violent test the matter was sorted, and the *Victoria and Albert* sailed on.[36] Peel had started the modern tradition of royal yachts as an asset for the nation which was crudely interrupted by Mr Blair and his incoming Government in 1997. A little later, perhaps from knowledge of the Isle of Wight gained on his own holiday there, Peel suggested to the Queen that she might buy Osborne to meet her need for an informal family home. He was becoming a courtier after all.

'Everything has gone off so well at Edinburgh, Perth and elsewhere,'[37] wrote the Queen to Lord Melbourne. But Scotland, as Peel knew, was not all Highland reels, bonfires on the hills, or even loyal Radical councillors. There was a good deal of 'elsewhere' where everything was certainly not going well. Peel's growing concern with working-class poverty was not limited to the study of such general statistics as existed or such anecdotes as came his way. He focused on particulars. He worried away at the facts until they were firmly planted in his brain; and out of the facts he traced a plan of action. The most striking example of this process was the large weaving town of Paisley just south and west of Glasgow.

Paisley, Scotland's fifth largest town, depended for employment on the weaving trade, organised in a large number of small businesses. The Paisley weavers may have been less nimble than their Continental competitors in adapting to changes in fashion but the main problem was the trade cycle. They depended on thousands of distant households whose expenditure fluctuated unpredictably. As the local historian put it, 'when the middle-class lady had to postpone buying a new muslin ball-dress and a new evening shawl, the Paisley weaver had to pawn his mattress'.[38] Trade was bad in 1837–8, up a little in 1839, down slightly in 1840.

In the second half of 1841 the roof fell in. More than half the merchants and manufacturers of the town went bankrupt. They carried down with them almost half of the Friendly Societies, which were the main means by which the weavers could save against adversity. Even the pawnbrokers failed. Farmers in the nearby countryside had to guard their fields of potatoes or turnips against hungry marauders.

There was a distinctive Scottish flavour to the distress of Paisley. The people of Paisley prided themselves on their high standard of education, their independence, their Kirk and the excellence of their local paper, the *Paisley Advertiser*. The 1834 English Poor Law had no counterpart yet in Scotland, so there was no workhouse. Relief was administered through a Relief Committee consisting of town councillors, lay volunteers and ministers of the Church of Scotland.

The number of destitute families stood at 15,000 during the winter of 1841–2, and funds quickly ran short. Local gentry from outside the town began to contribute. The Committee leaders who emerged reflected the politics of Scotland. The Provost of Paisley, Mr Henderson, was a strong Chartist; the Sheriff was a Tory from outside the town who feared a popular uprising; the Reverend Dr Burns was an eloquent critic of the Corn Laws. A deputation led by these men came to London and was received by Peel himself, flanked by Graham and Stanley. They explained the gravity of the crisis. Graham as Home Secretary did most of the talking in reply. He was hardly sympathetic. He asked them about the banking facilities in the town, believing that the Scottish one pound note might be responsible for destructive inflation. More woundingly, he referred to the Scottish appetite for whisky. For his part Dr Burns overdid his criticism of the Corn Law, which Peel and his colleagues were at the time planning to reform but not abandon.

The meeting led nowhere in particular but it lodged Paisley in the minds of Ministers. Peel asked for regular reports, and the local Member raised the question in Parliament. A new report from Paisley in February 1842 stated that there were now 17,000 men destitute; that the Relief Committee was rather too liberal in handing out help and too easy to hoodwink; that there was no immediate threat to public order, but this could worsen if relief funds entirely ran out; and that there was a need for a force of special constables to reinforce the local police.[39] This report galvanised Peel to dispatch an official, Edward Twistleton, an Assistant Poor Law Commissioner, to take a grip of the situation.

A curious episode followed. Twistleton needed money if he was to do any good. But there was no way that central government could provide money for the welfare of distressed citizens. The apparatus did not exist, and it would have been thought unacceptable to invent it. If for Paisley, why not for everyone? Such welfare payments by government would put intolerable burdens on the Exchequer, distort trade and postpone economic recovery. Peel had no intention of creating a welfare state to give taxpayers' money to the poor, or a national industrial policy to tell mill-owners where to weave their cloth. In these circumstances there were only two ways in which government could act, and Peel combined them for Paisley. The government, and in particular the Home Secretary, often used secret agents, not just to collect intelligence but to carry out any operations which Ministers favoured but which fell outside their normal powers. As Home Secretary Peel had reduced the use of such agents. Nevertheless he told Twistleton to exercise as quietly as possible an authority over Paisley which no law had provided. The hard-pressed community at first made no protest. For six weeks Twistleton acted as a virtual dictator in Paisley, reporting directly to Peel and Graham.

But powers were no use without money. Peel and Graham set themselves to work. The need was made even clearer by a memorial from the elders of the Kirk on 24 March:

There is a very general feeling of deep and settled discontent. Hopeless and worn out with either continued depression or often recurring distress, many have lost much of their wanted self respect, and a few all proper regard for the usual observance of religion and decencies of society. Their homes are sometimes the picture of extreme wretchedness. They are themselves often

wanting in change of dress, a kind of outfit formerly regarded as essential to
common decency in Scotland ... Your memorialists are labouring, some of
them beyond their strength, if possible to stem the tide which has been
bearing in upon them, and which is carrying before it much that has been
good in the wonted habits of society, but unsupported by means at all com-
mensurate to the task, they also are discouraged.[40]

Against this background Peel set out to raise money for Paisley from
the rich. He had done this before for distressed towns in Lancashire in
the 1820s, and remembered the technique. The Queen's generosity and his
own had to lead the way. On 24 March Twistleton was authorised to
inform the Paisley General Relief Committee that he had private funds
available, namely £500 each from the Queen and the Marquess of
Abercorn and £225 each from Peel, Graham and Stanley. With the money
came conditions on which Graham insisted. Relief should in future be
more closely supervised so that food was brought for children in need and
not squandered on drink; able-bodied men should be required to work.
As the next step Graham mobilised the London Manufacturers' Relief
Committee, which Peel had created in 1826 for relief in England, and a
further £12,500 (about half a million pounds in present money) flowed
from the Committee into Paisley. Twistleton emphasised at every turn
that this was private, not public, generosity, but it certainly would not
have flowed without strong pressure from Ministers.

Next, Peel asked the Queen to add a public gesture to her private generosity. She had already encouraged her ladies to wear Paisley shawls, but
that was hardly enough. On 7 May Peel wrote to her:

He had this day an interview with the Archbishop of Canterbury, the
Bishop of London and Sir James Graham on the subject of the destitute condition of the labouring classes in some districts of the country,
particularly in the neighbourhood of Paisley, and in some of the manufacturing towns and villages in Lancashire. The privations and sufferings in these parts of the country have been during the winter and
continue to be very great. The patience and submission with which
they have been hitherto borne have been exemplary in the highest
degree. The local funds for the charitable support of the sufferers are
in some cases nearly exhausted, and great apprehension is entertained

by the magistrates and others as to the consequences of a complete exhaustion of these funds.[41]

The Queen was asked to send a public letter to be read in churches and chapels asking for charitable contributions. Peel explained that this was intended not just to raise funds but to show sympathy with those who were suffering.

The Queen agreed; relief flowed; the children were fed. But as often happens gratitude was in short supply. Graham and his advisers had not lost their suspicions of Scottish fecklessness. They decreed that relief must take the form of rations of oatmeal bread and potatoes supplied in bulk by Government contractors based in Liverpool. But these were just the commodities which could best be supplied by local producers through local shops. The local Relief Committee pointed out that the Government's rules were driving the shops out of business. They pleaded that part of the relief should be provided as meal tickets which could be cashed locally, for goods such as soap as well as food. More than a thousand unemployed demonstrated in the town centre. But Twistleton was instructed to stick to official policy; the Provost and his colleagues on the Relief Committee resigned. Twistleton for six weeks had to act alone in Paisley. The distribution system which he established was actually more generous in its food allowance than under the old Relief Committee, but the system of distribution remained unpopular. Finally a compromise was reached. The Relief Committee was reinstated under Provost Henderson and allowed to pay one fifth of the allowance in cash. By this time one third of all the voluntary funds raised nationally was going to Paisley, and Graham secretly told the organisers not to reduce that proportion.

Twistleton returned to London in 1842. Trade slowly revived; the mills reopened. Graham set in hand a Scottish version of the Poor Law. Paisley was forgotten by most people, but never by Peel.* By stretching to the utmost the informal and secretive powers of government Peel and

---

* Nor by Disraeli. The present MP for Paisley, The Rt Hon. Douglas Alexander, points out that in his novel *Endymion* (written around 1880 but with a story cast at this time) Disraeli makes one of his characters advise the hero: 'Keep your eye on Paisley I am much mistaken if there will not be a state of things there which alone will break up the whole concern. It will burst it, Sir, it will burst it.'

Graham had just stopped short of open government intervention by subsidy to save Paisley. Of course Paisley was not alone; it was just the outstanding example of widespread suffering.

Historians argue whether Peel and Graham were moved to this exceptional effort by Christian compassion or by fear of an uprising against the ruling classes. But there is no contradiction. The two thoughts sit harmoniously side by side in Peel's letter to the Queen just quoted. The magistrates were worried about possible disorder, so Peel and Graham were worried too. Their whole conduct during the summer showed absolute determination that the Government should keep control of the country. They were a Conservative Government, and that was their first duty, as Lord Melbourne and most Whigs would have heartily agreed. But that does not rule out humanitarian compassion. Peel was usually a cool man when faced with human unhappiness, but the news from Paisley and the Lancashire towns touched him.

Such compassion for poverty shows convincingly in letter after letter of Peel's on all kinds of subject. It shows even more clearly in the way memories of the plight of the poor in the winters of 1841 and 1842 shaped what he did later. The ideas for action were already in his head; he was beginning to put them into effect with his Budget, the new Corn Law, and the tariff cuts, in the very weeks of most acute suffering. Knowledge of that suffering greatly sharpened his convictions and determination. It was not with trainloads of troops and acts of class repression that Peel wished to remedy the Condition of England. That wise historian G.M. Young summed it up: 'his frigid efficiency covered an almost passionate concern for the welfare of the people'.[42]

As we have seen, Peel and Graham were consistently firm in re-establishing order where it was in danger of breaking down. But they had no sympathy with employers who provoked the breakdown of order by paying miserable wages. Graham instructed General Arbuthnot in the North that while he must defend property against workers, and workers against intimidation by strikes, he must not use force to make strikers return to work. Indeed he should encourage employers to settle reasonable grievances. In Staffordshire Graham believed that the masters were more at fault than the men. Peel endorsed Graham's distinction between preserving public order and protecting employers against 'just and peaceable demands for a rise of wages'.[43]

There was one class of employer whom Ministers particularly criticised. In May 1842 an independent commission issued a famous Blue
Book on the employment of children in mines and factories. Lord Ashley
leapt once more into action on both fronts. Public opinion was particularly emphatic on the degradation suffered by women and children in the
mines. Peel congratulated Ashley warmly for his speech in June on what
Peel called 'the mining abominations'.[44] In Scotland in September with
the Queen Peel came across out-of-work miners who behaved well. He
suspected that the profits of mine-owners were high enough for them to
deal more generously with their workforce. Ashley's proposals prohibiting
the employment in the mines of women, girls and boys under ten were
supported in the Commons by Graham, and despite some bickering over
amendments quickly passed into law.

Meanwhile Peel had a wider argument on his hands, during which his
own emotions often overflowed. The argument continued to the end of
his premiership and beyond. Peel had to persuade his own supporters not
just to accept his 1842 measures, but to follow further down the path
which he had marked. In the cannonade of argument as Peel fired and
reloaded his artillery Paisley became his standard ammunition. The
Marquis of Ailsa lived not far away and ventured to grumble. Peel told
him, '[i]f I were a landed proprietor in the West of Scotland and saw
17,000 persons supported during the winter as in one Scotch town Paisley,
by charitable contributions I should seriously inquire whether such a state
of things was quite compatible with the security or at least the enjoyment
of property'.[45]

As usual Peel used Arbuthnot as a channel to the Ultras in the
Commons and Croker to reach the readers of the influential *Quarterly
Review*. These letters, carefully drafted and likely to pass from hand to
hand, were for Peel the nearest approach to radio or television broadcasts
today. To Arbuthnot, who reported dissatisfaction about farm prices on
the back benches, he hoped that those concerned would look at some
matters which were 'in truth more important to them and their property
than the fall in the price of stock or of pigs or of wheat'. He gave details
of the last letter he had opened before Arbuthnot's. It came from Paisley.
'It has required £600 a week beside poor rate to keep these people from
starving ... What is to be done with these people at Paisley during next
winter? They are not fit for emigration. There have been about 150

bankruptcies among the principal manufacturers of the town. No rents
are paid. No money can be raised, either by poor rates or voluntary contribution, within the district. What is to be the end of this?'[46] The answer
lay in increasing purchasing power. The inability of the poor to consume
depressed farm prices more than any tariff change.

To Croker in October he gave again the latest figures for Paisley, and
repeated the question 'what is to be done for the winter?'. Readers of the
Quarterly Review might like high farm prices. But they should 'rest assured
of this, that landed property would not be safe during this next winter,
with the prices of the last four years, and even if it were safe it would not
be profitable for long'. The Poor Rate, special help for poverty, and
diminished consumption would soon reduce the temporary gain of high
prices to producers. High prices and mechanisation were throwing 2,000
more hands out of work every day. 'These are the things I am more
anxious about than cattle from Vigo or the price of pork.'[47] Graham
wrote to him about a plan for moral education in schools; Peel would
have agreed with the comment of his usually pious Home Secretary.
'These instruments are not to be despised and have been too long neglected; but cheap bread, plenty of potatoes, low priced American bacon, a
little more Dutch cheese and butter, will have a more pacifying effect than
all the mental culture which any Government can supply.'[48]

The Ultras were not only selfish; they made no sense. Lord Kinnaird
complained to Croker that the price of hay had come down from fourteen to nine pence a stone – and in the next breath that he could not
afford to keep his Highland sheep. This was the sort of contradiction
which drove Peel to distraction. Worse was to come. As the summer of
1842 progressed it became clear that the harvest was going to be good. To
Peel and most people this was marvellous news. But the voice of lamentation was soon heard in the land, and from the kind of critic who most
exasperated the Prime Minister. Sir Charles Burrell, Conservative
Member of Parliament for Shoreham in Sussex, a prosperous agricultural
constituency, passed to the Chief Whip a grumble from his neighbours in
church against low prices, against imports and the proposed official
service of thanksgiving for the harvest. Peel was stirred. 'This is the first
intimation I have had that the thanksgiving for a good harvest was
deemed "inappropriate". The wheat crop of Sir Charles Burrell and that
of three or four of his neighbours who attend the parish church failed –

probably from want of draining and bad farming – and therefore we are not to thank God for a harvest which ... was providentially good.' Peel then fired his familiar salvo. 'If Sir Charles had such cases before him as I have, of thousands and tens of thousands in want of food and employment, at Greenock, Paisley, Edinburgh and a dozen large towns in the manufacturing districts, he would not expect me to rend my garments in despair if some excellent jerked beef from South America should get into the English market, and bring down meat from 7½ pence or 8 pence a pound.'[49]

In 1936 the unemployed workers of Jarrow in north-east England marched on London to protest against unemployment. For years after that, Jarrow became the symbol of a disaster which had tainted the reputation of a Conservative-dominated Government and which they must never on any account allow to happen again. Peel could justly say that he was not responsible for the hardships of 1841–2, but Paisley became the same sort of tragic symbol in his mind.

Peel's letters bristle with comments from a man who is sure he is right, addressed without ceremony to men less intelligent and well informed than himself. He counter-attacks without hesitation or tact. Yet these are precisely the men whose support he needed in Parliament and the constituencies. On other occasions Peel could be almost excessively roundabout and polite. But here, on the subject about which he felt most strongly, his caution deserted him, and he exclaimed what was in his mind.

Reading Peel's letters written at this time I am reminded of another Prime Minister for whom I worked closely for seven years, in Opposition and at 10 Downing Street. Like Ted Heath, Peel was stiff in manner and could take personal offence easily. Like Heath, he came from a background far removed from the traditional ruling class. Like Heath, he was greatly admired by a group of close colleagues and subordinates who enjoyed his company. Like Heath, he was genuinely and stubbornly concerned to improve the standard of living of the British people. Like Heath, he looked on them as one nation and he believed they could best be helped by reducing the burdens on them. Like Heath, he enjoyed detail and administration. Like Heath, he was impatient with contradiction, and was apt to lash out, particularly at his own supporters. Like Heath, he was conscious of the narrow and unacceptable face of some of those supporters on the sour Right of the Conservative Party.

There were many differences between the two men and indeed the context in which they worked. But when I read the letters and speeches of Peel and study his talents and tactics, success and failures, I hear an echo of that other voice.

Fourteen

Foreigners

———— ◎◡ ————

'Our cousin Jonathan is an offensive arrogant fellow in his
manner ... a treaty of conciliation with such a fellow,
however considered by prudence or policy to be necessary,
can in no case be very popular with the multitude'
*Lord Ashburton, after negotiating the north-east boundary of the United
States, 1842*

'Fifty-four Forty or Fight'
Slogan in the American presidential election, 1844

'Everything is very different to England,
particularly the population'
Queen Victoria's reflections on visiting France, 1843

'If you can keep peace, reduce expense, extend commerce,
and strengthen our hold on India by confidence in our
justice, kindness and wisdom you will be received here
on your return with acclamation a thousand times
louder ... than if you have a dozen victories to boast of,
and annex the Punjab to the overgrown Empire of India'
Peel to Hardinge, November 1844

Peel is best remembered for what he did in his own country – for Catholic Emancipation, for the Metropolitan Police, the Conservative Party, the great Budgets, the Corn Laws. Even well informed people suppose that in the background of these commotions foreign and imperial policy flowed in a steady stream, barely interrupted by changes of government, hardly requiring the attention of Peel as Prime Minister. On the contrary, Peel gave overseas affairs a large share of his thinking. He focused strongly on what seemed the three most important aspects: the governance of India and the shifting and precarious relationships with the United States and France.

The range of Peel's mind was not confined by the Atlantic and the Channel. He was Prime Minister of the most powerful country in the world. The way in which Britain used her military and naval power, the way she conducted her diplomacy and ruled her Empire, had a global significance of which Peel was well aware. The margin of Britain's superiority over others was much narrower than the margin of American superiority today. It depended for four or five decades of the nineteenth century on a mixture of naval supremacy and commercial boldness. But the questions in Peel's mind were not entirely different from those in American minds today.

Is there a general international interest? Are there specific moral objectives to which a powerful nation's strength should at least in part be dedicated? To what extent should a powerful nation accept constraints on the use of its power? Is it part of that nation's duty or interest to promote freedom and decent government in other countries? Should the tone of its diplomacy be loud and emphatic as befits its strength? Or quiet and conciliatory, in order to cultivate relationships of trust and good humour with other countries? Which choice is more likely to appeal to domestic opinion? In Peel's time British leaders argued different answers to these questions, as American leaders do now.

From the day he became Prime Minister in 1841 Peel found himself in the heat of these arguments. The pace had been set by Lord Palmerston, Foreign Secretary in Whig governments both before and after Peel's premiership, and eventually for ten years Prime Minister. Palmerston and Peel had been at Harrow together. Their views on essential matters were not far apart. Palmerston was a Whig, evolving into a Liberal, but with strong conservative instincts on most domestic matters. Peel was a Tory, evolving into a Conservative, but with a strong instinct for reform when the case was made. Both men looked for the centre ground in politics. The difference between the two was essentially of temperament. Both worked hard and were masters of detail; Peel, the son of a cotton spinner, paraded the fact whereas Palmerston, a Whig aristocrat, preferred to conceal it behind jokes and jolly stories. Palmerston led the permissive personal life of a Regency buck; Peel was a Victorian father of family, faithful to his wife and attentive to his children. Palmerston spoke, particularly about foreigners, in vivid, sometimes crude phrases which attracted popular opinion; Peel's long and often ambiguous sentences appealed to foreigners and to the elite. Palmerston believed in using Britain's strength, not just to advance her interests but (at least in Europe) to help the cause of reform and decent government. He did not mind humiliating an opponent whom he had worsted. His cartoon images, sometimes as a successful pugilist, sometimes lounging with a straw in his mouth, fitted his very English idea of himself. Through a highly successful career he trumpeted his successes to attract the public support in England which he held to the end of a long life.

To succeed Palmerston as Foreign Secretary in 1841 Peel chose as different a man as could be imagined. George Gordon, Earl of Aberdeen, was four years Peel's senior. He had already spent nearly thirty years of his life in foreign and colonial affairs, beginning as a special envoy in Vienna at the end of the Napoleonic War. He had witnessed the fearful slaughter at the battle of Leipzig in 1814. In 1834–5 he served as Peel's Secretary for War and Colonies. Like Peel, he was stiff and reserved in manner. His shyness masked a deep melancholy caused by extraordinary domestic tragedy; he had mourned the deaths of two wives, four daughters and a son. Perhaps more than any other politician of his day Aberdeen was genuinely reluctant in office. He was propelled forward by his own perceptive intelligence, by a tireless sense of duty and by the fact that everyone trusted him. He was not one of Peel's political confidants, for he lacked the necessary harsh grasp of the reality of politics. The link between the two men was more personal, but so strong that after Peel's death Julia wrote to Aberdeen, 'My beloved always talked to you as the friend whom he most valued, for whom he had the sincerest affection, whom he esteemed higher than any.'[1]

The absolute trust between the two men was one of the Government's outstanding assets. It did not mean that they always held the same views. Peel agreed with Aberdeen in rejecting Palmerston's boastful style of foreign policy. Both Prime Minister and Foreign Secretary believed in traditional diplomacy as a long-term technique for solving disputes and establishing the necessary understanding between great nations. Neither thought that it was part of Britain's job to force Britain's political traditions or institutions on other people. But these instincts led Aberdeen to believe in the good faith of others which Peel's natural caution questioned. Aberdeen rejected not just the idea of pre-emptive military action but even the strengthening of national defence. During a dispute with the

French Peel wrote briskly that one needed 'that charity which believeth all things' to accept the assurances of the French government, to which Aberdeen replied that 'charity should not only believe all things, but should never fail'.[2]

Equipped with a Foreign Secretary whose ability and experience concealed this degree of Christian innocence, Peel kept a close watch on the activities of the Foreign Office. He believed strongly in negotiation, but also that diplomacy should be conducted with firmness and where necessary backed by military strength. In combination the two men worked effectively together and achieved settlements which would probably have eluded the bluster of Palmerston. Aberdeen's final tragedy was that after Peel's death he was propelled into a role for which he was dramatically unsuited, that of Prime Minister leading the nation against Russia in the Crimean War.

The relationship between Britain and the United States in the 1840s was psychologically awkward. Far-sighted men like Peel glimpsed the huge potential of the still-new nation. Far-sighted Americans saw that their national security, peaceful expansion to the West and growing prominence in Latin America owed much to the supremacy of the Royal Navy. But these facts did not remove the impression in the United States that Britain was still trying to meddle arrogantly with their future – or in Britain that Americans were several sizes too big for their boots.

Against this background the unsettled nature of the border between the United States and Canada was dangerous. The possibility of another war with the United States (the third in less than seventy years) was not ruled out in Peel's Cabinet, but he was determined to prevent it. Canada was not yet established as the loyal and respected Dominion under the Crown which emerged during the nineteenth century. Arguments between French and British settlers in Canada, and between both and the British Crown, had loomed large in British politics during the last years of the Whig Government. The wishes of the inhabitants seemed uncertain. The Governor General had just alarmed Ministers and shocked the Duke of Wellington by admitting representatives of the French-speaking community to the government. On entering office Peel passed on to Aberdeen a cool view of Canada's future and Britain's responsibility:

Let us keep Nova Scotia and New Brunswick, for their geographical position makes their sea coast of great importance to us. But the connection with the Canadas against their will, nay without the cordial cooperation of the predominant party in Canada, is a very onerous one ... The advantage of commercial intercourse is all on the side of the Colony, or at least is not in favour of the mother Country ... If the people are not cordially with us, why should we contract the tremendous obligation of having to defend, as a point of honour, their territory against American aggression?[3]

Peel and Aberdeen set themselves to avoid this disastrous choice by resolving first the hottest dispute with the United States, namely the North-east Boundary which separated Canada from the states of Maine and Massachusetts. This had been left vague in the Treaty of Paris in 1783 which ended the American War of Independence. In 1833 the King of Holland, who had been asked to arbitrate, recommended a line which was favourable to the Americans, but which they rejected. The dispute became more important in practice as settlers crowded into the disputed area.

Peel was not happy with the man appointed by Palmerston to be British Ambassador in Washington, Mr Fox, who was said to be anti-American and to spend most of the day in bed.[4] Peel sent Lord Ashburton (who had just given him sober advice on income tax and the Corn Laws) to Washington as a special representative to negotiate on all outstanding matters with the Secretary of State, Daniel Webster. There was a flurry of excitement over old maps. American historians rummaging about in the archives of the French Foreign Ministry discovered a map belonging to Benjamin Franklin which showed the boundary falling roughly on the line claimed by the British. Asked to produce this map the Americans declined; another map then came to light on which the line was much more favourable to the Americans. Eventually in August 1842 Ashburton and Webster struck an old-fashioned compromise, seven-twelfths of the disputed area going to the United States, five-twelfths to Britain. Ashburton thought that the Americans only agreed to the compromise because they knew they were sitting on a disobliging map of which the British were likely to make a big issue. Aberdeen was content, pointing out that Ashburton had managed to push the boundary twenty-five miles further south from the St Lawrence River than the King of Holland's award of 1833. Palmerston in opposition was of course outraged at what he saw as a weak betrayal of Britain's interests, and poured out his scorn in the *Morning Chronicle*.[5] Lord Ashburton commented:

> Upon the defence of my treaty I am very stout and fearless, and they who do not like it may kill the next Hotspur themselves. It is a subject upon which little enthusiasm was to be expected. Our cousin Jonathan* is an offensive arrogant fellow in his manner ... By nearly all our people he is therefore hated, and a treaty of conciliation with such a fellow, however considered by prudence or policy to be necessary, can in no case be very popular with the multitude. Even my friends and masters who employed me are somewhat afraid of showing too much satisfaction with what they do not hesitate to approve.[6]

It was a good agreement, and Peel had no doubts about it. The rocks and forests in dispute were empty and barren compared to the prize of settled friendship with the United States. But a political battle had to be fought to ward off Palmerston, and Lord Ashburton did not understand political battles. The argument that Ashburton had let too much go was given wings by the fact that he had a rich American wife who was thought to have brought him plenty of property in that country. As a reward for his Treaty he was offered a viscountcy (that is, one step up in the peerage from his existing position as a Baron) and the red ribbon of the Order of Bath. He thought he deserved an earldom (two steps up). 'I did all I could', wrote Peel to Croker, 'to persuade Lord Ashburton that unusual extravagant reward for the Treaty would be injurious to him, to us and to the country – to the country as showing misplaced exultation on account of our differences, or rather some of our differences, with the United States having been terminated.'[7]

'Some of our differences' only. For a great stretch of unsettled frontier between the United States and Canada remained towards the West. In 1818 the two countries had agreed on the 49th parallel as the border through the central region as far as the Rockies. But beyond that lay the more valuable territory of Oregon and its Pacific coastline, into which

---

* Jonathan was at the time the American equivalent of John Bull.

both British and American settlers were beginning to move. In 1827 it had been agreed that both countries should jointly occupy the territory, but as settlement increased this was no longer satisfactory. Desultory negotiations through 1842 and 1843 failed to reach agreement. The issue boiled over in the US presidential election of 1844 when President Polk was elected on the catchy slogan 'Fifty-four Forty or Fight'. A boundary along the Fifty-four Forty latitude would carry the Americans well up the west coast of Canada towards Alaska, way north of Vancouver. But even prolonging the border along the 49th parallel to the sea was not good enough for Britain. This would deprive Britain of Vancouver Island, already in British hands, and of the entrance to the Columbia River.

Peel was not prepared to conciliate too far or too fast. 'I should not be afraid of a good deal of preliminary bluster on the part of the Americans,' he wrote to Aberdeen in September 1844. 'The best answer might be to direct the *Collingwood* to make a friendly visit when she has leisure, to the mouth of the Columbia.'[8] There followed a fierce war of words across the Atlantic, in which Peel and Aberdeen held their ground. But Peel refused to let the dispute spill over into something wider and more dangerous. The Mexicans, mired in their own quarrel with the United States, urged Britain to press her interests as far south as California. Aberdeen was tempted to stir up difficulties for the troublesome Americans and at one stage joined the French in urging the Mexicans to recognise the independence of Texas. But Peel opposed such manoeuvres, and also turned down a suggestion of special naval deployment in the Great Lakes. He did not want to seem weak or in a hurry, but his eye was on another reasonable compromise at the right time, so that the whole vast border between Canada and the United States could be agreed for ever.

These old-fashioned arguments about boundaries do not have much resonance today. But the remaining dispute between Britain and the United States sounds an echo in modern ears, though with the role of the two countries reversed. Britain had made the slave trade illegal for its own citizens in 1807 and abolished slavery in its colonies in 1833. As humanitarian ideas took hold and power passed to the middle class, Britain quickly became determined to stamp out across the world a trade from which British traders and plantation-owners had until recently hugely profited. In the Royal Navy Britain possessed a weapon well suited for this task. It seemed self-evident to all progressive thinkers that Providence had laid a duty on Britain to perform this task and provided the means to do so. Although Palmerston would not have used the phrase, he gloried in what the modern commentator Francis Fukuyama describes as 'benevolent hegemony'. It was good to have more power than any other country; it was even better to use that power for the benefit of mankind. The modern echo is obvious. The rhetoric of President George W. Bush has sounded the same note. To those who held this view the objections of foreign governments were morally despicable. By what authority, it was asked, did the frigates of the Royal Navy stop and search the vessels of other countries on the high seas? What was the legal basis for such action? By the supporters of Palmerston in the 1830s, as by supporters of President Bush after 2000, such questions were seen as pedantic and easily brushed aside.

Of course the parallel between now and then breaks down on practical examples. It did not occur to Palmerston even at his most vainglorious to impose a change of regime in another country by deploying military force. Even if Britain had possessed the means he would not have sent British regiments and gunboats to bombard Venice and free Milan from the Austrians, or rescue the Poles from the Russians. Except occasionally in his speeches, Palmerston did not lose his sense of proportion. The French revolutionaries and Napoleon had played with slogans about spreading freedom across the world, but used them to recreate their own tyrannies. That was not a path for Britain. But the slave trade was different. There seemed to be no downside. No one was killed by the Royal Navy's actions, the humanitarian case was overwhelming, and the instructions given to British naval commanders were strictly limited to stopping the trade.

Of course it did not look like this to other seagoing nations. To the Americans, nourishing their own idea of unique *American* righteousness, the arrogance of these British assertions was unacceptable. Some European countries had signed an agreement with Britain allowing a limited right of mutual search by sea. The United States refused to do this, but the Royal Navy's African squadron continued to search ships flying the Stars and Stripes in order to stop American slave-trading. American anger on the issue led Congress in the spring of 1841 to demand increased defence spending. Peel had no intention of abandoning the task of suppressing the slave trade, but characteristically on taking office he asked Aberdeen to check that the instructions to British naval officers ruled out any 'wanton visits from the sheer love and hope of gain'.[9] There was a danger of a clash at sea escalating into naval warfare. In their negotiations Ashburton and Webster did not solve the question of principle, but parked it on one side. It was agreed that each country would maintain an anti-slavery squadron off the African coast and the two forces would work together.

Palmerston in opposition was particularly virulent against what he saw as a weakening of the anti-slavery effort. He had enjoyed rubbing the noses of the Americans in their own misdemeanours as a nation where slavery still existed. But after the Ashburton Treaty triumphant British warships would no longer sail into New York harbour, towing behind them empty American slave ships whose human cargo they had just freed.[10] In practice the agreement was the only way forward. Britain was not going to renounce and other countries would not accept a special British prerogative on the high seas. The problem slowly shrank into insignificance as other countries bestirred themselves against their own traders. The most persistent slave-trading nation was Brazil, on which Aberdeen maintained strong pressure throughout his term of office.

These were tricky Anglo-American problems, but they lacked the intensity of Britain's dealings with France. Britain and an independent America were still feeling their way towards a relationship with a definite pattern. There was not yet enough history to guide their leaders in their dealings with each other. With France on the other hand there was too much history. The avalanche of memories and impressions down the centuries had already created that double relationship of respect and rivalry between Britain and France which persists today.

At the level of everyday politics the two countries had by 1841 begun to converge. Since the July revolution of 1830 in Paris both were parliamentary regimes under constitutional monarchs whose instincts were bourgeois and largely progressive. The politicians of Britain and France were increasingly middle-class; they served an electorate concerned with prosperity rather than military glory. Neither country had territorial ambitions in Europe; both in principle supported liberal European causes. This convergence has proved to be permanent. It led Britain and France to fight together as allies against Russia within four years of Peel's death, and against Germany twice in the twentieth century. But the convergence was far from self-evident in 1841. It looked fragile, as if it might at any time break down.

For the British the great accumulation of memory was of France as a permanent enemy with occasional truces. Sometimes France was ruled by a king, sometimes by a revolutionary republic, sometimes by an emperor. Now in 1841 it was run by bourgeois politicians in black coats – but all it seemed were intent on outwitting, defeating and if possible invading England. With these historical memories was associated a mass of popular ideas about the French, who were clever, frivolous and of course untrustworthy. To the French the English were slow, drunken, violent and of course untrustworthy. On both sides the prejudices were on the whole and at most times good-humoured. To each people the other was at most times ludicrous rather than detestable. But the persistence on either side of this mass of memory and prejudice meant that the relationship proceeded in a series of violent hiccoughs. The reconciliation of converging interests would be interrupted by angry disputes, during which public, press and politicians were inflamed so violently that there was talk of war.

One such passionate argument had just ended in the open humiliation of France. The French government under Thiers had backed the ruler of Egypt, Mehemet Ali, in his rebellion against the Sultan of Turkey. Mehemet Ali swept into Syria and with French backing threatened to establish a powerful regime in the Near East which would certainly not suit Britain. Palmerston organised the Royal Navy, assisted as we have seen by Midshipman William Peel, to bombard the Egyptians in Acre. He mobilised the autocratic powers of northern Europe, with whom in other contexts he had no sympathy. They joined in forcing Mehemet Ali to retreat to his home base in Egypt. When it came to the point Thiers had no intention of fighting for his protégé, but the French suffered humiliation and loss of office when his bluff was called.

The disappearance of Palmerston after the Whig defeat in the general election of 1841 was greeted with relief across Europe, but particularly in Paris. King Louis Philippe and his new Prime Minister, Guizot, set themselves to create a solid friendship with Britain under Peel which would prevent such moments of shame in future.

The Foreign Secretary, Lord Aberdeen, was enthusiastic for friendship with France, as for every exercise in peace-seeking diplomacy. Peel was much less well known to the French. In fact he shared neither the pacific enthusiasm of Guizot and Aberdeen nor the anti-French prejudices of most of his countrymen. He knew France well, but from a distance and through the glass of history and literature. He often read French books for weeks on end and was particularly a student of the French Revolution. Peel was far more familiar with French culture than most British politicians today. He shared Aberdeen's general enthusiasm for diplomatic initiatives and in particular for friendly relations with France; but he never banished from his mind questions over French motives and good faith. This was natural in a man whose boyhood and youth had been spent in a country fighting for its life against Napoleon.

At first Peel left the initiatives in the hands of his Foreign Secretary and his Queen. Victoria, already powerfully influenced by Prince Albert, agreed with Aberdeen about the need to improve relationships across Europe after the hurtful blustering of Palmerston. She had the added incentive that already a good number of the rulers concerned were her relatives. In particular King Louis Philippe's daughter was married to Victoria's uncle (and mentor), King Leopold of the Belgians. It was settled that the new relationship between Britain and France should be launched through an exchange of royal visits. In September 1843 the Queen accompanied by Aberdeen crossed the Channel and was entertained by Louis Philippe at the Château d'Eu near Le Tréport. It was the first time a British monarch had set foot in France since Henry VIII had met his counterpart on the Field of the Cloth of Gold in 1520. The King had taken great trouble over the arrangements for entertaining Victoria and Albert. Peel, watching from a distance, noted that he sent a very large order to England for cheese and bottled beer. He wrote to the Foreign Secretary, 'I hope you will have had calm weather so that you may enjoy these delicacies.'

Bottled beer or not, the Queen thoroughly enjoyed herself, though her comments were hardly penetrating. 'Our reception by the dear King and Queen has been most kind, and by the people really gratifying. Everything is very different to England, particularly the population.'[11] As a result of this visit Aberdeen invented the phrase '*entente cordiale*'. The expression was later used to describe a specific agreement reached between the two countries in 1904, but had been coined sixty years earlier. It is a more subtle expression than is sometimes supposed. There have been plenty of Anglo-French disagreements since Queen Victoria picnicked with Louis Philippe in the forest of the Château d'Eu; but 'understanding' does not exclude differences of view. These differences, though sometimes furious, have not destroyed the relationship. After all these years we are more or less comfortable with each other, despite the keen sense which each has of the other's failings.

Louis Philippe returned Victoria's visit next year at Windsor. He was particularly anxious to see Peel. In advance the Queen of the Belgians had been anxious that her father would eat too much, the particular danger being an English breakfast.[12] But this visit too went well. Afterwards Peel wrote Queen Victoria a charming letter saying that her personal character was responsible for its success. By now Peel was highly respected among practitioners of foreign affairs.[13] King Leopold wrote to his niece in June 1844, 'For your sake, for the good of England, and for the quiet of the whole earth, we must most devoutly pray that Sir Robert may remain for many many years your trusting and faithful Minister.'[14]

But these royal pleasantries were no longer decisive. For several centuries Britain and France had clashed with each other round the world as their sailors, merchants and emigrants found new opportunities to better themselves. France had lost Canada and India to Britain, and divided the Caribbean. They were beginning to divide Africa as the French moved into Algeria and Morocco, and the British pushed the Boers northwards from the Cape. The crunch between colonial powers in the centre of Africa was still several decades away. Thousands of miles further off the Pacific was a minor theatre for this competition; but it was in the Pacific that Britain's new understanding with France was put to its first painful test.

Queen Pomare of Tahiti had long been friendly to Britain. She had allowed the London Missionary Society to establish itself in her domain under the energetic leadership of George Pritchard, who was appointed British Consul. She refused entry to French missionaries. Indeed she had twice asked that Tahiti should be placed under British protection; but Palmerston's sense of adventure did not extend that far, and he declined.

The French were aggrieved by Queen Pomare's coolness towards them, but even more by the speed and thoroughness with which the British asserted control over nearby New Zealand. A French squadron was sent to the Pacific under the command of Admiral Dupetit-Thouras. When it reached Tahiti in the summer of 1843 the Admiral induced the reluctant Queen Pomare to ask for French protection. Pritchard was away in England. When he returned, with a carriage and a suite of drawing room furniture as a present for Queen Pomare from Queen Victoria, he found the French in control. In November the Admiral formally annexed Tahiti to France and arrested and expelled Pritchard.[15]

There was uproar in Britain. Back in London Pritchard addressed a crowded meeting of protest in Exeter Hall, the unofficial headquarters of evangelical Protestantism. Ashley wrote in his diary that 'grief and indignation cannot go beyond what I feel against the French aggressors in Tahiti'.[16] The outcry reached a climax in August 1844. Guizot quickly assured the British Government that the Admiral had acted without authority. But Peel, under strong pressure in Parliament and himself genuinely angry, found that inadequate. Earlier in the year he had spoken warm words of friendship about France in the Commons. Now his private comments to Aberdeen were scathing. He evidently saw the need to stiffen the Foreign Secretary's backbone. 'M. Guizot has himself alone to blame for what has occurred. If he chooses to send out expeditions to occupy every place where they can find the pretence for occupation and if the commanders of these expeditions occupy other places not contemplated by their Government and if M. Guizot has not the power or courage to disavow these, he is responsible for whatever may occur in consequence of such proceedings.'[17] Peel argued that we must consider our naval strength compared to that of France in case some local act of violence escalated into war. The French should not be allowed to presume upon our weakness.[18]

The French press and Assembly were equally inflamed. Behind the scenes Guizot and Aberdeen worked hard for a settlement. 'It would be difficult if you and I, two Ministers of Peace,' wrote Aberdeen, 'should be condemned to quarrel about a set of naked savages at the other end of the world.'[19] Louis Philippe was equally committed to peace and told Queen Victoria that he wished Tahiti 'au fond de la mer'.[20] Eventually he agreed to pay compensation out of his own pocket to the aggrieved Pritchard and the row subsided. Peel resumed his normal calm and summed up for Hardinge in India. 'We have had hard work to keep the peace. The public mind in each country was much excited and the selfish interests of Party and the violence of newspapers on each side of the Channel were near forcing two great countries into a war for the most trumpery cause of quarrel (excepting only so far as the point of honour was concerned).'[21]

More serious, because more closely related to the real interests of both countries, was the question of Spain. Whereas the clash over Tahiti looked forward to decades of Anglo-French rivalry over colonies, the Spanish dispute looked back over a century and a half of manoeuvring for power in Europe. Napoleon had tried to conquer Spain by force, and failed; but there was an older and more subtle way of asserting French influence in Madrid. Where armies had failed, a skilful marriage might succeed. Louis Philippe was a man of peace, but persistent and devious in advancing the aims of his country and of his own family.

Young Queen Isabella of Spain, though only thirteen years old, needed a husband, or at least that was the view of all the diplomats of Europe. The same was true of her younger sister. Plenty of young princes were available including the younger son of Louis Philippe, a Coburg relative of Prince Albert, and a Bourbon cousin of Spain's own royal family. It had been agreed long ago after the War of the Spanish Succession in 1714 that the crowns of France and Spain must be kept separate. This had been reaffirmed in 1834. So the front door was closed, but Louis Philippe and Guizot thought they had found a side door which would serve almost as well. Let Queen Isabella marry her Bourbon cousin. This was an exhausted royal breed; Isabella was sickly and the prince probably impotent. Let the Queen's sister the Infanta at the same time marry Louis Philippe's son, the Duc de Montpensier. No treaty would be broken, and with luck if Queen Isabella was childless her eventual successor on the throne of Spain would be her nephew, the grandson of Louis Philippe. Peel was angry when he heard. The scheme was, he wrote, underhand and dishonest. 'It might not breach any specific understanding, but it ran clear contrary to the spirit of the entente cordiale.'[22]

Patient but gloomy, Aberdeen again set to work, helped by Queen Victoria. The Queen and Prince Albert paid a second visit to Louis Philippe in the Château d'Eu in September 1845, with Aberdeen in attendance. In modern times the Queen would never take part in a negotiation of this kind on a state visit; but to Victoria it seemed natural. An agreement was reached. Any idea of a marriage between the Infanta and the

Duc de Montpensier was shelved, until Isabella Queen of Spain had not only married but had produced more than one child. Isabella's husband would be neither a French prince nor a Coburg. This deeply old-fashioned arrangement was welcomed by Queen Victoria and Aberdeen, and accepted by Peel. But the episode strengthened his belief that friendship with France, though desirable and indeed necessary, must be handled with caution and some mistrust.*

Such a combination of friendship and suspicion was bound to throw up real dilemmas. At moments of tension with France public attention turned to the state of our defences. We have seen that even a cool-headed man like Peel, even over a distant dispute like Tahiti, began to worry about naval preparations. No one thought in terms of a British invasion of France; many worried all over again about a French invasion of Britain. Yet it was not so much 'the many' who dominated this debate, as the one man who more than anyone else still living had brought about the defeat of Napoleon.

The Duke of Wellington was a member of the Cabinet and led for the Government in the House of Lords; he was also once again Commander-in-Chief of the Army. Both personally and constitutionally he held the key position in any discussion of national security. In 1844 the Duke was seventy-five. Younger men and women might laugh at his ideas on the Constitution or the economy, but on defence his prestige and authority remained absolute. Peel asked for his views and paid them respectful attention, being himself already increasingly alarmed. At the end of 1844 he wrote to Goulburn, the Chancellor of the Exchequer, about 'awful reports' on the state of the defence of the naval arsenals and dockyards. 'One would suppose that each was at the mercy of a handful of men and that it will require an enormous expenditure to give to each not complete but the most ordinary works of defence.'[23] At the same time he wrote to Stanley, Secretary of State for War, about the need for a great naval effort in 1845. Next summer the Duke wrote a formidable paper which he sent

---

* The agreement at Eu foundered in 1846. The French returned to their scheme once Palmerston was back in office, alleging that he was again favouring a Coburg prince. The two objectionable marriages took place behind Britain's back in October 1846. No one lived happily ever after. The Queen of Spain was miserable, Queen Victoria outraged and the French chased Louis Philippe out of his kingdom two years later.

direct to the Prime Minister. Compared to this subject 'all other interests of the country are mere trifles'.[24]

The Duke's argument ran as follows. All governments had in recent years neglected the defence of Britain, and the danger was hugely increased by the advent of steam. Steam had in effect built a multitude of bridges between Britain and all French ports stretching from Dunkirk to Bordeaux. From any of these ports an attack could now be quickly mounted against Britain, Ireland or the Channel Islands. In any future war the Navy's job would again be to blockade the French ports, but this time the sole aim would be to prevent an invasion. If a storm blew the blockading fleet away from the ports, our arsenals and main coastal cities would be helpless. Any one of them could be quickly stormed by a force of 25,000 men. The Duke drifted back into memories of his own sieges of Ciudad Rodrigo and Badajoz in Spain thirty years earlier, both stormed in a day or two. The Government should raise 100,000 men for the defence of Britain. If that was ruled out at present because it would cost £4 million, the militias should be organised and pensioners recruited.[25] Peel replied at length acknowledging the main case, and Ministers began to work out details of rearmament. A naval programme of £1 million had already been authorised early in 1845. Peel was concerned about cost, and also about the political difficulty of dealing with attacks from Palmerston. The Duke was vexed when Peel rebutted Palmerston's description of the country's helplessness but Peel feared that if he did acknowledge its essential truth he might simply encourage the French into rash adventures.

Lord Aberdeen lived in a different world, peopled by conscientious monarchs, skilful ambassadors and intelligent middle-class French Ministers. To most observers in Britain, and certainly to both Palmerston and the victor of Waterloo, reality lay not with Aberdeen's diplomatic comings and goings but with our defenceless harbours and cities threatened by a French army of 400,000 men.

The obvious parallel in our minds is with the rearmament debate in the 1930s when we were faced with the growing threat from Hitler. Wellington may seem a reasonable parallel with Churchill, and poor Lord Aberdeen with Neville Chamberlain. In that debate Churchill and those who called for rapid rearmament were proved right. But neither Louis Philippe, nor Napoleon III after him, in any serious way resembled

Hitler. Their word might be doubted, and their diplomatic manoeuvres resisted, but the idea that they were bent on invading Britain was a fantasy.

Aberdeen was alarmed at the alarm of his colleagues. The Duke's opinions were predictable; but Aberdeen found that both Peel and Graham had been

> converted into a policy of hostility and distrust ... It is my deliberate and firm conviction that there is less reason to distrust the French government and to doubt the continuance of peace at the present moment than there was four years ago ... It seems to me that we are now acting under the influence of panic, both with respect to the institutions of France and our own real condition, and such a course of conduct has a direct tendency to produce the very evil which it is intended to avert.[26]

Guizot had told him that Le Havre was completely at our mercy and that a couple of gunboats could bombard and destroy the place. Aberdeen felt so strongly that in September 1845 he offered his resignation. So long as dread of French invasion was regarded as a peculiarity of the Duke, no great harm was done. But now that Peel too shared this worry about what Aberdeen regarded as a chimera, he believed it would be best if he quickly stepped out of office, pleading grounds of ill health which were in fact genuine.

The Duke, though not often accused of panic, responded courteously but with confusion. For his next paper contained side by side the two contradictory positions which governed British attitudes to France. On the one hand he acknowledged that nothing could be settled in Europe, the Levant or anywhere in the world except by good understanding between the two countries. He also believed that the King and Guizot were wise men who sincerely wanted peace with Britain. But their naval preparation showed that the French were driven by deadly hostility towards us. These were feelings which we could not change. The Duke moved on to surer ground 'of which I think that my habits and pursuits have given me a little more knowledge than Lord Aberdeen has'.[27] He repeated his argument that steam had transformed all calculations. In steam as in sail we were stronger than the French, but steam would enable them to carry a large army quickly to our shores, and against that army we were helpless.

Peel could not afford to lose Aberdeen, the Foreign Secretary whom everyone liked, and Aberdeen did not press his resignation. He did not abandon the argument but carried it onto a more philosophical plane. Guizot wrote a long dissertation arguing that the old maxim *si vis pacem para bellum* (if you wish for peace prepare for war) was wholly out of date. Aberdeen agreed, and sent it to Peel for comment. This was hard on a Prime Minister wrestling with the Irish famine and entering the final drama of his political career. But Peel never left a question unanswered. He replied from Drayton on 17 October in his usual painstaking way, concluding with double negatives: 'I think it unwise, generally speaking, to waste the resources of a country during peace in preparation for war. But I greatly doubt whether, speaking of this country, the reverse of the axiom is true. I do not believe that there would be security for peace by our being in a state which would unfit us to repel attack without several months' preparation.' There had to be a middle way. He trusted Louis Philippe and Guizot as men of peace; but the King of the French at seventy-three would not last for ever and for whatever reason Guizot had spent huge sums on fortifying Paris and sustaining a large army.[28]

Peel and the Cabinet authorised a quick selective programme of rearmament and fortification. The defences of Portsmouth, Sheerness, Pembroke and the Thames estuary were improved. Harbours of refuge were sanctioned at Portland, Dover and Harwich. The effective strength of the Army had been increased by about 10,000, or almost a quarter, since 1841. Peel took a detailed interest in the equipment of ships of the line with heavier guns and screw propellers.[29]

Guizot eventually wrote a thoughtful memoir of Peel and throughout respected his integrity. For his part Peel sent Guizot in December 1845 a farewell letter which went beyond the ordinary. He wrote that the growing confidence between Britain and France had taught the two nations 'to regard something higher than paltry jealousies and hostile rivalries ... If it had not been for that confidence and esteem, how many miserable squabbles might have swollen into terrible national controversies.'[30] Anglo-French squabbles continued into the next century; but so did the convergence of interests between the two nations. The ambiguity of the *entente cordiale* remains to this day.

The British Empire expanded steadily during Peel's premiership, yet the

Government had no settled policy of increasing the proportion of the world marked red on the map. The notion that it was glorious or noble or profitable to annex large swathes of territory was not yet fashionable. Only one leading figure of the political world in Peel's time, Lord Ellenborough, dreamed in the manner of Kipling or Curzon, and as we shall see, little good did it do him. Palmerston, the epitome of an assertive foreign policy, measured Britain's greatness in terms not of annexed territories but of political strength sustained by naval and commercial superiority. The war with China which he started in 1839 was essentially a naval contest designed to open up the Chinese market, including the opium trade. The acquisition of Hong Kong by Britain, which was the most lasting result of that war, was an accident forced on Palmerston by the local British commander. To Palmerston, and to Peel after him, this barren rocky island inhabited by a handful of fishermen and smugglers was more likely to be a nuisance than an asset.

Peel was temperamentally even more reluctant to conquer. 'The Home Office is more important than India,' he once observed during a ministerial reshuffle, and he would have been surprised if anyone had questioned that judgement. It would never have occurred to Peel to visit any of Britain's overseas territories, or to launch a policy of deliberately increasing their size or number. Yet under him the Empire persisted in growing, almost entirely as the result of local initiatives. Because Cape Town was a crucial staging post on the route to India, the Cape Colony was settled in its hinterland. Because the Cape Colony was said to be threatened from the north, Natal was annexed in 1842. In New Zealand the Treaty of Waitangi had been signed with Maori chieftains in 1840, but its status was unclear. The New Zealand Company pushed ahead with settlement, inspired by commercial appetite and missionary zeal. Peel and Stanley, the Colonial Secretary, were reluctant to back settlement, for which the Treaty gave no authority. Peel would not 'undertake to dispossess by force and against the will of the inhabitants, the natives from certain lands desired by the New Zealand Company'.[31] He was equally reluctant to support the enterprise of James Brooke in Borneo.

A pattern established itself. Local commanders, missionaries or entrepreneurs occupied fresh territory, usually on the pretext of defending what they already had. By the time the government at home received this news, the fact was accomplished. Those concerned had significant backing at Westminster or in the City of London. Provided that no great further expenditure was needed it was easier for Ministers to acquiesce, often with a grumble, than to try to reverse the fact. In these years the Empire was acquired not so much in absence of mind as in absence of communications. Ministers had no opportunity to assert their natural caution; their men on the spot were not under effective control. Sometimes this caused real anxiety, even agony, in London, as Gladstone found much later in dealing with Gordon and the Sudan. Sometimes it suited both sides quite well.

India provided the biggest stage for this interplay of imperial enthusiasm on the spot and reluctance at home. The problem of communication was here at its most acute. There was no telegraph to India and no Suez Canal. Three or four months passed between the day when a British representative in India sent a report to London and the day when he received instructions based on that report. As Peel grasped more clearly than some of his colleagues, this meant that the Government had only two effective roles: to decide on the original policy, and, after the event, to approve or disapprove what their representatives had done. They could not hope to manage events week by week, even month by month; there was no alternative to trusting the man on the spot.

There was another complication peculiar to India. The man on the spot had two masters. British dominance in India had been established not by the British government, but by the East India Company under a charter originally granted by Queen Elizabeth I. It was as servant of the East India Company that Clive had drummed the French out of India and subdued their allies. But in practice the responsibility for providing troops and money fell on the British government. Although the House of Commons emptied when India was debated, a small group of enthusiasts in London kept a close watch on what was done there in Britain's name. By the India Act of 1784 Pitt had established a dual system. British India was ruled by a Governor General responsible to the Board of Control in London, consisting of directors of the East India Company presided over by a government Minister. The Board appointed and could dismiss the Governor General. Its president straddled the divide between the Company on the one hand and the Cabinet and Parliament on the other. This awkward division of power was badly shaken in Peel's time, and collapsed as a result of the Indian Mutiny in 1857. It was then replaced by the British Raj in its better-known form with a viceroy appointed by and responsible to the Cabinet and (from 1876) to his sovereign, the Empress of India.

One of Peel's first tasks as Prime Minister was to find a new Governor General for the Board to appoint in succession to Lord Auckland, whose term had come to an end. He consulted the Duke and the Queen and they all agreed: the right man was Edward Law, first Earl of Ellenborough. In domestic politics Ellenborough had for years held a central position as a liberal Tory. To the public he was best known for the duel he had fought with his wife's lover, Prince Schwarzenberg. Both men survived, but a court judgment forced the Prince to pay the aggrieved husband £25,000 in damages.

Ellenborough, aged fifty-one in 1841, had a reputation for arrogance, but also for eloquence and hard work.[32] In particular he had valuable experience of the Board of Control, under both Wellington between 1828 and 1830 and Peel in 1834–5. Writing to Wellington, Peel nursed a doubt. 'The only drawback would be a tendency to precipitation and over-activity, but I suppose he would have very good and steady advisers in India.' The Duke in reply did not think much of that point. The Council in India were civil servants who would hardly stand up to the Governor General, but 'I think you may rely upon Lord Ellenborough's sound sense and discretion, that he will avoid to involve himself and the public interest in difficulties, by well considering all the consequences which may follow any decision before he orders its execution'.[33] Rarely had the Duke's usual shrewdness in judging men so signally deserted him. Peel's fear of 'a tendency to precipitation' was an understatement. Ellenborough accepted the appointment with enthusiasm. 'It seemed to me like a dream,' he wrote, as he sailed to the East.[34]

Ellenborough was indeed a dreamer, the centre of each dream being his own position. He had no intention of acting as an obedient servant of the Government in London, let alone the directors of the East India Company. He asked to be military Commander-in-Chief as well as Governor General, but was not cast down when this was refused. His mind soared above such bureaucratic niceties. He intended to rule India 'as if I were its sovereign, having nothing to look to but India'. He regarded himself as the successor of the Mogul emperors. 'I must act like Akhbar and not like Auckland.'[35] On behalf of Queen Victoria of course, with whom he insisted on corresponding direct and whom he encouraged (anticipating Disraeli) to assume the title of Empress of India. Ellenborough disliked the restraints imposed by the dual system of government, ignored his Council and picked a quarrel with its legal member. He was one of the first to express alarm about the threat to India from Russia as she expanded rapidly eastwards. Like others after him he used that threat to justify his own policy of expansion.

Ellenborough was faced immediately on arrival with the opposite of expansion, namely the handling of retreat. The Whig Government had authorised an invasion of Afghanistan, which had gone disastrously wrong. 'I arrived here today', Ellenborough wrote to Peel from Madras on 21 February 1842, 'and received the disastrous intelligence from Kabul of the murder of Sir William Macnaghten, and the destruction of the British and native troops at that city.'[36] A force of 6,000 troops had been massacred by the Afghans. Sixteen Englishwomen were among more than a hundred hostages taken. Sir William Macnaghten, the British agent in Afghanistan, had been decapitated and his head paraded through Kabul as a symbol of victory with 'a portion of his mutilated body' stuffed in his mouth.[37] Peel was appalled, but one part of him was not surprised. He had always opposed the Afghan War as an example of Palmerstonian adventurism at its worst. 'I fear the possibility of a terrible retribution for the most absurd and insane project that was ever undertaken in the wantonness of power.'[38]

But emotions in London were for the moment irrelevant. Ministers could only hope that Ellenborough would show the sound sense with which the Duke had credited him. It was obvious even to the cautious Peel that the disaster at Kabul could not remain unavenged. He expected that Ellenborough would take decisive military measures, though he wrote on 5 September 1842 advising him to act cautiously and deliberately so as to avoid further disasters in British India itself.[39] Peel had appointed as President of the Board of Control his old friend from Ireland, William Vesey Fitzgerald, the man who by losing the Clare by-election in 1829 had pushed Peel and the country into Catholic Emancipation. But Fitzgerald was not well, and in any case by temperament felt subordinate to the Prime Minister. Peel took personal control of such policy-making as was practicable in London.

From the tone of his letter of 5 September Peel evidently expected that

Ellenborough would act boldly, even rashly. He was surprised that the Governor General hurled himself in the opposite direction. He ordered the military commanders to retreat at once from Afghanistan. He told Peel on 7 June that '[t]he Generals Nott and Pollock have not a grain of military talent. The latter has fallen into the hands of two or three young political assistants ... he would otherwise have been before this on the left bank of the Indus, and safe.'[40] *And safe* – that was the point. Ellenborough wanted the Army removed from danger, and safe under his own control. His correspondence shows that his main concern at this time was to establish his own personal authority against officers and civilians who he believed were intriguing against him.

If they had obeyed the Governor General's instructions to the letter the Generals would have taken the direct route out of Afghanistan through Quetta. This would have meant leaving the wretched hostages in Kabul to a grisly fate. General Pollock pointed this out to the Governor General. Ellenborough, recovering from his panic and encouraged by some military successes, gave the two Generals authority if they wished to retreat by way of Kabul. This meant in effect not retreating at all until they had freed the hostages. Peel and Fitzgerald, commenting helplessly from London, agreed that this equivocation put an unfair burden of choice on the Generals. Ellenborough was unloading onto men whom he despised the decision which was for him to take – was it worth putting the Army at risk again in order to rescue the hostages? But Nott and Pollock turned the Governor General's hesitation into success. Nott, ancestor of a distinguished Defence Secretary in Margaret Thatcher's Government, took the risk, swept north through Kabul, freed the prisoners and linked up with his colleague. Ellenborough talked about 'my victory' but Fitzgerald knew better. 'Nott and Pollock have set it all right.'[41]

Ellenborough celebrated success with grand proclamations, in one of which, by criticising Lord Auckland, he ensured the hostility of the Whigs at home. He began to quarrel with his own Council and thus by extension with the directors of the East India Company. He ordered his Generals to bring back from Afghanistan the gates of the Hindu temple of Somnauth, captured by a Mogul emperor eight centuries before. This was the sort of bogus gesture (the gates were replicas) which scored no points in India, but showed observers like Peel that Ellenborough was in the grip of those delusions of grandeur which, in Professor Gash's telling phrase, were 'India's subtle gift to successive Viceroys'.[42] It remained for Peel and his colleagues to defend in public Ellenborough's decisions and behaviour. The Duke of Wellington and the Queen did this with fervour, Peel and Fitzgerald with misgivings about the past and anxiety for the future.

Another victory was enough to bring Ellenborough down. The Amirs of Sind (whose main city was Karachi in modern Pakistan) had been compelled to allow the passage of British troops into Afghanistan in 1839, but their support had been equivocal. Ellenborough decided to force them into complete obedience. In reality this meant the annexation of Sind. He entrusted the task to General Napier, who in a celebrated display of classical learning telegraphed his quick success in one word, 'Peccavi'. He expected all his readers to construe the word correctly: 'I have sinned'. Neither Peel nor Fitzgerald nor the directors of the Company appreciated the witticism. They believed that the Amirs had been unfairly treated. Sensing this, Ellenborough complained that Fitzgerald had not given him enough support. Fitzgerald knew that the Government could not in practice disown Ellenborough whatever he did. 'In the present state of India he knows that he may play great pranks and threaten resignation every month.'[43] So he offered to resign himself. Peel would have none of this, but within four months Fitzgerald was dead. As his successor Peel appointed Ripon, who had over the years served along-side him (under different titles) as Chancellor of the Exchequer, Prime Minister and President of the Board of Trade.

By choosing a man he knew to be easily agitated and indecisive, Peel ensured that he would have to continue handling Indian policy himself. This meant controlling storms of indignation which blew with increasing force from opposite directions. Ellenborough was furious that the Government delayed its approval of the annexation of Sind. The direc-tors of the Company were furious with Ellenborough for what they saw as an arbitrary act of aggression, culminating in the imprisonment of the Amirs. Lord Ashley agreed with this criticism: 'I do indeed lament, I will not disguise it from you,' he wrote to Peel on 10 June 1843, 'that your own high minded and statesmanlike principles should be kept back or dis-coloured by those in whom you place confidence.'[44] Peel privately agreed, replying politely to Ashley and writing to Ripon on 13 August, 'In my opinion directions ought to be given without loss of time to treat the Amirs with every degree of consideration. We have taken their territories and despoiled them of their private property. Surely we need not inflict further punishment and privations.'[45]

The row between the directors and the Governor General overflowed its banks and for a few weeks flooded the political scene. The imprisonment of the Amirs of Sind was the pretext for releasing an antagonism which had gathered strength ever since Ellenborough reached India. Ellenborough was still smarting at criticism of his inept handling of the Afghan campaign. The directors saw that he treated them and their representatives in Calcutta with total contempt. In their anger the directors began to discuss among themselves the recall of Ellenborough. Peel had a difficult hand to play. He believed that Ellenborough had behaved foolishly over both Afghanistan and Sind. If he had been consulted he would almost certainly have vetoed the annexation of Sind. But the deal had been done, and it was not feasible to disavow it. He wrote to Ellenborough on 2 January 1844 justifying the time which Ministers had taken to consider the annexation before approving it.[46] He had already warned him not to write direct to the Queen on political matters.[47]

When it came to the crunch Peel made no effort to persuade the directors to hold back from dismissing Ellenborough. They took the final decision in April 1844. The Queen considered it unwise and ungrateful and 'would not be sorry if these gentlemen knew that this is her opinion'.[48] Even more indignant, the Duke of Wellington described the directors' actions as the most indiscreet exercise of power he had ever known.[49] Peel said as little as possible. He concentrated on picking up the bits and starting a new chapter in India with better chances of success. He joined in the necessary tributes to Ellenborough, persuaded his friend Hardinge to take the job, and induced the directors, who were half frightened of their bold deed, to undertake that they would give the new Governor General their full support.

Two vividly contrasting views of the right policy for Britain in India appear in letters written to Hardinge in 1844. Ellenborough wrote to him from Barrackpore on 15 April, in ignorance of the fact that at that very time the directors were nerving themselves to insist on his recall. As it happened Hardinge was Ellenborough's brother-in-law, and Ellenborough wrote in robust mode as to one of the family. He foresaw that the next war in India would be against the Sikhs in the Punjab. He hoped he could put this off for eighteen months. By then 'I should have an army which I could march to the Dardanelles'. He was mustering a total of 275,000 men at arms and planned to cross the Sutlej with rather more than 33,000 infantry, 7,000 cavalry and in all 162 guns. The Dardanelles might have to wait a bit. He foresaw an operation lasting two years which would secure the Punjab, Kashmir and Peshawar under the authority of the Queen as Empress of India. He needed a competent General, and hoped that his brother-in-law would throw up his career as a politician and come out to take command. 'Does not this excite your ambition?' Ellenborough's own ambition stretched beyond the natural boundaries of India. Once that was accomplished 'we have under our foot, whenever the state of Europe may permit us to take it, that country which has ever been the ultimate object of my desire, but of which I hardly dare to whisper the name — Egypt'.[50]

Napoleon had thought of Egypt as the gateway to India. It took Ellenborough to dream of India as the gateway to Egypt. Hardinge, a sober, disciplined man, showed the fantasy to Peel, who copied it marked secret to a handful of colleagues. Peel's comment came in another double negative: 'If the contents were known to the Court of Directors, it would not dissatisfy them with their recent letter of recall.' A new job had to be found at home for this dangerous dreamer, but nothing sufficiently glorious was available. 'His head had been so full of grand conceptions and schemes with great results that Post Offices and Privy Seals were beneath his notice.'[51]

Now the way was clear for Peel to set out his own ideas in India to Hardinge, a man he liked and trusted. He wrote, 'He [Ellenborough] will not infect the people of this country with the love of military glory. If you can keep peace, reduce expense, extend commerce, and strengthen our hold on India by confidence in our justice, kindness and wisdom you will be received here on your return with acclamation a thousand times louder and a welcome infinitely more cordial than if you have a dozen victories to boast of, and annex the Punjab to the overgrown Empire of India.'[52]

In October, Peel talked with the Russian Ambassador, Count Nesselrode, who had told him that Russia was worried by the extension of British power in Northern India. Peel read him some of Hardinge's first despatches, adding that 'the consolidation and improvement of the vast dominions we possess in India were objects much nearer your [i.e. Hardinge's] heart than the extension of our own Empire, or the gratification of the cravings of an army for more conquests and more glory'.[53]

That was the genuine voice of Peel, who saw empire in terms of expense and responsibility rather than profit and glory. But as Hardinge soon found, there was a dynamic behind the growth of empire which Peel could neither welcome nor withstand. The two reluctant imperialists Peel and Hardinge were denied the period of peaceful consolidation in India which they sought.

Fifteen

How Wonderful is Peel

'I suppose you are aware who is the person whom
you have shot?' 'Yes, Sir Robert Peel.'
*Inspector Tierney interviewing attempted assassin MacNaghton,** *
January 1843

'We cannot by mere force, by mere appeals to selfish
Protestant ascendancy principles, govern Ireland in a
manner in which a civilised country should be governed'
Peel to Hardinge, 1845

How wonderful is Peel
He changes with the time;
Turning and twisting like an eel,
Ascending through the slime
Punch, May 1845

'The small tradesman, clergyman or clerk has two or three
joints a week, instead of only one. He sometimes sees a
sirloin on his table. He can afford an occasional plum
pudding, and is not deterred from rice or fruit tarts by
the expensive appendage of sugar.'
The Times *points out that people have never had it so good,*
February 1846

On 20 January 1843 the Prime Minister was walking with his son
Frederick in Cockspur Street. He was stopped by a stranger and
asked if he had heard that his Private Secretary, Edward

---

* There are various spellings of his name. I follow Professor Gash and Peel himself. The judges
who named rules after him christened them the M'Naghten Rules. I do not know why.

Drummond, had been shot in Charing Cross. Peel hurried to Drummond's house. The bullet had passed through his back. At first it seemed that he would recover but he died five days later. The assailant, a man from Glasgow called Daniel MacNaghton, was at once arrested.

Drummond, at fifty-one, had in the manner of a first-class official become a friend of all the great men whom he had served – Canning, Ripon, Wellington and now Peel. Lord Melbourne remembered him as 'a very quiet, gentlemanly and agreeable man', which was about as high as you could get in Melbourne's vocabulary.[1]

The tragedy itself shocked and depressed Peel, but the aftermath caused even more alarm to those around him. The next day he told the Queen something he had just heard from the Home Secretary, Sir James Graham. 'On the Inspector Tierney going into the cell of MacNaghton this morning, he said to MacNaghton "I suppose you are aware who is the person whom you have shot?" He (MacNaghton) said: "Yes, Sir Robert Peel." '[2]

MacNaghton's mistake was not difficult to explain. In the days before the camera a man like Peel could become well known through the country without most people having the faintest idea what he looked like. Though they did not in fact look alike, Drummond and Peel were much the same age and often walked together in Whitehall. Indeed during the Queen's recent visit to Scotland Drummond had sometimes been driven in Peel's coach with Peel's coat of arms while the Prime Minister was with the Queen. MacNaghton had still been in Scotland at that time.

One way or another he had shot the wrong man.[3] The general alarm came close to panic. Assassination was in the air. There had been several attempts on the Queen's life. It was thirty-one years since Peel's predecessor as Prime Minister, Spencer Perceval, had been killed in the lobby of the House of Commons. Two questions excited the press and perplexed those immediately concerned. What were MacNaghton's motives, and what would be his fate? It emerged that he was a failed businessman with a set of deluded grievances against the police, the Jesuits and the Glasgow Conservative Party. At first Peel thought that he was exactly the sort of man whom conspirators might employ. But no evidence of conspiracy emerged, and attention turned to the simple question whether MacNaghton should hang. The Queen asked to be kept informed of every particular. Peel wrote, 'It will be most unfortunate indeed if the

Law does not attach its severest penalty to a crime so premeditated and so deliberately and savagely perpetrated as that of MacNaghton.'⁴ Peel added that MacNaghton was speaking to his jailer in a coherent, intelligent way, but his counsel would certainly plead mental illness. And so it proved. The judges accepted the plea of insanity and advised the jury to acquit.

The commotion which this verdict caused in legal circles led to more specific guidance than had hitherto been given; the MacNaghton Rules became the standard test for insanity long after MacNaghton himself had died, forgotten in an asylum. Peel bizarrely warned the Lord Chancellor that other feeble-minded individuals (he cited a naval captain and a lieutenant) were being tempted to threaten force to redress their own grievances in the belief that a weak judge and a foolish jury would see them right.⁵ The Queen's indignation drove her to much underlining: 'The ablest lawyers … allow and advise the Jury to pronounce the verdict of Not Guilty on account of Insanity while everybody is morally convinced that both malefactors [there was another similar trial at the time] were perfectly conscious and aware of what they did!'⁶ She worried about Peel's safety, and may not have been fully reassured when he told her that he was in the habit of walking home every night from the House of Commons and had met no difficulty.⁷

The political outflow from the attack on Drummond was poisonous. The atmosphere was already hectic. MacNaghton fired his pistol after weeks of virulent personal attacks on Peel by the Anti Corn Law League. Peel was personally blamed for the suffering caused by the recession. Instead of repealing the Corn Laws he had actually introduced a new one, with a lower wheat duty no doubt, but nothing but abolition would satisfy the League. Up and down the country he was vilified by the League's orators. In Manchester they had used a placard headed 'Murder'. In Sheffield a dissenting minister told of a man who was willing to kill Peel, adding that when Peel went to his grave there would be few to shed a tear. After Drummond's death both Chartist and Conservative newspapers accused the League, or at least some of its spokesmen, of incitement to kill.⁸

Less than a month after Drummond's death this tension exploded in the House of Commons. On 17 February 1843 Cobden accused Peel of being 'individually responsible for the present condition of the country . . . I tell him that the whole responsibility of the lamentable and dangerous state of the country rests with him.' The Conservative side of the House took this at once in the context of the attack on Drummond and created an uproar. Peel rose immediately and declared that he would never be influenced by menaces either in or outside the Commons. Cobden tried to explain himself. By 'individually' he had not meant 'personally' but had referred to the office which Peel held.[9] Peel crossly accepted that explanation, but Cobden resented Peel's insinuation that he had encouraged violence. The personal gap between the two men widened sharply just as their policies on free trade began to converge.

Julia Peel was hard hit both by Drummond's death and by the knowledge that her husband had been MacNaghton's chosen target. She collapsed; Peel had to withdraw from a visit by them both to the Queen at Windsor. For months the strain had been great. No doubt the carbines were still hidden in the tower at Drayton. After carrying herself with courage during the dangerous summer Julia was brutally reminded that the danger was not over, indeed that it would never come to an end so long as her husband was Prime Minister. It took her some months to recover. At the end of April Peel was writing to her from Whitehall:

> My own dearest love,
>   You must not be dispirited by occasional checks to your immediate and complete recovery. Depend upon it, all will go quite well. Your constitution is an excellent one. I wish I could have said this to you, instead of writing it.[10]

During the summer Julia regained her usual calm, in time to face a different and more agreeable test. In November the Queen and Prince Albert visited Drayton. This was a signal mark of royal favour and Peel was delighted. He took detailed trouble over the arrangements, sending Prince Albert one of the first examples of a railway timetable. The Queen drove from Windsor to Watford where the carriage was loaded onto a train which took her to Tamworth.[11] The Duke of Wellington and old Queen Adelaide were among the other guests. Peel was consulted about the decoration for the village adjoining Drayton. 'The best decoration for Fazely will be to have the children of the school drawn up − in line, all together and a shilling given to each child to make merry. I think the poorest of the poor should have some rejoicing, something to eat and drink at a given time. I have told the Mayor I would give one hundred guineas for this purpose.'[12] Prince Albert paid a visit from Drayton to Birmingham. No detail was too small for Peel. 'The Mayor is a hosier – of extreme political opinions – in fact, a Chartist ... no probability of any tumult or of any demonstration but one of respect personally towards the Prince, if his visit be clearly and manifestly unconnected with politics. An immense concourse of people must be expected ... Is the Mayor to accompany the Prince in the same carriage? The Mayor has no carriage.'[13] All went well on every count. In effect a new version of royal tours was being devised to match an increasingly varied society. George IV would not have ridden through Birmingham in a carriage with a Radical hosier.

Between 1841 and 1846 the Peels settled into a routine which separated them for much of each year. From February till August Peel worked in London, in his office in 10 Downing Street, but more often in the Commons, sleeping in the big empty house in Whitehall Gardens. Drayton was just too far to be reached comfortably at weekends, and in any case the custom of the British two-day weekend was not fully established. Julia would occasionally come to London for some great occasion. Peel spent as much as possible of the late summer, autumn and early winter at Drayton, using the comfortable new house for business meetings as well as social gatherings. When they were apart, husband and wife wrote affectionately to each other every few days. Peel combined a hearty appetite for work with genuine resentment at a way of life which separated him from his house, the Staffordshire countryside, his wife and the children who were her particular care.

My dearest love,

I am just returned from executing your botanical commission. I found a stephanotis and a plant which bears a yellow flower and grows over the house. It is called an Allamarda. I have hardly been able to get away for one hour, even from this table, for a week past, except to go to a Cabinet, a Council or the House of Commons. I am going to the House again now. It seems as if I was never out of it, so hurried is the interval between departure and return ... I have just come from Church and found entering this solitary but clean house, your dear letter. The things you kindly sent me, strawberries and potatoes and specially bright and fragrant flowers, came safely[14] ... Does everything look prosperous at Drayton? Tell me about your garden, the roses, the yew hedge, and all the rest. Everything of that kind will be interesting to me.

In her replies Julia hardly ever touched on politics:

My own dearest love,

I went out this morning with dear little Arthur for him to fish and to his great delight he caught seven small perch. Johnny caught about the same and they ate them today at their dinner. Robert and Johnny are just going out to ride.

In the same letter she asked him to find three or four of the large soft bouncy rubber balls which they had once seen, together with a proper cricket ball for the boys. Next April: 'This is a most lovely day, quite delightful to behold and to breathe. You inquire about dear little Arthur. He is looking so nicely and has wonderfully improved since he has been home. Dear little fellow! Somehow or other I know how to manage him.'[15]

The elder children by now needed more than soft balls and maternal clucking. Peel saw a lot of his eldest daughter Julia because she was usually in London with her husband Lord Villiers. Father and daughter were easy with each other and this companionship gave him much pleasure. They dined and sometimes went to church together. Peel trusted his son-in-law to choose his horses, a decision for which he later paid dearly. At the other end of the world William, still in his late teens, went through a dip in his naval career. The Royal Navy did not provide continuous excitement for a midshipman. He could not always be bombarding Acre or writing letters to be seen by the Duke of Wellington. Stranded in the sweaty Chinese Treaty port of Amoy in the summer of 1842, William had not heard from home for six months. Even worse was the fact that the first Opium War was over and there was nothing to do. 'The climate does not agree with me, it leaves me too weak to follow up with pleasure any studies, and as to the employment and excitement the duties of the service afford, you can pretty well guess on such a station as this in time of peace nothing can be more dull and uniform.'[16] The boredom did not last long; William was soon posted back home and in the following year was promoted to Lieutenant.

There was nothing the Prime Minister would or could do to advance his naval son's career. But he was still responsible for his younger sons. Frederick at Cambridge belonged to the fashionable Pitt Club, and with others had subscribed to pay for a band to drum up support for the Tory election candidate. In 1843 the election result was challenged in a petition and it was alleged that some of the money raised for the band had been used to bribe voters. The subscription list was in the hands of the petitioners, and there was the name of the Prime Minister's son. Peel wrote to Frederick to ask for the facts. 'I feel very confident that if any improper use whatever has been made of the money it must have been altogether without your sanction or knowledge.' This was indeed Frederick's firm contention, and the story faded away.[17]

The Peel children, well loved and cared for, with plenty of good food and country air were a healthy brood; but they could not be entirely immune from the epidemics which swept through Victorian England. In the autumn of 1844 Peel's youngest daughter Eliza caught scarlet fever. That was bad enough, but diphtheria might follow. For several desperate days at Drayton the twelve-year-old girl seemed close to death. Peel and Julia, banished from the Manor for fear of infection, lodged nearby in the steward's house. Peel was supposed to accompany the Queen on her autumn visit to Scotland, but asked Aberdeen to take his place. The crisis passed, Peel returned to his desk, and the rest of the family recovered their strength at Brighton.[18]

These were the crucial years of Peel's life. He never turned his back on his family, whose comings and goings were constantly on his mind. In his political career two processes were at work, or more precisely they worked against each other. Up to the last minute it was not certain which would prevail. On the one hand Peel's ability to absorb facts had never been so formidable. Equally strong was his determination that these facts, soberly perceived, should shape the decisions of his Government. On the two main questions in his mind, Ireland and poverty in Britain, the facts gradually persuaded him that specific actions were necessary. These perceptions and the actions which followed ran counter to his own past commitments and convictions. They also ran counter to the convictions and commitments of most of his followers in the Conservative Party.

This spelt trouble. Peel was the Queen's Minister, and had gradually won the Queen's support. In the old days that might have been enough when added to his own mastery of facts and powers of persuasion. But the Sovereign's influence was shrinking towards insignificance, and Peel's persuasiveness was limited by his stiff and self-righteous manner. It was now the House of Commons which counted, and in the House of Commons his followers rode with increasing dismay at each fence on the course which he devised for them.

Discontent with a Prime Minister and a government usually begins with silent discontent. The next stage is an incoherent and unco-ordinated grumble. Eventually the grumblers come together; a leader and a cause emerge; the decisive challenge is mounted. Between 1842 and 1846 Peel was running a race between his agenda and his weakening authority.

We can see how this double process of achievement and erosion of support was at work. Several of his colleagues, and in some moods Peel himself, noted it as the years passed and drew pessimistic conclusions. But he could not press on too fast. His ideas and plans took time to grow. They had not emerged fully armed from his brain when he travelled to Windsor in August 1841 to receive the Queen's commission. He was not ready then to repeal the Corn Laws or to alter the whole emphasis of government in Ireland. The facts worked their way inexorably but slowly through his mind. He needed time, more time than he was given. Yet it did not occur to him to turn back. Once they were clear in his mind, he planted the arguments in the minds of his followers. Their duty as followers was then in his view obvious. The approval of Parliament for his measures was necessary, but it would never have occurred to Peel that Parliament, let alone one party within it, possessed some supreme wisdom to which the Queen's Minister must subordinate his own views. That would indeed be the 'servile tenure' which he had rejected at the outset of his premiership. His followers had been warned, and had cheered the warning. The rest followed. He must work, work and work again to establish the facts, form his own conclusions, persuade his colleagues, inform the Queen and summon the Lords and Commons to their duty.

Like a headmaster supervising his pupils, Peel watched the Ministers in his Government, and intervened forcefully when he saw something amiss. One example shows an important characteristic. Peel was not by nature humanitarian, as can be seen from his attitude to capital punishment, to the slave trade, or to women and young people working in factories. But he was always keen to support respect for the law and to oppose abuse of it by the powerful or privileged. The Home Secretary who stopped magistrates from giving premature authority for the use of force against an unarmed crowd became the Prime Minister who accepted as absolute the right of jury trial in Ireland, and who intervened in the strange case of Lieutenant Munro.

The Lieutenant, faced with a charge of murdering a man in a duel, had simply disappeared for six months, and no one seemed to be looking for him. In December 1843 Peel wrote angrily to Hardinge, who was still Secretary at War —

> what possible reason can be assigned for not compelling any officer, so far as the Crown has the power of compulsion, to surrender himself to the laws of his country for the purpose of being placed upon his trial on a charge of murder? ... Suppose a common soldier or a common sailor was absent six months without leave — would he not be severely punished? Suppose his excuse was there was a criminal charge against me and therefore I absented myself, would such an excuse prevail? I really think this is a very important matter.[19]

But there is no end to the story — the file on record peters out without a conclusion.

Peel never lost his interest in public support for the arts. Some of his ideas were bizarre. In 1845 he wanted to pull down St James's Palace ('the present building [which of course remains] cannot long remain. It is a great blemish to the best part of London') and erect the new National Gallery on that site, which would be called the Royal Gallery. The Queen would be compensated by an enlargement of Buckingham Palace, which to appease traditionalists would be renamed St James's Palace.[20]

However, the Prime Minister's main interest was the economy. The word strategy is now abused, but in 1842 Peel had set out a strategy in the true sense of that word, namely a set of coherent measures designed to reduce poverty though increasing consumption.

The 1842 Budget had been the core of the strategy. Its benefits were slow to show. Officials took six months to set up the machinery for collecting income tax, and Customs duties produced less than expected because of the deep recession. As a result the Chancellor of the Exchequer, Goulburn, looking at 1843, had to budget for a deficit of just over £2 million, instead of the expected surplus of £½ million. But Goulburn, deeply cautious by nature, was reasonably optimistic. It was clear that once the revenue from income tax began to flow it would produce more than expected. The expense of Palmerston's war against China was being met by an indemnity from the Chinese government. Above all trade and industry were beginning to revive, and unemployment was dropping. Even in Paisley welfare payments in the form of outdoor relief were falling. Despite these favourable signs cautious Goulburn produced in effect standstill Budgets in both 1843 and 1844. Peel's strategy for reducing the cost of living had a long way to go, and the figures had to be right before he could safely make the next big move.[21] But as proof of confidence in March 1844 Goulburn was able to renew £250 million worth of Government stock at a lower rate of interest.

In this favourable moment a new British institution came to birth. *The Economist* newspaper still carries on each issue, albeit in tiny type, its founding statement of purpose in September 1843 – 'to take part in a severe contest between intelligence which presses forward, and an unworthy timid ignorance obstructing our progress'. Peel could not have put it better.

His economic thinking was throughout underpinned by a strong belief in a strong currency linked to gold. He had chaired the Committee in 1819 which had plumped for gold, and he believed that the later flow of facts confirmed his first opinions. In 1844 there was an opportunity to revise the Charter of the Bank of England. The system had not worked smoothly. There had been four financial crises since 1819, involving speculation, high prices, a flight of gold abroad, and over-issue of notes by the country banks, many of which had gone bankrupt. After discussion with the Bank and Goulburn Peel decided that the time had come to define more closely in statute the Bank's dual role as a holder of deposits and securities and as an issuer of notes backed by bullion. Out of this discussion came the Bank Charter Act of 1844, which also dealt with the controversial right of country banks to issue notes alongside the Bank of England. Peel took personal responsibility for deciding the shape of the Bill and for steering it through Parliament.

Peel continued to hold firmly the strict conservative view of currency which he shared with the Bank authorities. He showed no sympathy with the new banking school of Thomas Tooke and James Wilson. They were developing out of the earlier doctrines of Attwood in Birmingham (which old Sir Robert had supported) a sophisticated theory of credit management which gained ground in the next century. Peel was not tempted into complications. He stressed repeatedly the essential link between paper issue and the gold reserves. To prevent dangerous confusion his Bill provided that the Bank of England should be separated into distinct departments of issue and banking. The issue of notes should be related to specific amounts of bullion and securities, plus a modest allowance of £14 million as fiduciary issue, which should be not exceeded except in an emergency and with government permission. As regards the country banks, Peel admitted that if he were starting afresh he would favour a single issuing authority. But there was the problem of Scotland and Ireland; and anyway the country banks were popular and had many friends in the back benches of the Commons. So their right to issue notes was not abolished, but slowly squeezed by tight regulation.

Peel enjoyed this subject, not least because he understood it and many others did not. Before the Commons he relished the role of the avuncular academic, beginning his exposition with the question 'What is a pound?' which he answered at length. There was little parliamentary dissent and the press was favourable, apart from an inevitable argument about country banks.

Peel and public opinion in general regarded the Bank Charter Act as definitive, a final measure which closed debate. The Act provided a framework which lasted through the age of British commercial and financial pre-eminence up to 1914. In practice the framework succeeded because it turned out to be more flexible than Peel intended. Strictly interpreted it might have had a stifling deflationary effect on British expansion. But the Bank of England, the Treasury and the public found ways of bending the rules. For example in the financial crisis of 1857 the Treasury had to authorise a transfer of funds from the issuing to the banking departments of the Bank of England. More important, the discovery of gold in Australia and California together with the growth of cheques and other forms of credit transfer made it possible to live within rules which would otherwise have imprisoned the entrepreneur. Peel's figure of £14 million for the fiduciary issue, that is the amount of currency the Bank of England could issue over and above its holding of bullion and securities, was tiny for a country whose gross national income was about £500 million.[22] But in practice it turned out to be a reasonably comfortable arrangement – a highly respectable Act of Parliament carrying the trusted name of Peel, combined with practical arrangements to modify the rules when necessary.

For Peel there was a direct relationship between taxes, tariffs and banking on the one hand and the wellbeing of his fellow citizens on the other. For Lord Ashley, a man of equal persistence, that was all nonsense. Ashley carried in his head a simple interpretation of the will of God and of his own vocation. It was Ashley's sacred duty to relieve the suffering of those who worked in mines and factories, and for this overriding purpose Peel was his instrument. The two men looked at human misery with completely different eyes, and their eyes never met. Peel rejected Ashley's message but respected his integrity, and for good political reasons did his best to stay on terms with him.

The Home Secretary, James Graham, had in 1843 produced a mildly progressive Factory Bill which ran into fatal difficulty because of the education clauses attached to it. These were regarded as too favourable to the Church of England; no agreement was reached and the Government temporarily withdrew its Bill. In November 1843 the Cabinet decided to bring back a simplified factory measure without any education clauses. Graham's new Bill raised the age limit for children in factories from eight to nine years, and strengthened the factory inspectors, but kept the maximum of twelve hours of daily work for young persons and women. Ashley seized his moment, and moved to reduce the twelve hours to ten. In the fierce debates which followed it was generally accepted that whatever limit was accepted for hours worked by young persons and women would for practical purposes apply to men also. It would not be possible to operate factories for longer hours with men only.

The debate cut across party lines. Ashley, a Conservative, was supported by many who shared his humanitarian priority. They were joined by a considerable number of Conservative agriculturists driven by a strong grievance against the Anti Corn Law League. These country gentlemen thought that the manufacturers who were campaigning so hard against agricultural protection should taste some of their own medicine; political agitation should work both ways. If agricultural profits were to be squeezed by imported wheat as the League argued, then manufacturing profits should be squeezed by a tough factory law. Peel and Graham thought this was nonsense: could not the country gentlemen see how vulnerable the Corn Laws were to this kind of faction fighting?

But the main concern of Ministers was with the competitiveness of British industry. Of the total of national annual exports at £44 million, £35 million was in textiles. Ashley's amendment would cut seven weeks from the working year of British factories. In these circumstances manufacturers could only stay competitive by reducing wages. It was wrong therefore to regard the argument as one of cold heart against compassion. The wellbeing of factory workers was inseparable from the prosperity of their factories. The ten-hour amendment could renew the depression from which the country was emerging. It could frustrate all Peel had been trying to achieve for the standard of living of the poor in the 1842 Budget. In opposing Ashley he told the Commons 'I shall never forget as long as I live the situation of Paisley in 1841 and 1842'. From his Communist standpoint Engels was not impressed: 'There is something in these arguments, but they merely prove that the industrial greatness of England rests limply upon the barbarous treatment of the workers, the destruction of their health and the social physical and moral neglect of future generations.'[23]

Whatever their merit Peel's arguments did not work that day. Ashley's ten-hour amendment was carried by 179 votes to 170. A divided Cabinet met, and met again. Gladstone favoured a compromise, and there was talk of eleven hours. But Graham was in harsh mood; he would resign unless the Government held to twelve hours. Peel backed him, and after Easter confronted the Commons again. His speech on 10 May gave no ground. Peel restated the argument and was clear that if beaten he would resign. In the gallery the Russian Ambassador, coming from a different political tradition, was deeply impressed by the Prime Minister's uncompromising style. The imperious tone worked, the House reversed itself, and Ashley was defeated by an unexpected margin of 138 votes.[24] Greville wrote in his diary before the final vote, 'I never remember so much excitement as has been caused by Ashley's Ten Hour Bill, nor a more curious political state of things ... They [the Government] have been abandoned by nearly half their supporters and nothing can exceed their chagrin and soreness at being so forsaken.'[25] Yet when it came to the crunch the Conservative rebels were not yet able to contemplate a future without Peel.

But he had made a mistake. Peel disliked sentimental compassion masquerading as argument. He failed to see that warm-hearted sympathy has a place in politics. Margaret Thatcher made the same mistake. Both Prime Ministers were above all anxious to press home the arguments for their main policy. To deal with poverty Peel believed in cutting tariffs, Margaret Thatcher in curbing inflation and trade union power. They suspected specific measures to help the poor as unwelcoming and damaging diversions. In rebutting these they could appear insensitive and hard-hearted. So far from strengthening their main argument they weakened it. By forcing his backbenchers to reverse their vote Peel damaged his future power to persuade them. When the Ten Hour Bill eventually became law in 1847 the British textile industry did not crumble.

The fences on the political racecourse were now close together. Hardly had the row over the Ten Hour Bill died down when a new crisis blew up over the sugar duties. A warning sign hung over the whole question, since it was over sugar that the Whig Government had come to grief in 1841. For this reason sugar had been left out of the major tariff changes in 1842. But the subject could not be avoided indefinitely. The demand for sugar in an increasingly prosperous Britain was growing fast. The British West Indian plantations which had a virtual monopoly of supply could not produce enough. Sugar from Brazil was ruled out because of slavery. Sugar plantations without slaves were developing in Java and the Philippines and a lower tariff on foreign sugar could encourage their growth.

In June 1844 Goulburn proposed a complicated temporary scheme which would reduce the duty on non-slave sugar while retaining some preference in favour of the colonies. The plan was attacked for opposite reasons both by whole-hearted free traders and by the West Indian sugar lobby. An ingenious wrecking amendment by a Conservative backbencher called Miles managed to bring both sets of critics into the lobby against the Government, which was beaten on 14 June by twenty votes. The Government were back in the same position as over Ashley's Ten Hours. Peel, Stanley and Graham, baffled and angry, at first believed that they would have to resign. Goulburn, Gladstone and the Duke disagreed, thinking it absurd that the Government should fall on an intricate, incomprehensible matter which involved no principle. The Queen agreed, and Peel began to soften. A meeting of 300 Conservatives at the Carlton Club passed a resolution of general and cordial support for the Government. Peel was not impressed by soft words. He wrote to one of the rebels, Lord Sandon, 'I will not say more than that declaration of general confidence will not compensate for that loss of authority and efficiency which is sustained by a Government not enabled to carry into effect the practical measures of legislation which it feels to be its duty to submit to Parliament.'[26]

Peel agreed to a small concession towards the rebels, but essentially asked the Commons to think again. The Whigs objected, Disraeli twisted the knife, and Peel made a harsh, clumsy speech which Gladstone at his side thought was the Government's death warrant. Peel warned the Queen that the Government would probably lose the vote. In fact they scraped home by twenty-two.

During this political turmoil, Peel had to solve a family crisis. As we saw, John had been miserable in his first days at Eton and was still not thriving there. In March 1844 Peel received a letter from John's house-master, Edward Coleridge: 'Eton is not the best place for him ... his want of any desire for literary distinction ... my wish is that with your concurrence and at your convenience he may be removed from this place to one more likely to agree with his tastes and professional views.' Peel could hardly fail to concur, but the inconvenience rapidly grew. John, aged sixteen, was destined for the Army and Coleridge recommended a small educational establishment at Dover which pointed its pupils in this direction.

The Prime Minister's letter asking for a place for John provided an unexpected and a sweet opportunity to the headmaster of this Dover school, the Reverend F. Glover. Mr Glover held strong political views and here was a unique chance to further them. No longer need he confine himself to grumbling at Dover; he could rescue his country from impious disaster. He quickly fired a preliminary warning salvo: 'But, Sir, I think it right to inform you that the person who has the honour to address you is one who has thought it right, in his professional capacity to speak in severe terms of church measures introduced by you, and professionally of yourself.' Mr Glover then abandoned his studies and his pupils to compose and dispatch next day a further letter of twelve pages containing

A family thanks the man who brought them cheap bread

Stag at bay, after Landseer. Peel savaged by Disraeli and Bentinck . . .

. . . and finally stabbed by his friends.

Another Julia – Peel loved his daughter, but not escorting her to dances

The last carefree summer, 1845: the Queen, her mother, Albert, the Duke and Peel in Windsor Great Park

Lord John Russell fails the crucial test, while Peel waits, 1846

Manager Peel taking his farewell bow, 1846. Disraeli is being arrested by a Peeler.

Opposite page Very different men, but firm partners for nineteen years. The Winterhalter portrait of Peel and the Duke.

The two close friends at Peel's deathbed:
Sir Henry Hardinge (above) and Sir James
Graham (right)

'The Preaching of John Knox', by
Wilkie, on which Peel looked as
he lay dying, 1850

On the way to his downfall

Will he live? Rich and poor waiting for news in Whitehall Gardens.

a formidable indictment. Mr Glover's anger dated back to Catholic Emancipation in 1829, but his flames had been fanned into fury again by the proposal 'for the payment of superstitious Roman priesthood in Ireland'.[27] He enclosed a pamphlet so that the Prime Minister could study his views at greater length. His spiritual duty was clear: he could not accept Peel's son into his school unless Peel accepted his comments and principles.

Peel had no choice in his reply: 'Without reading the pamphlet which accompanies the letter, I beg leave to abandon my intention of placing my son under your charge ... I protest altogether against the condition you propose and withdraw the wish to commit my son to your care.' Peel must have been angry at Mr Coleridge at Eton for suggesting this bigot as a mentor for John. He might even have suspected that Coleridge had set a trap, though there is no evidence for this. In any case he had little choice but to ask Coleridge to forbear and take John back to Eton. 'I have spoken very seriously to John and have distinctly told him that my decision to place him in the Army is by no means absolute, but altogether dependent on the report which I may receive from you of his diligence and good conduct.'[28] Coleridge agreed, and John resumed his Eton career, which eventually delivered him as planned into the Army. The Reverend Glover, denied a place in history, paid a price for his boldness. His wife disapproved so strongly of his conduct that she could not sleep at night. She forced him to write Peel a letter of apology.

While wrestling with these domestic issues Peel could never forget Ireland. Nowadays it is hard to imagine the baleful influence of Ireland on the British scene. We have just lived through nearly forty years of troubles in Northern Ireland, now thankfully nearing a close. Hundreds of men and women have been killed, acts of unspeakable cruelty committed and the life of a province of our country disrupted by terrorism. But the impact of these troubles on the general life of Britain has been muted. The effort required from the British Army and the British taxpayer was substantial and painful – but never intolerable and (to my surprise) never rigorously questioned by most people. The political issues were a sideshow at Westminster. The British commitment was a nuisance but also a duty, and was performed without enthusiasm in that spirit.

Our great-grandparents lived through a period where, at the beginning of the twentieth century, the Irish question dominated British politics, disrupting British parties and government. In 1914 it brought the official Opposition close to civil disobedience and Ireland to the edge of civil war.

In Peel's time Ireland cast an even darker shadow. The numbers then were different from those with which we have lived. Ireland was much more significant. Whereas in total the population of England and Wales was just under fourteen million, there were nearly six and a half million Catholics in Ireland, comprising 81 per cent of that population.[29] This formidable community was faithful to and to a large extent guided by its priests under the authority of Rome. Though many Irish Catholics fought bravely in every war for the British Crown, their loyalty in Ireland itself was always doubtful and often non-existent.

The attempt to reproduce in Ireland the fundamental structure of English social life was doomed. The historian G.M. Young wrote shrewdly that 'the Irish difficulty went deeper than the philosophy of the age could teach. The twin cell of English life, the squire administering what everybody recognises as law and the parson preaching what everybody acknowledges to be religion, had no meaning in a country where the squire was usually an invader and the parson always a heretic.'[30] In a famous purple passage Disraeli in 1844 painted the same scene for the House of Commons: 'That dense population in extreme distress inhabits an island where there is an established church which is not their church and a territorial aristocracy the richest of whom live in distant capitals. Thus you have a starving population, an absentee aristocracy and an alien church, and in addition the weakest executive in the world. That is the Irish Question.'[31] This was the only occasion when Peel complimented Disraeli on a speech.

When Peel first went to Ireland as Chief Secretary in 1812, the danger of the situation was obvious and dire. The hostility of the Irish majority might, as in 1798, coalesce with the power of the French state with which Britain was at war, and bring disaster to Britain by the back door. Brought up with that fear, Peel slipped easily into the vocabulary and practice of coercion, and gained the reputation of 'Orange Peel'. He had learned the techniques of governing Ireland before he thought seriously about the underlying purpose of that government. Once he turned his mind to that problem he had to unlearn much of what he had picked up. The nightmare of a French invasion had faded, but Britain was still left with this mass of Irish Catholics within the Union preferring a faith which was detested for its false teaching and feared for its potential disloyalty. We have seen how Peel was moved by the facts to allow this Catholic majority to be represented in Parliament by men of their own faith. The Whig Government after 1832 had wrestled, often against opposition from Peel, to reform in the same spirit the system of local government in Ireland, and the finances of the unrepresentative Protestant Church of Ireland.

The situation in Ireland at the end of 1841 was relatively calm. For the time being Daniel O'Connell had lost his audience. But neither Peel nor anyone else felt that the calm could last. Reforms of some of the least defensible results of the Protestant ascendancy had produced a temporary quiet, but wise men knew it was not enough. Some lapsed into helpless pessimism; others like Peel groped for a better way.

And made mistakes along that way. Peel fumbled in the choice of men – unusual for one who usually assessed colleagues shrewdly and in 1841 assembled an outstandingly able Government. There was no problem about Sir James Graham as Home Secretary. Graham possessed the right mix of intelligence, honesty and determination. He could speak and write frankly to Peel, the more effectively because he was obviously subordinate. Graham's loyalty was that of a lieutenant helping his commander; there were no reservations or complicated ambitions on the side.

It was in appointing the Lord-Lieutenant in Dublin and the Chief Secretary that Peel made his mistake. It is easy to say this now, harder to work out who else would have been available and done better. But the choices of Earl de Grey as Lord-Lieutenant and Lord Eliot as Chief Secretary held up both the formation of policy and its execution. Neither man was stupid or dishonest. It was their differences which caused problems – de Grey being linked by conviction and marriage to the Protestant aristocracy in Ireland, Eliot combining liberal views with an impulsive nature. The two men never formed a team because each lacked the patience to work with the other. Instead of discussing and reconciling their differences they nursed grievances and complained about them to Peel and Graham.

The relationship between the Lord-Lieutenant and Chief Secretary was nowhere defined in statute. Each pair had to work out their own way of co-operating. The Lord-Lieutenant was by definition senior and outwardly held sway in Dublin as the Queen's representative. But because the Chief Secretary was often in London, he constantly met the Prime Minister and Home Secretary, sat in Cabinet and was active in the Commons. Politically the Chief Secretary held the inner track. Peel explained patiently and in detail to Eliot how he in his time as Chief Secretary had handled his relationship with the three Lord-Lieutenants with whom he had worked: 'we resolved not to disagree, and to defeat by our own cordiality and our own forbearance the mischievous efforts of those who are constantly trying, for their own purposes personal or political, to foment discord between the chief authorities in Ireland. It is an old Irish game, and played with consummate dexterity.'[32] But neither de Grey nor Eliot was capable of this suppleness. The Irish Lord Chancellor, Sugden, was no better. 'Even when Eliot is here, his advice or judgement is nil. Sugden has no knowledge of mankind ... their services here — honest and well-intentioned as they may be [are] nearly useless.'[33]

Before he received this letter from de Grey in June 1843 Peel had already asked Graham to crack the whip. 'It will be quite impossible to go on in the way we are now going with regard to Irish matters. Lord de Grey and Lord Eliot must tell us what they, in their official and collective capacity, advise ... [As it is] we are invited, not only to govern Ireland in detail, but to solve the difficulties arising from the discrepancies of opinion of those upon the spot.'[34] Graham tried to do what Peel asked, but despaired. His mind turned to ways of shifting Eliot. In fact compared to de Grey Eliot was closer in his views to the Prime Minister and Home Secretary; but to recall de Grey would be a much more difficult operation. Might Eliot be sent to govern Canada? asked Graham. Or possibly Providence might intervene. The Chief Secretary had to be in the Commons; Eliot was the eldest son of an Earl in the House of Lords. Graham wrote wistfully to Peel, 'Lord St German [Eliot's father] cannot be immortal, and there are some great advantages in an hereditary peerage.'[35] But Lord St German lingered on; de Grey and Eliot continued to differ and complain until de Grey retired on grounds of ill health in the summer of 1844.

The main differences between Peel and de Grey arose over patronage. This was no trifling matter. The Lord-Lieutenant on behalf of the Queen appointed men to a wide range of posts in the government, the judiciary and the professions. Some of these posts by law had to go to Protestants; the rest were at his discretion. Peel fastened on this fact as an instrument of the policy towards which he was moving. In his correspondence with de Grey on patronage in 1842 and 1843 we see clearly emerging for the first time Peel's vision for Ireland as a whole.

At great cost to himself Peel had reversed his own opinions and led Parliament in 1829 to open itself to Catholics. Catholic Emancipation was a fundamental change; it meant that the British State had renounced repression and exclusion of Catholics as the foundations of British rule in Ireland. The logic of this change could not be ignored. The Irish electorate was sending Catholics to Westminster; it followed that the Irish Government must find Catholics to serve in its own ranks, among judges and magistrates and in the professions. It should use patronage in the cause of conciliation. The Government must detach able Catholics from simple nationalism directed against the Crown and against all Irish institutions except their Church. This process would take time, and had hardly begun. The need seemed to Peel obvious. Yet here was the Lord-Lieutenant, by himself and without proper consultation with the Chief Secretary, making appointments on quite a different basis.

De Grey held to the ancient doctrine of Dublin Castle: those who were not with the Crown were against it and only Protestants could be trusted. De Grey did not bother to choose smooth words for this thought: 'Conciliation is a chimera,' he wrote to Peel in August 1843. 'I would not be deterred from doing what I thought right by any fear of their [Catholic] anger, nor would I do what I did not honestly believe to be right with any hopes of obtaining their praise.' Anyway, he went on, man for man there were no Catholics who could compete on merit with Protestants for important legal appointments 'except the two or three whose extreme opinions must prevent our employing them'. This prompted Peel to a full statement of his case. If Catholic candidates were inferior on merit, this was because Protestants had for years held a monopoly of experience and office. De Grey had not grasped the implication of Catholic Emancipation for the future of Britain in Ireland:

Every avenue to popular favour is opened, and if every avenue to royal favour be closed, we have done nothing by the removal of disabilities but organise a band of mischievous demagogues. You say that no favours will conciliate the great mass of the Roman Catholics. They will not conciliate a certain class of them; but it is a fearful prospect if

the whole body is so combined against the existing order of things that
nothing can soften or detach any part of it. I know not how it will be
possible in that case to conduct the Government of Ireland or to maintain the connexion with that country.

There must be 'Catholics of intelligence, tired of excitement and agitation' who would take the post. 'It is not the favour itself, but the favour as
indicative of the spirit and intentions of the Government, as a proof that
the old system of exclusion will not be rigidly adhered to, and that moderation in politics and abstinence from agitation has at least a chance of
reward.'[36] Notes on this file show that Graham, Stanley and Sugden saw
and strongly approved of these arguments. As a result de Grey appointed
a Catholic to a senior legal appointment. But it was hard grinding.
Protestants continued to get priority for promotion in the police. Eliot
told Peel that of twelve or fifteen Army promotions not one was
Catholic; Peel and de Grey continued to argue into 1844 about the small
proportion of Catholic barristers. De Grey could be outgunned on
particular appointments but was never persuaded of Peel's general case.

Conciliation had to be pursued consistently and over time if it was to
achieve Peel's aim of 'moderation in politics and abstinence from agitation'. But time was not limitless, and one man in particular was in a hurry.
When Peel took office Daniel O'Connell was sixty-six. He knew well that
the old Tories had a reputation for a hard line on Irish policy. Peel himself
had not lost his tough reputation despite Catholic Emancipation, and
O'Connell turned this to good effect. Disraeli gave the point a malicious
twist when he spoke of Peel as 'the same individual whose bleak shade fell
on the sunshine of your hopes for more than a quarter of a century'.[37] But
O'Connell did not know how Peel's bleakness was dissolving. Already in
1840 O'Connell had prepared for the arrival of a Conservative government, by founding the Repeal Association. But this was nothing to do
with the Corn Laws – this was for the repeal of the Act of Union.

O'Connell started slowly, for his influence had faded during the 1830s.
Only eighteen Repeal MPs were elected in 1841, compared to thirty-nine
in 1832. O'Connell himself lost his seat in Dublin City to a Conservative,
but was elected simultaneously for Cork County. He turned his attention
to building his Repeal Association from the grass roots, parish by parish,
mobilising the Catholic priests and tackling the reluctance of the Vatican

to see the politicisation of the Church.[38] He organised a series of mass meetings, which reached a climax in August 1843. The organisers claimed that a million Irish men and women gathered at Tara in County Meath, where the old Irish kings had built their palace. More objective observers calculated half a million, but the result was the same. These meetings became set piece triumphal processions for O'Connell, who addressed more than thirty of them. He also staged a three-day debate in the Dublin Corporation at which he spoke for four hours.[39] O'Connell in this way re-established himself as the voice of Ireland. His eloquence was as sweeping as ever, but he kept his precise demands within bounds. He did not press for a break with Britain, but argued that under the Crown Ireland must have her own parliament again, as before 1801.

The Government was at first relaxed. In July 1842 Peel warned de Grey not to pay too much attention to alarmist reports: 'Fifty thousand men are ready to come over from the United States to aid Irish patriots. This is very startling. But it is consolatory to hear that how they were to arrive was not mentioned.'[40] It was always awkward in Ireland to decide when to prosecute for seditious offences because only in Dublin was a jury likely to convict. Peel wrote to Graham in December 1841, 'when a country is tolerably quiet it is better for a Government to be hard of hearing than to be very agile in prosecuting'.[41] But in May 1843 the Lord-Lieutenant suddenly panicked at the prospect of endless mass meetings acclaiming O'Connell. Conscious that up to then he had thought that O'Connell was not worth noticing, de Grey argued that the growth of the Repeal movement had been sudden and astounding. But now, he added, Government must deal with this 'burst of audacity ... Every hour is adding fatal strength to the danger ... Let whatever you do be strong enough ... Let no morbid sensibility or mawkish apprehension of invading the Constitution be allowed to weigh.'[42]

The Duke of Wellington heard the trumpet call and pressed for immediate legislation against the Repeal Association. But there were two difficulties. The first, by now familiar, was that Eliot disagreed with de Grey. The other lay in the difficulty of drafting a Bill which would outlaw the Repeal Association in Ireland but leave untouched the Anti Corn Law League in England, whose language and tactics were similar. The Cabinet compromised. Peel made a strong but general declaration in the Commons in favour of maintaining the Union; but there was no ban on the Repeal movement or its monster meetings. As the autumn of 1843 wore on, the situation showed no signs of improving. Peel and Graham disapproved of the Irish Lord Chancellor's dismissal of magistrates. On the other hand the Irish authorities were extremely reluctant to prosecute examples of seditious speeches; they did not believe that juries would convict.* Graham thought that 'acquittals, with the facts clearly established, would be less dangerous ... I begin to despair of the Irish executive; it is not only asleep, it is dead.' The Duke of Wellington, now seventy-four, was equally gloomy, but he had a remedy which reached Graham's ears. 'I begin to suspect that the Duke wishes to go to Ireland and believes that the winds and the waves will obey him, and that in his presence there will be a great calm. I entertain an opposite opinion.'[43] So did Peel. The only circumstances in which it might be right to send the Duke would be armed rebellion or possible disloyalty in the Army.

Next month it became clear that O'Connell was planning another monster meeting at Clontarf, near Dublin. De Grey was in England, taking the waters at Buxton. The publicity for the Clontarf meeting was militant, even military in its language. Placards announced that 'repeal cavalry' would attend the meeting. The legal advisers of the Crown pointed out that there was now evidence to sustain a charge of treasonable conspiracy. The Cabinet agreed on decisive action. De Grey was to return to Dublin, ban the Clontarf meeting and prosecute O'Connell. There was real danger of a violent reaction. Graham organised troop and ship movements in case of need. But O'Connell was a lawyer who liked to stay within the law. He used his organisation to call off the Clontarf meeting as efficiently as he had summoned it. The Irish Government nevertheless proceeded to arrest him and half a dozen other Repealers on charges of conspiracy. Bail was given, and O'Connell instructed his followers to act patiently, quietly, legally. In the hands of the lawyers everything moved slowly. O'Connell was convicted in February 1844 and in

---

* It is striking that in our supposedly liberal twentieth century the Government faced with a similar problem had little difficulty in convincing itself and persuading Parliament to abolish jury trial for such offences in Northern Ireland. Peel and his colleagues do not seem to have considered this. They were too deeply rooted in traditional respect for the right to trial by jury, even for a seditious Irish peasant.

May sentenced to a fine of £2,000 and a year in prison. He appealed to the House of Lords, meanwhile occupying a suite in the house of the governor of Richmond prison in Dublin, where he was allowed to see whom he pleased. The law lords quashed his sentence in September, eleven months after Clontarf, and he processed once again in triumph to his house in Merrion Square.

But meanwhile the blaze had died down as suddenly as it flared up. There were no more mass meetings. After his arrest O'Connell behaved like a skilful old lawyer rather than a national martyr. He even modified his political demands. Peel refused to be stirred up by the clumsiness of the Irish executive in handling the trial or by the fact that the final acquittal was the work of the Whig majority among the law lords. O'Connell began to quarrel with his critics in the new organisation Young Ireland. Peel was at work on the policy of conciliation, persuaded that this was the only way to save the Union. Conciliation might not work but it had a chance. Peel had seized and was determined to keep the initiative. The Government in London could not silence O'Connell and his friends but it might conceivably outflank them.

Compared with born orators like O'Connell or Disraeli, Peel was clumsy in his handling of general concepts. For him, if conciliation meant anything it had to be expressed not at mass meetings or in great speeches but in practical measures. But practical measures needed to be based on careful and objective analysis. One Irish matter calling out for the Peel treatment was the relationship between landlord and tenant. To most observers this had up to then seemed a wholly intractable problem. There appeared to be no meeting place between the sacred right of property and the hopeless poverty of the Irish peasant. Peel in 1843 did not know the answer, but he did know he had to look for it. After consulting Graham and the Duke he asked a respected Whig landowner, Lord Devon, to chair a Commission to consider the law and practice of land occupation in Ireland. The Devon Commission began work early in 1844, but produced its report too late for Peel to act on it. The Devon report provided the framework for repeated efforts by successive governments to achieve agrarian reform.

As we have seen, government patronage was for Peel one necessary technique of conciliation. He continued to badger Graham and de Grey. 'We must discard', he wrote to Graham, 'the favourite doctrine of Dublin

Castle, you cannot conciliate your enemies, therefore give everything to the most zealous of your friends.'[44] This work became much easier when he could replace the ailing de Grey with an urbane diplomat, Lord Heytesbury, who agreed not only with Peel but also with Eliot. At last there was a coherent team working together in Dublin. This harmony continued after Eliot was at last elevated to the Lords in January 1845 and replaced by the faithful Chief Whip Sir Thomas Fremantle.

Peel was skilled in making constructive use of the work of his colleagues. To Eliot he owed much of the thinking behind the three major policy papers on Ireland which he circulated to colleagues in February 1844. His timing was influenced by a massive debate in the Commons originated by Lord John Russell. The debate caught the Government in an awkward position, halfway through reconsidering policy. Peel was determined to press on. Some of his proposals fell by the wayside. Eliot introduced a Bill to enlarge the Irish electorate. To dilute Protestant fears about the results of Catholic Emancipation the Irish forty-shilling freeholder had been deprived of his vote in 1829 and the threshold for voting fixed at £10. Three years later the English system had been rationalised in the Great Reform Bill and a £5 threshold introduced for English county seats. Eliot proposed to carry that threshold across to Ireland. But the Irish liberals objected, the discussion became bogged down, and the Government abandoned the Bill to concentrate on its more important proposals.

Another plan which faltered would have established new colleges in Cork, Galway and Belfast. These were to be non-denominational, but with provision for private financing of professorships of divinity. The Academic Colleges Bill passed the Commons without difficulty, but came to nothing, having run aground on the sensitivities of the Catholic Church, which had not been consulted.

The main focus of Peel's conciliation policy had to be the Catholic Church. He studied with a mixture of awe and repulsion its amazing dominance over four-fifths of the Irish population. This was a power unequalled in Britain or even perhaps in the rest of Europe. De Tocqueville had commented in 1835 on the 'unbelievable unity between the Irish clergy and the Catholic population' which he attributed not only to the fact that 'the clergy are paid by the people but also because all the upper classes are Protestant and enemies'.[45] The number of priests had risen, though not as fast as the population. There was an amazing burst of new church building between 1829 and 1846. Priests were active in O'Connell's Repeal movement. Peel noted that between twenty and thirty priests, but not one layman, had signed the original notification of the meeting at Clontarf. De Grey went too far when he said that 'every priest is a drill sergeant and every chapel an orderly room'.[46] Peel doubted the practicality of a general ban on political meetings because it would be evaded by priests holding meetings immediately after Mass.

At the heart of this problem lay the College for training priests at Maynooth, in County Kildare, fifteen miles from Dublin. Through Maynooth passed a high proportion of Irish priests. The numbers of students rose from 391 in 1826 to 438 in 1844. Of the four archbishops and twenty-three bishops who constituted the Irish hierarchy in 1844 all but seven had studied at Maynooth. Remarkably when Pitt founded the College in 1795 as part of his preparation for the Union, he gave it a grant of £8,000 from the British Exchequer. But that was at a moment of attempted conciliation, when it was expected that the Union would be quickly followed by measures to relieve Catholics of their legal disabilities. The grant remained unchanged. It was always controversial and by 1843 it was clear that it was either a hopelessly bad idea, or too small to produce a good effect. Eliot throughout held the second view, but it was not until after O'Connell's outbursts in 1842 and 1843 that Peel put the matter on his own agenda.

By then he had seen reports such as one written by Mr Kerman, resident magistrate for Sligo: 'The great supporters of the agitation among this body, and the most dangerous members of the Roman Catholic priesthood are young men who within the last five or six years have left the Catholic Seminary of Maynooth, and are now scattered about the country as curates.'[47] In his third memorandum on Ireland to the Cabinet in February 1844 Peel concluded that by leaving the Maynooth grant as it was they were 'sending out annually fifty spiritual firebrands, prepared for mischief by ourselves, to convulse the country ... The wit of man could not devise a more effectual method for converting them into sour, malignant demagogues, hostile to the law, from all sympathies of low birth and kindred, living by agitation, inclined to it and fitted for it by our eleemosynary but penurious system of education.'

Peel himself had no leanings towards Rome but he took a wider view than he had twenty years earlier. He wrote carefully to Lady de Grey, herself a sprig of the Irish Protestant aristocracy. Roman Catholicism was the religion of over half of Christendom; 'it has therefore, as it exists in Ireland, the sympathies of many powerful countries, and it is therefore equally consistent with the precepts of our own religions, and with the dictates of justice and sound policy, not to presume too much of our own infallibility'. Translated out of Peel's prose this meant that the popular English slogan 'No Popery' made no sense in Ireland. Peel's aim was political. He wanted to raise the social and intellectual level of the priesthood. He aimed to detach by persuasion and generosity as many Catholics, priests and laymen, as possible from the Repeal movement and persuade them to take a constructive part in the life of the community.

Something might be done through Rome. Even the staunch Protestant de Grey suggested an approach to the Pope. Metternich, Chancellor of Austria and in his own view the main protector of stability in Europe, was ready to put in a word at the Vatican. He wanted for his own reasons to dissuade the Church from letting its priests foment revolution in Ireland. Peel did not expect much of this and he was right. The main move towards the Catholic Church must come in the form of generous finance — private and public. The private endowment of Catholic chapels and benefices could be encouraged by setting up a new and impartial board with a Catholic majority to administer such endowments. There was no particular difficulty in Parliament over the Charitable Trusts Bill, which provided for this, but all depended on the co-operation of the Church. Archbishop Murray of Dublin agreed to serve on the Board, and held to this decision despite intense pressure from O'Connell and the Repealers. They urged the Vatican to disown the Archbishop and the new Board, but the Vatican stayed neutral and other Catholic bishops joined Murray on the Board. This was the sort of success which Peel relished — practical, fair-minded, the result of careful drafting and skilful persuasion. It might still be possible to kill Repeal by kindness.

Public generosity to Maynooth from the British taxpayer was much more difficult. Graham and the new Lord-Lieutenant, Lord Heytesbury, were set to work. In November 1844 the Cabinet began to discuss a scheme for reorganising Maynooth and increasing the annual grant from £9,000 to £25,000. There was no decision, largely because Gladstone said he was bound to oppose the scheme. Peel was prepared to wait, but not for ever. A powerful storm was blowing up from all the Protestant churches in England, Scotland and Wales. The new Tractarians in the Church of England hated State involvement in Church matters; all true Protestants hated any encouragement to Popery.

Once the Government's intention was announced hostile petitions began to pour in. Protest meetings were held. During the four months from February to May 1845 the House of Commons received more than 10,000 petitions against the Maynooth Bill carrying a million and a quarter signatures.[48] An anti-Maynooth committee was set up at Exeter Hall. The press too was generally hostile, fastening on the rapid change in Peel's views. *The Times* had supported him against O'Connell, but could not swallow Maynooth. Peel's unpredictability undermined confidence. It mattered more that British statesmen could be trusted, said *The Times*, 'than that the Maynooth students sleep in one bed'. *Punch*, then in Radical mode, supported Maynooth but with contempt:

> *How wonderful is Peel*
> *He changes with the time;*
> *Turning and twisting like an eel,*
> *Ascending through the slime.*
> *He gives whatever they want*
> *To them who ask with zeal*
> *He yields the Maynooth grant*
> *To the clamour for repeal!*[49]

Despite the uproar the Cabinet endorsed the proposal and Peel was determined to press on with the necessary Bill. Gladstone resigned in February 1845. His reasoning was characteristically abstruse. It was not that he opposed the Maynooth Bill; indeed he supported it. But in his first book on Church and State he had argued strongly against State interference in Church matters. Maynooth was an example of such interference; he would be false to his own reputation if as a member of the Government he supported a measure of a kind he had once denounced. Peel greatly valued Gladstone's work at the Board of Trade, but had little time for this complicated scruple, remarking unhelpfully that no one could remember what Gladstone had written in 1838.

Peel persevered. At the second reading on 11 April he argued, '[y]ou must break up, in some way or another that formidable confederacy which exists in that country against the British Government and the British connexion. I do not believe you can break it up by force ... You can do much to break it up by acting in a spirit of kindliness, forbearance and generosity.'[50] In one quarter at least the words found an enthusiastic echo. Indeed by now there was no hesitation in the Queen's wholehearted support for her Prime Minister. She wrote to King Leopold on 15 April:

> My beloved Uncle
>   Here we are in a great state of agitation about one of the greatest measures ever proposed. I am sure poor Peel ought to be *blessed* by all Catholics for the manly and noble way in which he stands forth to protect and do good to poor Ireland. But the bigotry, the wicked and blind passions it brings forth is quite dreadful, and I blush for Protestantism![51]

Peel had the votes, but they were not Conservative votes. The language he had just used was new and largely unwelcome to the benches behind him. During the long debates on the Bill in April and May Peel made little effort to humour them. Conciliation of Ireland was more important than conciliation of his backbenchers. Peel relied on the Whigs to see the Bill through, but he paid a price. In the Commons the fiercest attack on Peel came from Macaulay, who strongly supported Peel's Bill but followed the line of criticism in most of the press. Peel was in trouble, Macaulay argued, because he was contradicting his own negative past. 'You are doing penance for the disingenuousness of years ... Explain to us why, after you have goaded Ireland to madness for the purpose of ingratiating yourselves with the English, you are now setting England on fire for the purpose of ingratiating yourself with the Irish.'[52] This was a brilliant attack which left its author self-satisfied. 'How white poor Peel looked while I was speaking.'[53]

Macaulay's charge was difficult to refute, and Peel hardly tried. He was above all anxious to get the Bill through, and worried that on some technical point the Whigs might combine with his Tory rebels to defeat it. He averted that danger by humble words and skilful tactics. In April 1845 the Bill passed the Commons easily by a proportion of about two to one, but the Conservatives had been split in half. This was a formidable result.

Graham saw the consequence for the Government. 'The Bill will pass,' he wrote to Hardinge in India, 'but our party is destroyed.'[54] Peel too wrote to Hardinge at this time; he focused on Ireland rather than on the future of his Government. 'Come what will I am sure we are in the right, we can prevent the carrying of Repeal by force, we can probably prevent actual disturbance, and bloodshed from monster meetings. But we cannot by mere force, by mere appeals to selfish Protestant ascendancy principles, govern Ireland in a manner in which a civilised country should be governed.'[55]

The Ten Hour Factory Bill, sugar, Maynooth – there was no doubt in the spring of 1845 that Peel's Government was in deep trouble with its own supporters. Greville wrote, 'The disgust of the Conservatives and their hatred of Peel keep swelling every day, and what Ministers expect is that on some occasion or other they will play Peel a trick ... The truth is that the Government is Peel, that Peel is a reformer and more of a Whig than a Tory, and the mass of his supporters are prejudiced, ignorant, obstinate and selfish.'[56] That was the partisan view of an old-fashioned Whig; but Graham too thought that the Conservative backbenchers were by now not only unruly but hostile.

The truth was more complicated. The three big revolts of 1844 and 1845 were not the first. The Government had met trouble in the Commons as early as 1842, for example over the import of cattle. We think now in terms of an organised government policed by Whips, facing an organised Opposition, and possibly challenged from time to time by an organised rebel faction within its own ranks. But the whole concept of organisation on any scale was new in the Parliament of 1841. We have seen how varied and haphazard were the constituency campaigns in the 1841 election. Candidates bearing the same party label had been elected after saying all manner of diverse things to their electors. It was not realistic to suppose that once elected these men would suddenly forget their different pledges, fuse their contrasting ideas and act as a disciplined whole.

Nowadays a Member of Parliament is first and foremost a politician. The House of Commons in 1841 was full of businessmen and professional people, squires, sugar merchants, cotton manufacturers, sons and brothers of peers who happened to be Members of Parliament. There was no disguise. They did not pretend otherwise. They saw no reason why they should forget their personal convictions and the interests of themselves and their friends when they cast their votes in the Commons.

Of course such independent-mindedness, left to itself, would lead to anarchy. In the eighteenth century anarchy had been avoided by the power and patronage of the Crown. The King's Government could be carried on because the Crown could rely on a cohort of friends. These were men bought and persuaded by one means or another to support the government. They counterbalanced the awkward independent tendencies of men like Wilkes and Fox, or indeed the backwoodsmen of the Tory country Party. But now the patronage of the Crown was evaporating and its political power virtually gone. In 1845 the Queen and Prince Albert let it be known that they would not in future seek to influence the result of any election in Windsor. If even Windsor under the Castle walls was beyond the Crown's reach, how on earth was the Queen's Government to be carried on? The answer was party discipline. This discipline gradually asserted itself as the decades passed, but it was distinctly immature in the Parliament of 1841.

It is easy to understand the bad-tempered grumbling of Peel and Graham as their parliamentary problems increased. We can see now that they were working in a period of difficult transition from one form of parliamentary equilibrium to another; but to Peel and Graham it was just cussedness.[57] After Maynooth Peel wrote caustically to Croker that the rebels were not voting on the merits of his proposal: 'Tariff, drought, 46s a quarter for wheat [a low price] quicken the religious apprehension of some; disappointed ambition, and the rejection of application for office, of others.'[58] Peel had no appetite for concessions to such people, but their number could be reduced by firm leadership. After the sugar crisis he wrote to Hardinge in India, 'I would not admit any alteration in any of these Bills. This was thought very obstinate and very presumptuous – but the fact is people like a certain degree of obstinacy and presumption in a Minister.'[59]

That is true, but obstinacy cannot be the only or even the main weapon in the armoury of a Prime Minister. He has to be able to consult and conciliate those who know much less than himself about each issue but whose support he needs. As early as June 1843 Ashley had grasped the point: 'Peel has committed great and grievous mistakes in omitting to call his friends frequently together to state his desires and rouse their zeal. A few minutes and a few words would have sufficed; men would have felt they were companions in arms; they now have the sentiment of being followers in drill.'[60] This is an excellent description of the modern art of party management. It was practised in our time by such masters as Harold Macmillan or Harold Wilson and neglected by such brave and intelligent leaders as Ted Heath and (in their decline) Margaret Thatcher and Tony Blair. Peel was ready to teach his followers, and the teaching sessions were long and frequent; but to concede, to charm and reward them was beyond his skills and contrary to his convictions.

The grumbles of the agricultural interest grew louder. The Anti Corn Law League had sent missionaries into the countryside, believing that tenant farmers could be persuaded that the Corn Laws were simply a device for keeping up the rent they had to pay. This was a mistake. The farmers were provoked into organising themselves in the opposite direction. An Essex clergyman, Mr Cox, started the new movement in November 1843, and a thousand farmers gathered before Christmas in the Saracen's Head at Chelmsford. It was a robust occasion, at which their chairman proclaimed 'that such a flame will be lighted up in Essex as will extend to the other counties, and show to the League that they have raised a body more powerful than themselves'. Societies were quickly formed in other counties, and the farmers decided to set up a central office in London. The landlords were slower off the mark, but forty or fifty gathered in February 1844 at the Duke of Richmond's house in Portland Place. They decided to link up with the tenant farmers. In this deferential age it was agreed by both sides that the Dukes of Richmond and Buckingham should lead the merged organisation, but that half the management committee should always be tenant farmers. After this discussion 'the deputation of tenant farmers withdrew, much gratified with the proceedings of the day'. The new central Agricultural Protection Society, usually known as the Anti League, secured rooms at 19 Old Bond Street, appointed a secretary and set to work.[61]

So Peel's critics gathered strength. It did not follow that his Government was doomed. The independent spirit of backbenchers made it difficult for the Government to pass its measures but it also made it difficult to co-ordinate a revolt. The Whigs themselves were divided on most issues. Within the Conservative ranks different currents ebbed and flowed. The backbenchers must have sensed that outside Parliament among the people as a whole Peel's stock was steadily rising. He was a national figure and there was no Conservative in the Commons who could rival his reputation.

No one was more conscious of this than his most vehement and consistent opponent. Benjamin Disraeli had now gained the ear of the House of Commons. This was not because of the handful of aristocratic friends whom he gathered together under the name of Young England. The concept of an alliance between the aristocracy and the working class to form One Nation was an agreeable entertainment in his novels, but hardly more. George Eliot described it as 'a sort of idyllic masquerade, to grow feudal fidelity and veneration by an artificial system of manure'.[62] Disraeli had won an audience by his own brilliant debating techniques. He set himself to destroy the man who had refused him a job, and who represented a pragmatic administrative approach to politics which was at odds with his own romanticism.

Disraeli studied Peel's history, his weaknesses, his appearance, his mannerisms. Disraeli did not bother with other Ministers, he had one target. He did not worry about intellectual consistency. On Ireland for example, Peel's movement towards conciliation in the Maynooth Bill fitted Disraeli's own earlier analysis, and attracted some of his Young England friends. But from Disraeli it evoked one of his fiercest attacks on grounds which had nothing to do with Ireland. 'We have a great Parliamentary middleman. It is well know what a middleman is: he is a man who bamboozles one party and plunders the other, till having obtained a position to which he is not entitled, he cries out "let us have no party question, but fixity of tenure".' He invited the Commons to find a remedy 'by dethroning the dynasty of deception, by putting an end to the intolerable yoke of official despotism and Parliamentary imposture'.[63]

To this and half a dozen other attacks of similar savagery Peel had no effective response. He had achieved command of the House of Commons for two decades by mastering each subject under discussion, not by flair or wit. Peel's style was clear but long-winded. His speeches were earnest. They bulged with facts, figures and quotations. They radiated a painful integrity, even or particularly during his changes of view. Disraeli by contrast was quick, funny, unscrupulous and devastating. 'The right honourable gentleman caught the Whigs bathing and walked away with their clothes. He has left them in the full enjoyment of their liberal positions and is himself a strict conservative of their garments.'[64] The combination of witty, sometimes whirling words with a sallow expressionless face scored heavily night after night. But this was not decisive. Disraeli knew that he could not yet lead the Conservatives against Peel. His eccentric talents won him an audience, but not yet a following. The flamboyant Jewish novelist, with his odd wife and unsatisfactory money affairs, was the man to bait Peel, but not to replace him.

What mattered to Peel was the progress of his underlying plans. He could put up with occasional defeat in the Commons. He could even pull his hat down over his eyes in the Chamber and endure Disraeli, so long as he was not frustrated in doing what he thought necessary on the two great matters, Ireland and the economy. If that happened he would resign and damn the consequences. But it had not happened yet, and in the real world away from the debating chamber the country was prospering. Peel decided that after two standstill years the 1845 Budget could repeat the boldness of 1842. This meant renewing the income tax, and using the expected surplus of £3.4 million to hack away again at tariffs. The price of sugar had already been brought down. Duties were now completely abolished on 430 of the 813 remaining articles, including the crucial raw cotton. The main beneficiaries were the new industries which increasingly needed to import raw materials from abroad.

By February 1846 *The Times*, by no means a consistent friend of Peel, was describing the changes which it saw:

> The small tradesman, clergyman or clerk has two or three joints a week, instead of only one. He sometimes sees a sirloin on his table. He can afford an occasional plum pudding, and is not deterred from rice or fruit tarts by the expensive appendage of sugar. There are two candles instead of one on the table ... the children do not go so long out at elbows ... when the family becomes a little too large for the home ... the father either himself builds another room, or gets his landlord to build them with a rise of rent.[65]

Of course little of the prosperity came from Government measures, as Peel acknowledged in his Budget speech. Nor did all the small tradesmen have a vote or any influence on divisions in the House of Commons. Nor did the new prosperity reach the slums and the workhouses. Yet Peel could write confidently to Hardinge about the state of the country. He had just received a report on the situation in the North from General Brotherton, the same officer who had commanded there in 1842. Then the General had reported dangerous strife, now complete tranquillity. Peel described his critics to Hardinge:

> They cannot deny that trade is prosperous — that the public are con-tented — that the labourer has a greater command than he ever had over the occasions and comforts of life — that Chartism is extinguished or at least fast asleep, that the Church is stronger than it ever was except for its own internal stupid differences and controversies — that the revenue is so prosperous that our calculations of deficiency are con-stantly baffled, that our monetary system is sounder than it has ever been — and yet that there has been boundless activity in commerce and all speculation is of gain — that even land is increasing because of the prosperity of commerce — but [and here the scars show] we have reduced protection to agriculture and tried to lay the foundation of peace in Ireland, and these are offences for which nothing can atone.[66]

The critics were tiresome, but their noise was ineffective so long as the country flourished. In June 1845 Peel and Julia rode with the Queen down the course at Royal Ascot, and attended her ball at Windsor Castle in the evening. Julia reported to young Frederick that they danced Sir Roger de Coverley and minuets till one in the morning. It was a lovely day.[67]

Sixteen

Martyrdom

'There was a dead silence'
*In Cabinet after Peel announced his decision to repeal the Corn Laws,
21 December 1845*

'This night you will select the motto which is to indicate
the commercial policy of England. Shall it be "advance" or
"recede"? Which is the fitter motto for this great
Empire? ... is this the country to shrink from competition?
Is this the country to adopt a retrograde policy? Is this the
country which can only flourish in the sickly atmosphere of
prohibition? Choose your motto "Advance" or "Recede".
Many countries are watching the selection you may make.'
Peel in the Commons, 2 February 1846

'Let men stand by the principle by which they rise, right or
wrong ... Do not then because you see a great personage
giving up his opinions – do not cheer him on, do not give
him so ready a reward to political tergiversation. Above all,
maintain the line of demarcation between parties.'
Disraeli in the Commons, 22 January 1846

'In relinquishing power I shall leave a name, severely
censured I fear by many ... I shall leave a name execrated by
every monopolist who ... clamours for protection because
it conduces to his own individual benefit; but it may be that
I shall leave a name sometimes remembered with
expressions of good will in the abodes of those whose lot it
is to labour, and to earn their daily bread by the sweat of
their brow, when they shall recruit their exhausted strength
with abundant and untaxed food, the sweeter because it is
no longer leavened by a sense of injustice'
Peel in the Commons, 29 June 1846

By mid August 1845 Ministers were already writing to each other about the rain. This was not gossip to fill a letter. In those days bad summer weather was not just a threat to holidays or sporting events, but a major political hazard. A wet summer meant a poor harvest, higher food prices and political trouble. Graham at his desk in the Home Office reported a dark cold day, more like November than summer, and wrote to Peel, 'I know not that the state of affairs is really sound when Ministers are driven to study the Barometer with so much anxiety, but under no law will it be found easy to feed twenty five million crowded together in a narrow space, when Heaven denies the blessings of abundance.'[1]

As summer moved into autumn, it became clear that the real problem did not lie with the flattened Midland cornfields which Peel noticed from the train. The wet weather was encouraging potato blight, on the Continent, in England, but above all in Ireland, where the potato crop failed almost everywhere. As the fungus spread, Ireland paid heavily for its dependence on the crop. Most potatoes looked shiny and wholesome when harvested, but began to rot within days.

There was nothing extraordinary about talk of famine in Ireland. As Chief Secretary Peel had by the standard of the time dealt competently with the famine of 1817. First reports were usually wrong. 'There is such a tendency to exaggeration and inaccuracy in Irish reports that delay in acting on them is always desirable.'[2] But by the time he wrote this to Graham on 13 October he recognised that Government action would be needed.

Five days later Peel was conferring at Drayton with Dr Lyon Playfair, a well known chemist who had studied in Germany under the great Liebig. With two other scientists Playfair formed a Scientific Commission which went at once to Ireland to investigate. After only two days Playfair wrote to tell Peel that so far from being exaggerated the situation was actually much worse than the public supposed. Half the potato crop of Ireland had already been destroyed or would shortly perish. The scientists set out to discover a way of preventing the potatoes from rotting once harvested, or if that was not possible of turning spoiled potatoes to good use. This proved a vain hope. Detailed suggestions were circulated to landlords and the clergy for distribution to tenants. Diseased potatoes were to be mashed, dried and mixed with other meal to make wholesome bread.

Neither these nor a multitude of other suggestions worked in practice. The diseased potatoes were just not usable. From that point on disaster was inevitable.

But men had to try. On 3 November the Lord-Lieutenant, Lord Heytesbury, received a deputation of Irish notables who produced a set of proposals to avert calamity, drawn up by Daniel O'Connell. Some of these, such as a ban on the use of grain for distilling whiskey and brewing beer, were familiar from earlier famines when they had proved largely irrelevant. More eye-catching was the proposal to stop the export of grain and other foodstuffs to Britain. This seemed at first sight common sense. The sight of ships loading grain for export while Irish families starved seemed outrageous; armed guards had to be provided to protect the shipments from attack. But the decision of Ministers to reject a ban on exports was not entirely unreasonable. An Irish tenant had two overriding needs: food for his family and rent to save them from losing their land. Their diet was overwhelmingly based on the potato, and his wife was unused to baking bread from grain. The rent depended on cash from the sales of produce. Cut off the exports to Britain and for lack of income the tenant might face eviction or find himself entirely at the mercy of the landlord. The notables also proposed the opening of the ports to food from the colonies without duty, and the provision of employment through public works. Peel had already made up his mind on the first point, and begun to act on the second.

The Cabinet set up a Relief Commission under the chairmanship of Sir Randolph Routh, a genial old Roman Catholic with long experience of supplying the Army. Skilled rather than brilliant, he had been in charge of the commissariat at Waterloo. The Relief Commission was instructed to form local committees to raise money for famine relief. They were to set up local employment schemes, to work with the Board of Works in making new roads, and to provide for hospitals to cope with the fever which was expected to follow the famine. But above all they were to receive, store and distribute the maize which the Government was to buy from the United States.

This last was Peel's personal initiative, which he pushed through without much collective discussion. Peel shared the prevailing doctrine of laissez-faire. In the end the famine would be ended through the benevolence of God in providing a better harvest, and through the free working of the market. If Government contradicted that market system, either by providing massive relief from public funds or by interfering with trade, it would postpone the recovery, and further weaken the fragile Irish economy. But at a different level of reality Peel was faced with the prospect of mass starvation once stocks of food ran out and could not be replaced. There was no market in American maize (called Indian corn at the time) so there would be no interference with normal trade. Bypassing the Treasury and the cumbersome machinery of military procurement, Peel arranged for Barings to buy £100,000 worth of maize, confidentially, and at different points in the United States so as not to send up the price.

Purchase was easy compared to distribution. The Admiralty at first could provide only two steamers to take the maize from Cork to unsatis-factory little harbours on the west coast close to the greatest need. Poor Law officials refused to help, pleading the narrow way in which the Poor Law Act defined their duties. There was another bureaucratic problem of a kind beloved by the Treasury in all generations. The maize was meant to relieve distress caused by the potato disease. But how could one distin-guish between potato-related disease and the normal distress which was widespread in Ireland even when the potatoes were in good shape? One can imagine the zeal with which officials identified this difficulty. The problem became more baffling the further one travelled from London, and at the point of actual suffering was insoluble.

The maize began badly. It was at first rejected by people who remem-bered uneatable meals distributed by government at the last famine in 1831. Because it was bright yellow it was called 'Peel's brimstone'. There were riots in workhouses which introduced it; it was greeted by weeping and wailing in Limerick and Waterford. But within weeks the maize became immensely popular and the Government prepared a halfpenny pamphlet with advice on cooking it.

Popularity quickly brought its own problems. There was not nearly enough maize to go round. It was estimated that the lost potato crop was worth £3.5 million; American maize worth £100,000 could not go far to fill that gap. Peel had planned to release the maize sparingly, and only when in a particular district the price of food rose above a certain level. This concept, like many benevolent notions of the time, wrongly assumed that Ireland had a functioning market economy.

The import of maize continued through the summer of 1846. The

Government began to consider whether more maize should be bought to maintain supply to the food depots which Sir Randolph Routh had set up. By this time Peel was fighting for his life at Westminster, and Sir Randolph had to reckon with the Treasury in its purest and least merciful form, embodied in the Assistant Secretary Charles Trevelyan. Young, handsome, an intense evangelical, Trevelyan was wholly devoted to hard work. By his outstanding ability he quickly came to dominate the organisation of relief. Trevelyan's integrity and energy masked two difficulties: he did not approve of the Irish, and was dogmatically devoted to the doctrines of the free market. He was not on good terms with Peel, whom he had annoyed three years earlier by publishing under a pseudonym in the *Morning Chronicle* two long letters based on an earlier visit to Ireland. Peel too believed in free trade and the functioning of the market, but people were suffering, these benevolent forces took time to muster their strength, and meanwhile Peel bought maize for Ireland in 1845 and 1846, just as he had mobilised help for Paisley in 1842. These were the limited concessions he was ready to make at the expense of his theoretical beliefs to relieve human hardship. It is hard to believe that if Peel had retained power he would have allowed Trevelyan to close the food depots and refuse any further purchase of maize. The new Whig Government was more to Trevelyan's taste and fully approved his determination to wind up the relief effort.

It was clear by late summer of 1846 that the potato harvest would fail again. To Trevelyan the second harvest failure was an argument not for extending the public relief effort but for quickly ending it, so that the inevitable future hardship would be tackled correctly, that is by commercial enterprise and private charity. Sir Randolph Routh was in despair. 'You cannot answer the cry of want by a quotation from political economy. You ought to have 16,000 tons of Indian corn.'[3] But the man on the spot pleaded in vain, the gentlemen in Whitehall knew best, and Ireland descended into the abyss. Much of the suffering would have happened under any government, but no one died of starvation while Peel was in power.

Back in the autumn of 1845 neither Peel nor his Home Secretary, James Graham, believed that the import of American maize went to the heart of the matter. The two men quietly decided to double the stakes on the table. Faced with the need to allow the import of grain for a particular emergency, Peel decided to go for the complete though not immediate abolition of the Corn Laws. Faced with an economic disaster in Ireland, he tackled it by creating a political convulsion in the whole country. Faced with the hostile murmurings of some supporters, he responded with a policy which broke his Government and tore apart his party.

The link between repeal of the Corn Laws and the suffering Irish was far from clear. The case for a temporary suspension was strong, so that any available foreign wheat could enter the ports duty-free. But a temporary suspension was not the same as permanent repeal. Peel had to argue that once the Government suspended the duty it would be impossible to reimpose it once the famine was over, given the state of the debate on the subject. But this was essentially a circular argument. It amounted to saying that the Corn Laws should be repealed because he and others now thought that they were no longer justified. In reality Peel was using the dramatic reality of the Irish famine to propose a change which he already believed was needed. Without the famine he might have launched the same struggle a year or two later; but famine or no famine, Peel believed the struggle was necessary.

To simple observers Peel's decision to go for repeal looked like panic. Some, like the Duke of Wellington, attributed it to loss of nerve: 'Rotten potatoes have done it all. They have put Peel in his damned fright.'[4] Disraeli detected a devious pretence by a man who had long ago decided to betray his followers. 'Now I think it is a false famine and the question is not ripe enough for his fantastic pranks. He is so vain that he wants to figure in history as the settler of all the great questions; but a parliamentary constitution is not favourable to such ambitions; things must be done by parties, not by persons using parties as tools – especially men without imagination or any inspiring qualities, or who, rather, offer you duplicity instead of inspiration.'[5]

Neither description fits Peel's mind or character. The reversal of view was not the result of sudden panic or a long-standing plot. As with Catholic Emancipation, Peel changed his mind under the compulsion of what seemed to him overwhelming evidence. Peel's intellect was not original, but it gave him a powerful tool for analysing facts and views put to him by others, and then for acting on that analysis. His conscience made it difficult for him to arrest this process or to deny its results simply because of danger to himself. He had run a great risk in 1829 by recognising that the Clare election would make Ireland ungovernable without Catholic Emancipation. He ran an even greater risk in 1845–6 by concluding that the Corn Laws were no longer sustainable. But he would not have been Peel if he had denied the arguments in both cases once they were overwhelming in his mind. Nor was it in his nature to hold out against those who told him that it was his duty to direct the change himself, even though this greatly increased the danger to his own reputation.

On 31 October and 1 November, because he was suffering from gout, Peel asked the Cabinet to meet in his house in Whitehall Gardens instead of Downing Street. For the second meeting he tabled a paper:

> If we can place confidence in the reports which we have received there is the prospect of a lamentable deficiency of the ordinary food of the people in many parts of Ireland, and in some parts of this country, and of Scotland. The evil *may be* much greater than present reports lead us to anticipate ... The calling of Parliament ... compels an immediate decision on these questions. Shall we maintain unaltered, shall we modify, shall we suspend – the operation of the Corn Laws ... ? Can we vote public money for the sustenance of any considerable portion of the people on account of actual or apprehended scarcity, and maintain in full operation the existing restrictions on the free import of grain ... ? I am bound to say my impression is that we cannot ...[6]

This put the question without answering it. Peel's practical proposal that week was to recall Parliament, to open the ports to grain, suspending temporarily all except a nominal duty, and to ask Parliament after the Christmas recess to consider 'a modification of the existing law'. He did not go into details as to what that permanent modification might be. But on such occasions there is sometimes a buzz, an atmosphere in the room, which those present understand even though nothing explicit is said. Colleagues could sense that the Prime Minister was going for broke. He had written as much to Lord Heytesbury in Dublin on 15 October. 'The remedy is the removal of all impediments to the import of all kinds of human food – that is, the total and absolute repeal for ever of all duties on all articles of subsistence.' Peel's friends remembered how in 1842 he had made clear that for him the change they were then making in the Corn Laws was the last chance for that policy. In March 1845, before anyone had a bad word to say about potatoes, after listening to Cobden denounce the Corn Laws in the Commons, Peel had said to Sidney Herbert sitting beside him: 'You must answer this, for I cannot.'

'The total and absolute repeal for ever of all duties on all articles of subsistence.' It was a huge conclusion, coming on top of the main repeal and reduction of other duties already achieved in the 1842 and 1845 Budgets. And a radical conclusion even for the twenty-first century. For there is no talk of reciprocity in any of Peel's measures. No country was required to open its own markets to British textiles in return for the ability to supply wheat to Paisley and Stockport. The British market was to be free whether or not other countries followed Britain's example. Peel believed that Britain could afford this unilateral generosity because of her position of competitive advantage. He was more concerned with the British consumer than with the British producers, who could, he believed, look after themselves. But that kind of advantage has not been enough for most countries. Even those governments which parade most often their theoretical commitment to free trade act, for example in world trade rounds, as if this commitment is conditional on others joining them down the same path. The city states of Hong Kong and Singapore perhaps come closest to following Peel's example, by opening the market to others regardless of what others do.

We have traced the political events and arguments which brought Peel to this climax. The rest is a story of battle – battle to achieve free trade and to safeguard it once achieved. But it is worth pausing briefly to consider the wider background. Peel lived in an age dominated by the thinking of Newton. He inhabited a universe of systemic harmony and immutable rules of science. As a Christian he believed that God had created these rules and systems and administered them through his Providence. Humans could only hope to glimpse the workings of Providence, but must hold back from selfish or prejudiced actions which distorted the purposes of God and the natural harmony of the universe. A corrupted currency clearly fell into that category – hence the return to gold in 1819. So did the attempt to distort the natural flow of trade between countries endowed with different resources and skills – hence the need to remove tariffs from 1842 to 1846. Peel accepted that a statesman had to recognise existing interests. He must reckon with the delays and compromises needed to overcome them. These were all part of the story of human imperfection. Peel did not believe like Macaulay and other optimistic mid-Victorians in the inevitability of progress for example, in automatic economic growth year by year. Stability was itself a prize, hard to achieve in a world of ruthless trade cycles and variable harvests. More than that, improvement was possible provided that the leaders of a country worked with and not against the nature of the system of which under God they were part.

But the colleagues were not ready. The crisis was too sudden and Peel's underlying proposal too absolute. Only three Ministers, Graham, Aberdeen and Herbert, supported him in full on 1 November. Most argued for delay, some were openly opposed. Lord Stanley wrote on 2 November that he was absolutely against repeal; Peel's holding reply simply said, accurately but misleadingly, that he had not actually proposed repeal. Peel was always particularly concerned with the young men whose friendship with him was that of disciples. Gladstone was out of office because of his pernickety behaviour over Maynooth. Herbert was on side. That left Lord Lincoln, whose father and sponsor in Parliament, the Duke of Newcastle, was a ferocious Protectionist who was bearing down heavily on his son. Lincoln proposed the kind of compromise that comes from a troubled spirit. Ministers should maintain the Corn Laws for a short time, but decide privately that on the eve of the next general election (due in 1848 at the latest) they would announce that the next Parliament would be asked to consider immediate or gradual repeal. Peel swept this aside impatiently; it would be impossible for Ministers to defend the Corn Laws when they had already decided to replace them.[7]

Ministers settled down to a bout of correspondence with each other which led nowhere. Peel busied himself with the purchase of grain from America. The reports from Lord Heytesbury, from the potato scientists and from private individuals, showed Ireland continuing to slide downhill. Peel was vexed by the irresolution of his colleagues, but decided to leave them until the end of the month to find some courage.

His hand was forced by an unexpected intervention from outside government. Lord John Russell belongs to the second rank of British Prime Ministers. It is hard to remember anything notable about him. Diminutive in stature, he was usually represented by cartoonists as a small boy with a big head and an even bigger black hat. A brother of the Duke of Bedford, he belonged at the heart of the Whig aristocracy, but as we have seen with instincts more radical than most of his friends and relations. He was not an exciting man. He had neither Palmerston's jovial ferocity nor Peel's painstaking mastery of issues. Few people either liked or disliked Lord John with any intensity. But he was always around, persistent and mildly irritating with his nasal, unattractive voice. Russell's tactical dexterity brought him some prizes, leading eventually to five rather empty years as Prime Minister.

The Corn Laws were almost as divisive an issue for the Whigs as for the Conservatives. The Whigs were well aware of the persuasive power of the Anti Corn Law League, but old gentlemen like Melbourne and vigorous landlords such as Palmerston were not keen to sacrifice traditional beliefs or interests because Cobden could gather a crowd and make a noise. Some form of agricultural protection was seen by a good many Whigs as a necessary bulwark for the landed interest on which the stability of England rested. Lord John thus took something of a gamble when on 22 November he wrote from Edinburgh an open letter to his constituents in the City of London telling them that he had changed his views. He now favoured total repeal. 'Let us ... unite to put an end to a system which has been proved to be the blight of commerce, the bane of agriculture, the source of bitter divisions among classes, the cause of penury, fever, mortality and crime among the people. The Government appears to be waiting for some excuse to give up the present Corn Laws. Let the people by petition, by address, by remonstrance, afford them the excuse they seek.'

Lord John's letter made it impossible for Ministers to continue writing to each other without a decision. The timing suited Peel well. He had already decided that he must bring the Cabinet to the crunch by the end of November. He summoned them again on 26 November and tabled yet another paper, this time answering one of the questions he had set them at the beginning of the month. Yes, he now definitely proposed suspension of the Corn Laws. Yes, suspension meant looking hard at the system to be adopted when the temporary suspension came to an end. But he believed that this review was best carried out by others than himself.[8]

Peel warned the Queen at Osborne that it would be tough going in Cabinet. As usual she and Albert had no doubts: 'At a moment of impending calamity it is more than ever necessary that the Government should be strong and united. The Queen thinks the time is come when a removal of the restrictions upon the importation of food cannot be successfully resisted. Should this be Sir Robert's own opinion the Queen very much hopes that none of his colleagues will prevent him from doing what it is right to do.'[9]

But what Peel proposed was exactly what most of the Cabinet did not want. They wanted both Peel and (in some form) the Corn Laws to continue. He was now proposing no Peel and (in effect) no Corn Laws. Peel bombarded them with powerful memoranda, pressing now for an immediate decision. The Duke of Wellington, deaf, unhappy and seventy-seven, gave his reply from Stratfield Saye on 30 November. His loyal confusion emerged clearly as one paragraph contradicted another. The Duke believed that the continuance of the Corn Laws was essential to agriculture, particularly in Ireland. The Government should wait a year before deciding on repeal. Repeal would turn the landed interest against the Government. They should not hesitate to suspend the law temporarily if that was necessary to avoid real hardship. But what was truly important was that the Queen's Government should be carried on by Peel. If Peel felt that he could only carry on if his recommendations were accepted, then the Duke would support him.[10]

Peel sent this letter to Stanley but could hardly have expected it to impress that keen mind. 'The reasoning does not strike me as very conclusively or logically leading to the result, and I do not think the course adopted by him [the Duke] could be adopted by anyone else.'[11] Stanley was right. The Duke's sense of priorities was leading him to support a measure of which he disapproved. But there was no comfortable refuge for any of them in this storm.

On the same day that the Duke wrote, the debate was moved to a different plane by a lesser member of the Cabinet. The Chancellor of the Exchequer, Henry Goulburn, was hard-working, sensible and in the nicest possible way Peel's creature. Of Peel's closest political friends, he was less definite than Aberdeen, Graham or Hardinge. His knowledge of Ireland, where he had, like Peel, served as Chief Secretary, had brought the two men together. Trusting his loyalty completely, Peel made Goulburn one of his executors. It is among Goulburn's papers in Woking that one finds the small paraphernalia of jottings and notebooks which a man like Peel, who formed his views pen in hand, inevitably leave behind them. Politically Goulburn played a part which in the modern Conservative Party belongs to the Party Chairman; from time to time he took it upon himself to articulate the worries and woes of the Party's closest supporters.

At the end of November Goulburn felt that he could no longer keep silent on the Corn Laws. One crucial factor was being ignored. Peel had deliberately concentrated on the merits of the matter. Goulburn on balance believed in the Corn Laws, but to him that was not the main point. Peel was now about to destroy a system which he and his supporters had set up and promised to sustain. The real point was good faith. Goulburn began his letter by saying that he usually deferred to Peel's judgement and entirely trusted his motives. He moved on to strong language. He acknowledged that Peel had been cautious rather than robust in defending the Corn Laws. But this made things worse, for people would be the more ready to believe that he had all the time been planning their destruction, and was guilty of treachery and deception. They doubted the relevance of the Irish famine to this question. The personal reputation of Ministers would be undermined. Worse would be the effect on the Conservative Party. Goulburn still lived in the shadow of the imagined nightmares of 1832:

> The Party of which you are the head is the only barrier which remains against the revolutionary effects of the Reform Bill. So long as that party remains unbroken, whether in or out of power, it has the means of doing much good, or at least of preventing much evil. But if it be broken in pieces by a destruction of confidence in its leaders (and I cannot but think that an abandonment of the Corn Laws would produce that result) I see nothing before us but the exasperations of class animosities, a struggle for pre-eminence, and the ultimate triumph of unrestrained democracy.[12]

Goulburn was right about the breaking of the Party. If that was a mortal sin, Peel was about to commit it. But Peel had a different faith. He had refused to give undertakings that protection would remain for ever. Indeed, as long ago as 1839 he had given a warning, 'Unless the Corn Law can be shown to be consistent [with] the condition of the labouring class, the Corn Law is practically at an end.'[13] There is a close parallel, perhaps not surprising, between this cautionary statement and Peel's similar statement in advance of his about-turn on Catholic Emancipation. In both cases he warned that his support for the traditional Tory cause depended on the test of the national interest, which it might fail. If his supporters had galloped all over the place in the 1841 election shouting protectionist slogans to win their seats, that was their business. In Peel's private mind the Corn Laws had been on probation for several years, and his own judgement had steadily tilted against them. The choice now facing Ministers as a result of the Irish famine brought the period of probation to an end. The Corn Laws had failed the test of national interest, and must go. In the end the national interest must prevail over Party considerations.

Peel made a final effort to persuade his colleagues in Cabinet. On 2 December he wrote to the Queen that he was hopeful of success; two days later he was gloomy. Two days later a story in *The Times* reported that the Cabinet had agreed to an immediate and total repeal of the Corn Laws. This fabrication added to his difficulties with public opinion, which on both sides of the argument was now feverish.* On 5 December, Peel told the Queen that he had failed. This was not, he explained, because a majority had turned against him. On the contrary all except Stanley and the Duke of Buccleuch were willing to accept his proposal. But they did so out of loyalty to Peel, not out of conviction. This was too fragile a basis for success. Peel told the Queen that he must resign. The royal couple were appalled. Long gone were the antagonisms of the Bedchamber crisis of 1839; Peel was now a trusted friend to an extent inconceivable today.

Nowadays Prime Ministers come and go. The monarch may feel some inner satisfaction or sadness as they take leave, but this will be a minor emotion. Even the most powerful Minister is a transient being chosen by the electorate, whose relationship with the Sovereign is formal rather than deep. The premiership in 1846 was moving towards this state of affairs from the traditional role of the Prime Minister as the monarch's personal choice. Victoria had to accept this change, but it ran against her inherited

---

* Nearly forty years later George Meredith made this story the centre of his novel *Diana of the Crossways*. The heroine is determined to overcome male prejudice and establish her career as a writer. Her lover is a Minister. She lures him into telling the secret, and then late at night, accompanied by her maid, bustles off to confide in a famous editor. He promises secrecy and publishes at once. She loses both story and lover.

ideas and strong personal emotions. The result was a more intense relationship with most of her Prime Ministers than would be conceivable
today. She had been devoted to Melbourne, and had resented having to
send for Peel; now she relied heavily on Peel, and resented the uncertainties of a future without him. She persuaded him to spend that weekend at
Osborne, and with Prince Albert they went over the ground. Prince
Albert asked why with a majority of 100 in the Commons Peel could not
continue on course. Peel answered that the Duke of Buccleuch would
carry half Scotland with him, and Stanley in the Lords could do formidable harm, not least in bringing about defections in the Royal Household.
The pressures from the League were intense, and might begin to focus on
other Radical targets, for example the Army, the game laws and the
Church. To avoid serious harm the issue of the Corn Laws must be
settled quickly, and this would only be done by someone other than
himself.

The royal couple asked for advice on how the Queen should proceed.
Peel said that Stanley could not form a protectionist government, which
would lead to insurrection or riots. The Queen should send for Lord
John Russell, and Peel would support him in repealing the Corn Laws. In
a bout of nostalgia, the Queen wanted to recall Lord Melbourne, though
she must have known that a revival of their old comradeship was impossible. She was persuaded instead to send the old man a note saying that
her first instinct had been to invite him to Osborne to advise her, but this
was asking too much of his health. Lord Melbourne characteristically
replied that the journey would indeed have been inconvenient, since he
had a horror of the sea. To him a voyage from Portsmouth to Ryde was as
formidable as crossing the Atlantic. The choice of Lord John Russell was
in fact inevitable. On 10 December Peel wrote the Queen a letter pledging
his support for the general principle of repeal, which she was authorised
to show to Lord John.[14] Lord John Russell was to be the man for the great
deed.

There was no reason at that stage to suppose that Lord John Russell
would fail. True, his would be a minority Government at least until the
next election, but with Peel's support he would be able to handle the
immediate crisis. Peel himself had mixed feelings. He felt himself once
again to be the right pilot in extremity, but extremity had not yet quite
arrived. There was nothing hypocritical in his desire for rest at Drayton.

The need for rest had become real.

There was something wrong with Peel. It went beyond mere tiredness. He had run the premiership in a way which would wear down the strongest constitution:

> I defy the Minister of this country to perform properly the duties of his office – to read all that he ought to read, including the whole foreign correspondence; to keep up the constant communication with the Queen *and the Prince*; to see all whom he ought to see; to superintend the grant of honours and the disposal of civil and ecclesiastical patronage; to write with his own hand to every person of note who chooses to write to him; to be prepared to every debate, including the most trumpery concerns; to do all these indispensable things, and also sit in the House of Commons eight hours a day for 118 days.

So he described it in one letter to Arbuthnot. 'It is impossible for me not to feel that the duties are incompatible, and above all human strength – at least above mine.'[15] More than once in 1845 and 1846 Peel complained to Gladstone of physical pain in his head. He suffered from nosebleeds, headaches and earache, all of which probably stemmed from a shooting accident in the 1820s. He described the sensation as like the noise of boiling water in his head. 'Few know', he wrote to Graham, 'what I have been suffering from noises and pain in the head.'[16] The long spells of duty in the Commons eight or nine hours in a night had become a penance, not least because of their tedium. He felt the energy seeping out of him.

Even Peel admitted that Lord John's letter from Edinburgh to his constituents had been a dexterous move. But now, with the ball at his feet, Lord John proved slow and clumsy. He failed to catch the mood of the moment. The country, Parliament and the Queen were keyed up for great happenings. Ordinary attitudes and allegiances were already in suspense. It was a time for swift leadership. Instead Lord John for a fortnight handled the formation of a new government with a leisurely ineptitude characteristic of the Duke of Newcastle in the eighteenth century or an Italian politician in the twentieth. Ireland was sliding, the country in an uproar, the main parties divided; Lord John concentrated on the game of trying to reconcile the ambitions and prejudices of individual grandees. Through the Queen he tried to pin Peel down to supporting a particular proposal; but Peel did not want to conspire with the Whigs, and preferred to rest on the general support for repeal which he had already offered.

Lord John's main problem, which in different forms was to vex him for many more years, lay with Palmerston. Palmerston was not afraid of anyone, and certainly not of the leader of his party. He would gladly return to the Foreign Office but would not accept any other position. This prospect cast gloom into many hearts. King Louis Philippe wrote anxiously to the Queen; she and Albert knew already that under Palmerston British foreign policy was a rough ride, particularly for themselves and the Courts of Europe. But none of these could prevent his return. Palmerston gave the Queen a bland assurance about his strong support for the *entente cordiale* with France. Gradually it seemed that the difficulties were sorted out.

During this period Julia stayed at Drayton in growing distress. Kind neighbours fed her with false unhappy rumours, for example that Sidney Herbert had deserted Peel. Peel wrote affectionately several times a week. He thought that one way and another it would not be long before they would be able to spend more time together. Meanwhile he admitted that there were plenty of unjust and untrue reports. A familiar theme reappeared in a letter of 15 December. 'How can those who spend their time in hunting and shooting and eating and drinking, know what were the motives of those who are responsible for the public security, who have access to the best information, and have no other object under Heaven but to provide against danger and answer the general interests of all classes?'[17]

On 18 December Lord John told the Queen that he could accept her invitation to form a government. The next day the project was in ruins. Lord Grey, son of the Prime Minister who had carried the Reform Bill, refused to serve if Palmerston was Foreign Secretary. He considered that this appointment would be fraught with danger for the peace of Europe. He wanted Cobden brought into the Cabinet. Lord Grey and Palmerston dug in. Lord John thought both were indispensable. On 20 December he told the Queen that he had failed. The Whigs had turned out to be, as Macaulay put it, 'mauvais coucheurs'. The Queen, who had just arranged to hold a painful parting interview with Peel, now sent for him in much more cheerful mood.

Peel's interview with the Queen at Windsor on the afternoon of 20 December 1845 changed the course of his life. Before 5 December he had been Prime Minister as a result of the general election of 1841, which had given him a majority in the Commons. Now he was Prime Minister again through an older and simpler process: the Queen had chosen him. He was scornful of Lord John's futile comings and goings, keeping the Queen hanging about while he dickered with all and sundry. A *Punch* cartoon showed tiny Lord John standing like a page before the Queen, who told him 'I'm afraid you're not strong enough for the place, John.'[18] Precisely; Peel was made of different metal. Without consulting anyone, he at once agreed to form a government. He put exhaustion behind him and sum-moned up energy for a last enterprise. He was now prepared to stand by the Queen and had thrown aside all other considerations. He added: 'There is no sacrifice that I will not make for Your Majesty, except that of my honour.' He told the Queen that he would go at once to Parliament, lay his measure before it and say: 'Reject it, if you please; there it is.'[19]

All the old difficulties remained, but Peel had a new determination to overcome or ignore them. Before he left for Windsor he had as a precau-tion summoned his colleagues to an immediate meeting that evening. They assembled in Downing Street at half past nine. Peel addressed them in his new mode. There were no more pleas, no more cogent memoranda. He was not asking them for advice or agreement. He was the Queen's Minister. Whatever support they might give or withhold, he would go to Parliament and propose the necessary measures. There was a dead silence. Ministers took stock of the new Peel and of each other. Eventually Stanley broke the silence, declaring that he must still resign. His ancestors the Earls of Derby had held sway over Lancashire and the Isle of Man long before there was a Hanoverian on the throne in London. Of all those present Stanley was the least likely to change his mind because of a royal decision. He did not care hugely about the Corn Laws and had no personal animosity against Peel; but he had given his word for protection and did not mean to break it. His parting words to his ministerial colleagues were 'we cannot do this as gentlemen'.[20]

The Duke of Wellington was different, a gentleman certainly, but a soldier first. Though deaf, he could still hear a trumpet call as well as any man. He declared that he thought the Corn Law was a subordinate con-sideration; what counted now was the service of the Queen. Once loaded and pointed in the right direction Wellington was still a formidable political force. Attention turned to the Duke of Buccleuch: would he stick to his previous decision to resign? The Scottish Duke was agitated, havered, asked for time. Peel wrote him a stern note saying the question was not the Corn Laws but whether the present Ministers should serve the Queen or hand over to Lord Grey and Cobden. The Duke of Buccleuch stayed.

Peel carried his new mood into the Christmas recess. Gladstone agreed to take Stanley's place at the Colonial Office. After an emotional meeting he and Peel clasped hands and whispered encouragement to one another, each saying 'God Bless You'.[21] Peel wrote to Princess Lieven, 'It is a strange dream. I feel like a man restored to life after his funeral service has been preached.' Not all the preaching had been funereal. The heady feeling of popular admiration was beginning to lift Peel above the ordinary ebb and flow of parliamentary life. That great definer and worshipper of romantic greatness, Thomas Carlyle, dedicated his Life of Oliver Cromwell to Peel as a man capable of true leadership.

Leadership required a broad vision. Although Peel believed in mastering detail, he did not allow detail to master him. The crisis in Ireland brought into focus the thoughts which had long been maturing in his brain. Rates of duty and details of agricultural compensation were necessary themes, but as part of a new concept of harmonious society. On Christmas Eve in 1845 he shared this concept with the man best equipped to sympathise. Prince Albert wrote a memorandum recording their conversation:

> Sir Robert has an <u>immense scheme in view;</u> he thinks he shall be able to remove the contest entirely from the dangerous ground upon which it has got — that of a war between the manufacturers, the hungry and the poor against the landed proprietors, the aristocracy, which can only end in the ruin of the latter; he will not bring forward a measure upon the Corn laws, but a much more comprehensive one. He will deal with the whole commercial system of the country. He will adopt the principle of the League, <u>that</u> of <u>removing all protection and abolishing all monopoly</u>, but not in favour of one class, and as a triumph over another, but to the benefit of the nation, farmers as well as manufacturers.[22]

Peel admitted to Prince Albert that the Irish famine had upset his timetable. He had intended to persuade his party before the next general election to move to this national plan. He filled in a few of the details. The countryside would be relieved of the cost of legal administration and the Poor Laws. A rural police force would be established on the lines of the Metropolitan Police in London, paid for from central funds. When the railway boom subsided, landowners might be helped by state loans to improve their estates. All monopolies and restraints on trade would be abolished.

Peel needed emotional and well as intellectual fuel to sustain his intensified sense of mission. Intellectually he had been persuaded that the Corn Laws could no longer be justified. The emotional impulse came from his personal view of the condition of England. The misery of Paisley and Stockport in the recession of 1842 crops up again and again in his letters and speeches. He was indignant against any who ignored or took lightly that suffering. Peel was not alone in his analysis or his indignation – many shared it and put forward their own answers. Disraeli, particularly eloquent in his novel *Sybil*, found a fantastic remedy in an alliance between the working class and the traditional aristocracy, as we have noted. Engels, hard at work in Manchester, used it to lay one of the foundation stones of Marxism. Ashley thought legislation on factory hours was the key. The Benthamites laboured away at bureaucratic schemes for the greatest good of the greatest number. Peel had his own distinct remedy and, unlike the others, possessed at that moment the power to achieve it. He was convinced that the condition of England was best improved by lowering the prices which ordinary men and women paid for their food and other necessities. This conviction, which had produced the 1842 and 1845 Budgets, gained fervent intensity in his mind as he approached the inner citadel of protectionism. As the danger to his own position increased, so did his determination.

So also did support from public opinion. Not by all measurements, for the Protectionists did well in the early by-election of 1846; but these tended to be in county seats which supporters of Peel resigned because of pledges made for protection. There was a strong protectionist press, led nationally by the *Morning Post*, a strong free trade press including the *Morning Chronicle*. Most of these stayed with their traditional opinion, but in the middle between them the tide flowed for Peel. In November 1845

Punch published a cartoon with Peel as the tricky opportunist Knave of Spades holding a sword marked 'to Cut Both Ways'. By July 1846 *Punch* hailed Peel as the theatre manager, taking his farewell benefit, as bouquets are thrown onto the stage and a protesting Disraeli is arrested by the police. *The Times*, which under Delane as editor enjoyed huge influence, was not warm to Peel personally but supported repeal. It summed up the position as follows:

> History should also record a fact more striking than the present colli-sion of parties in Parliament, or of opinion in the clubs. While the Carlton is indignant, the Conservative pettish, and many boudoirs plaintive, there is a slow and gradual mutation taking place in the minds of the community ... men do not augur any evil from the pro-posed changes. Previous experience has taught them that great changes can be effected in England without damaging the character or safety of our institutions.

Though some Tories found it hard to admit, Peel's evident integrity and long experience rallied support for his measures. Lockhart, the editor of the *Quarterly Review*, though protectionist, found even in quarters not at all kindly to Peel a sort of vague feeling that somehow or other he must govern England. This feeling of trust grew rapidly as winter turned through spring to summer, and the night trains carried copies of Peel's speeches to local papers in every town and city of the Kingdom.[23]

The campaign against the Corn Laws had reached unlikely corners of the Kingdom, for example the rural fortresses of Dorset. Thomas Hardy, aged six, was equipped with a wooden sword. He dipped it into the blood of a newly killed pig and marched about the garden shouting 'Free Trade or Blood!'[24]

In January 1846 Peel persuaded his colleagues to support a much wider scheme than anything he had put to them in November or December. He proposed to the Commons on 22 January a final repeal of the Corn Laws, one last great tariff reform combined with compensation for agriculture. He acknowledged that quite apart from the Irish famine his general opinion on protection had changed. Once again he was the proud pilot. But he showed clearly his new, defiant mood. 'I will not take the helm with mutilated power and shackled authority. I will not stand at the helm during such tempestuous nights as I have seen if the vessel be not allowed fairly to pursue the course which I think she ought to take ... Sir, I do not wish to be the Minister of England; but while I have the high honour of holding that office, I am determined to hold it by no servile tenure.'[25]

Peel was received that day in silence by his own party, but opposition had so far been muted. Peel's mastery of the Commons was still so massive that once again he seemed certain to prevail over his grumbling critics. Later that evening the scene changed. Disraeli was starting to dazzle. In one of many gibes he compared Peel to the admiral of the Sultan, who when appointed to command the Turkish fleet, at once steered it into the enemy port and betrayed his master. In the serious part of his speech Disraeli pinned down the real political difference between Peel and himself. 'Let men stand by the principle by which they rise, right or wrong ... Do not then because you see a great personage giving up his opinions – do not cheer him on, do not give him so ready a reward to political tergiversation. Above all, maintain the line of demarcation between parties.'[26] That was the crunch of an argument between party loyalty and the national interest which continues today.

Peel changed his tactics. On 27 January he introduced his detailed proposals in a speech of three and a half hours, packed with details such as he alone could master. Probably only Prince Albert, sitting in the gallery, gained the full benefit. On the Corn Laws he proposed to reduce the duties gradually, abolishing them finally in February 1849.[27] But this conclusion was wrapped up in a mass of other matter. In his incomparable narrative of those debates Disraeli later described how Peel used detail that night to lull opposition:

This remarkable man who in private life was constrained and often awkward, who could never address a public meeting or make an after dinner speech without being ill at ease, and generally saying something stilted or a little ridiculous, in the senate was the readiest, easiest, most flexible advocate of men. He played upon the House of Commons like an old fiddle. And tonight, the manner in which he proceeded to deal with the duties on candles and soap while all were thinking of the duties on something else; the bland and conciliatory way with which he announced a reduction of the import on boot fronts and shoe leather; the intrepid plausibility with which he entered into a dissertation on

the duties of foreign brandy and foreign sugar while visions of deserted villages and reduced rentals were torturing his neighbours, were
all characteristic of his command over himself, and those whom he
addressed.[28]

But now the protectionist reaction was in full spate. Protectionist
Societies had sprung up across the country, trying to emulate the Anti
Corn Law League in putting the opposite case. Their pressure was felt in
particular by Conservative MPs who had given protectionist pledges in
1841. One of those resigning his seat as a matter of principle was
Gladstone, who felt he had pledged himself to his patron at Newark, the
Duke of Newcastle. That passionate Protectionist also hounded his own
son Lord Lincoln out of the Nottinghamshire county seat, thus depriving
two of Peel's ablest Ministers of their places in Parliament. One loyal
Peelite accepted a junior post to provide the Government with a political
by-election victory in the prestigious Westminster seat – and lost. He
wrote ruefully, 'Disraeli in full dress uniform, Lord John Russell in full
toga, and a Leaguer in rags met and polled together. This is the key to the
problem.'[29] Croker, after more than thirty years of political friendship,
quarrelled and broke with Peel. Lord Melbourne, presuming in old age
on a faded friendship with the Queen, remarked during dinner at
Windsor that repeal was 'a damned dishonest act'[30] and was distressed
when she told him to change the subject.
     The difficulty for the Protectionists was to find a leader – a difficulty
which led Peel to tell the Queen on 30 January that he doubted that his
party would break up. Stanley was the obvious choice, eloquent, a great
name, and staunch in his views. But Stanley did not have the necessary
zest for organisation and detail. He had resigned from the Government
but he had too many other interests, his racehorses, his translation of
Homer and his huge estates in Lancashire, to be involved in petty Party
matters. He sat by his own wish in the Lords, not the Commons. So far
from undermining the Government which he had just left he encouraged
Gladstone, his successor as Colonial Secretary. In short, Stanley at this
critical stage still felt too grand to serve protectionist purposes.
     Disraeli was too new and, to put it mildly, too odd. He was beginning
to gain the cheers and laughter of the rebels. The combination of quiet
voice with outrageous wit was already captivating; but his origins and

background still told against him.

In February 1846 Disraeli found the Protectionists a leader. Lord George Bentinck was also odd, though his oddities were not at first fully apparent. He was rich, the younger son of a duke, a king of the turf, grandson of one Prime Minister, nephew of another. Bentinck was not an orthodox Ultra. He had started as a Whig and strongly favoured Catholic Emancipation and relaxing restrictions on Jews. But his main concern was with honesty, and his violent temper was directed against those who he thought were crooks. He had made his reputation by exposing the Derby scandal of 1844 when a four-year-old won the race pretending to be a three-year-old. He had followed Peel loyally, but it now appeared that Peel was deceiving him. He is reported to have summarised his views on the Corn Laws as follows: 'I keep horses in three counties, and they tell me that I shall save fifteen hundred a year by free trade. I don't care for that; what I cannot bear is being sold.'

But unlike most of his colleagues on the back benches Bentinck knew that he had to support the simplicity of this view with detailed evidence. Only in this way could the Protectionists make an effective stand against Peel, the master of facts and figures. Bentinck began to study the statistics of trade and production. He combined this appetite for details with a violent temper. On a day when he made a speech he refused to eat anything until he had delivered it. Hungry and angry, he was a difficult man to cross in the small hours of the morning of a Commons debate. He had never spoken to Disraeli before 1846, but Disraeli quickly spotted in these qualities the makings of a Party leader. The two men used meetings of the Protectionist Society to mobilise support. Lord George pressed successfully for the creation of a Protectionist Party with its own management and Whips. When the detailed parliamentary debates began in February Lord George became the acknowledged leader of that party, relying heavily on Disraeli as his chief of staff.

Dramatic news from the East suddenly darkened the scene. Peel's hopes for a peaceful, prosperous India, justly governed by Britain at minimum expense, were wrecked by the Sikhs. In December 1845 they stormed across the Sutlej from the Punjab attacking the British position with an army of 65,000 men and 150 pieces of artillery. Lord Ellenborough, now safe at home but still excitable, proclaimed that the Empire was in danger. 'In India a lost battle is a lost Empire', he wrote to

Peel, 'where forces so large are engaged.'[31] In choosing Hardinge to succeed Ellenborough as Governor General Peel had said goodbye to a close friend who could have helped him at home, but confided India to a safe pair of hands. Nevertheless he waited anxiously for news.

Hardinge had real trouble with his Commander-in-Chief, Sir Hugh Gough, whom he described as brave and active but incompetent, without the capacity for order or administration. Hardinge himself was up with the troops at one critical moment. 'During the night there was great despondency amongst the officers. I lay down amongst the men. It was excessively cold. I had not eaten, and had been on horseback twenty-four hours, and the poor fellows were suffering from thirst. The CinC came to me about midnight and said the army was in a most critical and perilous state.' The two men decided to discard any idea of retreat and to counter-attack vigorously next morning.[32] The Sikhs were driven back across the River Sutlej, but the fighting was tough. On 24 February, after congratu-lating Hardinge on the success of his defensive battles, Peel wrote: 'Your loss has been very severe. It demonstrates the extent of the danger, and the necessity for unparalleled exertion. We are astonished at the numbers, the power of combination, the skill and courage of the enemy.' He ended: 'God bless you, my dear Hardinge. Excuse my hurried letter. I am fighting a desperate battle here; shall probably drive my opponents over the Sutlej; but what is to come afterward I know not.'[33] Now Hardinge had to carry the war across the river and reach a settlement with the Sikhs. Through the coming weeks India could never be far from Peel's thoughts.

Peel trusted his Foreign Secretary, Lord Aberdeen, just as he trusted Hardinge in India. But it was not in Peel's nature to leave foreign affairs to the Foreign Secretary. He worried about the stormy relationship with the United States. At the beginning of Peel's premiership the Ashburton Treaty had fixed the boundary between the US and Canada as far west as the Rockies. But that left in dispute the future of Oregon, where both British and American farmers had settled, and in particular of Vancouver with its splendid harbour. President Polk, who took office in excited mood in March 1845, claimed that the American claim to Oregon was clear and unquestionable. Every American voter studied the latitudes on the maps; as we have seen, Polk's election slogan had been 'Fifty-four Forty or Fight'. The agitation spread across the Atlantic. Lord Ellenborough, again excited, volunteered to go as Governor General to

Canada in case there was need to fight the Americans. (Peel sent him to the Admiralty, remarking drily to the Queen that this should give him ample scope for his martial genius.)

Peel kept a firm grip on the diplomacy. His naval son William was sent to the area to give a personal report. As in earlier dealings with France, Peel stiffened the language of the Foreign Office when reacting to American bluster. But he had no intention of going to war. He could hardly have foreseen the time when the United States would take the baton from Britain and lead the world in free trade, but the Americans as trading partners and grain producers were already important. Peel lacked Palmerston's zest for showy diplomatic victories. Aberdeen reached a satisfactory compromise with the Administration after the Queen had made a conciliatory reference to the subject in her speech to Parliament in January. But would the US Senate ratify the new Treaty? Peel waited as anxiously for news from Washington as from the Punjab.

On 9 February Peel moved in the Commons that his tariff proposals be considered by a committee. On this formal motion hinged a debate which lasted over twelve nights. The length of the debate proved that the Protectionists were now fully organised to put forward their strength. The quality of oratory was not high. Bentinck spoke powerfully for two hours after nibbling some dry toast. He showed the depth of his recent homework, and rebuked Prince Albert for having sat in the gallery for the earlier debate.

Peel's speech on 16 February summed up the man as well as his message. Peel was determined to show that the reduction of tariffs produced prosperity. The Commons were bombarded with a mass of detailed argument backed by statistics. They were used by now to his little foibles. 'The arrangement of his coat tails, next to beating the red box, forms the most important part of his rhetorical accessories,' wrote Disraeli in his novel *Tancred*.[34]

They were told all about feathers. 'It seems a small article, but trade consists of an aggregate of small articles.' He had reduced the duty on foreign feathers in 1842. He had been told that this was the most hardhearted measure ever introduced and that the English and Irish farmers who produced feathers would be ruined. What happened? One correspondent who complained had just written again. In 1845 he had imported more than 250 tons of feathers from St Petersburg and 50 tons from elsewhere in Europe. He had been able to reduce the price of the feather beds which he made, and many more had been sold. He was better-off, and was now actually buying more feathers from Ireland than before.

Peel moved from feathers to fundamentals. One of his themes was melancholy. Once again he asked the House to remember the gloomy winters of 1841 and 1842. 'Are these winters effaced from your memory? From mine they never can be.' These sad times might come again. Providence might once again decide to punish the land with hardship. They should anticipate that day now at a time of comparative prosperity by 'trampling on every impediment to the free circulation of the Creator's bounty'. Then if hardship came they could at least be sure that it had not been 'aggravated by laws of man, restricting in the hour of scarcity the supply of food'. This was a strangely negative way of phrasing his appeal, but it reflected the strain of Tory pessimism in Peel's nature.

The main message of the speech was confident, even triumphant. By boldness Britain could now assert its leadership of the world. This was not a philosophy for the narrow-minded or faint-hearted. 'This night you will select the motto which is to indicate the commercial policy of England. Shall it "advance" or "recede"? Which is the fitter motto for this great Empire? Survey our position; consider the advantage which God and nature have given us, and the destiny for which we are intended. The discoveries of science, the improvement of navigation, have brought us within ten days of St Petersburg and will soon bring us within ten days of New York.' After listing other advantages, 'And is this the country to shrink from competition? Is this the country to adopt a retrograde policy? Is this the country which can only flourish in the sickly atmosphere of prohibition? Choose your motto "Advance" or "Recede". Many countries are watching the selection you may make. Determine for "Advance" and it will be the watchword which will animate and encourage in every state the friends of liberal and commercial policy.' He listed some of the watching countries – Sardinia, Naples, Prussia, France – and then, reflecting his priority of the moment: 'Can you doubt that the United States will soon relax its hostile tariff and that the friends of a freer commercial intercourse – the friends of peace between the two countries – will hail with satisfaction the example of England?'[35] Well, yes, it was possible to doubt the last point; with ups and downs the stubborn American tariff took a century to crumble. But there was no doubting the strength of the trumpet call. Peel's speech of 16 February 1846 with all its clumsy phrasing must rate as one of the founding documents of globalisation and free trade.

It had less effect on his immediate audience. The Whips told Peel, and Peel told the Queen, that the benchmark for success would be a majority of 100. The House divided at three o'clock on the morning of 28 February 1846. Two hundred and twenty-seven Liberals voted with Peel, so did 112 Conservatives; 231 Conservatives and 11 Liberals voted against. The Government majority was thus 97.

The Queen put the best face on it. 'The division is a very good one, though three more would have looked better, but ninety-seven is in fact a hundred.' Next day Prince Albert was more cautious: 'There appear certain supporters of the Government only 112 out of 658 members of the House. This does not look like a strong Government. But this division has arisen from circumstances which can hardly reappear, and there is a moral strength in the government which must tell more every day.'[36]

Letters did indeed pour in to Peel praising his speech of 16 February. The eloquence of loyal backbenchers was in full play. 'I can't sleep', wrote Mr Moffatt, MP, at three a.m., 'before expressing my delight at your speech this evening. I have never before perfectly understood the effect of eloquence ... That speech has landed the measure.' The detailed debate during March in fact changed little. The Government majority on Second Reading of the Bill on 27 March was only 88. Peel spoke on lines by then familiar, through strong Protectionist heckling.

From time to time Peel believed that some of the dissident MPs would return to loyalty. But Bentinck and Disraeli had given them a voice, organisation and hope. If Conservatives in the Commons could sustain night after night a substantial rebellion against the Government, surely an even stronger offensive could be mounted in the Lords. The rebels contemplated enthusiastically the endless acres of protected wheat owned by the peerage, the likelihood of Whig votes against repeal, and the possibilities of using the traditional right of access by peers to the Queen. As fruitless weeks passed Peel became more gloomy but gloom in no way weakened his determination. As usual he wrote freely to Hardinge in India. On 4 April:

The position of the Government is an extraordinary one. On the great question, the Corn Bill, though we carried the first motion by a majority of 97, we had only 112 Conservatives in the division. 112 Conservatives compose little more than one sixth of the House of Commons. Deduct 40 official men it would appear as if our independent strength did not much exceed 70 members.

We have two Cabinet Ministers – Gladstone and Lincoln – as yet without a seat. Rous beaten in Westminster by Evans – Lincoln beaten in his own county – many friends retiring rather than violate implied engagements, and their places in the counties supplied by opponents.

I have threats of resignation from Lord Delawarr, Lord Bexley, Lord Forester, and other Peers in the Queen's Household – fixed intentions to resign, I should say, rather than menaces. I know not how I shall replace them. I doubt if I could before the Second Reading in the Lords.

However, we are still the Government – have the confidence and most kind and cordial support of the Queen. I think Lord John Russell has lost ground from hesitation and vacillation as to the acceptances of the Government when it was offered to him, with the assurance of my cordial support on the great measure which he would come in to carry. He has lost ground also from throwing up the Government after he had accepted it for no better reason than that one ill-conditioned obstinate gentleman opposed the appointment of another, not to the Cabinet but to a particular office.[37]

While Bentinck and Disraeli hoped that the Lords would block repeal, their minds were turning to another possibility. If they could not kill the Bill, they could kill the Government which had produced it. They were particularly keen to destroy the Prime Minister. For this revenge they needed an issue on which they could persuade their forces to vote with their traditional Whig enemies. The Government must be defeated on a major matter. Peel would then be forced either to resign, or to dissolve Parliament and hold an election, at which the Protectionists would hope to strengthen their hold on natural Conservative seats.

Such an issue came quickly to hand. A new wave of crime and disorder had troubled Ireland for several months. The Lord-Lieutenant in Dublin and Graham at the Home Office proposed to revive some traditional powers which had been allowed to lapse. This required legislation, and a Bill was prepared. It gave the Lord-Lieutenant power to proclaim disturbed districts, deploy extra police and enforce a curfew.

The contents of this Life and Property Bill were not savage or extraordinary. The Bill started in the Lords and passed there without difficulty. Graham introduced it in the Commons on 20 March. Irish Members were strongly opposed, but it was a measure which in normal times all Conservatives and many Whig MPs including Lord John Russell would have supported. But these were not normal times. The Irish Bill and the Corn Law Bill were now simultaneously before the Commons, competing for time. In the days before the parliamentary guillotine was invented, the opportunities for delay were great. The month of April and half of May passed without serious progress in the Commons on either Bill. Tempers flared; Peel's brother Jonathan became involved in violent argument which almost led to a duel with Bentinck. No seat could be found yet for Gladstone, but Lord Lincoln, standing in a by-election for Lanarkshire, squeaked in by eleven votes.

In the committee stage of the Commons, historical analogies were flung to and fro. Peel was accused of paving the way for revolution like the French Finance Minister Turgot. Peel retorted on 5 May that what had been meant as a sarcasm was actually a compliment. 'If the doctrines of Turgot had been applied at an earlier period – if taxation had been equal and if various privileges of the aristocracy had not been insisted on, the revolution of France would not have precipitated, or the evils of that eventful period incurred. Does not my honourable friend feel that it was the unjust insisting on by gone privilege that led to that revolution?'[38] This was the Conservative case against the Corn Laws: it was a mistake to hang on to privilege for too long if you were interested in a stable society.

The Whigs were increasingly tempted by this prospect of voting out the Government through alliance with the protectionist rebels against the Irish Bill. On 15 May the Corn Law Bill was finally presented for Third Reading, its last stage in the Commons. Disraeli used the occasion for the greatest of his speeches against Peel. He spoke for three hours, with a tremendous climax in the last twenty minutes. He fastened on the undoubted truth that Peel's was not an original mind: 'His life has been a great appropriation clause. He is a burglar of other intellect ... there is no statesman who has committed political petty larceny on so great a scale.'

The final blow was the mightiest: 'I know, Sir, that all confidence in public men is lost. But Sir I have faith in the primitive and enduring elements of the English character. It may be vain now in the hindsight of their intoxication to tell them that there will be an awakening of bitterness. But the dark and inevitable hour will arrive.' Then they would remember those who were not afraid 'to struggle for the good old cause – the cause with which are associated principles the most popular, sentiments the most entirely national, the cause of labour, the cause of the people, the cause of England!'.[39] The meaning was obscure, the effect tremendous.

Peel rose after midnight. This was for him the climax of a personal effort, the last occasion before the die was cast on the greatest decision of his life. But he could hardly get going. The Protectionists screamed and hooted for a quarter of an hour. He began to defend repeal as being in the national interest. When he turned once again to defend his personal integrity, the jeers and shouts overwhelmed him. He stopped, his eyes filled with tears, the Whigs on the front bench opposite thought he was about to break down. But Peel was not going to be routed in the assembly of which he had so long been the master. He turned particularly to his fellow Conservatives. He was acting as a good Conservative, in the interests of the Crown, Church and aristocracy. It could not be in the Conservative interest that landlords and farmers should carry the odium of an indefensible system. It was essential to show the people that Parliament worked for equity and justice. Then: 'I have a strong belief that the greatest object which we or any other government can contemplate should be to elevate the social condition of that class of the people with whom we are brought into no direct relationship by the exercise of the elective franchise.'[40] Disraeli would never have framed such a clumsy sentence, but it was the core of what Peel was about. The workers of Paisley and Stockport had no vote; but it was essential to the national (and incidentally the Conservative) interest that their lot should be improved.

The duel with Disraeli that night was not quite over. Peel never handled his tormentor with any skill. He seldom deployed in speech the ironical humour which often appeared in his letters and conversation. He had no quick talent available to match Disraeli's wit. His own emotions were deep but ponderous, whereas Disraeli the magician easily conjured up emotion to sharpen his flashing rhetoric. But that evening Peel made a remark to which Disraeli felt he had to reply. Peel said in his speech that if the Honourable Member for Shrewsbury had for thirty years before 1841 despised him in the way he had described that night, it was odd that he had been ready to take office under Peel in that year. When Peel had finished, Disraeli got up to deny that he had ever solicited office. Peel then simply repeated his point, taking no notice of Disraeli's denial.

Disraeli had told the lie before to his constituents in Shrewsbury in 1844. But it was a huge gamble to repeat it in the presence of the man who could prove it was false. Where that night was the crawling letter which Disraeli had written in 1841 pleading for a job? This is one of the poignant mysteries of Victorian politics. The letter still existed, for Peel had showed it to Lord Lincoln. But where was it on the night of 15 May? Perhaps Peel had it with him, but mislaid it in the mass of documents which he usually assembled in front of him when speaking. Perhaps he had left it in Downing Street and had no time to send for it. There is a story that he sent a runner to fetch it. Perhaps, indeed probably, he simply thought it beneath his dignity to trade personal insults with a man he despised. In any case he missed the trick. If he had read out the letter, rammed the point home and proved Disraeli a liar before that audience that night, the political effect would have been formidable. But that was not the speech Peel wanted to make.[41] * At four o'clock in the morning of Saturday 16 May the Corn Bill achieved its Third and final Reading with a majority of 98 votes. The magic 100 still eluded the Government. The Bill passed to the Lords.

Behind the scenes Peel had great difficulty in organising the Government's case for the Lords debate. No one was keen to move the Second Reading. Lord Ripon (the former tearful, irresolute Prime Minister Lord Goderich) agreed under pressure to take on the task, then withdrew. Letters flowed, different possibilities were canvassed, but in the end of course the work fell to Wellington. The difficulty for the Duke was that insofar as he understood the policy, he disagreed with it. 'I entertain a different opinion upon the whole issue. I am really ignorant of all details and of the grounds on which the Bill is founded and has been supported in the House of Commons by you and others. But I shall read as

---

* I am told that Robert Birley, Headmaster of Eton, when preaching to the boys used Peel's forbearance that night as an example of Christian charity in politics.

many of your speeches as I can find between this and next Thursday.'[42]

From this unpromising start the Duke built up his campaign. He made it clear to colleagues that if the Lords messed about with the Bill this would create a constitutional crisis, in which the powers of the House would be called into question. It is fascinating to speculate what would have happened if the Lords had thrown out or crippled Peel's Bill. In their current mood neither Peel nor the Queen would have hesitated to create peers to force their hand. Would the crisis of 1910 have been brought forward to 1846? On this and many other occasions their Lordships owed a big debt to the Duke of Wellington.

Peel supplied detailed briefing. The Duke was spurred on by his detestation of what he called the 'blackguard combination' of Whigs and Protectionists against the Government, and by a genuine conviction that the Lords must not on such a matter oppose the will of the Commons. If Stanley had at this stage bothered to lead an organised group of protectionist peers the result might have been different. But he did not match the determination of the Government. The Duke did well; Julia Peel called on him and thanked him tearfully. The proceedings in the Lords became desultory.

In these weeks the affairs of India were never far from Peel's mind. The Sikhs were brave adversaries but Lord Hardinge wore them down. After a bloody victory at Ferozshah a peace treaty was signed. Hardinge did not go so far as to annex the Punjab and his moderation was attacked in England and in India. Peel was robust in his defence, and Hardinge repeatedly thanked the Prime Minister for having turned the tables on his critics. Hardinge's moderation after victory exactly fitted Peel's instincts. 'It is justly thought that it adds a lustre to the skill and valour displayed in the military achievements. It is ten times more gratifying to the public mind than the annexation of the Punjab would have been.' Even the Protectionists, he reported, were temporarily distracted by patriotic pride away from their preoccupation with corn. He also believed that the display of strength and moderation would have the right effect on the Americans. 'What has taken place on the banks of the Sutlej will have its influence on the banks of the Oregon.'[43] Peel's dislike of vainglory showed itself remarkably when he took time to alter the proposed proclamation of thanks for victory over the Sikhs. He explained to the Queen:

[c]onsidering the sanguinary nature of great battles and that (however just the cause) many thousands forfeit their lives through no fault of their own, too direct a reference to the special intervention of Almighty God is not very seemly. When Lord Jocelyn brought the resolution of thanks to Sir Robert Peel on Wednesday last, Sir Robert Peel altered them in this sense. They almost make it appear, as they were originally drawn, that the fire of artillery on the confused mass of Sikhs, after they had been driven into the Sutlej, had been directed by Divine Providence, and was an agreeable sight to a merciful Creator.[44]

It is impossible to imagine Palmerston, or indeed Disraeli or Margaret Thatcher, making this change.

The long struggle for repeal of the Corn Laws was nearing its end. The Whigs in the Lords were scampering all over the place, but Lord John Russell in a rare display of leadership brought them to heel. Having written the Edinburgh letter he could hardly continue as Party leader if the Whig peers brought down the Government by opposing repeal. Once he made this clear on 23 May they agreed to support the Bill. The Protectionists now acclaimed Lord Stanley as leader of their party, but they could not by themselves muster the votes in the Lords to block repeal.

Increasingly their thoughts turned away from victory to revenge. There was a chance of beating the Government in the Commons on another Factory Bill introduced by Ashley, but the Government survived. It became clear that the real challenge would come at the Second Reading of the Irish Life and Property Bill. The Whigs had overcome their hesitation and were ready to reverse their earlier position and join in defeating the Government on the Bill – but only once the Corn Law Bill was safely through the Lords. Lord George Bentinck had difficulty with those Protectionists who by instinct favoured the coercing of Ireland by any available means. He had to use the argument that the Government could not be serious about the Irish Bill because they had failed to press it quickly through Parliament. Anyway, Ministers, and in particular the Prime Minister, could no longer be trusted on anything.

When the Second Reading began on 8 June there was not much to say about the actual merits of a thin Bill. But Lord George managed to work himself into a tantrum. Plunging back twenty years, he accused Peel of having chased and hunted Canning to his death in 1827, by refusing to support Catholic Emancipation even though he had changed his mind in favour of Emancipation as early as 1825. The venom of this attack threw Peel, who did not immediately reply, off balance. He asked Lord Lincoln to wait after the debate while he wrote his usual note to the Queen of the day's proceedings. As in the quiet of early morning the two men walked arm-in-arm up Whitehall to Peel's house, Peel told his disciple that he felt the slur on his honour was so great that he must challenge Bentinck to a duel; would Lincoln act as his second? They paced up and down the empty street arguing the matter. Eventually Peel went to bed, and next day agreed to forget a duel and reply to Bentinck in the Commons. Disraeli tried to prolong the argument, but finally, having consulted old letters and newspaper cuttings, Peel made on 19 June a detailed statement which satisfied the House. Peel had not changed his mind on Catholic Emancipation until after the Clare election in 1828 and had acted in good faith when declining to serve with Canning a year earlier.[45]

The episode raised the general temperature yet higher. The Duke's friend and factotum Charles Arbuthnot reported to Peel on 10 June: 'His blood is up. He is most anxious that you should defeat the abominable combination against you, and he feels that you will be able, if you hold high language and if you resolve not to be overcome. The vile and black-guard attacks of Lord George Bentinck have done good. Everybody, save the most rabid portion of the Protectionists, is disgusted.'[46]

But resolution and high language were not going to prevail against the votes now stacking up against the Government in the Commons on the Irish Bill. Ministers began to discuss what they should do after defeat. The Bill had not at the outset been regarded as crucial for Ireland, but Peel thought it was now inconceivable to acquiesce in its failure and carry on regardless. The Duke argued strongly for dissolving Parliament if they were defeated and forcing an election. Cobden, trying to overcome years of mutual dislike, wrote a friendly letter on 23 June to Peel. He advised that Peel, if defeated, should go to the country on the cry of 'Peel and Free Trade'. 'Are you aware of the strength of your position with the country ... Practical reforms are the order of the day, and you are by common consent the practical reformer. The condition of England question – there is your mission. You represent the Idea of the Age, and it has no other representative among statesmen.'[47]

Never before or after were the Duke of Wellington and Cobden likely to give identical advice, but Peel brushed it aside. He judged that no election forced on that basis would produce a stable government with a coherent set of policies and clearly identified supporters.

This was a realistic assessment, but the real resistance lay deep inside Peel. Exaltation and exhaustion joined to form his mood. It was one thing as the Queen's Minister to force through a great necessary and popular measure in an atmosphere of high drama. It was quite another to pick up the pieces afterwards, to negotiate with tricky Lord John Russell, to get agreement on a manifesto or to woo ignorant Protectionists back into the fold with a sprinkling of baronetcies and minor jobs. He was simply not willing to start up again the routine processes of party politics. The retention of power and the reconstruction of his party were secondary compared to the great matter which, at huge personal cost, he was about to accomplish. Peel was giving his all; to ask for more was too much.

While they waited for the parliamentary vote the gossips were active. The Lord Chancellor's wife went out to breakfast and told the company, ignorantly but as it turned out accurately, that if the Prime Minister were beaten he would resign. 'I cannot of course be responsible for the follies of Lady Lyndhurst ... Many people assert that which is untrue solely for the purpose of getting a short-lived notoriety. If the pretence of knowing Cabinet secrets made Lady Lyndhurst a lioness at a breakfast for three hours, that probably was sufficient fame for her. The exposure of her ignorance would probably not take place until the breakfast was over.'[48]

The crucial vote took place after one o'clock on the morning of Friday 26 June 1846. Lord George and Disraeli had been less successful than they had hoped in drawing Protectionists to vote against the Irish Bill in which most of them believed. More Protectionists voted with the Government than voted against it. But those who abstained and those who voted against the Bill were enough in alliance with the Whigs and the Irish to defeat the Government by seventy-three votes.

Disraeli described the scene with a romantic novelist's licence, imagining the sadness in Peel's heart as he watched the gentlemen of England pass into the lobby to vote against him, 'the Manners, the Somersets, the Bentincks, the Lowthers and the Lennoxes ... They trooped on: all the men of metal and large-acred squires, whose spirit he had so often quickened and whose counsel he had so often solicited in his fine Conservative speeches in Whitehall Gardens.' Disraeli listed the names of otherwise unknown gentry with Shakespearean fullness and then described Peel receiving the news of defeat: 'Sir Robert did not reply or even turn his head. He looked very grave, and extruded his chin as was his habit when he was annoyed and cared not to speak. He began to comprehend his position, and that the emperor was without his army.'[49]

Disraeli supposes that up to the last moment Peel had thought he might survive. Probably Peel had no such illusion, though the hostile majority was bigger than he expected. Something had just happened two hours before the vote which outweighed defeat. Two drowsy parliamentary clerks had mumbled out at the Table of the House of Commons that the Lords had passed the Corn and Customs Bills. The Corn Laws were repealed. Peel wrote to Hardinge that he was satisfied. 'We have fallen in the face of day and with our front to the enemies.'[50] The great enterprise had been accomplished; Britain's future commercial and economic course had been set.

The Queen received in the same box on 26 June both items of news from Westminster. 'In one breath, triumph and defeat. Those abominable, short-sighted and unpatriotic Protectionists.' She had already written in her journal of 'that dreadful Disraeli' and now added 'to turn out the Minister who has carried the Corn Law, and in fact done so great a work these last five years is really dreadful'.[51] It was a beautiful afternoon. The Queen and Albert walked in the grounds overlooking the sea at Osborne waiting for Peel to arrive by special train; then they rested in a tent. When he appeared Peel seemed remarkably cheerful. He explained the reasons for his resignation. They persuaded him to stay for two nights; throughout he kept his high spirits. He was waiting anxiously for news from Washington about ratification by the US Senate of the Oregon Treaty. The Queen was used now to Peel's long-windedness both in speech and on paper, so different from the chattiness of Lord Melbourne in her early years. The Queen's usual comment on the speeches which Peel sent was that they were long – but so very noble. An audience with Peel could last two or more hours. To an increasingly serious monarch this thoroughness made him trustworthy. Now he was going, this time probably for good. Peel said that it seemed like a dream that he was out of office, at which the Queen observed 'a very bad dream'. Soon she would have to deal again with Lord John Russell, who was 'such a contrast to Sir Robert Peel who was in such good spirits in spite of everything, whereas poor Lord John seems to be torn in pieces by the number of people he (very unwisely) consults and the number of applications for office'.[52]

On Monday Peel announced his resignation in the Commons. A big crowd lined Whitehall and cheered him all the way from his house to the Commons, arriving a little breathless. As one observer saw it, he 'walked up to the House; colder dryer, more introverted than ever; yet to a close gaze showing the fullest working of a smothered volcano of emotions'.[53] There were no histrionics as the words passed into history. Briefly by his standard, he reviewed the acts of his administration. He looked forward on Ireland – 'I do not hesitate now to say that in my opinion there ought to be established between England and Ireland a complete equality in all civil municipal and political rights.' After mentioning the Bank Charter Act and the Sikh War, he praised his Foreign Secretary, Aberdeen, picking out a particular characteristic: 'He has dared to avow that he thinks in a Christian country there is a moral obligation upon a Christian minister to exhaust every effort before incurring the risk of war.' Palmerston, sitting opposite, would have got the point. Peel had just heard that the US Senate had ratified the Oregon Treaty, and reminded the House of Commons of its terms. Then, he turned to the Corn Laws. To the amazement of the House he singled out for praise a man whom until very recently he had regarded with hostility, even bitterness. 'The name which ought to be associated with the success of those measures is the name of Richard Cobden.' Peel moved towards a clumsy but powerful and prophetic climax:

> In relinquishing power I shall leave a name, severely censured I fear by many who on public ground deeply regret that severance [with his sup-porters] not from interested or personal motives, but from the firm conviction that fidelity to party engagements – the existence and maintenance of a great party – constitutes a powerful instrument of government: I shall surrender power severely censured also by others, who from no interested motive, adhere to the principle of protection considering the maintenance of it to be essential to the welfare and interests of the country. I shall leave a name execrated by every monop-olist who from less honourable motives clamours for protection because it conduces to his own individual benefit; but it may be that I

shall leave a name sometimes remembered with expressions of good will in the abodes of those whose lot it is to labour, and to earn their daily bread by the sweat of their brow, when they shall recruit their exhausted strength with abundant and untaxed food, the sweeter because it is no longer leavened by a sense of injustice.

Peel left the Commons by a side door to avoid the growing crowds. He was immediately recognised and men took off their hats. The cheering crowd made a lane through which he walked home. The cheering continued long after he entered his house.[54]

In exceptional political careers there comes a point where talent and personality fuse with the handling of a particular matter to produce something different. Someone hitherto known for hard work or eloquence or courage or other qualities rises above such assessments and becomes extraordinary. For the rest of his life after 1846, Peel found himself in that position. Peel had paid a great price for a great achievement, and thus become a great man. The last speech proved it all. Thanks to Victorian technology, the cheap newspapers and the reading rooms Peel's peroration quickly entered the public consciousness.

Press comment next day was mixed. 'There are some victories', wrote the *Northampton Mercury*, 'which are necessarily fatal to the conqueror.' *The Times* led those who were critical of Peel's final speech and in particular the praise of Cobden. The *Leeds Mercury* complained that Peel was 'the most inconsistent of statesmen. He has not only changed his opinion on some points but on every point. He has not changed to some degree, but he has swung round to the very opposite point of the compass. We should feel incomparably greater pleasure in cheering him as a glorious martyr to the country's good. But facts are notorious ... We must be content to look on him with wonder and regret.' But even the *Leeds Mercury* admitted that the current of public opinion was running strongly in Peel's favour. Public addresses were prepared thanking Peel for his services. The address from Bradford was signed by over a thousand professional men, shopkeepers and other tradesmen.[55]

A working man wrote from Nottingham to thank Peel for 'unfettering the Staf of Life to the poor man ... Be assured that you do dwell in the hearths of thousands for ever utering those memerable words.'[56]

Seventeen

Not Broken At All

'Clear, strong blue eyes which kindle on occasion, voice
extremely good, low tones, something of *cooing* in it,
rustic, affectionate, honest, mildly persuasive ... a vein
of mild fun'

Carlyle on first meeting Peel, 1848

T he ferocity of the debate on the Corn Laws in 1846 meant that
the arguments on both sides soared beyond reality. In hard practical terms the outcome was neither as miraculous nor as disastrous
as the partisans had supposed. The immediate effect of repeal brought no
quick help to Ireland through the bitterly cold winter of 1846–7. The
incoming Whig Government dismantled Peel's maize import scheme and
public works programme. What was lacking in Ireland was not food but
money for the people to buy food. The new Government tried to solve
the problem by a big extension of the Irish Poor Law to include outdoor
relief. But this depended on local funding which was simply not available.
The sequence of famine and disease followed its tragic course without
regard to the debates and decisions at Westminster.

Economic historians differ on the effects of repeal on British farming
and the national economy. Home production of wheat, barley and oats
fell sharply in England and Wales. Farm costs were rising, particularly
wages and rents, and because of repeal and the availability of imports,
farmers could not recoup these costs by raising their prices. Some moved
into livestock farming, taking advantage of the rising demand for meat
from a more prosperous population.[1] There was a huge increase in the
import of corn into Britain, from 251,000 tons in 1843 to 1,749,000 tons

in 1847. But because of the economic context this had the effect of averting a big price increase in the price of bread rather than at once reducing it.[2] Bread prices fluctuated for several years to come, but its relative cost fell as the general standard of living rose.

In the short term the outflow of gold to pay for these imports forced the Bank of England to put up interest rates from 2.5 per cent (March 1845) to 10 per cent (October 1847). The resulting deflation led to pressure to suspend Peel's 1844 Bank Charter Act. But in the longer term repeal was rightly regarded as a watershed. The Whig Government followed up with the repeal of the Navigation Acts which had provided protection for British shipping. The economic news steadily improved. Income per capita began to increase. Imports and exports almost doubled between 1844–6 and 1854–6. In 1851 it was revealed that for the first time more Britons were living in towns than in the countryside.[3] In that year the Great Exhibition attracted six million visitors to London, and proved that Britain had become the workshop of the world.

In the late 1870s the onrush of duty-free wheat across the Atlantic at last overwhelmed the British farmer. Disraeli was then Prime Minister, but it never occurred to him to reinvent agricultural protection. Peel's work was irreversible.

The 1846 summer at Drayton was sunny. Peel found 'the day too short for my present occupations, which consist chiefly in lounging in my library, directing improvements, riding with the boys and my daughter, and pitying Lord John and his colleagues'.[4] At last he was learning to lounge. He wrote elaborately to the Queen 'from this place of profound tranquillity and repose, presenting such a contrast with all that has been recently passing'. He thanked her for her kind confidence in all the time they had passed together. He reminded her of her promise to send him a royal family portrait. 'He hopes they will be in that simple attire in which, when he has the frequent happiness of being admitted to your private society, he has seen Your Majesty and the Prince.' In short, he wanted them in smart casual.[5]

These were genuinely happy days for Peel. The lounging did not last. His passion for hard work soon channelled his energy into a dozen different purposes; but for a few weeks while the Queen and Peelites mourned, the Protectionists rejoiced, and Lord John wrestled with Ireland, Peel was genuinely at ease with his Staffordshire acres, his pictures, his family and himself.

'We had a glorious merrymaking yesterday – all my labourers and their wives, 125 in number, dined under a tent – their children were feasted at the Inn at Drayton. The evening was past in Bowls – skittles – quoits – cricket – football – and above all dancing – which was kept up by old and young – on the green sward in front of our windows till long after it was dark. It was a very pretty sight.'[6]

Peel was writing just six weeks after his final resignation as Prime Minister. That harvest merrymaking set the tone for the next four years of his life. Politics went on of course, but he was no longer at the centre of the stage and had no appetite for political anticlimax. Peel busied himself with draining his land, negotiating improved leases with his tenants, and writing to Prince Albert about plans to entertain them with more music and dancing such as the Prince had offered his estate workers at Osborne.[7]

Peel enjoyed the role of paterfamilias, keeping his scattered children in touch with each other. Their eldest son Robert was working as an amateur diplomat: 'we are thus disposed of Robert at Berne – Frederick making a tour of France alone ... John is here [having managed to progress from unhappiness at Eton into the Army] very sick of barrack duty and full of ardour for taking the field against the Drayton partridges. Arthur has gone to Eton. Your Mama and Eliza at Cromer on the coast of Norfolk – but intending to return to Drayton next Saturday.' That was the roll-call communicated to William in the autumn of 1847. There was always a special warmth in Peel's dealings with this distant son. 'I earnestly hope that everything is prosperous with you, that you like your ship, your officers and crew and your station. Your letters are received by all of us with the greatest interest.' But also sometimes with anxiety. 'Your Mama sometimes feels they are written in low spirits, but I tell her they are the natural expression of feelings which separation from home and the loneliness of command must occasionally inspire.'[8]

Peel stayed closely in touch with political events, both at home and abroad, particularly in France. He showed surprisingly generous sympathy for tricky old King Louis Philippe after he had been chased out of France in 1848. Peel entertained the exiled King at Drayton, offered him a secret

loan, and discussed French affairs at length with Guizot. He read French
socialist tracts and worried at the influence they would have on the suffering poor.⁹ An old theme still dominated his talk: 'what struck me above
all in the conversation of Sir Robert Peel', wrote Guizot, 'was his constant
and passionate preoccupation with the state of the working classes in
England'.¹⁰

Peel could now find time for the intellectual exercises outside politics
which fitted his active argumentative mind. History was full of puzzles to
be sorted out. Was it true, for example, that the Romans practised human
sacrifice? Peel thought not, though the relevant passages in Livy were
ambiguous. He argued the point with Lord Mahon, who became his literary executor.¹¹ Macaulay was brought into the argument and the correspondence bustled on for a year and a half. More practically, Peel served
as an energetic member of Prince Albert's Commission preparing the
Great Exhibition of 1851.

Peel had time now to show friends and acquaintances round his
pictures in the gallery at Whitehall Gardens. In April 1847 he gave a
party there for celebrities of art and literature. Dickens, Thackeray,
Turner and Landseer turned up, as did the Prime Minister Lord John
Russell. The greeting between the two political opponents was described
by one of the guests as 'as pleasing a picture as any which adorned the
walls'.

Peel as Prime Minister had helped needy artists and writers with
public grants, and he now continued this generosity from his own pocket.
Dickens had for years disliked Peel, but now, like the magazine *Punch*
and many others of similar views, he swung sharply in his favour. 'I
little thought once upon a time', he wrote, 'that I should ever live to praise
Peel. But Disraeli and that Dunghill Lord [presumably Lord George
Bentinck] have so disgusted me that I feel disposed to champion
him ... and should have done so even if he hadn't shown to a starving
artist such delicate attention and compassion as he showed to Haydon.'¹²
Peel's generosity to Benjamin Haydon was well publicised by the
painter himself, who was notoriously difficult to help. Peel had given him
money at intervals since 1830 and commissioned a large portrait of
Napoleon. Haydon repeatedly complained that Peel had not given him
enough; Peel replied by sending more. Haydon finally committed suicide
in 1846. Peel's letters were read out at the inquest, and the coroner

commented that his kindness 'must speak to the heart of a great many thousand persons'.

Peel enjoyed talk, whether among scientists and men of letters invited to Drayton or at the dinner tables of London. Carlyle had for years persuaded himself from a distance that Peel was a hero, a leader of men, almost to be compared with Cromwell or Frederick the Great. He met Peel for the first time at a London dinner in 1848:

> He is toward sixty and, though not broken at all, carried especially in his complexion, when you are *near* him, marks of that age: clear, strong blue eyes which kindle on occasion, voice extremely good, low tones, something of *cooing* in it, rustic, affectionate, honest, mildly persuasive ... Reserved seemingly by nature, obtrudes nothing of *diplomatic* reserve. On the contrary, a vein of mild fun in him, real sensibility to the ludicrous, which feature I liked best of all.[13]

Peel was not a man for epigrams or shafts of glittering wit, but he enjoyed telling stories. Some of these clustered round Lord Stowell, long ago Peel's senior colleague as Member of Parliament for Oxford University. Stowell, who was notoriously mean, had addressed young Peel on a traditional obligation of the two Members for the University. They were expected to present to the Bodleian Library bound copies of Hansard, the record of parliamentary debate. The two Members of Parliament shared the expense. Lord Stowell proposed that the junior Member should carry the whole cost. Peel was taken aback, but Lord Stowell explained that this new arrangement would save Peel a lot of money. He himself would not last long, and Peel would then sit as senior Member for decades yet.

Peel had gathered round him a band of young disciples who provided a devoted and ready audience. Some, like Gladstone, Eliot and Herbert, were already launched on successful careers; the ambitions of others, like Smythe and young Gregory from Ireland, soon withered away. Peel was particularly generous in friendship with Lord Lincoln, who needed it. His wife ran away with another man and his father, the dreaded Duke of Newcastle, undermined his son's career at every turn.

But these were not young men to be satisfied with stories round the table, or speculations on what might have been – or even with talk among the scientists and diplomats gathered at Drayton. They were men of action. They had tasted the chief pleasure of politics – to serve in an effective government with a clear sense of direction. They wanted to work like that again – if possible under Peel their old leader but, in any case, to work. They did not feel sad, discredited or out of touch with the electorate. On the contrary the Peelites did well in the general election of 1847; it was the protectionist group of the Conservative Party under Bentinck and Disraeli which suffered losses.

There were two ways in which the block of ninety Peelite Members in the House of Commons might regain office and start proper work again. Some talked of reconciliation within the Conservative Party; some flirted with the idea of alliance with the Whigs. Neither tactic had any charm for Peel. He did not admire Lord John Russell and in particular thought his policy in Ireland unimaginative in the desperate months of famine. Neither man could be expected to serve under the other. Peel did not want to destroy the Government. His main concern was to preserve free trade, together with the banking system which he saw as its necessary companion. He quickly advised Charles Wood, Chancellor of the Exchequer, on the handling of the financial crisis in the winter of 1847.

Lord George Bentinck died in 1848, and Disraeli began the long process of hypnotising the protectionist Conservatives into abandoning protection. But this process was still at an early stage. In the winter of 1849 there was even talk of the Whig Government introducing a low, five-shilling fixed duty on foreign corn. Peel was alarmed; he leaned on Ministers, and the idea disappeared. Second-rate though they might seem to Peel, these Whig Ministers were for the moment the best guarantee for free trade. Peel discouraged all suggestions from Gladstone and other Peelites for reuniting the Conservative Party to bring the Government down.

The underlying reason for Peel's political aloofness was more personal. Party warfare had no more charm for the man who had once been a master of party tactics. Nowadays he travelled more often round the country and was treated almost like royalty, as a man above politics. When he arrived by train at Darlington in September 1847, the Union Jack was flown from the station roof, church bells pealed, and shops closed early in his honour. In Liverpool a month later the programme of his visit was published in advance in *The Times*. Peel made the point himself when speaking at the public library in Tamworth in January 1849. He now preferred talking about matters on which there was general agreement.

He had achieved his main aim in spite of the party system. Indeed he had acquired a unique national standing by defying that system. In 1845 and 1846 he had tasted the pains of martyrdom, and was now conscious of its pleasures. If he went back into the political arena he would have to negotiate, manoeuvre, compromise all over again. He was free now of the grubbiness of everyday political life, and had no intention of muddying himself again. This might be tough on his friends and supporters, but they must find their own way in the new political world which had been born in 1846.

Peel therefore used the House of Commons not for immediate tactical purposes but to deepen his own thinking on the main issues and press home his conclusions. His speeches at this time lacked the drama which goes with a great political occasion but were among his most thoughtful. For example, his views on Ireland had continued to move sharply towards conciliation, as he explained to the Commons in January 1849. He argued that the potato disease and the famine had not created the tragedy of Ireland but exposed its realities. He set out a programme of change which focused on the land problem as described by his own Devon Commission. Because of the collapse of agriculture many estates were insolvent or debt-ridden. A commission should take these estates and entrust them to capable managers who could shift from potatoes to farming cattle and cereals. In private he argued for settling finally the relationship between the State and the Catholic Church, even if this meant going well beyond Maynooth and endorsing all clergy from public funds. In a series of friendly talks he urged Lord Clarendon, the new Lord-Lieutenant, to act boldly along these lines.[14] If there had been no potato disease a Peel Government, re-elected in 1847, might have acted as boldly on these Irish questions as on free trade.

In August 1849 Peel returned to the Scottish Highlands with Julia and their youngest daughter Eliza. They rented from Lord Lovat a beautiful house fifteen miles west of Inverness, perched on a rocky island in the River Beauly. As often during Peel's Scottish visits, the weather was bad. He shot less nowadays but greatly relished the wild scenery and the expeditions to romantic beauty spots. He made elaborate travel plans for young William to join them on leave from the Navy. Julia wrote to Bonham that she had never seen her husband so happy.[15]

Eighteen

The Final Fall

'You will not advance the cause of constitutional
government by attempting to dictate to other nations' ...
'If you succeed I doubt whether or not the institutions that
take root under your patronage will be lasting.
Constitutional liberty will be best worked out by those
who aspire to freedom by their own efforts. You will
only overload it by your help, by your principle of
interference.'

Peel in the Don Pacifico debate, 29 June 1850

'Everyone seems to have lost a personal friend'

Queen Victoria on Peel's death

'I feel if possible additional melancholy – as if every link as
it comes, connected with the fond idol of my heart, was
breaking away. I fondly loved – I respected – I admired him
– I lived life for him – then think what a Blank is here –
how gladly would I now lie by the side of his hallowed
remains in that sacred vault.'

Julia Peel to Goulburn, 28 August 1850

By 1850 Palmerston had replaced Peel as the best-known figure active
in British politics. Returning to the Foreign Office in 1846, he had
again given the Courts of Europe, including the Queen and Prince
Albert, the tough ride which they feared. Worse still from their angle, he
had been successful. He had sympathised with the new nationalist movements in Europe and watched with satisfaction the collapse of the old
regimes on the Continent in 1848, the year of revolutions. Metternich and
Louis Philippe were gone, the Austrian Emperor and the King of Prussia
were humiliated, but Palmerston prospered. He worked hard and in his

own sphere was as great a master of detail as Peel; among the public he built his reputation as a carefree Englishman scornful in a general way of the antics of foreigners and concerned above all else to keep Britain strong and dominant in world affairs.

Palmerston's weakness was a tendency to overplay his hand. When in 1850 Don Pacifico, a British subject of dubious reputation, suffered losses in a Greek riot and claimed compensation from the Greek Government, Palmerston brushed aside an offer of French mediation which he had in theory accepted, and ordered a British fleet to blockade Piraeus. Opposition peers in the House of Lords passed a critical motion. The Government countered by arranging for the Radical MP Roebuck to table a motion in the Commons in support of Palmerston. The stage was prepared for the Don Pacifico debate, one of the set pieces of Victorian oratory.

Two points were in doubt: the effect on Palmerston's reputation, and whether the Peelites would join the main protectionist opposition in voting against him. Peel himself felt awkward at any thoughts of allying himself with Disraeli. He knew that Palmerston was in the wrong, but he was anxious that the Whig Government should not fall and let the Protectionists into power. He was keen to speak on a different day from Disraeli, and was much vexed when an arrangement to that effect fell apart.[1] Palmerston rose to the occasion. In a speech of four hours on the night of 28 June he deployed his professional mastery. He famously proclaimed that a British subject, like a Roman citizen of old, could rely wherever he was on the watchful eye and strong arm of England to protect him against injustice and wrong, declaring proudly, 'Civis Romanus sum.' Palmerston transformed a weak case into a personal triumph.[2]

Peel rose after midnight. No one was sure what line he would take. He had (like the Prime Minister, Lord John Russell) snoozed through part of Palmerston's speech. He had listened to Disraeli, who would turn out later to be a Palmerstonian Prime Minister but who on this occasion took a high moral line against the Government. Gladstone recorded afterwards that when Disraeli sat down Peel murmured approval. Yet it was known that Peel was very reluctant to do anything which would help to bring down the Whig Government. Aberdeen, Peel's close friend and former Foreign Secretary, from genuine indignation felt strongly against

Palmerston's opportunism. He had argued that case with Peel, but met little success.

Nevertheless, when pressed to the point, Peel could not dodge the genuine moral and political issue. Palmerston was again banging about in the world, as if loud diplomacy was the same as strength. He praised Palmerston's speech, but set out to counter his general policy on philosophical grounds. The points which Peel made resound in a different form among us today. We argue now whether it is right to use force on behalf of democratic change in other countries. Peel was clear: 'You will not advance the cause of constitutional government by attempting to dictate to other nations ... If you succeed I doubt whether or not the institutions that take root under your patronage will be lasting. Constitutional liberty will be best worked out by those who aspire to freedom by their own efforts. You will only overload it by your help, by your principle of interference.' He took the example of China, still topical today. The Government was sending a particularly verbose Radical MP to represent Britain in Canton. 'Shall we instruct Dr Bowring to read to the Chinese people at Canton lectures on political economy? ... Shall we invite him to instruct the people of China in their duties towards themselves ... or is it wise to live at peace with China and to make allowance for these peculiar institutions under which the people live, and with which we have no concern?'*

Don Pacifico and his compensation claims were left far behind as Peel restated his fundamental view of the right foreign policy for Britain. He felt that he had won the battle for free trade; but alongside free trade Britain needed a peace-seeking diplomacy. The two went together; Palmerston had got it wrong:

> If you appeal to diplomacy let me in the first place ask what is this diplomacy? It is a costly engine for maintaining peace. It is a remarkable instrument used by civilised nations for the purpose of preventing war. Unless it be used to appease the angry passions of individual men, to check the feelings that rise out of national resentments – unless it be

---

* Six years later Dr Bowring helped to ignite the Arrow War between Britain and China, which led to another parliamentary crisis for Palmerston, followed by yet another personal triumph.

used for that purpose, it is an instrument not only costly but mischievous. If then, your application of diplomacy be to fester every wound, to provoke instead of soothing resentments, to place a Minister in every court of Europe for the purpose not of preventing quarrels or of adjusting arguments, but for the purpose of continuing an angry correspondence and for the purpose of promoting what is supposed to be an English interest of keeping up conflicts with the representatives of other Powers, then I say that not only is the expenditure upon this costly instrument thrown away, but this great engine, used by civilised society for the purpose of maintaining peace, is perverted into a cause of hostility and war.

Peel's last speech was not one of his greatest and he had a muted reception. Observers were as interested in his tactics as in what he said. He was ill at ease in aligning himself with Disraeli and the Protectionists. But his sense of the merits of the argument prevailed, and his last words in the Commons were as eloquent as any in defining how the greatest power in the world should handle its dealings with others.

Julia, in Whitehall Gardens that night, was not feeling well but she waited up for Peel. He returned exhausted at three in the morning. As usual he wound up his watch, and retired to his dressing room. He stayed there longer than usual. Julia went to him and found him saying his prayers. He said he thought his speech had gone well.

Next morning Julia was still feeling ill, and did not get up as usual to make his breakfast. But she read his speech, and wrote him a note saying she thought it was excellent. He sent a note back, that he was never so happy as when she approved of something he had done. When Julia got up later in the morning she found him still in the house, but about to leave. He had to attend a meeting of the Commission on the 1851 Exhibition that afternoon. He also wanted to fit in a ride in the Park before they dined with the Jerseys. The Commission was examining a fascinating plan by Paxton, the Duke of Devonshire's celebrated gardener at Chatsworth, to house the Great Exhibition in a great glass palace in Hyde Park. After the meeting Peel went home briefly, promised Julia he would not be late, kissed her goodbye and at about five o'clock set out on his ride. He signed his name in the visitors' book at Buckingham Palace, and rode slowly up Constitution Hill towards St George's Hospital, now the Lanesborough Hotel.

There were different opinions on the horse which Peel was riding. He had bought it several weeks earlier from a friend. His son-in-law had tried it out and thought it suitable. Peel's own coachman had his doubts. It later emerged that an earlier owner had got rid of it because of its kicking and bucking. A young man who knew its reputation actually recognised the horse in the Park. He thought of warning Peel, but Peel's well known stiffness to strangers put him off. Peel himself had ridden the animal each evening for about eight weeks without mishap. Peel was perhaps too big a man to be an ideal horseman, but he had been riding regularly without trouble for fifty years.[3]

As Peel paused to greet two young ladies of his acquaintance his horse began to plunge, kick and swerve. It threw Peel over its head and he fell to the ground. The horse stumbled on top of him, striking and crushing his back. Bystanders hurried to help, and a Mrs Lucas took him home to Whitehall Gardens in her carriage. Peel fainted as he was carried into the house. The pain was so great that doctors and family decided not to take him upstairs. Pillows and later a water mattress were brought. The dining room table became Peel's bed, and the apparatus of a sick room accumulated round him.

He lay within sight of his favourite pictures – David Wilkie's painting of John Knox preaching, and the five Reynoldses, including Dr Johnson in old age. There, in front of the tall windows overlooking the garden by the side of the Thames, Peel struggled for life for just over three days.

The kick of the horse had broken Peel's collarbone and several ribs. Fragments of shattered bone caused severe haemorrhage and produced a swelling below the left shoulder blade as large as a hand could cover, which pulsated and shifted its position with the action of the heart. So much is certain. The family would not allow a post-mortem, so the exact extent of Peel's injuries remains unknown. Fifteen leeches were applied to allay the inflammation, but they only exhausted the patient. Bandages were tied round his chest and arms to prevent movement, but they produced unbearable pain.

The accident happened on Saturday evening, 29 June. Within a few hours all London had heard of Peel's fall. It was four years to the day since he had resigned as Prime Minister. That evening he saw Julia but was allowed no other visitors. There was no improvement on Sunday or Monday. A stream of carriages arrived bearing callers to leave good wishes, including Prince Albert and twice the Duke of Wellington. Julia collapsed; two of their children, William and Eliza, ran the household and sent to Rome for their eldest brother, Robert. Peel tossed and turned, sometimes delirious. He muttered the names of Hardinge and Graham; Hardinge spent Monday night by his side.

A crowd began to gather in the street, mainly of working people. They filled Whitehall Gardens through Monday night and Tuesday, scrutinising the medical bulletins which were fastened to the gates of the house. Police were posted to control and guide them. Nothing quite like this had been seen in London before. The crowd stood silent, hoping for better news than anyone could give. The Queen wrote to her uncle, 'Thank God he is better again this morning, but I fear still in great danger. I cannot bear even to think of losing him; it would be the greatest loss for the whole country and irreparable for us, for he is so trustworthy and so entirely to be depended on.'[4]

On Tuesday morning Peel slept for four hours. When he woke up he took tea and broth and said he was in less pain. He even walked round the room. Two hours later there was a relapse, probably because pneumonia set in. His breathing became difficult; the pulse became faster and weaker. At half past six the doctors abandoned hope. The Bishop of Gibraltar, an old friend, administered the Sacrament to Peel and Julia. The family were admitted one by one to say goodbye. Peel, very weak but by now in little pain, gave his blessing to each in turn. Julia was led away. For two hours Peel lay unconscious, in the company of his three brothers, three of his sons, his son-in-law, Hardinge, Graham and the doctors. Just after eleven o'clock on the evening of 2 July 1850 Peel died.

The farewells in Parliament next day were eloquent, none more than that of his opponent Stanley. The Duke of Wellington, in a choked voice, spoke of Peel's passion for truth. Graham could not speak, silenced by tears. Gladstone quoted Walter Scott:

> *Now is the stately column broke*
> *The beacon light is quenched in smoke*
> *The trumpet's silver voice is still*
> *The warden silent in the hill*

The French Assembly adjourned, uniquely, as a sign of respect.

For some of these politicians the mourning was conventional. For others the emotion was out of the ordinary. For Gladstone, Aberdeen, Hardinge, Lincoln and Graham the loss was absolute. The dead man had taught them what they knew about the taking of decisions, the process of government, the handling of Parliament. More important they had learnt from him about the clash between courage and consistency, the place left open in politics for generosity, long-term thinking, and high standards in public life.

What struck these men and all political commentators was not their own feelings, but those of the people. Peel had never been a democrat. He had opposed parliamentary reform. He was strongly against universal suffrage and the ballot. He thoroughly disliked pressure brought to bear on Parliament by outside bodies. Yet it was precisely among those outside politics, the millions without a vote, that the loss of this difficult, austere, uncharismatic Conservative was most deeply felt.

To them the repeal of the Corn Laws and the courage shown in achieving it were something extraordinary. It fell outside the usual run of politics. Its author deserved a special farewell. Shops and factories closed. Peel's last speech was reprinted in a penny pamphlet. All over the country subscriptions were started for statues, reading rooms, memorials of many kinds. In his birthplace, Bury, 4,000 subscribers raised £3,052 for his memorial, many of them in sums of a penny, threepence or sixpence.[5]

After a tiff with Peel a leading Ultra, Sir Edward Knatchbull, had written 'it will be found when he dies, that no Minister ever possessed fewer friends or would be personally less lamented'.[6] Rarely can a prophet have been so confounded. The sophisticated as well as the Ultras were surprised: 'I thought he had a great hold on the country,' wrote Greville, the prince of in-house gossip, 'but had no idea it was so deep and strong and general as now appears.' Macaulay recorded, 'Once I little thought that I should have cried for his death.' Aberdeen wrote to Princess Lieven three days after Peel's death. 'A great light has disappeared from amongst us. Never did I know such universal grief exhibited by every description of person; high and low, rich and poor, from the Queen to the common labourer; all feel alike and with good reason, for his services were equally rendered to all.'[7]

The Queen wrote to her uncle, 'Poor dear Peel is to be buried today. The sorrow and grief at his death are most touching, and the country mourns over him as over a father. Everyone seems to have lost a personal friend.'[8]

Although Peel's memorial tablet is modest by Victorian standards, it dominates the interior of the parish church of Drayton Bassett. There by his own wish he was buried on 9 July. There was room at the service only for family and close friends and allies. The churchyard and the park at Drayton Manor were crowded with families from the estate, and from the big Midland towns nearby. It was a cold, wet day. Across the country, in Manchester, Birmingham, Liverpool, Bristol, Leeds, Wolverhampton and Bury, mills stopped work. Shops closed, and in seaports flags on ships were lowered to half mast.[9]

The tears of the nation brought no comfort to Julia, for her own tears were devastating. She had been led away from the deathbed and was not present during Peel's final hours. In the weeks that followed her despair poured out in letters to Goulburn, Graham and Aberdeen. Her personal grief was distorted by her quarrel with the new Baronet, their eldest son Robert, now back from Rome. She disapproved of his way of life and distrusted his judgement. In hysterical terms she appealed to Goulburn as Peel's executor to go to Drayton at once and stay there as long as possible. She was worried that the servants would let the new Sir Robert look at Peel's private papers and in particular his correspondence with her.

Peel had organised everything: she was at a loss in all practical matters without him. On 20 August, seven weeks after his death, she wrote, 'My beloved love was ever exact, and had a peculiar facility in all his arrangements.' But these practical worries were caught up in an awful emptiness. 'Every moment as it heavily passes reminds me of him, who on earth I can never see again – and I feel such despair. I cannot as yet bear up against my overwhelming grief – in God is my trust, for vain is the help of man! I am not well – but my desolate heart is what I feel is destroying me – my God have pity on me.' The words spilled straight from the heart to the pen, without any sense of order or composition – and this to a dry politician who had been Peel's personal friend, not hers.

His angelic disposition – his true religious feeling – his kindness and benevolence of heart – his noble charities – his unselfishness, sense, judgement, discretion I am not able, or fit to live without him, I am not good enough to follow so bright a pattern of God's holy work. I am sad and depressed and you must forgive my melancholy. <u>Where is the cure?</u> I devote my thoughts much to prayer – but I require strengthening more ... I no longer like living now.'[10]

To Aberdeen: 'I am sure you will forgive my writing to you. I can hardly say why I do – but in truth – I am so unhappy. My beloved one always talked of you as <u>the</u> friend, whom he most valued.'

Julia, the General's daughter, had for a quarter of a century served as her husband's staunch ally, keeping herself at one remove from his political life, but providing the comfort, loyalty and perceptive love within a family which had meant so much to him. He returned that love with a devotion unique in his life. Julia did not realise how total her dependence had become. When her support was suddenly removed, she collapsed. At the end of August she was still prostrate. 'I feel if possible additional melancholy – as if every link as it comes, connected with the fond idol of my heart, was breaking away. I fondly loved – I respected – I admired him – I lived life for him – then think what a Blank is here – how gladly would I now lie by the side of his hallowed remains in that sacred vault.'[11]

Nineteen

Epilogue

———— ✒ ————

*A*t one level there is no mystery about the man. He sits in the sun by the window at Drayton, feeding the partridges as they come forward clucking across the grass. In London he comes back late and weary from the Commons to the big new empty house in Whitehall Gardens and feels its loneliness. A few evenings later he shows his guests proudly round the Dutch masterpieces in his gallery. He shuffles his feet awkwardly in front of the Queen at Windsor. He eats a shade too greedily, cutting the jellies with a knife. He spreads his coat-tails and talks at length in Cabinet, at even greater length in the Commons, occasionally giving a vowel a Staffordshire value. He compels his audience because he has thought more fully and clearly than they about whatever is discussed. At night when the House is not sitting he reads and writes hour after hour until it is time to climb upstairs, wind his watch, say his prayers and get into bed, resting beside Julia or thinking of her.

Peel was born rich and died rich. He had the means to create for his life a background which suited his temperament. He was devoted to his wife; he loved and worried about his children. He went to church, and believed in an Anglican God and in God's Providence; he had no patience with disputes about doctrine or other Church matters. He was genuinely interested in painting and architecture, recognising talent and sharing without originality the tastes of his time.

So far this is the portrait of an estimable but not extraordinary man. To it must be added the faults which kept Peel at a distance from most of those whom he met. His stiffness was not just an awkwardness of manner. He was warm to his family and to a small circle of close friends, but to the rest of the world Peel was cold. O'Connell's famous remark that Peel's smile was like the silver plate on a coffin was not merely the gibe of a political opponent. Peel was not moved by emotional compassion. He believed in sense, not sentiment. He was not persuaded by the sufferings of boys in factories. He showed no interest in the anti-slavery movement. He supported the 1834 Poor Law and the workhouses which it established. He despised the sentimentality of George IV in pressing for mercy to be shown to criminals facing the gallows. In the scale of outward human sympathy for individual suffering Peel stands at the opposite end from Shaftesbury, Dickens and Wilberforce.

To this chilly temperament Peel added an excessive preoccupation with his own righteousness. He changed his mind on two dramatic occasions, Catholic Emancipation and the repeal of the Corn Laws. Each time public feelings ran spectacularly high. He was particularly vulnerable to accusations of bad faith and betrayal. Throughout his career he resented these charges with exceptional bitterness. He kept assuring himself and the world that he was acting out of true conviction and perfect good faith. This was true; when others saw it differently, Peel piled up further indignant assurance. To the examples already given we can add what he wrote to Ellenborough. 'I feel that confidence in the result [of the 1842 Budget] which must always accompany the consciousness of acting from pure and honourable motives and the deep conviction that the course taken is a wise and just one.'[1]

This self-righteousness marked out Peel even in a profession where self-righteousness is common. George IV used his powers of mimicry to imitate his Home Secretary's moralising speeches. At the end Disraeli found it easy to attack Peel's moral eminence because Peel had that eminence so high. Peel was a prig and paid the price.

If that was the sum of the story it would be worth telling only as a cautionary tale. But in that case the crowds would not have gathered round the house where Peel lay dying, the bells would not have tolled across the country or the factories closed. Peel was saved from his chilly self-righteousness by the relentless working of an honest mind; facts and figures were the fuel which drove it. His appetite for them was insatiable from the first days of his career to the last. To a greater extent than any of his predecessors he demanded them on every subject up to the moment when he made a decision. He was contemptuous of colleagues or opponents who entered an argument armed with only prejudice or sentiment.

But before he could take action on them the facts had to be tested against the beliefs operating at the back of Peel's mind. While scornful of all theological dogma, he believed in a God whose Providence shaped the world. As a Tory patriot he believed in good order, in the rights of property, in the institutions of his country. As the founder of the new Conservative Party he believed that these institutions were best protected not by resisting change but by measuring it to the needs of the moment.

Out of this fusing of facts and beliefs came a formidable legacy of actions which shaped his generation, and therefore our own. Peel invented our modern police force, which became a model for the world. He reorganised the criminal justice system, which remained harsh but became rational. He established a banking system based on gold which was criticised at the time and later for its deflationary bias, but which helped to create the confidence necessary for an extraordinary economic expansion.

Peel's legacy to the Conservative Party is controversial. That is not surprising, since he formed the modern Conservative Party and then wrecked it. There was nothing sensational about the strategy which was embodied in the Tamworth Manifesto of 1834. Peel abandoned the dramatic pessimism with which others and sometimes he himself had opposed the Great Reform Bill. All was not lost; the monarch, the House of Lords, the castles of dukes and the palaces of bishops were not after all doomed. Peel saw what could be built for the Party out of the ruins of electoral defeat in 1832. He was not himself the organiser of the Carlton Club, the constituency associations, or the machinery for registering the new voters. But he defined the appeal of the new Party based on selective and constructive opposition and the gradual enlisting of sober men of property.

The victory of 1841 proved the success of his strategy, but Peel exaggerated the willingness of his followers to be led down strange paths. After five years of growing discontent most of them broke away, preferring to remember their convictions and election pledges on the Corn Laws. They could not prevent repeal, but within days they pulled down the man who had forced it through with Whig votes.

The Conservative Party then dwelt in the wilderness. They snatched at occasional glimpses of office, but were not actually in control of events for any length of time until Disraeli's victory in 1874. Disraeli had preached that if the Constitution was to work a man must above all stick to his party. Those who accepted that doctrine and believed that party unity was an overriding good were bound to condemn Peel for being what Marxists later called a 'splittist'. Bagehot and Trollope as outsider commentators were joined in this condemnation by party leaders such as Salisbury, Rosebery and Balfour. For all of these the merits or demerits of repealing the Corn Laws were less important than the moral failure of Peel to realise that he was not the man to carry it through.

But of course political life is not so simple. The reputation of political parties has plunged downhill since those comments were made. Party loyalty remains a useful tool, but it would be impossible to persuade this generation that it is a prime virtue. Disraeli realised this clearly enough. Having preached the doctrine of loyalty to Protectionists, he deserted protectionism as soon as he reasonably could. For Disraeli it was more important to dish Peel than to save or restore the Corn Laws. By enlarging the franchise in the 1867 Reform Act Disraeli reversed another traditional stance of his party. He accomplished his own transformation with a tactical skill of which Peel in 1846 was not capable. Disraeli's sleight of hand in 1867 dismayed some of his supporters, but this time there was no split and no later condemnation. For Disraeli brought to his party a wealth of wit and style which has established his reputation among modern Conservatives well above that of Peel. He is easily quoted, for his words are memorable and sometimes wise. Little is remembered of his actions, for few of them were memorable. Disraeli in power bought a dominant share in the Suez Canal, made Victoria Empress of India, and played the part of elder statesman at the Congress of Berlin. These were spectacular rather than substantial events; they shone and he is remembered.

Disraeli also presided over disastrous defeats in the Zulu and Afghan Wars. Apart from the 1867 Reform Act it is hard to remember a single notable accomplishment by Disraeli at home, though phrases from his speeches or novels trip easily from the tongue. Putting aside his earlier falsehoods and intrigues, Disraeli learned to be respectable. He presided over a middle-class party practising free trade, a party which Peel would have immediately recognised as descended from Tamworth.

I do not grudge Disraeli his place in the dictionaries of quotations or the speeches of our party leaders. They are always in search of style, and their advisers direct them to the supreme stylist. But while Disraeli spun the phrases which survive, Peel clumsily and sometimes unattractively took the actions which underpinned Britain's strength and prosperity. One Nation is a phrase derived from one of Disraeli's novels; it describes a sense of direction established by Peel.

Throughout his career Peel's thoughts returned constantly to the question of Ireland. He began as the hard, competent administrator of the Protestant ascendancy, sharing many of the prejudices and fears of the landowning minority which he was sent to protect. Once the facts forced him to accept in 1829 that Catholics could no longer be excluded from the House of Commons, the logic of that decision gradually transformed his thinking. He realised that Catholics must somehow be brought into the Government and judiciary of Ireland. This meant tackling the relationship between landlord and tenant and changing the whole relationship between the Government and the Catholic Church. In the Maynooth debate he set out the principles on which he would work. They represented an even greater reversal of his views than the repeal of the Corn Laws, since he had campaigned more strenuously for the Protestant ascendancy than he ever campaigned for the 1815 Corn Law.

I do not doubt that a Peel government re-elected in 1847 would have brought forward something like a Home Rule Bill for Ireland. Gladstone became the heir to Peel's Irish policy. No one will ever know whether successful Irish Home Rule in the nineteenth century would have averted partition and civil war and allowed Ireland to evolve into a commonwealth monarchy like Canada, with a Catholic majority rather than minority. Probably not; probably there was already too much history separating the two sides of the Irish Sea. But it is hard to imagine that if Peel and Gladstone had had their way and reconciliation had been consistently pursued, the outcome would have been worse for Ireland than what she actually endured in the twentieth century. Ireland has entered the twenty-first century with far brighter prospects thanks to the peace process in the North and a sudden explosion of prosperity in the Republic based on free trade within the European single market. Peel would have approved heartily of both these efforts.

In his latter years Peel's main concern had been with the condition of England and in particular the problems of poverty in our industrial towns and cities. The concept of tariff reduction had been pioneered by

Huskisson and supported by Peel long before in the 1820s. In those days it was a concept coolly argued by intelligent men. The notion of applying that concept wholeheartedly to the main citadel of protection, namely the Corn Laws, bumped up against the political facts of life, namely the power of the agricultural interest. But the recession of 1842 and three years later the Irish potato famine changed the discussion so far as Peel was concerned. He stopped calculating a balance. He convinced himself that the idea with which he had sympathised for twenty years must be given full and dramatic expression in the repeal of the Corn Laws. The political risks had not disappeared, but to Peel in his new state of mind at the end of 1845 they could no longer be decisive.

Peel did not go to Paisley (as a modern Prime Minister might) or appear in public with tears in his eyes alongside the unemployed weavers. He did not return to Ireland with words of broken emotion in sympathy with the hungry tenants as he inspected heaps of diseased potatoes. Instead he stayed at his desk at Drayton or in Whitehall. He assembled the facts as best he could. He then mobilised his own powers of persuasion to bring round his colleagues and Parliament to the action which he thought necessary. He did not lose the habit of cool argument, but this was now overlaid by emotion. Of course he wanted to have it both ways, to preserve his political position while achieving his objective. As it became clear that these two might be incompatible he had no hesitation about the choice. In his exalted mood it was much more important to repeal the Corn Laws than to save his premiership. By this choice he destroyed his own political position and sent his party into the wilderness; but he gained something which he had never consciously sought, namely popularity among the great mass of people as the man who brought them cheap bread.

The real test came two years later.

The Chartist movement under its leader, Fergus O'Connor, planned a gigantic demonstration on Monday 10 April 1848 in support of its political demands. A petition with five million signatures was to be presented at Westminster by a huge crowd which would first gather on Kennington Common in south London. There had been many such demonstrations and petitions in the ten years of the Chartist movement's life, but this one was to be different. For in the first months of 1848 Europe was convulsed with revolution. The French King had lost his throne, and in these opening weeks of the Second Republic Paris was full of revolutionary talk. Metternich, the man who more than anyone stood for conservative Europe, had fled from Vienna in disguise. Parts of Germany, Italy, Spain, Hungary and Poland were in revolt. The Chartist plan was to install a National Assembly which would replace Parliament until the demands in the Charter became law. The Queen left London for Osborne. Even members of the Cabinet believed that by Monday evening Britain would be under a provisional government.

This was the Duke of Wellington's last great hour; he was seventy-nine. As Commander-in-Chief he made the necessary arrangements. Two hundred thousand Chartists were expected. Twelve thousand soldiers were discreetly posted at strategic points. Cannons were placed on the Thames bridges, though the Duke turned down Prince Albert's suggestion that the Tower guns should be moved. But the protection of order was basically in the hands of 4,000 police officers and 85,000 special constables. The police officers belonged to Peel's twenty-year-old force, the specials were recruited from all layers of the society which Peel, more perhaps than any other individual, had helped to shape. Only 150,000 Chartists turned up on Kennington Common. They were outfaced by the police and abandoned the idea of a march on Westminster. The petition was trundled to Westminster in a cab. In the afternoon it began to rain, the crisis passed, and the Duke ordered the soldiers back to barracks. There was trouble later in London and northern cities and a large number of arrests; but the big danger was over.[2]

In Paris killings began seriously in June and most of Europe remained in turmoil. The British had shown themselves immune from the revolutionary infection. This was not because they led contented lives; on the contrary, many sympathised with the Chartist demands. But after 1846 they knew that in England change could come about without revolution. The political system under strong leadership could operate against powerful interests for the benefit of the people as a whole.

The Great Exhibition of 1851, which Peel had helped to prepare, symbolised the national background of confidence. What the historian Geoffrey Best called 'a rich vein of national self-congratulation' may sometimes grate on us, like one of Peel's self-righteous speeches. But there was justification, particularly for those like Peel who had lived through the Napoleonic Wars and the tense days of Peterloo and the Reform Bill riots.

In foreign affairs Peel wove together the two contrasting strands of British diplomacy. By instinct Peel belonged to the school which valued diplomacy, disliked noise and was conscious of the miseries of war. He was disgusted by the expensive showmanship of Palmerston. He understood the huge coming importance of the United States and unlike Palmerston was willing to make concessions in order to establish a sound relationship with the United States. In India he tried to pull back from the policy of expansion until the Sikhs forced Hardinge into another war. He allowed Aberdeen and Queen Victoria to found the *entente cordiale* with France, but unlike Aberdeen he was not prepared to trust the French beyond a certain point. He accepted the need to spend more on the Royal Navy and on the defence of our coasts and harbours. In Peel's last speech in the Don Pacifico debate he argued against imposing our own political philosophy on other countries by force.

But arguably Peel's greatest legacy was to the world as a whole. We have seen how, when his own mind cleared on free trade, he proclaimed the message not just to Britain but to all trading nations. Britain should adopt the motto 'Advance, not recede' so that others could follow. Britain was then the world's leader. The home market was growing with the population. There were bound to be voices to argue that the main economic purpose of government should be to secure that market for the British producer by keeping out, for example, European or North American wheat and South American beef. Peel saw that in the long run the world market was infinitely more important; it was in Britain's interest to lower trade barriers and encourage others to do the same. Peel went one step further than his predecessor Pitt, for he did not insist on reciprocity. Negotiated commercial treaties were fine but the case which Peel made for free trade in Britain did not depend on other countries following our example. It was in the interests of the British consumer and of competitive British manufacturers that British barriers should come down anyway.

Peel was thus well ahead of many politicians and much public opinion today. The intricate bargaining processes of the European Commission and the World Trade Organisation are politically inevitable. Public opinion in most countries still believes that barriers should only come down as part of a bargain; reciprocity rules. To Peel such bargaining was not central to the argument. There were no foreign concessions as a counterpart to the repeal of the Corn Laws because none were needed.

No one rushed to follow Britain's example, with temporary variations. France and the United States remained staunchly protectionist. Germany came to birth behind a tariff wall. As the British Empire grew and foreign countries kept up their barriers there was a temptation to forget Peel and try to establish a protected market for British goods wherever the Union Jack flew. In return Britain would give preference to food and raw materials flowing in from her Empire. To Joseph Chamberlain and his successors at the start of the twentieth century this bargain would have political consequences. From it, the enthusiasts believed, would emerge a greater Britain, much of it self-governing in the form of White Dominions, able to match in wealth, cohesion and determination as well as naval strength anything that could be achieved by a united Germany or an expanding United States. Wider still and wider would her bounds be set. It was a noble imperial vision which attracted great men; but there would have been a price to pay. The vision could only be realised if Britain turned away from Peel's concept of free trade.

Once again the argument convulsed the Conservative Party. Its leader, Arthur Balfour, determined at all costs to avoid what he saw as Peel's disaster in splitting the Party, hedged his bet. He just preserved Party unity but wobbled his way into the electoral annihilation of 1906. After the Great War voices were again raised in the Party against free trade. Beaverbrook and Leo Amery achieved a modest success for imperial preference in the Ottawa Agreements of 1932. But during the years of greatest British power Britain had resisted the temptation to renounce free trade. Gladstone followed where Peel had led, and was in turn followed by Asquith, Lloyd George and Conservative free traders like Churchill. The doors of the British market were kept open, and the whole world gained.

After the Second World War leadership passed to the United States. After 1945, in an unmatched display of statesmanship, the Americans enshrined the principles of free trade in the post-war settlement and the institutions which embodied it – the World Bank, the International Monetary Fund and the GATT (General Agreement on Tariffs and Trade). Within Europe, six countries, now expanded to twenty-seven, went further by proclaiming a single European market. They marred this with an agricultural policy setting up indefensible barriers to limit access to that market from outside. The United States too has been slow to practise what it preaches. In the world as a whole the negotiations and the arguments continue, now covering services as well as goods and agriculture.

But there is no doubt about the way we are all going, albeit in clumsy lurches. New technology, and in particular the explosion in communications, makes free trade only one element in globalisation. Within the discussion of globalisation there are disagreements and reactions, but alternative models are not easy to find. No one, least of all the Chinese Communists, finds charm in the Soviet model which once (it is hard to remember) attracted much of the world. The nationalist (or French Gaullist) model has a pulling power for countries in an early stage of development. The unpopularity of American foreign policy masks to some extent the extraordinary success of the United States economy. So the waves ebb and flow, but there can be no real doubt about the direction of the tide.

That direction was initially set by Peel. He did not invent the doctrine of free trade. Adam Smith was a more rigorous thinker, Cobden a more eloquent communicator. Many share the credit. But Sir Robert Peel was in undisputed charge of the crucial country at the crucial moment. He was a doer, happiest when putting ideas into action. As G.M. Young wrote, 'Like an able artificer, Peel always thought with his hands.' He turned his hands to good purpose when he plumped for free trade.

If Peel had been different, less stiff and awkward, more devoted to Party unity, less intellectually honest, he might have stayed with protection, as Disraeli and the country gentlemen urged. He might have wobbled like Balfour sixty years later. He might have refused to respond to the Queen's final appeal from Windsor when Lord John failed to form a government in the days before Christmas 1845. These would all have been rational decisions for a lesser man. Then Britain would have been very different, and so would the world. No doubt at some stage the arguments for free trade and globalisation would with the help of technology have shone through the murk of narrower thinking. But as it happens it was Robert Peel who held the torch and pointed the way.

Acknowledgements

I have written this book in longhand, over three years, on many tables.

On an ancient oak table here at Westwell, surrounded by tagged books and folders of increasingly untidy notes. These hours have been eased with cups of coffee, and punctuated by calls to recapture my wife's errant sheep.

Or on the kitchen table in our house in Hammersmith, work beginning as soon as the croissant crumbs had been brushed away. In a conference room on calm evenings in the City at Hawkpoint, who provided the space and a delicious seafood supper. At the top of a pink library tower looking across olive and fig trees towards the mountains of Castile, at the invitation of Catali and Tristan Garel-Jones. In an elegant converted farmhouse with views over the Cairngorms most generously lent by Anthea and Thomas Gibson. Or in a room at Chatham House in St James's Square set aside for me by the Director, Victor Bulmer Thomas. To the providers of all these tables, and the hospitality with which they loaded them, I give warm thanks. They furnished the surroundings in which it was possible to learn about Peel, enjoy his company, and get used to his faults.

Peel's papers are scattered through many different institutions, each with its own flavour. I am deeply grateful to Her Majesty the Queen for permission to use the Royal Archives. To work in the Round Tower at Windsor is to join a social as well as a scholarly activity. Under the kindly supervision of the Registrar, Pamela Clark, and the Deputy, Jill Kelsey, the scholar is allocated a room where the requested volumes are already prepared. At eleven o'clock a bell tinkles, and all are summoned to elevenses in a common room. There they are joined by personalities of the Castle, including the man whose continuous duty is to wind the clocks throughout the estate. At Windsor I studied the diaries of Queen Victoria, who possessed the skills of a natural journalist; in her letters and diaries she chronicled without self-consciousness her own transition from harsh critic of Peel to fervent admirer.

The bulk of Peel's own papers are gathered at the British Library in London. My thanks are due to all those at the Library who helped my research assistant and myself over many days. They have created a thoroughly efficient and pleasant atmosphere. The coffee is excellent and a glass of wine taken in the forecourt on a summer evening can stimulate good argument over a knotty problem of interpretation.

I am grateful too to the custodians of the other treasure houses of Peel papers. The National Archives at Kew contain the Home Office papers, which vividly convey a portrait of the disturbed and often violent Britain seen through the reports of Peel's officials, correspondents and spies. Here I was indebted to Roger Kershaw for his help. The Surrey Archive holds the papers of Henry Goulburn, Peel's Chancellor of the Exchequer, close friend and executor. There we found the small brown notebooks in which Peel kept a record of his travels and jotted down occasional thoughts, for example his theological doubts. The 5th Earl Stanhope (formerly Lord Mahon) was Peel's literary executor, and in the Stanhope papers, formerly at Chevening and now in the Kent archive at Maidstone, we found Peel's musings on Robert Walpole and on the question whether the Romans indulged in human sacrifice.

The Duke of Wellington was a central figure in Peel's story. I am grateful to Lord and Lady Douro for their advice and hospitality at Stratfield Saye, and to Her Majesty's Stationery Office, by whose authority the University of Southampton have care of most of the Duke's papers. I am particularly grateful to Mrs K. Robson at the University of Southampton for her guidance.

I relied throughout on the forbearance and helpfulness of the House of Lords Library. Forbearance, because the librarians did not ask for books back unless they were specifically needed; helpfulness, because they seemed ready without hesitation to follow any new trail in which I was interested – for example fetching a ladder and identifying high up in a corridor the big batch of pamphlets on Ireland prepared for Peel when he went to Dublin as Chief Secretary at the age of twenty-four.

The Library of the Travellers Club has for fifty years been special in my life as a haven for quiet thought. Our Librarian, Sheila Markham, and the Library Committee were most co-operative, particularly in generous interpretation of the rules for borrowing books.

An author feels particularly vulnerable at two points: at the beginning of a project, when he needs encouragement, and at the end when he needs advice from people willing to read his draft. Graham Goodlad, who teaches history at St John's College, Southsea drove me home one evening in 2004 after I had spoken at the College. I did not realise until then that he had written a particularly useful sixty-page textbook on Peel in the Collins Flagship series. I am grateful for his encouragement, and most recently for his advice on the draft. At the same early stage I received practical encouragement from Stephen Lees and Peter Fox at the Cambridge University Library; Stephen Lees interrupted his own research on disappearing Members of Parliament to guide me along. Cambridge was indeed helpful throughout. Adam Green, Assistant Archivist at Trinity College, dealt courteously with my question about Peel's inquisition into the finances of the College living at Monks Kirby. I am grateful to the Master of Trinity for a bed on my visits, and to Nick Humfrey and Andrew Davies for providing my research assistant with floor space. Lively exhortation, mostly on postcards, came from fast-talking, quick-thinking Andrew Robinson at Eton, who arranged for me to use the Marten Library. The Provost, Eric Anderson, from his expert knowledge of Sir Walter Scott supplied colourful material on the visit of George IV and Peel to Edinburgh in 1822.

From Oxford I was helped over two animated lunches by Brian Young at Christ Church, and by the College Archivist, Judith Courthoys — though we are still baffled by the exact origin of the large notice in nails, NO PEEL, on the door leading up to Christ Church Hall.

I had plenty of other help in tackling the early stages of Peel's life. My son Philip and my research assistant visited his birthplace at Bury in Lancashire, and I am grateful for the help given them by Penny Farrell of the Bury Library. Christopher Tyerman, Rita Boswell Gibbs and Margaret Knight were equally helpful over Peel's time at Harrow.

By chance I recently met Niall Ferguson in expansive mood just after the publication of his last book, *The War of the World*. I at once snapped up his offer to read Peel in draft. It has been good of him to honour this promise so fully. Warm thanks also go to Sandra Wilson who made the same rash offer at a meeting at Cumberland Lodge and to Katrina Ramsey, whose commitment was ratified at a memorable supper in Stepney Green.

Peel among other things was a country squire. Beneath the overlay of modern urban settlement Tamworth retains the flavour of the market town which Peel represented in Parliament, together with the villages of Fazeley and Drayton Bassett close to Drayton Manor. Even more than the church where he lies buried, the solid red-brick cottages which he built bear witness to his interest. That local interest is alive today thanks to the Peel Society, whose publications and museum at Middleton House have been of great help to me. The Society is sustained by the determination of Mr and Mrs Norman Biggs and now their son Edward. Together with Nigel Morris, Vice Chairman, they have been hospitable and enthusiastic from the beginning. I hope that this book may attract new support for the Peel Society.

Thanks to Norman Biggs I twice visited the modern Drayton Manor, now an amazing theme park on the site of the house which Peel built and in which he entertained Queen Victoria. I have tried to convey both the contrast and the link between what Peel created at Drayton and what stands there today. This is the achievement of that formidable West Midlands entrepreneur George Bryan. George Bryan received me twice, kindly helping forward my interest in the past without diverting his attention more than was necessary from the excitement of the present. I am grateful too to Christine Colloby, the local historian who showed us round Drayton Bassett and its church.

Working through the huge mass of primary material on Peel is like fishing the Atlantic with a single rod. You cannot be sure what, if anything, you will find that is both new and interesting. Whenever we achieved this my research assistant and I christened the result a 'nugget'. One wall of my study is covered with scraps of paper, fastened with bluetack, on each of which he has transcribed a 'nugget' with its original reference, so that I shall not fail to include each of them as I write the story.

But inevitably I owe a huge amount to those who have already written about Peel. The acknowledged master is Norman Gash, whose two volumes published in 1961 and 1972 cover the whole life clearly and with immense sensitivity. They remain a great read. Professor Gash, who was born in 1912, lives in retirement on the outskirts of Langport in Somerset. On my first visit I was encouraged by his view that it was high time that Peel the politician was described by a politician. Later, when my project was under way, I invited him out to tea in his neighbourhood. Wrongly interpreting this as a slight on the tea which he had provided on my first visit, he produced in response not just tea but a traditional Madeira cake of much distinction. This time we went over particular points, for example the character of Julia Peel, on which he lighted my path.

Dr Boyd Hilton of Trinity College Cambridge has tackled Peel from a more severe and analytical angle. His book *The Age of Atonement*, his many articles, and now his contribution to the New Oxford History of England, *A Mad, Bad, and Dangerous People?* are compulsory reading for any student. Early on Dr Boyd Hilton gave me lunch at our College, sketched the different theories in the academic world about Peel and suggested what I might read to clear my mind. As with Professor Gash, I planned a return match which went slightly awry. My research assistant and I failed to find either taxi or tube to carry us in anything like time to the Covent Garden restaurant to which I had invited Dr Boyd Hilton. He had made the journey from Cambridge solely for this purpose. Eventually, very late, we found him, patient, puzzled, but ready to clear up a number of points which had baffled me, notably on the relationship between Peel's changes of policy and his belief in a Providence with whose workings men should meddle as little as possible.

A student sitting for a scholarship may decide to consult the winner of last year's scholarship. In that spirit I approached William Hague, whose *William Pitt the Younger* had recently scored such a success. William was most welcoming. He gave me plenty of practical advice on research, writing and marketing, some of which ('buy the books, don't borrow') is perhaps best suited to those who are already established winners. Another politician who helped was Gordon Brown. I went to see him at the Treasury on a matter related to prisons. I soon found myself discussing Peel in relation to the doctrines of the Church of Scotland and the ethical views of Adam Smith. Gordon put me in touch with Douglas Alexander, then just promoted to the Cabinet as Transport Secretary, but more important to me as Member of Parliament for Paisley, the Scottish town which for Peel became the symbol of industrial poverty. Douglas helped me with local literature and pointed me towards the local museum and the excellent local Studies Library under the direction of David Weir, to whom I am most grateful.

Peel's fourth son, Arthur, was given a peerage after serving as Speaker of the House of Commons from 1884 to 1895, and it is from him that the present Earl Peel is descended. Judy and I have enjoyed Willie Peel's hospitality at Eelmire in the North Riding of Yorkshire. On his staircase we admired the portrait of Peel by Lawrence, and in the drawing room an even finer Lawrence of Peel's father the 1st Baronet. Georgina Stonor gave me brisk and valuable guidance on several points, and helped in particular with the Wellington papers at Southampton. Mrs George Thorne, the granddaughter of Speaker Peel with her son Robin and other members of the family kindly entertained us to tea at Chilton House near Aylesbury, where we picked up much family gossip. Robert Floyd helped with advice about the Floyd family and Edward Cazalet dug out early photographs of Whitehall Gardens, which his forebears bought after Julia's death.

The Reverend Jonathan Peel came from Norfolk to lunch at the Travellers Club and lent me a large manila envelope full of letters between Peel and his children. The most attractive of these were from his favourite son, William, as he followed a naval career across the world. Some of them, dated after Peel's death and written to William's mother and brother, are outside the scope of this book. I believe they would justify a specific study of William, the first naval holder of the Victoria Cross, whose promising career was cut short by smallpox caught during the Indian Mutiny when he was thirty-four. These crisp, fragile letters from the Mediterranean, China, the Crimea, Egypt and the Sudan, the lines crammed together to save space in a handwriting more modern and legible than his father's, are a dramatic reminder of the range of this young Victorian life.

Peel was the last Prime Minister not to be photographed. Cartoons and caricatures showed people what he looked like and influenced what they thought about him. Simon Heneage and Kenneth Baker, were generous in steering me through this fascinating mass of material and allowing me to use examples from their impressive collections. Throughout I have been guided by two senior statesmen of the publishing world, namely my editor at Orion, Ion Trewin, and my agent, Michael Sissons. Both have built great reputations over many years and are entitled now to dignified repose. But they have exerted themselves persistently on behalf of Peel and myself. This has been a particular blessing and they know how grateful I am. The team of Orion, Bea Hemming, Katie Hambly, Tom Graves and Linden Lawson, added the necessary mix of professionalism and good humour.

I am grateful to many people for help on particular points: to Bob Morris, a former colleague at the Home Office, for a shrewd paper on the early days of the Metropolitan Police; to the Governor of the Bank of England on the historical value of the pound; to Dr Cliff on behalf of James Lock and Co. on Peel's hats; to Margaret and Anthony Young for their hospitality in York; to Francis Russell on Peel's pictures; to Charlotte Stevenson for lending me her copy of the *Private Letters*; to Michael Brock for his wisdom on the Great Reform Bill; to Claire Tomalin, William Fittall, Malcolm Williams, Sir John Birch; to Martin Wolf for educating me on the history of globalisation. To Jill Pellew for her book on the nineteenth-century Home Office; to Colonel Brook and Paul and Hilda Willard for welcoming me back to Chevening; to Professor G.W. Jones for advice on Private Secretaries; to Christopher Tugendhat, Mark Stuart, Ferdinand Mount, Tristam Hunt, Rosemary Baird (Curator at Goodwood), Carey Chung (Government House Librarian, Isle of Man), Timothy McCann (West Sussex County Archives), Peter Sheppard, Asa Briggs, Maggie Bird (the Metropolitan Police Librarian), Edward Pearce, David Marsh, David Weir (Paisley Library).

Three years is a long time to entertain in your house as exacting a guest as Robert Peel. My family have put up with his presence among us with great forbearance, only rationing occasionally the number of Peel references allowed during meals. Much more than that, my wife Judy flung herself into the double task of researching and describing Peel's collection of pictures, and finding many of the illustrations for this book. My son Philip was outrider to the enterprise, visiting on my behalf Bury, Paisley and the newspaper library at Colindale. For this help and particularly for the forbearance I owe my family yet another huge debt.

Pauline Glock has through this time continued her usual work for me at Hawkpoint, off Bishopsgate in the City. On top of this she nobly volunteered to type my manuscript onto the necessary computer. She cannot have guessed at the outset how much work this would involve. My scribbles have gone through many revisions. The epic of the footnotes must have by itself filled many wearisome hours. For Pauline this meant long hours of extra work, and many weekends spent with Peel as well as her own husband and family. She has carried all this with great good humour; her common sense has steered us out of many a difficult corner. I am enormously in her debt.

Near the beginning of this project I found myself talking about Peel with Edward Young, a friend of my son Philip. Ed had studied Peel at Eton and had asked me if I would like to see his A Level notes. He had gone on to take a First in History at Clare College, Cambridge and at the time of this conversation had just passed his twenty-second birthday. From that conversation a partnership developed which transformed the nature of this book. Ed suggested a rigorous plan for research, a large part of which he has carried out on my behalf. His high academic standards and ingenuity never flagged and he continued his brisk advice from across the Atlantic while taking up a scholarship on International Relations at Yale. I knew from the beginning that I would enjoy writing about Peel. Ed's enthusiastic part in the enterprise has greatly increased that enjoyment.

Bibliography

MANUSCRIPTS AND ARCHIVES

British Library
Peel Papers: Add. Mss. 40181–40617

Bury Public Library
Miscellaneous Peel Papers: A52 PEE; A76.2 PEE; G76.2 BUR; R31.1 JON

Christ Church College, Oxford
Archive XLVIII a45

Kent County Archives, Maidstone
Stanhope Papers: S4

National Archives, Kew
Audits and Accounts: AO 2/13
Distress at Paisley: HO 45/345
Disturbances 1821–30: HO 41/7–8
Home Office Correspondence 1821–30: HO 43/31–39
Irish Correspondence 1815: HO 100/4
Police Recruitment Order: MEPO 2/38
Private and Secret: HO 79

Parliamentary Papers
House of Commons Reports and Committees

Private Collection (Revd J. Peel)
Miscellaneous Peel Family Letters

Royal Archives, Windsor Castle
With the permission of Her Majesty Queen Elizabeth II
Georgian Archive
Melbourne Archive
Queen Victoria's Journal
Victorian Archive

Southampton University Archives
With the permission of HMSO
Wellington Papers

Surrey History Centre
Goulburn Papers: 304/A1–A2

Trinity College, Cambridge
Monks Kirby Archive

PUBLISHED SOURCES

W. Cobbett, *Rural Rides* (London, 1830)
Correspondence and Diaries of J.W. Croker, 3 Vols, ed. L.J. Jennings (London, 1884)
Diaries of 15th Earl of Derby, ed. J. Vincent (Oxford, 2003)
Disraeli's Letters, Vol. IV, ed. J. Gunn (Toronto, 1982)
B. Disraeli, *Coningsby, or the New Generation* (London, 1900)
B. Disraeli, *Endymion* (London, 1881)
B. Disraeli, *Lord George Bentinck: A Political Biography* (London, 1852)
B. Disraeli, *Sybil, or the Two Nations* (Oxford, 1956)
B. Disraeli, *Tancred* (London, 1900)
Gladstone Diaries, 14 Vols, ed. M. Foot and H. Matthew (Oxford, 1974)
Greville Memoirs 1817–1860, ed. L. Strachey and R. Fulford (London, 1938)
T.C. Hansard, *Parliamentary Debates from 1803* (London, 1803–)
A. Jameson, *Companion to the most celebrated Private Galleries of Art* (London, 1844)
Journal of Mrs Arbuthnot, 2 Vols, ed. F. Bamford and the Duke of Wellington (London, 1950)
The Letters of Lady Palmerston, ed. T. Lever (London, 1957)
Letters of Queen Victoria 1837–1864, 3 Vols, ed. A.C. Benson and Viscount Esher (London, 1908)
R. Mudie, *A Historical Account of His Majesty's Visit to Scotland* (Edinburgh, 1822)
R. Peel, *Memoirs*, 2 Vols, ed. Lord Mahon and E. Cardwell (London, 1856)
R. Peel, *Speeches by Sir Robert Peel at Glasgow* (London, 1837)
R. Peel, *The Speeches of Sir Robert Peel* (London, 1853)
R. Peel, The Tamworth Manifesto as reproduced in *The Historical Significance of the Tamworth Manifesto* (Peel Society publication, 1986)
The Private Letters of Sir Robert Peel, ed. George Peel (Murray, 1920)
Sir Robert Peel from his Private Papers, 3 Vols, ed. C.S. Parker (London, 1899)
Punch, or the London Charivari (London, 1841–)
The Diary of Frances, Lady Shelley, 2 Vols, ed. R. Edgcumbe (London, 1912–13)

BOOKS AND ARTICLES

P. Adelman, *Peel and the Conservative Party 1830–1850* (London, 1989)
M. Arthur, *Symbol of Courage* (London, 2004)
W.O. Aydelotte, 'The Country Gentleman and the Repeal of the Corn Laws', *English Historical Review*, 1967
W. Bagehot, *Biographical Studies* (London, 1881)
K. Baker, *The Prime Ministers: An Irreverent Political History in Cartoons* (London, 1995)
D. Beales, 'Peel, Russell and Reform', *Historical Journal*, 1974
G.F.A. Best, *Temporal Pillars* (Cambridge, 1964)
R. Blake, *The Conservative Party from Peel to Thatcher* (London, 1985)

R. Blake, *Disraeli* (London, 1966)

P. Brett, 'Political Dinners in early nineteenth-century Britain: Platform, Meeting Place and Battleground', *History*, 1996

A. Briggs, 'Middle-Class Consciousness in Politics 1780–1846', *Past and Present*, 1956

M. Brock, *The Great Reform Act* (Aldershot, 1993)

M. Brock and M. Curthoys, *The History of the University of Oxford*, Vol. VI (Oxford, 1997)

W.R. Brock, *Lord Liverpool and Liberal Toryism: 1820–1827* (London, 1967)

W.H.L. Bulwer, *Sir Robert Peel: An Historical Sketch* (London, 1874)

Cambridge History of British Foreign Policy, Vol. II (Cambridge, 1923)

O. Chadwick, *The Victorian Church* (London, 1966)

J. Chambers, *Palmerston: The People's Darling* (London, 2004)

J.C.D. Clark, *English Society 1660–1832: Religion, Ideology and Politics during the Ancien Regime* (Cambridge, 2000)

S. Clark, *Paisley: A History* (Edinburgh, 1988)

L. Colley, *Britons: Forging the Nation 1707–1837* (London, 1996)

L.W. Cowie, *Sir Robert Peel 1788–1850: A Bibliography* (Westport, 1996)

J.M. Crook, 'Sir Robert Peel: Patron of the Arts', *History Today*, 1966

T.L. Crosby, *English Farmers and the Politics of Protection 1815–52* (Hassocks, 1977)

T.L. Crosby, *Sir Robert Peel's Administration 1841–1846* (Newton Abbot, 1960)

R. Davis, 'The Tories, Whigs and Catholic Emancipation 1827–1829', *English Historical Review*, 1982

R. Davis, *Wellington, Peel and the Politics of the 1830s and 1840s* (Southampton, 2002)

T. Dickson and T. Clark, 'Social Concern and Social Control in nineteenth-century Scotland', *Scottish Historical Review*, 1986

D. Eastwood, 'Peel and the Tory Party reconsidered', *History Today*, 1992

F. Engels, *The Condition of the Working Class in England* (Oxford, 1958)

E.J. Evans, *The Forging of the Modern State: Early Industrial Britain 1783–1870* (Harlow, 2001)

E.J. Evans, *Sir Robert Peel: Statesmanship, Power and Party* (London, 1991)

S. Evans, 'Thatcher and the Victorians', *History*, 1997

R. Fairley (ed.), *Jemima – the Paintings and Memoirs of a Victorian Lady* (Edinburgh, 1988)

N. Ferguson, *The World's Banker: The History of the House of Rothschild* (London, 1998)

D.R. Fisher, 'The Sugar Crisis of 1844 reconsidered', *Historical Journal*, 1975

R.F. Foster (ed.), *Oxford History of Ireland* (Oxford, 1989)

A. Gambles, 'Rethinking the Politics of Protection: Conservatism and the Corn Laws 1830–1852', *English Historical Review*, 1998

N. Gash, *The Historical Significance of the Tamworth Manifesto* (Peel Society publication, 1986)

N. Gash, *Mr Secretary Peel: The Life of Sir Robert Peel to 1830* (London, 1961)

N. Gash, 'Peel and the Party System', *Transactions of the Royal Historical Society*, 1951

N. Gash, *Pillars of Government and other Essays on State and Society c.1770–c.1880* (London, 1986)

N. Gash, *Politics in the Age of Peel: A Study in the Technique of Parliamentary Representation 1830–1850* (Sussex, 1977)

N. Gash, *Sir Robert Peel: The Life of Sir Robert Peel after 1830* (London, 1972)

V.A.C. Gatrell, *The Hanging Tree: Execution and the English People 1770–1868* (Oxford, 1996)

G. Goodland, *Peel* (London, 2005)

F.P.G. Guizot, *Sir Robert Peel. Etude d'histoire contemporaine* (Paris, 1856)

F.P.G. Guizot, *Mémoires pour servir à l'histoire de mon temps*

W. Hague, *Pitt the Younger* (London, 2004)

F. Herrmann, 'Peel and Solly', *Journal of the History of Collections*, 1991

B. Hilton, *The Age of Atonement: The Influence of Evangelicalism on Social and Economic Thought c.1785–1865* (Oxford, 1988)

B. Hilton, *Corn, Cash, Commerce: The Economic Policies of the Tory Governments 1815–30* (Oxford, 1980)

B. Hilton, 'The Gallows and Mr Peel' in T.C.W. Blanning and D. Cannadine (eds), *History and Biography* (Cambridge, 1996)

B. Hilton, *A Mad, Bad, and Dangerous People? England 1783–1846* (Oxford, 2006)

B. Hilton, 'Peel: A Reappraisal', *Historical Journal*, 1979

B. Hilton, 'Peel, Potatoes, and Providence', *Political Studies*, 2001

B. Hilton, 'The Ripening of Robert Peel' in M. Bentley (ed.), *Public and Private Doctrine: Essays Presented to Maurice Cowling* (Cambridge, 1993)

W. Hinde, *George Canning* (London, 1973)

A. Howe, *Free Trade and Liberal England 1846–1946* (Oxford, 1997)

P.D. James and T.A. Critchley, *The Maul and the Pear Tree* (London, 1987)

B. Jenkins, *Henry Goulburn, 1784–1856: A Political Biography* (Liverpool, 1996)

R. Jenkins, *Gladstone* (London, 1996)

T.A. Jenkins, *Sir Robert Peel* (Basingstoke, 1996)

B. Kemp, 'Reflections on the Repeal of the Corn Laws 1830–1852', *Victorian Studies*, 1962

D. Kerr, *Peel, Priests and Politics: Sir Robert Peel's Administration and the Roman Catholic Church in Ireland 1841–6* (Oxford, 1982)

C. Kindelberger, *A Financial History of Western Europe* (London, 1984)

G. Kitson Clark, *The Making of Victorian England* (London, 1962)

G. Kitson Clark, *Peel and the Conservative Party: A Study in Party Politics* (London, 1929)

T. Lever, *The Letters of Lady Palmerston* (London, 1957)

E. Longford, *Wellington*, 2 Vols (London, 1969–72)

G.I.T. Machin, 'Resistance to Repeal of the Test and Corporation Acts', *Historical Journal*, 1979

J. Mathieson, *British Slavery and its Abolition* (London, 1926)

T.E. May, *The Constitutional History of England* (London, 1861–3)

D.N. McClostrey, *Enterprise and Trade in Victorian Britain* (London, 1981)

T.S. McKeown, 'The Politics of Corn Law Repeal and Theories of Commercial Policy', *British Journal of Political Science*, Vol. 19, No. 3 (1989), pp. 353–80

G. Meredith, *Diana of the Crossways* (London, 1885)

J. Micklethwait and A. Wooldridge, *A Future Perfect* (New York, 2000)

N. Mitford (ed.), *The Ladies of Alderley 1841–50* (London, 1938)

J. Morley, *Life of Gladstone*, 3 Vols (London, 1903)

J. Morley, *The Life of Richard Cobden* (London, 1903)

W.P. Morrell, *British Colonial Policy in the Age of Peel and Russell* (Oxford, 1930)

R. Morris, 'Peel and the New Police' (unpublished paper)

J. Morrow, 'The Paradox of Peel as a Carlylean hero', *Historical Journal*, 1997

I. Newbould, 'Peel and the Conservative Party 1830–1850; a study in failure?', *English Historical Review*, 1983

P. Norton (ed.), *The Conservative Party* (Hemel Hempstead, 1996)

Oxford Dictionary of National Biography (Oxford, 2004)

Oxford History of the Prison (Oxford, 1995)

J. Prest, *Lord John Russell* (London, 1972)

L. Radzinowicz and R. Hood, *History of English Criminal Law*, Vols I–V (London, 1986)

D. Read, *Peel and the Victorians* (Oxford, 1987)

T. Renton, *Chief Whip* (London, 2004)

J. Ridley, *Lord Palmerston* (London, 1970)

Lord Rosebery, *Sir Robert Peel* (London, 1899)

G. St Aubyn, *Queen Victoria* (London, 1991)

R.C. Shipkey, *Robert Peel's Irish Policy 1812–1846* (New York, 1987)

T.C. Smout, 'The Strange Intervention of Edward Twistleton: Paisley in Depression, 1841–3',
    The Search for Wealth and Stability: Essays in Economic and Social History Presented to M.W. Flinn, ed.
    T.C. Smout (London, 1979)

R. Steward, *The Foundation of the Conservative Party 1830–1867* (London, 1978)

W. Thomas, *The Quarrel of Macaulay and Croker* (Oxford, 2000)

R. and I. Tombs, *That Sweet Enemy* (London, 2006)

G.O. Trevelyan, *Life and Letters of Lord Macaulay* (London, 1876)

A. Trollope, *Framley Parsonage* (London, 1861)

A. Trollope, *The Three Clerks* (London, 1858)

A. Trollope, *The Warden* (London, 1855)

C. Tyerman, *History of Harrow School* (Oxford, 2000)

A.N. Wilson, *The Victorians* (London, 2002)

H. Wilson, *A Prime Minister on Prime Ministers* (London, 1997)

C. Woodham-Smith, *The Great Hunger* (London, 1962)

W. Vamplew, 'The Protection of English Cereal Producers: The Corn Laws Reassessed',
    Economic History Review, New Series, Vol. 33, No. 3 (1980)

M.E. Yapp, *Strategies of British India 1798–1856* (Oxford, 1980)

G.M. Young, *Victorian England: Portrait of an Age* (Oxford, 1936)

P. Ziegler, *King William IV* (London, 1971)

P. Ziegler, *Melbourne* (London, 1976)

Notes

CHAPTER 1: FROM COTTON
TO THE COMMONS (PP.5–13)

1 *Peel Papers*, 40605, fol. 7
2 Bury Public Library, A52 PEE
3 Gash, *Mr Secretary Peel*, pp. 20–4
4 *Peel's Papers* (ed. Parker), Vol. I. p. 7
5 Tyerman, *History of Harrow School*, pp. 140–66
6 Ibid., p. 152
7 Gash, *Mr Secretary Peel*, p. 48
8 Ibid., pp. 54–7
9 Ibid., p. 57
10 *Peel's Papers* (ed. Parker), Vol, I, p. 22, G. R. Dawson to Revd Mark Drury, 19 November 1808
11 Christ Church Archives, XLVIII, a45, ff. 68–71, George Chinnery to his mother, 20 November 1808

CHAPTER 2: NOT A TIMID MAN
(PP.14–23)

1 Hinde, *Canning*, p. 237
2 Gash, *Mr Secretary Peel*, pp. 68–9
3 *Peel's Papers* (ed. Parker), Vol. I, p. 27
4 Gash, *Mr Secretary Peel*, p. 69
5 Bury Public Library, G76.2 BUR
6 *Peel's Papers* (ed. Parker), Vol. I, p. 28
7 *Peel Papers*, 40605, ff. 16–17, Cyril Jackson to Robert Peel, 1 April 1810
8 *Peel's Papers* (ed. Parker), Vol. I, pp. 28–9
9 *Stanhope Papers*, S4/16, William Bathurst to Lord Mahon, 19 November 1850
10 Gash, *Mr Secretary Peel*, pp. 75–9

11 Ibid., p. 81
12 Peel, *Speeches at Glasgow*, pp. 49–52
13 Hinde, *Canning*, p. 247
14 *Dictionary of National Biography*, Lord Liverpool
15 Gash, *Mr Secretary Peel*, pp. 87–9
16 Ibid., pp. 89–91

CHAPTER 3: ORANGE PEEL
(PP.24–46)

1 *Peel Papers*, 40280
2 *Peel's Papers* (ed. Parker), Vol. I, p. 38
3 Ibid., Vol. I, p. 47
4 *Peel Papers*, 40605
5 Gash, *Mr Secretary Peel*, pp. 103–5
6 *Peel's Papers* (ed. Parker), Vol. I, p. 38
7 Ibid., Vol. I, p. 86
8 *Croker Correspondence* (ed. Jennings), Vol. I, pp. 75–6
9 Gash, *Mr Secretary Peel*, p. 115
10 Ibid., pp. 108, 116
11 *Peel's Papers* (ed. Parker), Vol. I, p. 106
12 Woodham-Smith, *The Great Hunger*, p. 42
13 *Peel's Papers* (ed. Parker), Vol. I, p. 20
14 Gash, *Mr Secretary Peel*, p. 152
15 *Dictionary of National Biography*, Daniel O'Connell
16 Shipkey, *Peel's Irish Policy*, p. 164
17 Gash, *Mr Secretary Peel*, p. 163
18 Ibid., pp. 164–6
19 *Peel's Papers* (ed. Parker), Vol. I, p. 194
20 Ibid., Vol. I, p. 140
21 Ibid., Vol. I, p. 149
22 Gash, *Mr Secretary Peel*, pp. 172–3

23 *Peel's Papers* (ed. Parker), Vol. I, p. 223
24 Ibid., Vol. I, p. 231
25 Ibid., Vol. I, p. 152
26 Cowie, *Bibliography*, p. 275
27 *Peel's Papers* (ed. Parker), Vol. I, p. 207
28 *Parliamentary Record*, 26 April 1816, Cols 26–7
29 Peel, *Speeches*, Vol. 2, p. 631
30 Gash, *Mr Secretary Peel*, p. 197
31 Chambers, *Palmerston*, p. 87
32 *Peel Papers*, 40281 fol. 99, Peel to Richmond, 2 March 1813
33 Gash, *Mr Secretary Peel*, p. 210
34 Shipkey, *Peel's Irish Policy*, p. 195
35 Gash, *Mr Secretary Peel*, pp. 211–18
36 Shipkey, *Peel's Irish Policy*, p. 3
37 Gash, *Mr Secretary Peel*, p. 226
38 *Peel's Papers* (ed. Parker), Vol. I, p. 227
39 Ibid., Vol. I, p. 161
40 Ibid., Vol. I, pp. 164, 278
41 Ibid., Vol. I, p. 256
42 Ibid., Vol. I, p. 286
43 Gash, *Mr Secretary Peel*, p. 236

CHAPTER 4: BULLION AND A BRIDE (PP.47–61)

1 *Peel's Papers* (ed. Parker), Vol. I, p. 287
2 Gash, *Mr Secretary Peel*, p. 232
3 Hilton, *Mad, Bad, and Dangerous People*, p. 259
4 Hilton, *Age of Atonement*, pp. 23–4
5 Hilton, *Corn, Cash, Commerce*, p. 48
6 Kindelberger, *Financial History*, p. 63
7 Morley, *Gladstone*, Vol. II, p. 465
8 Hilton, 'Peel: A Reappraisal', p. 590
9 *Private Letters* (ed. G. Peel), pp. 29–35
10 Ibid., pp. 37–8
11 Wilson, *A Prime Minister on Prime Ministers*, p. 53
12 Gash, *Mr Secretary Peel*, p. 261
13 *Croker Correspondence* (ed. Jennings), Vol. I, p. 170
14 Ibid., Vol. I, p. 176
15 Ibid., Vol. I, pp. 84–5

CHAPTER 5: THE DISTURBANCE FILE (PP.62–80)

1 Quotation attributed to Lady Hamilton Dalrymple by Dr E. Anderson, Provost, Eton College
2 *Peel's Papers* (ed. Parker), Vol. I, p. 319
3 Evans, *Forging of the Modern State*, pp. 189–98
4 Gash, *Mr Secretary Peel*, p. 351
5 *Disturbances*, HO 41
6 *Peel's Papers* (ed. Parker), Vol. I, p. 415
7 *Private and Secret*, HO 79/124-S, Hobhouse to Byng, 1 May 1826
8 *Disturbances*, HO 41/7
9 Parliamentary Papers 1822 IV (Police of Metropolis)
10 Gash, *Mr Secretary Peel*, p. 313
11 Radzinowicz, *History of English Criminal Law*, Vol. I, pp. 564–5
12 Gash, *Mr Secretary Peel*, p. 299
13 Ibid., p. 299
14 Radzinowicz, *History of English Criminal Law*, Vol. I, pp. 568 *et seq.*
15 Hansard, *Parliamentary Debates 1827*, Vol. 12, Cols 393–411
16 Radzinowicz, *History of English Criminal Law*, Vol. I, p. 574 n. 24
17 Gatrell, *The Hanging Tree*, pp. 569 *et seq.*
18 Hilton, 'The Gallows and Mr Peel', pp. 88–112
19 *Peel's Papers* (ed. Parker), Vol. I, p. 337
20 Ibid., Vol. I, pp. 315–17
21 Ibid., Vol. II, pp. 146–8
22 Gash, *Mr Secretary Peel*, p. 323
23 *Oxford History of the Prison*, p. 94
24 *Home Office Correspondence*, HO 43/37/f. 219
25 *Peel's Papers* (ed. Parker), Vol. I, pp. 400–2

CHAPTER 6: PARTRIDGES, PICTURES, PARENTHOOD (PP.81–9)

1 *Private Letters* (ed. G. Peel), p. 44
2 Ibid., pp. 53–86
3 Gash, *Mr Secretary Peel*, pp. 270–2

4 Heermann, *Peel and Solly*, p. 92
5 Jameson, *Companion to the most celebrated Private Galleries of Art*, p. 126
6 *Jemima* (ed. Fairley)
7 *Peel Papers*, 40342, ff. 293–4; ff. 320–1
8 *Peel's Papers* (ed. Parker), Vol. I, pp. 322–3
9 *Peel Papers*, 40343, ff. 1–22

CHAPTER 7: POLICE (PP.90–108)

1 Longford, *Wellington*, Vol. II, p. 13
2 *Private Letters* (ed. G. Peel), pp. 91–6
3 *Peel's Papers* (ed. Parker), Vol. I, p. 477
4 Ibid., Vol. I, p. 452
5 Steward, *Foundation of the Conservative Party*, p. 35
6 Gash, *Mr Secretary Peel*, p. 433
7 *Peel's Papers* (ed. Parker), Vol. I, p. 467
8 Ibid., Vol. II, p. 17
9 Gash, *Mr Secretary Peel*, p. 421
10 *Croker Correspondence* (ed. Jennings), Vol. I, p. 365
11 Gash, *Mr Secretary Peel*, p. 448; Hinde, *Canning*, pp. 459–60
12 Gash, *Mr Secretary Peel*, p. 452
13 Steward, *Foundation of the Conservative Party*, p. 29
14 Ibid., p. 36
15 Hilton, 'The Ripening of Robert Peel', p. 69
16 *Peel's Papers* (ed. Parker), Vol. II, p. 128
17 Hansard, 15/4/1829
18 James and Critchley, *The Maul and the Pear Tree*, pp. 18–24
19 Gash, *Mr Secretary Peel*, p. 501
20 *Police Recruitment Order*, MEPO 2/38, No. 547
21 Morris, 'Peel and the New Police'
22 *Croker Correspondence* (ed. Jennings), Vol. II, pp. 19–20
23 Lever, *Letters of Lady Palmerston*, p. 196
24 Machin, 'Resistance to Repeal of the Test and Corporation Acts', pp. 115–39
25 Clark, *English Society*, p. 532
26 Hilton, 'The Ripening of Robert Peel', p. 69

CHAPTER 8: THE CATHOLIC BREAK-THROUGH (PP.109–129)

1 Gash, *Mr Secretary Peel*, p. 521
2 *Wellington Papers*, WP 1/940/14
3 Peel, *Memoirs*, Vol. I, p. 119
4 *Private and Secret*, HO 79/4, July 1823
5 *Peel's Papers* (ed. Parker), Vol. I, p. 426
6 *Peel Papers*, 40311, fol. 315, Peel to Canning, 17 April 1800
7 Hilton, 'The Ripening of Robert Peel', p. 70
8 *Croker Correspondence* (ed. Jennings), Vol. I, p. 419
9 *Peel's Papers* (ed. Parker), Vol. II, p. 54
10 *Wellington Papers*, WQ 1/989/9
11 Peel, *Memoirs*, Vol. I, pp. 365–6
12 *Peel's Papers* (ed. Parker), Vol. II, p. 88
13 Ibid., Vol. III, p. 93
14 Ibid., Vol. II, p. 94
15 Ibid., Vol. II, p. 109
16 Ibid., Vol. II, p. 100
17 *Peel Papers*, 40343, fol. 348
18 Brock and Curthoys (eds), *History of Oxford*, Vol. VI, p. 58
19 Gash, *Mr Secretary Peel*, pp. 562–3
20 Cowie, *Bibliography*, p. 809
21 Brock and Curthoys (eds), *History of Oxford*, Vol. VI, p. 58
22 Ibid., Vol. VI, p. 59
23 Brock, *Great Reform Act*, p. 56
24 Peel, *Memoirs*, Vol. I, p. 342; Gash, *Mr Secretary Peel*, pp. 564–5
25 Peel, *Memoirs*, Vol. I, p. 346
26 Ibid., Vol. II, pp. 343–50
27 Gash, *Mr Secretary Peel*, p. 570
28 Hilton, 'The Ripening of Robert Peel', p. 77
29 Ibid., pp. 75–7
30 Gash, *Mr Secretary Peel*, p. 578
31 Longford, *Wellington*, Vol. II, p. 185
32 Gash, *Mr Secretary Peel*, p. 580
33 Peel, *Memoirs*, Vol. II, p. 116
34 Gash, *Mr Secretary Peel*, p. 598
35 Blake, *The Conservative Party*, p. 22
36 Cowie, *Bibliography*, p. 101

37 *Croker Correspondence* (ed. Jennings), Vol. II, p. 15

CHAPTER 9: REFORM OR REVOLUTION? (PP.130–156)

1 *Journal of Mrs Arbuthnot* (ed. Bamford and Wellington), pp. 230, 239, 358
2 Brock, *Great Reform Act*, pp. 18–29
3 Ibid., pp. 27–8
4 Ibid., p. 47
5 Ibid., p. 63
6 *Private Letters* (ed. G. Peel), p. 115
7 Gash, *Mr Secretary Peel*, p. 614
8 Longford, *Wellington*, Vol. II, p. 207
9 *Private Letters* (ed. G. Peel), p. 119
10 Ziegler, *William IV*, p. 150
11 Ibid., p. 153
12 Brock, *Great Reform Act*, p. 91
13 Ibid., p. 93
14 Ibid., p. 117
15 *Peel's Papers* (ed. Parker), Vol. II, p. 169
16 Brock, *Great Reform Act*, p. 129
17 *Croker Correspondence* (ed. Jennings), Vol. II, p. 78
18 Ibid., Vol. II, p. 105
19 Hilton, *Mad, Bad, and Dangerous People*, p. 424
20 Gash, *Sir Robert Peel*, p. 13
21 Brock, *Great Reform Act*, p. 186
22 Ibid., p. 192
23 Ibid., p. 209
24 *Private Letters* (ed. G. Peel), p. 135
25 Gash, *Sir Robert Peel*, p. 24
26 *Croker Correspondence* (ed. Jennings), Vol. II, p. 137
27 Ziegler, *William IV*, p. 204
28 Brock, *Great Reform Act*, p. 217
29 Ibid., p. 218
30 Gash, *Sir Robert Peel*, p. 29; Ziegler, *William IV*, p. 236
31 *Croker Correspondence* (ed. Jennings), Vol. II, p. 113

CHAPTER 10: THE HUNDRED DAYS (PP.157–188)

1 Gash, *Sir Robert Peel*, pp. 40–1
2 *Croker Correspondence* (ed. Jennings), Vol. II, pp. 189–90
3 *Private Letters* (ed. G. Peel), pp. 139–43
4 Ibid., pp. 139–46
5 Stanhope Papers, S4/9, Peel to Mahon, 23 December 1833
6 *Peel's Papers* (ed. Parker), Vol. II, p. 212
7 *Croker Correspondence* (ed. Jennings), Vol. II, p. 204
8 Longford, *Wellington*, Vol. II, p. 284
9 Cowie, *Bibliography*, p. 107
10 Longford, *Wellington*, Vol. II, p. 248
11 *Peel's Papers* (ed. Parker), Vol. II, p. 227
12 Longford, *Wellington*, Vol. II, p. 290
13 Gash, *Sir Robert Peel*, p. 64
14 Ziegler, *William IV*, p. 242
15 *Dictionary of National Biography*, Stanley
16 *Greville Memoirs*, 21 February 1835, Vol. III, pp. 162–3
17 Gash, *Sir Robert Peel*, p. 76
18 Cowie, *Bibliography*, p. 108
19 *Greville Memoirs*, Vol. III, p. 97
20 Ziegler, *William IV*, p. 257
21 Longford, *Wellington*, Vol. II, p. 303
22 Goulburn Papers, 304/A2/Box 6 (travel notebook)
23 Blake, *Disraeli*, p. 114
24 Text in Peel Society publication, *The Historical Significance of the Tamworth Manifesto*
25 Gash, *Sir Robert Peel*, p. 98
26 Blake, *Disraeli*, p. 121
27 Trollope, *Framley Parsonage, passim*
28 Jenkins, *Peel*, p. 400
29 Gash, *Pillars of Government*, p. 10
30 Disraeli, *Coningsby*, p. 177
31 Steward, *Foundation of the Conservative Party*, p. 142
32 *Croker Correspondence* (ed. Jennings), Vol. II, p. 255
33 Gash, *Sir Robert Peel*, p. 102
34 *Peel's Papers* (ed. Parker), Vol. II, p. 275

35 *Goulburn Papers*, 304/A2/Box 6
36 Morley, *Gladstone*, Vol. I, p. 172
37 Chadwick, *Victorian Church*, pp. 164 *et seq.*
38 Private letter from Mr Green, Assistant Archivist, Trinity College, 18 November 2004
39 *Greville Memoirs*, Vol. III, p. 171
40 Gash, *Sir Robert Peel*, p. 117
41 *Peel's Papers* (ed. Parker), Vol. II, pp. 306–10
42 Ibid., Vol. II, pp. 296–7
43 Cowie, *Bibliography*, p. 107

CHAPTER 11: CONSTRUCTIVE OPPOSI-
TION (PP.189–218)

1 Gash, *Sir Robert Peel*, p. 130
2 Longford, *Wellington*, Vol. II, p. 312
3 Ibid., Vol. II, p. 312
4 *Peel's Papers* (ed. Parker), Vol. II, p. 323
5 Longford, *Wellington*, Vol. II, p. 313
6 *Private Letters* (ed. G. Peel), p. 158
7 Ibid., p. 155
8 Ibid., p. 156
9 *Croker Correspondence* (ed. Jennings), Vol. II, p. 280
10 Gash, *Sir Robert Peel*, p. 168
11 Ibid., p. 169
12 Mordaunt Crook, 'Patron of the Arts', p. 10
13 Gash, *Sir Robert Peel*, pp. 167–79
14 Ibid., p. 170
15 *Goulburn Papers*, 304/A2/7
16 *Croker Correspondence* (ed. Jennings), Vol. II, p. 301
17 *Peel's Papers* (ed. Parker), Vol. II, p. 325
18 Gash, *Sir Robert Peel*, p. 150
19 *Peel's Papers* (ed. Parker), Vol. II, p. 329
20 Hansard, 11 April 1845
21 Hilton, *Age of Atonement*, p. 231
22 *Peel's Papers* (ed. Parker), Vol. II, pp. 331–3
23 Gash, *Sir Robert Peel*, p. 154
24 Ibid., pp. 154–6
25 Ziegler, *William IV*, p. 290
26 *Goulburn Papers*, 304/A2/7
27 *Croker Correspondence* (ed. Jennings), Vol. II, p. 306

28 *Stanhope Papers*, S4, Notebook
29 *Peel's Papers* (ed. Parker), Vol. II, p. 349
30 Gash, *Sir Robert Peel*, pp. 200–5
31 Gash, *Pillars of Government*, p. 156
32 Brett, 'Political Dinners', p. 546
33 Gash, *Sir Robert Peel*, p. 216
34 St Aubyn, *Queen Victoria*, p. 107
35 RAVIC/QVJ/1839: 5 April
36 Ziegler, *Melbourne*, p. 292
37 Ibid., pp. 260–1
38 RAVIC/QVJ/1839: 10 April
39 St Aubyn, *Queen Victoria*, pp. 96 *et seq.*
40 RAVIC/QVJ/1839: 7 May
41 St Aubyn, *Queen Victoria*, p. 109
42 RAVIC/QVJ/1839: 12 May
43 *Peel's Papers* (ed. Parker), Vol. III, p. 396
44 Jenkins, *Goulburn*, p. 280
45 *Peel's Papers* (ed. Parker), Vol. II, p. 405
46 Ibid., Vol. II, p. 400
47 Ziegler, *Melbourne*, p. 276
48 *Peel's Papers* (ed. Parker), Vol. II, p. 410
49 William Peel letter dated 5 November 1840 in the possession of the Revd Jonathan Peel
50 *Peel's Papers* (ed. Parker), Vol. II, p. 452
51 *Private Letters* (ed. G. Peel), pp. 170–1
52 Ibid., p. 165
53 St Aubyn, *Queen Victoria*, p. 138
54 *Peel's Papers* (ed. Parker), Vol. II, p. 432
55 Ibid., Vol. III, pp. 408–9
56 Gash, *Sir Robert Peel*, p. 263
57 Ziegler, *Melbourne*, p. 357

CHAPTER 12: VICTORY (PP.219–241)

1 Gash, *Sir Robert Peel*, p. 196
2 *Peel Papers*, 40616, ff. 198–9
3 *Peel's Papers* (ed. Parker), Vol. II, p. 467
4 Steward, *Foundation of the Conservative Party*, p. 142
5 Gash, *Sir Robert Peel*, p. 265
6 *Peel's Papers* (ed. Parker), Vol. II, p. 475
7 Engels, *Condition of the Working Class*, p. 75
8 Guizot, *Peel*, pp. 83–4
9 *Croker Correspondence* (ed. Jennings), Vol. II, p. 335
10 Gash, *Sir Robert Peel*, p. 250

11 *Peel's Papers* (ed. Parker), Vol. II, p. 480

12 Gash, *Sir Robert Peel*, pp. 268–70

13 St Aubyn, *Queen Victoria*, p. 154

14 *Letters of Queen Victoria*, Vol. I, pp. 198–9

15 Gash, *Sir Robert Peel*, p. 258

16 *Letters of Queen Victoria*, Vol. I, p. 311

17 Ibid., Vol. I, pp. 320–2

18 St Aubyn, *Queen Victoria*, pp. 155–6

19 *Letters of Queen Victoria*, Vol. I, pp. 333–4

20 Ibid., Vol. I, p. 320

21 Ziegler, *Melbourne*, p. 347

22 Gash, *Sir Robert Peel*, p. 293

23 St Aubyn, *Queen Victoria*, p. 155

24 *Letters of Queen Victoria*, Vol. I, p. 337

25 *Peel's Papers* (ed. Parker), Vol. II, p. 461

26 Steward, *Foundation of the Conservative Party*, p. 120

27 Gash, *Pillars of Government*, p. 129

28 Hilton, *Mad, Bad, and Dangerous People*, p. 590

29 Gash, *Sir Robert Peel*, pp. 279–80

30 Ibid., p. 283

31 *Croker Correspondence* (ed. Jennings), Vol. II, p. 335

32 *Peel's Papers* (ed. Parker), Vol. II, p. 486

CHAPTER 13: THE WELFARE OF THE PEOPLE (PP.242–270)

1 Gash, *Sir Robert Peel*, pp. 295 *et seq.*

2 *Peel's Papers* (ed. Parker), Vol. II, pp. 490–1

3 Ibid., Vol. II, pp. 500–2

4 Gash, *Sir Robert Peel*, p. 303

5 Morley, *Gladstone*, Vol. I, p. 248

6 *Croker Correspondence* (ed. Jennings), Vol. II, p. 379

7 *Peel's Papers* (ed. Parker), Vol. II, p. 518

8 *Private Letters* (ed. G. Peel), p. 191

9 Guizot, *Mémoires*, p. 344

10 Gash, *Sir Robert Peel*, p. 309

11 *Peel's Papers* (ed. Parker), Vol. II, p. 507

12 Ibid., Vol. II, p. 520

13 Ibid., Vol. II, p. 521

14 *Private Letters* (ed. G. Peel), p. 196

15 *Disraeli's Letters*, Vol. IV, 12 August 1842

16 Gash, *Sir Robert Peel*, p. 362

17 Read, *Peel and the Victorians*, p. 124

18 Gash, *Sir Robert Peel*, p. 319

19 *Peel's Papers* (ed. Parker), Vol. II, pp. 528–30

20 *Greville Memoirs*, 13 March 1842

21 Gash, *Sir Robert Peel*, p. 320

22 *The Ladies of Alderley* (ed. Mitford), p. 35

23 *Croker Correspondence* (ed. Jennings), Vol. II, p. 385

24 *Peel's Papers* (ed. Parker), Vol. II, p. 527

25 Gash, *Sir Robert Peel*, p. 341

26 *Private Letters* (ed. G. Peel), p. 201

27 Ibid., p. 203

28 Ibid., p. 204

29 *Letters of Queen Victoria*, Vol. I, p. 425

30 Gash, *Sir Robert Peel*, pp. 342–3

31 *Private Letters* (ed. G. Peel), p. 202

32 Gash, *Sir Robert Peel*, p. 345

33 *Peel's Papers* (ed. Parker), Vol. II, p. 542

34 *Private Letters* (ed. G. Peel), pp. 209–10

35 RAVIC/AB/12

36 *Peel's Papers* (ed. Parker), Vol. III, p. 200

37 *Letters of Queen Victoria*, Vol. I, p. 427

38 Clark, *Paisley*, p. 95

39 *Disturbances*, HO 45/345

40 *Distress at Paisley*, HO 45/345

41 RAVIC/A12/55

42 Young, *Victorian England*, p. 44

43 Gash, *Sir Robert Peel*, p. 350

44 *Peel's Papers* (ed. Parker), Vol. II, p. 354

45 Ibid., Vol. II, p. 527

46 Ibid., Vol. II, p. 532

47 *Croker Correspondence* (ed. Jennings), Vol. II, pp. 389–90

48 *Peel's Papers* (ed. Parker), Vol. II, p. 541

49 Ibid., Vol. II, p. 532

CHAPTER 14: FOREIGNERS (PP.271–297)

1 Cowie, *Bibliography*, p. 44

2 Gash, *Sir Robert Peel*, p. 496

3 *Peel's Papers* (ed. Parker), Vol. III, p. 389

4 Gash, *Sir Robert Peel*, p. 499

5 *Croker Correspondence* (ed. Jennings), Vol. II, pp. 398–9

6 Ibid., Vol. II, p. 395

7 Ibid., Vol. II, p. 400

8 Cowie, *Bibliography*, p. 117

9 Gash, *Sir Robert Peel*, pp. 489–9

10 Chalmers, *Palmerston*, p. 224

11 *Letters of Queen Victoria*, Vol. I, p. 490

12 Ibid., Vol. I, pp. 21–3

13 *Peel's Papers* (ed. Parker), Vol. II, p. 162

14 *Letters of Queen Victoria*, Vol. II, p. 19

15 *Cambridge History of British Foreign Policy*, Vol. II, pp. 182–5

16 Gash, *Sir Robert Peel*, p. 508

17 *Peel's Papers* (ed. Parker), Vol. II, p. 394

18 Gash, *Sir Robert Peel*, p. 511

19 Tombs, *That Sweet Enemy*, p. 341

20 *Letters of Queen Victoria*, Vol. II, p. 25

21 *Peel Papers*, Peel to Hardinge, 40474/171

22 Gash, *Sir Robert Peel*, p. 513

23 *Peel's Papers* (ed. Parker), Vol. II, p. 196

24 Ibid., Vol. II, p. 202

25 Ibid., Vol. II, p. 202

26 Ibid., Vol. II, p. 405

27 Ibid., Vol. II, p. 406

28 Ibid., Vol. II, p. 410

29 Gash, *Sir Robert Peel*, pp. 523–4

30 *Peel's Papers* (ed. Parker), Vol. II, p. 411

31 Crosby, *Peel's Administration*, p. 129

32 *Dictionary of National Biography*, Ellenborough

33 *Peel's Papers* (ed. Parker), Vol. II, pp. 576–7

34 *Dictionary of National Biography*, Ellenborough

35 *Dictionary of National Biography*, Ellenborough

36 *Peel's Papers* (ed. Parker), Vol. II, p. 581

37 Crosby, *Peel's Administration*, Ch. 4

38 *Peel's Papers* (ed. Parker), Vol. II, p. 580

39 Ibid., Vol. II, p. 588

40 Ibid., Vol. II, p. 588

41 Ibid., Vol. II, p. 598

42 Gash, *Sir Robert Peel*, p. 483

43 *Peel's Papers* (ed. Parker), Vol. III, p. 3

44 Ibid., Vol. III, p. 8

45 Ibid., Vol. III, p. 9

46 Ibid., Vol. III, pp. 18–19

47 Gash, *Sir Robert Peel*, p. 487

48 *Letters of Queen Victoria*, Vol. II, p. 9

49 Gash, *Sir Robert Peel*, p. 490

50 *Peel's Papers* (ed. Parker), Vol. III, p. 30

51 *Peel Papers*, Peel to Hardinge, 40474/172

52 Yapp, *Strategies of British India*, p. 51

53 *Peel Papers*, Peel to Hardinge, 40474/168

CHAPTER 15: HOW WONDERFUL IS PEEL (PP.298–332)

1 *Letters of Queen Victoria*, Vol. I, p. 460

2 Ibid., Vol. I, p. 456

3 Gash, *Sir Robert Peel*, p. 364

4 *Letters of Queen Victoria*, Vol. I, p. 457

5 Ibid., Vol. I, p. 473

6 Ibid., Vol. I, p. 469

7 *Peel's Papers* (ed. Parker), Vol. II, p. 555

8 Read, *Peel and the Victorians*, p. 120

9 Gash, *Sir Robert Peel*, p. 367

10 *Peel's Papers* (ed. Parker), Vol. II, p. 229

11 Ibid., Vol. II, p. 215

12 Ibid., Vol. II, p. 574

13 *Letters of Queen Victoria*, Vol. I, p. 507

14 *Private Letters* (ed. G. Peel), pp. 227, 237, 230, 240, 243

15 Ibid., pp. 239, 255

16 Letter dated 6 July 1842 in the possession of the Revd Jonathan Peel

17 *Peel Papers*, 40608, fol. 211

18 Gash, *Sir Robert Peel*, p. 455

19 *Peel Papers*, 40474, ff. 112–13

20 Crook, 'Peel: Patron of the Arts', p. 5

21 Gash, *Sir Robert Peel*, p. 372

22 Hilton, *Mad, Bad, and Dangerous People*, p. 550

23 Engels, *Condition of the Working Class*, p. 199

24 Gash, *Sir Robert Peel*, pp. 438–44

25 *Greville Memoirs*, 31 March 1844

26 *Peel's Papers* (ed. Parker), Vol. III, p. 152

27 *Peel Papers*, 40608, ff. 243–302

28 *Peel Papers*, 40608 (3), pp. 243–300

29 Kerr, *Peel, Priests and Politics*, p. 42

30 Young, *Victorian England*, p. 44
31 Hansard, 3rd series, LXXII, 1016
32 *Peel's Papers* (ed. Parker), Vol. III, p. 42
33 Ibid., Vol. III, p. 13
34 Ibid., Vol. III, p. 39
35 Ibid., Vol. III, p. 43
36 Ibid., Vol. III, pp. 56–89, 104
37 Hansard, 3rd series, LXXXIX, 567, 11 April 1845
38 Kerr, *Peel, Priests and Politics*, pp. 76–80
39 *Dictionary of National Biography*, O'Connell, p. 16
40 *Peel's Papers* (ed. Parker), Vol. III, p. 37
41 Ibid., Vol. III, p. 37
42 Ibid., Vol. III, p. 46; Kerr, *Peel, Priests and Politics*, p. 81
43 *Peel's Papers* (ed. Parker), Vol. III, p. 63
44 Ibid., Vol. III, pp. 53–4
45 Kerr, *Peel, Priests and Politics*, p. 37
46 Ibid., p. 91
47 Ibid., p. 83
48 Read, *Peel and the Victorians*, p. 141
49 Ibid., pp. 142–3
50 Peel, *Speeches*, IV, pp. 497, 521
51 *Letters of Queen Victoria*, Vol. II, p. 36
52 Read, *Peel and the Victorians*, p. 140
53 Trevelyan, *Life of Macaulay*, Vol. II, p. 158
54 Gash, *Sir Robert Peel*, p. 477
55 *Peel Papers*, 40474, 314–16
56 *Greville Memoirs*, 5 and 6 April 1845
57 Fisher, 'Sugar Crisis of 1844', pp. 279–302
58 *Peel's Papers* (ed. Parker), Vol. III, p. 176
59 *Peel Papers*, Peel to Hardinge, 40474/254
60 Steward, *Foundation of the Conservative Party*, p. 183
61 Crosby, *English Farmers*, pp. 133–5
62 Steward, *Foundation of the Conservative Party*, p. 186
63 Hansard, 3rd series, LXXIX, 565–6
64 Hansard, Disraeli, 28 February 1845
65 *The Times*, 24 February 1846
66 *Peel Papers*, Peel to Hardinge, 40474/316
67 *Private Letters* (ed. G. Peel), p. 267

CHAPTER 16: MARTYRDOM (PP.333–370)

1 Gash, *Sir Robert Peel*, p. 533
2 *Peel's Papers* (ed. Parker), Vol. III, p. 233
3 Woodham-Smith, *The Great Hunger*, pp. 54–93
4 Longford, *Wellington*, Vol. II, p. 363
5 Blake, *Disraeli*, p. 223
6 Peel, *Memoirs*, Vol. II, p. 145
7 *Peel's Papers* (ed. Parker), Vol. III, p. 231
8 Peel, *Memoirs*, Vol. II, p. 182
9 RAVIC/C44/6
10 Peel, *Memoirs*, Vol. II, p. 199
11 Ibid., Vol. II, p. 236
12 Ibid., Vol. II, p. 200
13 Hilton, 'Reappraisal', p. 599
14 *Letters of Queen Victoria*, Vol. II, p. 48
15 Gash, *Sir Robert Peel*, p. 526
16 *Peel's Papers* (ed. Parker), Vol. III, p. 457
17 *Private Letters* (ed. G. Peel), p. 275
18 Chambers, *Palmerston*, p. 238
19 RAVIC/C 44/78
20 *Dictionary of National Biography*, Stanley
21 Morley, *Gladstone*, Vol. I, p. 286
22 RAVIC/C 44/94
23 Read, *Peel and the Victorians*, p. 158
24 Information from Mrs Claire Tomalin
25 Peel, *Speeches*, Vol. IV, p. 709
26 Blake, *Disraeli*, p. 227
27 Gash, *Sir Robert Peel*, p. 570
28 Disraeli, *Bentinck*, p. 70
29 *Peel's Papers* (ed. Parker), Vol. III, p. 354
30 Ziegler, *Melbourne*, p. 358
31 *Peel's Papers* (ed. Parker), Vol. III, p. 302
32 Ibid., Vol. III, p. 298
33 Ibid., Vol. III, p. 301
34 Disraeli, *Tancred*, p. 78
35 Peel, *Speeches*, Vol. IV, p. 685
36 *Peel's Papers* (ed. Parker), Vol. III, p. 342
37 *Peel Papers*, 40475, ff. 199–202
38 Peel, *Speeches*, Vol. IV, p. 685
39 Blake, *Disraeli*, pp. 236–7
40 Gash, *Sir Robert Peel*, pp. 589–90
41 Ibid., p. 590
42 *Wellington Papers*, Wellington to Peel, 19 May 1846

43 *Peel's Papers* (ed. Parker), Vol. III, pp. 317–19
44 RAVIC/A 18 (29)
45 Gash, *Sir Robert Peel*, pp. 595–8
46 *Peel's Papers* (ed. Parker), Vol. III, p. 361
47 Gash, *Sir Robert Peel*, p. 601 and Morley, *Cobden*, p. 426
48 *Peel's Papers* (ed. Parker), Vol. III, p. 362
49 Disraeli, *Bentinck*, p. 301
50 Peel, *Memoirs*, Vol. II, p. 310
51 RAVIC/QVJ/1846: 22, 26, 27 June
52 RAVIC/QVJ/1846: 28 June
53 Prest, *Lord John Russell*, p. 215
54 Gash, *Sir Robert Peel*, p. 604
55 Ibid., pp. 240–1
56 Read, *Peel and the Victorians*, p. 239

CHAPTER 17: NOT BROKEN AT ALL
(PP.371–378)

1 Vamplew, 'The Corn Laws Reassessed', pp. 393–5
2 Ferguson, *The World's Banker*, p. 449
3 Hilton, *Mad, Bad, and Dangerous People*, pp. 629–30
4 *Peel's Papers* (ed. Parker), Vol. III, p. 458
5 RAVIC/C 25/29
6 Letter 10 September 1846 to William Peel, in the possession of Revd Jonathan Peel
7 Gash, *Sir Robert Peel*, p. 682
8 Letters in the possession of Revd Jonathan Peel

9 Gash, *Sir Robert Peel*, p. 685
10 Guizot, *Peel*, p. 78
11 *Stanhope Papers*, 54/12
12 Read, *Peel and the Victorians*, p. 249
13 Gash, *Sir Robert Peel*, 662
14 Ibid., p. 642
15 Ibid., p. 696

CHAPTER 18: THE FINAL FALL
(PP.379–387)

1 Morley, *Gladstone*, Vol. I, p. 369
2 Ridley, *Lord Palmerston*, p. 387
3 Gash, *Sir Robert Peel*, p. 697
4 *Letters of Queen Victoria*, Vol. II, p. 252
5 Bury Library, *Miscellaneous Peel Papers*
6 Steward, *Foundation of the Conservative Party*, p. 183
7 *Peel's Papers* (ed. Parker), Vol. III, p. 553
8 *Letters of Queen Victoria*, Vol. II, p. 256
9 Gash, *Sir Robert Peel*, p. 215
10 *Goulburn Papers*, 304/A2/10
11 *Goulburn Papers*, Lady Peel to Goulburn, 28 August 1850

EPILOGUE (PP.388–397)

1 Jenkins, *Peel*, p. 108
2 Hilton, *Mad, Bad, and Dangerous People*, p. 613

Index